THE ESCHATOLOGY OF 1 PETER

The author of 1 Peter regards Christian suffering as a necessary feature of faithful allegiance to Jesus, which precedes the full restoration and vindication of God's people. Much previous research has explored only the cause and nature of suffering; Kelly D. Liebengood now addresses the need for an explanation for the source that has generated this particular understanding. If Jesus truly is God's redemptive agent, come to restore His people, how can Christian suffering be a necessary part of discipleship *after* his coming, death and resurrection, and what led the author of 1 Peter to such a startling conclusion? Liebengood analyzes the appropriation of shepherds, exodus and fiery trials imagery and argues that the author of 1 Peter is dependent upon the eschatological programme of Zechariah 9–14 for his theology of Christian suffering. This book will interest those studying the New Testament, Petrine theology and early Christianity.

KELLY D. LIEBENGOOD is Associate Professor of Biblical Studies at LeTourneau University, where he also serves as Director of the Center for Global Service Learning. He is co-editor, with Bruce W. Longenecker, of *Engaging Economics: New Testament Scenarios and Early Christian Reception* (2009).

SOCIETY FOR NEW TESTAMENT STUDIES

MONOGRAPH SERIES

General Editor: Paul Trebilco

157

THE ESCHATOLOGY OF 1 PETER

SOCIETY FOR NEW TESTAMENT STUDIES

MONOGRAPH SERIES

Recent titles in the series

The Eschatology of 1 Peter

Considering the Influence of Zechariah 9–14

KELLY D. LIEBENGOOD

CAMBRIDGE
UNIVERSITY PRESS

CAMBRIDGE
UNIVERSITY PRESS

32 Avenue of the Americas, New York NY 10013-2473, USA

Cambridge University Press is part of the University of Cambridge.

It furthers the University's mission by disseminating knowledge in the pursuit of education, learning and research at the highest international levels of excellence.

www.cambridge.org
Information on this title: www.cambridge.org/9781107566163

© Kelly D. Liebengood 2014

First published 2014
Reprinted 2014
First paperback edition 2015

A catalogue record for this publication is available from the British Library

Library of Congress Cataloguing in Publication data
Liebengood, Kelly D., 1970–
The eschatology of 1 Peter : considering the influence of Zechariah 9–14 / Kelly D. Liebengood.
    pages   cm. – (Society for new testament studies monograph series)
Includes bibliographical references and indexes.
ISBN 978-1-107-03974-2 (hardback)
1. Bible. Peter, 1st – Criticism, interpretation, etc.   2. Eschatology – Biblical teaching.
3. Suffering – Biblical teaching.   4. Bible. Zechariah – Relation to Peter, 1st.   5. Bible.
Zechariah IX–XIV – Criticism, interpretation, etc.   I. Title.
BS2795.6.E7L54   2013
227′.9206 – dc23   2013027677

ISBN 978-1-107-03974-2 Hardback
ISBN 978-1-107-56616-3 Paperback

CONTENTS

ACKNOWLEDGMENTS

Without the care, support, encouragement, generosity and sacrifice of a number of significant people in my life, this project never would have come to its completion.

I am grateful to Alan Tomlinson, who inspired me to pursue biblical studies – mostly through his infectious passion for the text that he loved sharing with anyone who would listen to him.

It was a tremendous privilege to do the bulk of my research for this book at a place as special as the University of St Andrews. Many of the most intellectually stimulating and satisfying moments of my life were experienced in the environs of St Mary's College, where I was surrounded by some of the most outstanding people I have ever met. It is with a profound sense of gratitude, then, that I wish to acknowledge the following persons and institutions which to one degree or another made that experience possible.

Our move from Costa Rica to Scotland was enabled by the love and generous financial support of our parents, Robert and Linda Forbes, Dr DeeAnna Liebengood, Pete Liebengood and V. Michael Schreiber. The same can be said of Mike and Jody Schreiber. We also wish to thank our UWM team, anchored by Grace Evangelical Presbyterian Church and the Rev. William Vogler, who also provided generous support and incessant encouragement throughout our time in both Costa Rica and Scotland.

Additionally, I am grateful to the University of St Andrews, and in particular St Mary's College for granting me a PhD Scholarship from 2006 to 2009.

My officemates in the Black Room and the Roundel broadened my horizons well beyond my own research interests, giving me a well-rounded education while in Scotland. In particular I wish to thank my Red Roofs companions, Aaron Kuecker, Luke Tallon and Kevin Diller, with whom I enjoyed exercising both body and mind. Additionally, Daniel Driver, Margaret Ramey, Mariam Kamell, Timothy Stone, Patrick Egan and Matt Farlow offered many engaging and insightful conversations.

I am grateful to Professor Alan Torrance, Professor Markus Bock-muehl, Mark Elliott, Nathan McDonald, and Grant Macaskill for their leadership and contribution to the Scripture and Theology Seminar, which has profoundly impacted the way that I think about my own approach to the Bible.

Bruce Longenecker was the kind of supervisor that every PhD student wishes for: he was diligent, reliable, insightful, encouraging and above all hospitable.

Professor Richard Bauckham and Joel Green both made significant contributions to my thesis as they filled in for Dr Longenecker while he was on sabbatical. And Kelly Iverson graciously brought my thesis to full gestation upon Dr Longenecker's departure from St Andrews. I am particularly grateful for his diligence, his keen eye for details and his insightfulness.

Professors Tom Wright and David Horrell were the kind of examiners that all doctoral students dream of when they submit their work for appraisal. Their thoroughness, insight and critical engagement made this book much better than it would have been without their feedback – but this should not be understood to mean that they are liable for any of its shortcomings! I especially want to express my appreciation for David Horrell, who since the day I met him has graciously welcomed me into the world of Primopetrine scholarship, and who embodies so many of the qualities of the scholar that I hope to become.

The Parish Church of the Holy Trinity nurtured us while in St Andrews, and we are especially grateful to Rory and Annice MacLeod for their kind hospitality.

I also wish to extend my appreciation to my colleagues at LeTourneau University for their support as I finished up the last stages of this book. In particular, I wish to thank Provost Philip Coyle, Associate Provost Steve Mason, Vice President Robert Hudson and Department of Theology Chair Pat Mays for their support of my scholarship.

Finally, it is difficult if not impossible to express with words the profound gratitude I feel towards my children, Chloe, Caleb, Caedmon and Campbell, as well as my wife, Marietta, who accompanied me while I put pen to paper, constantly giving me much-needed perspective, encouragement and grace. It was never easy; but because it was with you, it was never too hard.

For this reason, I dedicate this book to my family.

TABLES

1

INTRODUCTION

The principal aim of this study is to discern what has shaped the author of 1 Peter to regard Christian suffering as a necessary (1.6) and to-be-expected (4.12) component of faithful allegiance to Jesus Christ.[1] That 1 Peter declares suffering to be a normative reality for faithful followers of Jesus is not a novel idea in the earliest church traditions. In fact, several NT witnesses affirm this central message of 1 Peter. In the Jesus Tradition, for example, Jesus warns that those who choose to follow him will face opposition from family and compeers, and even be accused of wrongdoing (e.g. Mark 8.34; 13.9–13; John 15.18–27). In Acts 14.22, would-be followers of Jesus are reminded that tribulations are requisite for those who wish to enter the kingdom of God. Statements made by Paul seem to indicate that one of the central components of his teaching was that tribulations (for the sake of Jesus) were part and parcel with faithful Christian discipleship (e.g. 1 Thess. 3.3–4; Phil. 1.28–30; 2 Thess. 2.3–12). And the overall narrative of Revelation depicts Christian suffering as a necessary part of a wider eschatological programme (e.g. 3.10; 6–19).

These witnesses, however, offer little (if any) insight into how the early church actually arrived at such a startling conclusion regarding Christian suffering, except perhaps to suggest that the idea originated with Jesus independent of any scriptural precedent. I will argue that 1 Peter offers a unique vista into the way in which at least one early Christian witness came to conclude that Christian suffering was a necessary feature of faithful allegiance to Jesus Christ.

All abbreviations are in keeping with the Society of Biblical Literature standards.

[1] Throughout this study I have qualified 'suffering' with the adjective 'Christian' to underscore that what 1 Peter specifically has in view is suffering that comes as a result of one's allegiance to Jesus Christ. It is important to note that this study, and 1 Peter for that matter, is not offering a comprehensive theodicy but rather an explanation of suffering that is integrally related to Christian discipleship.

1.1   Suffering in 1 Peter: a survey of the literature

Since suffering is one of the principal themes of 1 Peter, it is no surprise that studies on the subject (whether tangentially or intentionally) are legion.[2] Most recent comprehensive investigations, however, tend to limit their scope to two particular aspects of suffering in 1 Peter: (1) its cause and nature, and (2) the strategies that the author of 1 Peter employs in order to enable his addressees to respond in faithfulness.

Prior to the ground-breaking observations of E. G. Selwyn (*The First Epistle of St. Peter* (1946)) most assumed that the addressees of 1 Peter were suffering because of Roman imperial proscription. As a result, scholars seldom questioned the nature of suffering, and instead attempted to discern whether this official programme of persecution came under Nero, Domitian or Trajan. Selwyn, however, led the way (at least in the English literature) in observing that the language used to describe the suffering in 1 Peter reflected sporadic and localized slander and social discrimination rather than physical persecution characteristic of Roman policy.[3] This astute observation opened the door for a reconsideration of the socio-historical context of the letter, and more particularly the cause and nature of suffering.

John Elliott, who was the first to apply a social-scientific perspective to 1 Peter, began a new conversation in 1 Peter studies with his monograph *A Home for the Homeless* (1981). His unique approach to 1 Peter yielded an equally unique explanation for the cause of suffering, which he argued can be explained in three words: πάροικος (2.11), παρεπίδημος (1.1; 2.11) and παροικία (1.17). According to his analysis, these key terms regularly refer to people living in a literal foreign land as actual resident aliens in a condition of social estrangement.[4] A literal reading of these three key terms served as the basis for Elliott's reconstruction of the social setting of 1 Peter. According to Elliott, the addressees of 1 Peter found themselves in a precarious situation because *some* among them were literal πάροικοι and παρεπίδημοι (1.1; 1.17; 2.11) in Asia Minor *before* becoming Christians. In other words, they were suffering because of their

---

[2] The words πάσχω and πάθημα occur sixteen times in 1 Peter – five in reference to Jesus (2.21,23; 3.18; 4.1; 5.1), and eleven in reference to Christian suffering (1.11; 2.19,20; 3.14,17; 4.1,13,15,19; 5.9,10).

[3] E.g. 1 Pet. 2.12; 3.9; 3.16; 4.4; 4.14. See Selwyn 1958: 47–56, esp. 55, for his full argumentation.

[4] His lexical analysis includes biblical as well as extra-biblical usages such as inscriptions and Graeco-Roman literature. See Chapters 1 and 2 of Elliott 1981, and especially his summary *ibid.*: 48. For a detailed and updated summary of his position see also 2000: 101–3, 312–16, 457–62, 476–83.

social status as resident aliens prior to joining the fellowship of Christ followers. In response to this social alienation, Elliott argued that the author of 1 Peter employs the metaphor 'household of God' (οἶκος τοῦ θεοῦ; 4.17; 2.5) in order to 'reinforce the group consciousness, cohesion and commitment' – in other words, to offer a home for the homeless.[5]

Elliott's work generated a number of responses, many of which questioned his lexical analysis and his reconstruction of the letter's occasion, and which sought to examine further the strategy of the letter. Perhaps the most significant response to *A Home for the Homeless* was Reinhard Feldmeier's *Die Christen als Fremde* (1992).[6] Feldmeier offered an extensive analysis of the terms πάροικος and παρεπίδημος in both the context of 1 Peter as well as within the wider Graeco-Roman world (including philosophical works and Second Temple Jewish texts),[7] and concluded that their usage in 1 Peter is based primarily upon OT references to the dispersed people of God, and therefore ought to be understood as metaphors which point to the addressees' (new) favourable status with God, a status which also generates misunderstandings and conflict with their compeers.[8] In essence, Feldmeier turned Elliott's work on its head: οἶκος τοῦ θεοῦ, rather than being the chief metaphor of the letter and the author's strategy for reducing alienation, is instead the basis for the addressees' estrangement within society.[9] What is more, Feldmeier contended that the *Fremde* motif, understood in relation to the dispersed people of God in the OT, rather than being the cause of alienation is in fact 1 Peter's strategy both for consoling as well as for instructing the addressees with respect to their new obligations and lifestyle.[10]

Troy Martin and Steven Bechtler also offered challenges to Elliott's proposal, while additionally contributing new insights into the strategy of 1 Peter.[11] Martin argued not only that 'diaspora' (1.1) is the controlling metaphor of the letter, but also that it is the organizing principle for its compositional structure.[12] What is more, Martin maintained that the author of 1 Peter has taken over the metaphor of 'diaspora' in order to orient his addressees with respect to their new eschatological journey,

---

[5] Elliott 1981: 107; for full argumentation see *ibid.*: 101–266. In the same year that Elliott's work appeared, in a monograph entitled *Let Wives Be Submissive: The Domestic Code in 1 Peter*, David Balch (1981) argued that 1 Peter's strategy was targeted more towards assimilation rather than (sectarian) group cohesion. The two engaged in a number of responses, which later became known as the Balch–Elliott debate. For a summary of the debate and a nuanced response see Horrell 2007.
[6] Others of note are Chin 1991; Bechtler 1998; and Seland 2005.
[7] Feldmeier 1992: 8–104.   [8] *Ibid.*: 169–74.   [9] *Ibid.*: 203–10.
[10] *Ibid.*: 133–74, 175–91.   [11] Martin 1992; Bechtler (1998).
[12] Martin 1992: 144–267. For a more detailed discussion of Martin's proposal see §6.2.

which is a result of their new birth.[13] Bechtler similarly recognized that
1 Peter speaks of the Christian life as a kind of transition period, which
he described as 'temporal liminality': 'Christian life is . . . an existence
"betwixt and between" history and the eschaton.'[14] Bechtler maintained
that this concept of temporal liminality 'contains within it one very important element of the letter's total answer to the problem of the suffering of
the addressees'.[15]

Elena Bosetti's monograph *Il Pastore* (1990), astonishingly, is the
only comprehensive study to date of the pastoral motif in 1 Peter. In
her analysis she noted that 1 Peter's appropriation of shepherd imagery
has been relatively ignored, and in turn demonstrated that it serves a
key role in the overall strategy of the letter and is integrally connected
to the expectations of Jewish restoration eschatology.[16] However, as I
will argue in more detail in Chapter 3, because she neglected to analyze
comprehensively the eschatological shepherd tradition of Zechariah 9–
14 and note its unique contribution, she was unable to make a connection
between the shepherd imagery and the theology of Christian suffering in
1 Peter. In other words, for Bosetti, the shepherd imagery gives comfort
to suffering Christians, tells us something about the identity of Jesus, and
helps give scriptural warrant for his suffering and death – but it does not
offer any help in determining how our author arrived at the conclusion
that he makes in the letter regarding Christian suffering.

Additionally, I draw attention to J. de Waal Dryden's *Theology and
Ethics in 1 Peter* (2006). Dryden argues that 1 Peter is a paraenetic letter
concerned with forming Christians seeking faithfulness to God in the
midst of suffering and temptation.[17] Of the five paraenetic strategies that
Dryden identifies in the letter, his most significant and original contribution was to demonstrate that story (or narrative) is a strategic and integral
part of the letter, working at the substructure level:[18] '[b]efore giving [the
addressees of 1 Peter] moral instructions, [the author of 1 Peter] gives
them a moral vision that places them in a moral universe. He does this
by depicting not simply ontological statements about how the world is,
but weaving together a *story* of how the world is'.[19]

---

[13] *Ibid.*: 153.   [14] Bechtler 1998: 134; for full argumentation see *ibid.*: 109–78.
[15] *Ibid.*: 134.   [16] Bosetti 1990: 10, 259–80, 117–58.
[17] Since the work of Lohse (1954), many Primopetrine scholars have abandoned the
once popular composite theory and concluded that 1 Peter is paraenetic in nature.
[18] Dryden 2006: 66. I highlight this first element because, arguably, all the other elements
(remembrance, construction of a corporate identity, moral instruction and Jesus as moral
exemplar) can all be subsumed under the 'narrative' strategy. Saying that 1 Peter has
narrative elements is not the same as saying that 1 Peter narrates a story.
[19] *Ibid.*: 64.

These investigations into the source and nature of Christian suffering in 1 Peter and into the strategy employed by the author have enhanced our understanding of 1 Peter. And as any good investigation should, they also generate further questions. For example, with respect to the various strategies that have been proposed, is there a relationship that can be discerned between the *Fremde* motif (Feldmeier), the notion that the 1 Peter addressees are on an eschatological journey (Martin), the concept of temporal liminality (Bechtler), shepherd imagery (Bosetti) and story (Dryden)? In other words, is there some way that these elements of 1 Peter's strategy can be synthesized? The most glaring lacuna in all of the works mentioned above, however, is that they have not sought to discern where the author of 1 Peter might have derived his strategy. If, for example, 'diaspora' (as understood by Martin) is in fact the controlling metaphor, how did the author of 1 Peter arrive at such a conclusion? If liminality is a key response to the addressees' situation, does our author give us any indication regarding where this notion of the Christian life came from? Are we able to discern what has led the author of 1 Peter to the particular narrative he develops in the letter? These questions are particularly important because the OT prophetic material, which is said to have shaped the author's understanding of τὰ εἰς Χριστὸν παθήματα (1.11), seems to suggest that when God's redemptive agent emerges he will immediately usher in peace and justice.[20] What has led the author of 1 Peter to conclude otherwise?

Surprisingly there are only two studies that comprehensively have sought to discern the source behind 1 Peter's theology of Christian suffering – Helmut Millauer's (1976) *Leiden als Gnade*, and Mark Dubis' (2002) *Messianic Woes in First Peter*.

Millauer's work was, in part, a challenge to the consensus within German scholarship which regarded the theology of 1 Peter as dependent upon Pauline theology.[21] Focusing on the particular theme of suffering,

---

[20] As I will explain in §6.1, I translate τὰ εἰς Χριστὸν παθήματα as 'the suffering until [the second coming] of Christ'.

[21] The following comment by W. G. Kümmel (1975: 424) is representative of the consensus:

> 1 Pet presupposes... Pauline theology. This is true not only in the general sense that the Jewish-Christian readers, the 'people of God' (2:10), are no longer concerned about the problem of the fulfilment of the Law, but also in the special sense that, as in Paul, the death of Jesus has atoned for the sins of Christians and has accomplished justification (1:18f; 2:24). Christians are to suffer with Christ (4:13; 5:1), obedience to the civil authorities is demanded (2:14f), and the Pauline formula ἐν Χριστῷ is encountered (3:16; 5:10, 14). The frequently advanced proposal that 1 Pet is literarily dependent on Rom (and

Millauer sought to demonstrate that 1 Peter's theology of suffering was derived not from Paul (or deutero-Pauline theology) but rather from two *Vorstellungskomplexe*: (1) the election tradition of the Old Testament and Judaism (e.g. Qumran and Second Temple Literature), and (2) the Synoptic tradition. In particular, Millauer identified three themes in 1 Peter which were derived from the election tradition: (1) suffering as πειρασμός, (2) the juxtaposition of suffering in the present with rejoicing in the future and (3) suffering as judgment and purgation of the elect.[22] From the Synoptic tradition, Millauer argued, 1 Peter develops the notions of (1) suffering as a Christian vocation, (2) suffering as 'blessing', and (3) joyfully responding to suffering in the present.[23] In Millauer's view, this complex of ideas which are found in these two traditions was the raw material which the author of 1 Peter ingeniously fused together to form his distinct theology of Christian suffering: 'Aufgrund dieser verschiedenen Traditionen kommt der 1 Peter zu einer eigenen Leidensdeutung: das Leiden des Erwaehlten in der Gemeinschaft mit Christus ist als Berufung in die Nachfolge Gnade.'[24] According to Millauer, the nexus which brings the complex of ideas together is the *Nachfolgetradition* (*imitatio christi*) of the Synoptics: Christ, the elect one, faithfully embodies the election tradition and becomes the example of how to live loyally to God.[25]

Although Millauer was successful in demonstrating differences between Pauline and Primopetrine theologies of suffering,[26] and in showing parallels between the Synoptic tradition and 1 Peter,[27] his overall thesis is problematic for at least three reasons. First, as is often characteristic of the history of traditions approach, Millauer traces the development of words and ideas from their earliest usage to their appearance in NT traditions, assuming that the Synoptic tradition and the author of 1 Peter have the same access to and notions of these texts, words and ideas, but without demonstrating this to be the case. Second, he is unable to explain in a satisfactory manner what has compelled or governed the author of 1 Peter to interact with this particular complex of ideas among the many he could have chosen in the two traditions and why the author presents

Eph) is improbable because the linguistic contacts can be explained on the basis of a common catechetical tradition. But there can be no doubt that the author of 1 Pet stands in the line of succession of Pauline theology, and that is scarcely conceivable for Peter, who at the time of Gal 2:11 was able in only a very unsure way to follow the Pauline basic principal of freedom from the Law for Gentile Christians.

[22] Millauer 1976: 15–59, 105–33, 135–44, 165–79.
[23] *Ibid.*: 61–104, 145–64,179–85.   [24] *Ibid.*: 187.   [25] *Ibid.*
[26] See, e.g. *ibid.*: 38–44, 85–7.   [27] *Ibid.*: 69–76, 146–59.

his theology of suffering in the fashion that he has. In other words, what is it that brought these six particular themes together? Finally, and most significantly, it is unclear how the election tradition and the Synoptic tradition are relevant to the situation that the author of 1 Peter is addressing. How does the complex of ideas in these two traditions, which explain the suffering of God's people prior to or concomitant with the appearance of God's chosen redemptive agent, adequately explain Christian suffering *after* the coming, death and resurrection of Jesus Christ and prior to his second coming?

Although Mark Dubis does not interact with Millauer, this is precisely the point that he addresses in his *Messianic Woes in First Peter*. For Dubis, the best way to explain Christian suffering after the coming, death and resurrection of Jesus Christ is to read 1 Peter against the backdrop of the messianic woes tradition of 'early Judaism'.[28] In his analysis of 1 Pet. 4.12–19, the primary focus of his study, Dubis identifies seven themes which are paralleled in the messianic woes tradition of Judaism: (1) the necessity of 'fiery trials' for God's people prior to restoration (1 Pet. 1.6; 4.12);[29] (2) suffering which is directly related to one's allegiance to the Christ and part of God's eschatological programme (4.13; 5.1; 1.11);[30] (3) the spirit of glory as a sign of the restoration of God's people (4.14);[31] (4) lawlessness and apostasy during the messianic woes (4.15–16);[32] (5) judgment that begins with 'the house of God' (4.17);[33] (6) God's sovereign protection of those who undergo the messianic woes (4.17);[34] and (7) the exhortation to trust God for eschatological deliverance (4.19).[35] According to Dubis, these parallels suggest that the theology of suffering found in 1 Peter was dependent on the messianic woes tradition.[36]

The strength of Dubis' study is the manner in which he relates suffering to Jewish eschatological restoration expectations. Dubis rightly notes that the themes of suffering and glory are integrally linked to notions of exile and restoration. But, as I will detail in Chapter 4, his overall approach is ultimately unsatisfying. First, he has unduly dismissed the OT as a viable source for the kind of theology of suffering that 1 Peter offers. Second, in the place of the OT, Dubis has constructed a particular strand of messianic woes from a variety of texts within the Second Temple period and then noted the parallels that this construction shares with

---

[28] Dubis 2002: 186.   [29] *Ibid.*: 62–95.

[30] I.e. he interprets τὰ εἰς Χριστὸν παθήματα καὶ τὰς μετὰ ταῦτα to be references to the messianic woes tradition. *Ibid.*: 96–117.

[31] *Ibid.*: 118–29.   [32] *Ibid.*: 130–41.   [33] *Ibid.*: 142–62.

[34] *Ibid.*: 163–71.   [35] *Ibid.*: 172–85.   [36] *Ibid.*: 186–91.

1 Peter. In the process, he has failed to address adequately the variety of perspectives regarding the 'messianic woes' that these Second Temple texts offer, especially with respect to when suffering is to occur and who is to undergo the suffering. Additionally, he has not demonstrated the availability of these texts or their notions regarding suffering. And finally, he does not adequately demonstrate how his findings in 1 Pet. 4.12–19 relate to the overall strategy of 1 Peter.

In my view, there remains a compelling and comprehensive explanation for the source that has generated 1 Peter's theology of Christian suffering. In other words, if Jesus truly is the Christ, God's chosen redemptive agent who has come to restore God's people, then how can it be that Christian suffering is a necessary part of discipleship *after* his coming, death and resurrection? What led the author of 1 Peter to such a startling conclusion, which seems to runs against the grain of the eschatological hopes and expectations of Jewish restoration theology?

1.2   Thesis stated in brief

I will argue that as we trace the argumentation of 1 Peter, and the appropri-ation of imagery and OT texts, we can discern dependence upon Zechariah 9–14 for our author's understanding of Christian suffering. Said in another way, I will argue that the eschatological programme of Zechariah 9–14, read through the lens of the Gospel, functions as the substructure for 1 Peter's eschatology and thus his theology of Christian suffering.

1.3   Methodological issues

1.3.1   What is a 'substructure' and how do we find it?

In order to advance my thesis, it will be essential that I explain what I mean by the term 'substructure'. In this regard it will be necessary to survey the work of two scholars who have been influential in using the term, yet in distinct fashions, and who also have contributed to several assumptions that I maintain regarding the way in which the OT shapes NT theology and discourse.

In his seminal work *According to the Scriptures: The Sub-structure of New Testament Theology* (1952), C. H. Dodd sought to demonstrate that NT authors were dependent upon the OT in order to elucidate their understanding of the kerygma:[37] 'the Church was committed . . . to a

---

[37] I do not agree with Dodd (1952: 12) when he states that the kerygma is 'pre-theological' and 'does not bring us very far on the road to that reflective and reasoned presentation of the truth of the Gospel which is Christian theology'.

formidable task of biblical research, primarily for the purpose of clarify-
ing its own understanding of the momentous events out of which it had
emerged, and also for the purpose of making its Gospel intelligible to
the outside public'.[38] One of Dodd's unique contributions in *According
to the Scriptures* was to draw attention to a body of OT passages, which
he called *testimonia*,[39] that were called upon in the process of explaining
the significance of the Christ event.[40] In his investigation Dodd points
to 'fifteen instances where there are grounds . . . for believing that New
Testament writers were working upon a tradition in which certain passages of the Old Testament were treated as "testimonies" to the Gospel
facts, or in other words as disclosing that "determinate counsel of God"
which was fulfilled in those facts'.[41] In the course of analyzing the fifteen
testimonia, Dodd observed that while the NT authors may have agreed
upon the exegetical value of a particular passage in the OT, they nevertheless did not agree in the precise material that they included in their
discourse. In other words, Dodd argued, the NT authors do not appear to
have been working from anthologies (at least not in the way that Rendel
Harris imagined) or with mere proof-texts. Instead, Dodd suggests, 'there
were some parts of scripture which were early recognized as appropriate
sources from which *testimonia* might be drawn'.[42] This hypothesis led to
Dodd's second significant contribution, an analysis of the wider context
of the *testimonia*, upon which he concluded that the selected OT passages were understood as *wholes*, and that particular verses or sentences
were quoted from them rather as pointers to the whole context than as
constituting testimonies in and for themselves.[43] For Dodd then, in light
of these judgments, it follows that 'the attempt to discover just how the

[38] *Ibid.*: 14.
[39] Throughout his work Dodd distances himself from Rendel Harris' work on *testimonia*,
emphasizing that the quotation of passages from the OT is not to be accounted by the
testimony books. Instead, he argues that the composition of testimony books was the result
of the work of early biblical scholars.
[40] For Dodd (*ibid.*: 29–30; 61–110), any two passages that are cited by two or more NT
authors independently are considered *testimonia*.
[41] *Ibid.*: 57; for full analysis see *ibid.*: 28–60. The fifteen passages are: Ps. 2.7; Ps.
8.4–6; Ps. 110.1; Ps. 118.22–3; Isa. 6.9–10; Isa. 53.1; Isa. 40.3–5; Isa. 28.16; Gen. 12.3;
Jer. 31.31–4; Joel 2.28–32; Hab. 2.3–4; Isa. 61.1–2; and Deut. 18.15,19.
[42] *Ibid.*: 60.
[43] *Ibid.*: 126. See *ibid.*: 61–110 for full argumentation. In Chapter 2 I will show how
Zechariah 9–14 functioned in this manner. In the course of his investigation Dodd (*ibid.*:
72) highlights a particular cluster of *testimonia* (Joel 2–3, Zechariah 9–14 and parts of
Daniel), which he labels 'apocalyptic-eschatological', that he argues were employed in
order to indicate 'that the crisis out of which the Christian movement arose is regarded as
the realization of the prophetic vision of judgment and redemption'. In Chapter 2 I will
analyze the 'prophetic vision of judgment and redemption' in Zechariah 9–14 and trace its
reception in Second Temple Judaism and in the NT.

Old Testament was employed to elucidate the *kerygma* in the earliest period accessible to us and in circles which exerted permanent influence on Christian thought, is one which we are bound to make in seeking the *substructure* of New Testament theology'.[44]

Richard Hays (*The Faith of Jesus Christ: The Narrative Substructure of Galatians 3:1–4:11*) has advanced significantly the discussion regarding the way in which the OT shapes NT theology, arguing in particular that Paul's letters are 'best understood as the product of an underlying narrative bedrock'.[45] Hays' key observation is that a number of interpreters, including Dodd, have offered readings of Paul that stress various aspects of what he calls 'the narrative substructure' of Paul's theology, but have failed to develop an interpretation of Paul that roots his theology in story.[46] Drawing on the work of Nothrop Frye, Paul Ricoeur and Robert Funk, Hays argues that

(1)   There is an organic relationship between stories and reflective discourse [i.e. letters]...which not only permits but also demands restatement and interpretation in non-narrative language.

(2)   The reflective statement does not simply repeat the plot (*mythos*) of the story; nevertheless, the story shapes and constrains the reflective process because the *dianoia* [the meaning of the *mythos* or sequence of the story when seen as a whole] can never be entirely abstracted from the story in which it is manifested and apprehended.

(3)   When we encounter this type of reflective discourse, it is legitimate and possible to inquire about the story in which it is rooted.[47]

---

[44] *Ibid.*: 27. Italics mine. Lindars (1961) and Juel (1988) have advanced Dodd's work in significant ways, the former highlighting the exegetical techniques and practices which paralleled the Dead Sea Scrolls (DSS) while also tracing the development of particular doctrines in the early church, the latter arguing that Jesus' messiahship was the starting point for OT exegesis. For a critique of Dodd 1952 see Albl 1999: 27–32. It is notable that in the midst of his critique of Dodd, Albl (*ibid.*: 32) grants that Dodd offered two especially valuable contributions with his study: (1) the suggestion that NT writers had an entire 'plot' in mind when they cited a passage, and (2) the notion of a substructure which undergirded NT theology. I wish to point out that Dodd is certainly not the last word regarding OT appropriation in the NT; neither does he offer an exhaustive account of the subject. However, I find his foundational observations (i.e. *testimonia* read as wholes and viewed as sources for elucidation of the gospel and its implications) to be helpful in understanding at least one way in which the OT is appropriated in the NT.

[45] This description is taken from Longenecker (2002: 3). For an appraisal of the narrative approach to Pauline theology by several leading Pauline scholars see *ibid.*

[46] Hays 1983: 9. For a full discussion see *ibid.*: 9–14.

[47] *Ibid.*: 28. Brackets not original to Hays.

For Hays, then, there are two components within Paul's letters: (1) the reflective discourse and (2) the substructure which undergirds, supports, animates, constrains the logic of, and gives coherence to, Paul's argumentation.[48]

At this point it is important to clarify the distinctions between Dodd and Hays. For Dodd, between the 'ground plan' (the kerygma) and 'the theological edifice' (the discourse of the NT) lies the substructure, which consists of the *testimonia* (a body of recognized OT passages) that present a narrative which elucidates the 'gospel facts'.[49] Hays, on the other hand, argues that the pattern of the Christ story (i.e. the gospel) 'governs the selection and interpretation of OT texts rather than vice versa': 'Paul's superstructure is constructed on the basis of the Christological story, and the OT texts that Paul draws into the discussion, rather than determining the shape of the theological development, are used in a highly eclectic fashion and reinterpreted in light of the story.'[50] In this book, I hope to demonstrate that (at least in the case of 1 Peter) a mediating position is more likely, in which the gospel (i.e. the Christ story) and prominent OT passages *(testimonia)* mutually generate theological reflection and discourse. Thus, the gospel brings clarity to OT texts and OT texts in turn give clarity to the gospel. But, as we will see, the gospel and the OT passages do not just work together to give theological meaning to the events of Jesus' life but also (and perhaps more significantly) mutually function to provide Christians with a sense of identity and vocation. There is, then, an ecclesial trajectory.[51]

To be clear then, when I use the term 'substructure', I am referring to the way in which the Christ story (i.e. the gospel) and OT texts mutually generate theological understanding and reflection which undergird, animate, support, constrain the logic of and bring coherence to the discourse (in 1 Peter) regarding Jesus and the church. Following Dodd, then, in Chapter 2 I will demonstrate that Zechariah 9–14 was a prominent and influential block of scripture in the early church, which served as a significant source for understanding the gospel and its implications for the church. Additionally, following Hays, I will demonstrate how the Christ story has shaped the way in which Zechariah 9–14 was read, in particular the way in which the figures of Zech. 9.9–10; 11.4–17; 12.10; and

---

[48] I am indebted to Longenecker (2002: 6) for this language.
[49] Dodd 1952: 12–13.   [50] Hays 1983: 63–4.
[51] In consequent work, Hays (1989: 86) stresses Paul's 'ecclesiocentric hermeneutic'. For example, he writes (Hays 2005: 222) that Paul was 'engaged in a hermeneutical project of re-presenting the Christ-story in relation to the needs of the church'. For a comprehensive development of Paul's 'ecclesiocentric hermeneutic' see Hays 1989: 84–121. Dodd (1952: 111–14) also touches on this point.

13.7 have been conflated in the Passion Narratives. In Chapters 3 to 6, I hope to show how Zechariah 9–14, read through the lens of the gospel, undergirds and shapes the discourse of 1 Peter.

Hays has demonstrated the fruitfulness of looking at the narrative aspects of Paul's thought; I would like to suggest that a similar approach to 1 Peter will likewise yield fruitful results. As I have already stated, in this book I will argue that by looking at Peter's argumentative strategy, as well as his appropriation of OT texts and imagery, it is possible to discern a substructure that has generated his theological reflection with regard to Christian suffering. I should state clearly from the start that I am particularly interested in the substructure of Peter's eschatology and theology of Christian suffering, and am not attempting to explain the substructure of the letter as a whole, nor will I be claiming to provide any keys to the compositional or rhetorical make-up of the letter. What remains in this section, then, is to offer a model for how one discerns such a substructure.

As I have already mentioned, Hays argues that there is an organic relationship between narrative and reflective discourse.[52] Drawing from Frye and Ricoeur, Hays suggests that narrative consists of two component parts (which share the same substance):[53] *mythos* (the linear plot or sequence of events) and *dianoia* (the theme or meaning of the sequence of events seen as a whole).[54] He stresses that the *dianoia* is not abstracted from the *mythos* but is instead an organic property of the narrative.[55] Drawing from Funk, Hays further suggests that Paul writes in the mode of recapitulation, in which he unveils theological implications by drawing his readers to their foundational traditions (i.e. the Christ story and Israel's scriptures). 'In order to make his point, he must allude to the key events of the story, because the *dianoia* is discovered only in the narrative pattern.'[56] He adds that '[w]e therefore can expect that the structure (*the mythos*) of the story will appear most visibly at the points where Paul is elucidating the theme (*dianoia*) of the story by repeating what he has already told his readers on some previous occasion'.[57] He concludes by arguing that this 'mode of recapitulation' means that we must look not only to Paul's hymnic and confessional passages but also to argumentative recapitulation for traces of Paul's foundational story.[58] With these

---

[52] Hays 1983: 21–9.   [53] *Ibid.*: 23.
[54] Hays (*ibid.*: 22–4) draws these terms from Frye.
[55] Hays 1983: 23.   [56] *Ibid.*: 27–8.
[57] *Ibid.*: 28. Or, I would add, by pointing to what the author already assumes the readers to know (i.e. Zechariah 9–14 read through the lens of the Passion Narrative tradition).
[58] *Ibid.*: 28.

assumptions in place, Hays proposes that reflective discourse, such as the kind we might also find in 1 Peter, can be governed in decisive ways by a story that 'may find only allusive, fragmentary expression within the discourse'.[59]

With this in view, Hays suggests two phases of enquiry in order to identify the foundational story that shapes reflective discourse: '[W]e may first identify within the discourse allusions to the story and seek to discern its general outlines . . . [T]hen, in a second phase of inquiry we may ask how this story shapes the logic of argumentation in the discourse.'[60] In this book, Chapters 3, 4 and 5 will seek to demonstrate the way in which Peter alludes to the eschatological programme of Zechariah 9–14. In Chapter 6, I will relate these findings to the strategy and structure of 1 Peter, and demonstrate the way in which Zechariah 9–14 has functioned as the substructure of 1 Peter's eschatological programme and as the source for the theology of Christian suffering.

Since identifying allusions will be an essential component of discerning the substructure of 1 Peter's eschatology and theology of Christian suffering, it will be necessary for me to explain what I mean by the term 'allusion' and to establish a basis for responsible adjudication.[61]

At the most fundamental level an allusion 'involves (1) the use of a sign or marker [within a given text] (2) that calls to the reader's mind another known text (3) for a specific purpose'.[62] Ziva Ben-Porat, a literary critic who has done extensive work on allusion theory, helps to amplify this basic definition with the following:

> a literary allusion is a device for the simultaneous activation of two texts. The activation is achieved through the manipulation of a special signal: a sign (simple or complex) in a given text characterized by an additional larger 'referent'. This referent is always an independent text. The simultaneous activation of the two texts thus connected results in the formation of intertextual patterns whose nature cannot be predetermined.[63]

For Ben-Porat, the 'special signal' or 'sign' can be a sentence, phrase, motif, pattern or idea. She describes the process of interpreting allusions in the following four moves:

---

[59] *Ibid.*: 22.   [60] *Ibid.*: 29.

[61] I am indebted to Jauhiainen (2005: 18–36) and Ahearne-Kroll (2007: 23–37) for their helpful discussions regarding the way in which allusions can be defined and adjudicated.

[62] Thompson 1991: 29.   [63] Ben-Porat 1976: 107–8.

(1)   The reader recognizes the marker (or sign or special signal) in the text under examination.

(2)   The reader identifies the evoked text that contains the marker.

(3)   The reader modifies his or her interpretation of the signal in the alluding text on the basis of the marked sign.

(4)   The reader activates the evoked text as a whole in an attempt to form connections between the alluding text and the evoked text, which are not necessarily based upon the markers. For Ben-Porat, this final step is 'the particular aim for which the literary allusion is characteristically employed'.[64]

Ben-Porat's definition of allusion, then, forms the basis for the way in which I will be interpreting perceived allusions in 1 Peter. The definition, however, raises a question regarding the relationship between the author, the text and the reader. While it is common for biblical and literary scholars to focus exclusively either on authorial intent, text forms or the reader, I will take a mediating position in this volume.[65] In my view, while it is impossible to prove without a doubt the intentions of an author of a biblical text, it is also problematic to bracket out at least some concern for the author, not least because an allusion (as I have defined it) implies that there is in fact an author who has placed the sign or marker in the text under examination.[66] The task, then, is to demonstrate responsibly the plausibility of an allusion, in part by ruling out other possible readings, and also by attending to the cultural, social and scriptural-theological contexts which surrounded the composition of the text in order to minimize the possibility of misreading the sign and the allusion. As Juel has noted, historical enquiry 'can provide constraints on imaginative readings of the text: Given knowledge of the first century, some readings are implausible'.[67] In other words, as a reader I have the

---

[64] *Ibid.*

[65] I am indebted to Ahearne-Kroll (2007: 24–9), who perceptively articulates the relationship between the three approaches.

[66] Ahearne-Kroll (*ibid.*: 25) makes a similar point:

> Demonstrating the relative probability of an evocation by appealing to the text's signals involves the author to a certain extent because the author wrote the words and constructed text as it stands. So when one makes a claim about an evocation in the text, one is implicitly making a claim about the intention of the author, or at least about the possibility that the author intended such an evocation.

Additionally, Hays (1989: 29) points out that '[t]he concept of allusion depends both on the notion of authorial intention and on the assumption that the reader will share with the author the requisite "portable library" to recognize the source of the allusion'.

[67] Cited from Wagner 2002: 12. Wagner (*ibid.*: 12–13) also points out that 'knowledge of exegetical techniques and traditions available . . . can open our eyes to new interpretive possibilities'.

responsibility to respect the text in its own context and to demonstrate that the evocation is historically plausible. Additionally, given that steps (3) and (4) in Ben-Porat's definition are more subjective in nature, it is also my responsibility to give a satisfying account regarding the way in which I understand the two texts to be working together, by using persuasive reasoning that demonstrates reasonable plausibility based upon a set of criteria. As Jauhiainen argues: 'The key issue is not how we discover or identify allusions, but rather how we are able to argue that our reading of the text makes the most sense.'[68]

In my judgment, Hays' seven-fold criteria for discerning the presence of an allusion are still the best available.[69] I would like to emphasize, as Hays does, that biblical interpretation is more art than science.[70] I do not think it is possible to establish criteria that will 'prove' that an allusion exists.[71] To borrow a line from Thompson, the value of these criteria 'lies in assisting the judgment of relative probability'.[72] These criteria help determine whether an allusion is within the historical and literary realm of possibility, but they can never prove it to be the case. The argumentation of this study, then, has been organized in such a way as to demonstrate, in one way or another, that the thesis I am putting forth fulfils the seven-fold criteria put forth by Hays. It will be important to lay

[68] Jauhiainen 2005: 34. Additionally, he argues (*ibid.*: 33) that the reader's main task is to give 'a satisfying account . . . which includes an account of the rhetorical end for which the marked sign is utilized' that consists of 'an appeal to perceived verbal and thematic parallels, or to other such criteria'. Note also Wagner (2002: 13), who remarks that '[o]ur interpretations are shaped by and ultimately responsible to the judgments and sensibilities of larger communities of readers'. Thus, broadly speaking, I am following N. T. Wright's critical realist approach as outlined in *The New Testament and the People of God* (1992: 61–4, 98–109).

[69] Hays 1989: 29–32. For critiques of Hays' seven-fold criteria see Evans and Sanders 1993; Porter 1997; and Beker 1993. Wagner (2002: 11) has responded to Porter's critiques of Hays by stating that he 'misses the mark when he criticizes Hays for failing to offer a rigorous set of criteria, as if interpretation were simply a matter of hitting on the right methodology. While methodological rigor is crucial for certain purposes, it fails miserably as a strategy for reading literature, particularly for such metaphorically-charged literature as Paul's letters.'

[70] So also Wagner 2002: 5–13; Jauhiainen 2005: 33–5; Ahearne-Kroll 2007: 24–9.

[71] So Hays (2005: 30):

> The identification of allusions and especially echoes is not a strictly scientific matter lending itself to conclusive proof, like testing for the presence or absence of a chemical in the bloodstream. The identification of allusions, rather, is an art practiced by skilled interpreters within a reading community that has agreed on the value of situating individual texts within a historical and literary continuum of other texts. The 'yes' or 'no' judgment about any particular alleged allusion is primarily an *aesthetic* judgment pronounced upon the fittingness of a proposed reading . . . The ability to recognize – or to exclude – possible allusions is a skill, a reader competence, inculcated by reading communities.

[72] Thompson 1991: 36.

out those seven tests now, described in relation to the thesis of this study, and initially in the form of a question:

(1) Availability: Was Zechariah 9–14 available to Peter and/or his readers? In what way was Zechariah 9–14 available (i.e. MT, LXX, via the Passion Narratives, etc.)? This is the most basic of necessities for establishing an allusion, but often overlooked (especially, in my view, with respect to 'Messianic Woes' scholarship).

(2) Volume: What is the degree of verbal correspondence between the alleged allusion and the precursor text? This can be determined by evaluating two features. First, '[t]he degree of verbatim repetition of words and syntactical patterns';[73] and second, 'the distinctiveness, prominence or popular familiarity of the precursor text'.[74] In this regard, I have chosen to expand this criterion to include conceptual correspondence if and when the concept found in the precursor text is distinct enough to rule out other possible texts.[75] As we will see in Chapter 2, Zechariah 9–14 was all of these things – it was unique, prominent and, arguably, familiar to many who knew the Passion Narrative.

(3) Recurrence or clustering (multiple attestation): How often does Peter elsewhere allude to the same scriptural passage? The assumption of this criterion is that the influence of a particular precursor text upon an author usually manifests itself in a cumulative fashion. 'In other words, the case for an alleged [allusion] becomes stronger if the author has a pattern of drawing on the text or its larger context elsewhere.'[76]

(4) Thematic coherence: How well does the alleged allusion fit into the line of argument that Peter is developing?[77] Does the proposed precursor text fit together with the point that Peter is making in the near context and within his argument as a whole? Does the alleged allusion connect with the way in which the author appropriates other precursor texts? Does it bring coherence to the text or better explain the logic of the passage and the letter as a whole?

---

[73] Hays 2005: 35.   [74] *Ibid.*: 36.
[75] This emendation concurs with Ben-Porat's broad understanding of what constitutes a sign or marker.
[76] Wagner 2002: 12.   [77] Hays 2005: 38.

(5) Historical plausibility: Could Peter have intended the alleged meaning and could his first-century readers have understood it? How did other people contemporaneous to Peter read Zechariah 9–14? How are their readings similar? How are they different? Are there any techniques or tendencies that accompany a reading of Zechariah 9–14? What are the hermeneutical assumptions about reading Zechariah 9–14 as Christian scripture? As Hays has noted, '[t]he use of this criterion requires of us a broad historical construction of the hermeneutical horizon and reader-competence of [the author] and his first-century readers.'[78]

(6) History of interpretation: Have others 'heard' the same allusion? Regarding this criterion, Hays points out that '[w]hile this test is a possible restraint against arbitrariness, it is also one of the least reliable guides for interpretation . . . An investigation of the history of interpretation can extend the range of possible readings . . . but it can also lead us to a narrowing of the hermeneutical potential of . . . inter-textual collocations. Thus, this criterion should rarely be used as a negative test to exclude proposed echoes that commend themselves on other grounds.'[79]

(7) Satisfaction: Does the reading offer a satisfying account of the intertextual play? Does the proposed allusion illuminate the reading of 1 Peter as a whole? Does it help explain other features of the text? Does the proposed allusion provide exegetical value in interpreting 1 Peter?

I must stress that when I use the term 'allusion' I mean a *literary* allusion.[80] This is in contradistinction to what Ben-Porat has called an 'allusion in general', which is 'a hint to a known fact' that is not intended to activate steps 1 to 4 in the interpretative process.[81] Additionally, I should mention that I make a slight distinction between an allusion and an echo.[82] In my view, broadly speaking an echo is a sub-species of allusion – a more oblique sign or special signal that points to the influence of the precursor text. More specifically, an echo (of a particular precursor text), at least in the way that I will be using the term, is only

---

[78] *Ibid.*: 42.   [79] Hays 1989: 31.

[80] Note my discussion below regarding the complex manner in which biblical texts can be accessed, including via memory and even liturgy.

[81] Ben-Porat 1976: 108.

[82] For a helpful discussion regarding the way scholars have distinguished between allusions and echoes see Moyise 2000: 18–25.

discerned once allusions to the same precursor text have been identified and explained. In this regard, echoes have a deictic function: that is, they point to intertextual play, reinforcing and affirming allusions that have been perceived elsewhere in the alluding text.[83]

1.3.2   Foundational assumptions regarding the composition of 1 Peter

Before proceeding to the thesis proper, it will be helpful to reveal a number of assumptions that I have regarding the composition of 1 Peter, which have influenced my handling of the data, as well as the shape of my argumentation.

1.3.2.1   Authorship and date of composition of 1 Peter

Judgments concerning the authorship and the date of composition of 1 Peter are integrally related, and are also shaped by questions regarding the literary integrity and the historical setting of the letter.[84] Generally, scholars have argued either that 1 Peter was written by the apostle Peter (or by means of Peter's amanuensis, Silvanus; 5.12), or that 1 Peter is a pseudonymous document, perhaps written by someone within a 'Petrine circle' of disciples in Rome.[85] Much in keeping with the argumentation of Achtemeier, I find it difficult if not impossible to situate 1 Peter within a precise historical setting, which makes adjudicating between the two positions problematic at best.[86] If one is persuaded that Peter stands behind the letter in some way (whether independently or with the help of Silvanus), then the letter was most likely completed prior to or just after his martyrdom (c. 64–5 CE).[87] Perhaps the most challenging evidence against this position, however, is the 'Babylon' reference in 1 Pet. 5.13.

---

[83]   Thus, I do not follow scholars such as Sommer (1998: 16), who contends that an echo signals a preceding text but has little or no effect on the reading of the marker.

[84]   For the complexity of the issues pertaining to authorship and date of composition and how they are related to literary integrity and 1 Peter's historical setting see, e.g., Michaels 1988: lv–lxvii; Achtemeier 1996: 39–50; and Elliott 2000: 118–31.

[85]   For a helpful summary of the arguments of the positions see Elliott 2000: 118–30. Richard's (2004: 413) claim that 'modern scholarship, employing linguistic, social, and theological factors, is virtually unanimous in arguing for pseudonymity' is certainly an overstatement (e.g. Jobes 2005; Green 2007a).

[86]   Achtemeier (1996: 42) concludes his survey by commenting that '[e]vidence to solve definitively the question of the authorship of 1 Peter remains unavailable'.

[87]   Regarding the tradition which claims that Peter died at the hands of Nero, see Jerome's comments in Ceresa-Gastaldo 1988: 72–4. For a nuanced and qualified defence of Jerome's comments see Bockmuehl 2007. For Silvanus as the author of 1 Peter, see Selwyn 1958: 9–17. For the use of secretaries in letter writing, the cooperative nature of letter writing and the practice of shaping letters through multiple drafts see Richards 2004. For reasons to reject the notion of Petrine school see Horrell 2002.

Ever since the seminal article by Hunzinger ('Babylon als Deckname für Rom und die Datierung des 1. Petrusbriefes' (1965)), many scholars have concluded that 1 Peter must have been written after 70 CE (and thus after Peter's death), since 'Babylon' (5.13) only became a reference to Rome in extant Jewish and Christian literature after the destruction of the temple in Jerusalem. Recently however, Lutz Doering has suggested that Hunzinger's conclusions at times have been misappropriated by those who have used his research to argue for a post-70 CE date for 1 Peter. First, he notes that evidence for the identification of Rome as Babylon is 'sparser and less unambiguous than sometimes claimed by those relying on Hunzinger'.[88] Second, he suggests that the force of the Babylon reference in 1 Peter is more likely a qualification of Rome as ultimately responsible for the persecution and dispersion of God's people, akin to the Babylonian exile – and not a reference to Rome as the temple destroyer per se.[89] The main point in all of this is that 'Babylon' is likely not being used in the same way that it was in extant Christian and Jewish literature (highlighted in Hunzinger) after the fall of the Jerusalem temple in 70 CE.[90]

If one judges that the letter is pseudonymous, following the argumentation of Elliott, it was most likely composed no later than 92 CE.[91] In my view, given the paucity of evidence, and because the scope of my proposal makes it unnecessary, I am unwilling (if not also unable) to make a definitive judgment regarding the authorship and date of composition of 1 Peter, except to place it within the second half of the first century CE.[92] In the present volume, then, I have not concerned myself with the historical figure of Peter who exists outside of the letter. Instead I have chosen to focus on Peter who manifests himself within the letter – that is, the author who is revealed as we interpret 1 Peter.[93] Taking my cues from the text itself, and placing the author within the wider cultural, theological and historical realities which encompassed early followers of

---

[88] Doering 2009: 233.   [89] *Ibid.*
[90] For my reading of Babylon in 1 Pet. 5.13 see §5.1.   [91] Elliott 2000: 134–8.
[92] Not everyone gives due force to the fact that the paucity of evidence can work both ways in either confirming or denying Petrine authorship. As Michaels (1988: lxvii) has commented, 'the traditional view that the living Peter was personally responsible for the letter as it stands had not been, and probably in the nature of the case cannot be, decisively shaken'.
[93] On this distinction between the author (of the letter) and the historical figure (writer) see Nehamas (1986: 689), who argues that the author, while not identical to the writer, must, however, be 'a plausible historical variant of the writer'. Jobes (2005: 325–38) demonstrates that 1 Peter evidences Semitic interference, which suggests that the author wrote Greek as a second language.

Jesus between 64 and 92 CE, I have sought to focus on what Zechariah 9–14 might contribute to the interpretation of 1 Peter. For convenience I will refer to the author as Peter, as he has identified himself at the beginning of the letter (1.1).[94]

1.3.2.2 Appropriating biblical texts

Even with a cursory reading of 1 Peter one easily discovers that the OT has a profound influence on the letter. In his comprehensive analysis of Primopetrine hermeneutics William Schutter observes that '[n]othing is quite so significant as the variety of ways [that OT] materials have been handled'; Peter conflates OT texts, gathers OT texts around a single idea, assumes that readers will pick up on the wider text-plot cited, and interacts with exegetical traditions in existence.[95] And yet, in spite of this fact, we know very little about the way in which Peter accessed and appropriated the OT apart from what we can discern from the letter itself. For example, in a recent survey regarding the Septuagint textual tradition in 1 Peter, Jobes concludes that '[t]he author of 1 Peter seems to be . . . familiar with a Greek form that is . . . the same as the critically-reconstructed Septuagint text'.[96] In other words, from the standpoint of presentation, Peter frequently draws from the LXX.[97] But this does not necessarily indicate that Peter's theological reflections were exclusively generated from the LXX. In fact, Peter's appropriation of the Stone tradition in 1 Pet. 2.6–8, his dependence upon MT Proverbs 10.12 in 1 Pet. 4.8, as well as his eclectic usage of OT passages (as noted by Schutter and others) all suggest a more complex process of reflection and appropriation.

Having engaged the work of a number of biblical scholars, especially in relation to the use of the OT in Paul and the Gospels, it seems myopic in my view to propose that an NT author like Peter (who composed the letter within the period outlined above) would have access to the OT exclusively through either the LXX tradition, or the MT, or testimony books, or *excerpta*,[98] or memory. In fact, all of these modes of appropriation are well documented in the first century.[99] Given the paucity of information

---

[94] Again, for purposes of this volume this assumes no relationship with the historical figure Peter the apostle.
[95] Schutter 1989: 43.   [96] Jobes 2006: 332.
[97] See below for more on the LXX tradition.
[98] For the distinction between testimony books and *excerpta* in the literature see Lincicum 2008.
[99] For ways in which the wider Graeco-Roman world accessed and engaged with written texts see J. H. Humphrey 1991; Harris 1989; Bowman and Woolf 1994; see also Henzser 2001, with emphasis upon Jewish literacy in Roman Palestine; for the relationship between

regarding Peter, I propose as a working assumption that we are not able to rule out a complex process of appropriation that might include memorization and meditation of OT passages (including text-plots), interaction with a collection of *excerpta* (both personal as well as from tradition), reflection upon early Christian traditions such as the Stone Testimonia and the Jesus Tradition, as well as direct access to written texts including the LXX and MT traditions.[100] Additionally, we must also consider the possible influence of early Christian liturgy and the way that it could have shaped how people interpreted the OT in light of the Christ story. For example, as we will see in Chapter 2, the Passion Narratives likely influenced the way in which some early Christians read/heard Zechariah 9–14.

Although this approach may not allow for as precise a methodology for adjudicating the appropriation of an OT text as some would like, it does nevertheless reflect the complex world of texts, readers and theological reflection in the first-century world of Christianity.[101]

Having said this, when considering allusions in 1 Peter, my starting place will be to analyze the critically reconstructed Greek OT with its available variant readings, which in the case of Zechariah is Ziegler's work in the Göttingen Septuagint.[102] I acknowledge that the Greek OT was in a state of flux in the first century. The Göttingen Septuagint offers a working hypothesis for what Peter and the Anatolian Christians were likely reading, one that will be maintained unless there is good reason to adopt another reading. With that in view, I will also compare the LXX

books and reading in early Christianity see Gamble 1995; Millard 2000. Regarding testimony collections anthologies, and *excerpta* see Hatch 1889; Hodgson 1979; Albl 1999; Koch 1986: 247–55; Stanley 1992; Lim 1997; Tov 1995; White 1990; Abasciano 2007; note especially the concise survey by Lincicum 2008. Regarding memorization in education see Safrai 1976; see also 2 Macc. 2.25, and Augustine, *De Doctrina Christiana* 2.30. For the relationship between memorization and writing see Gerhardsson 1998; Achtemeier 1990; Jaffee 1992, 1994, 2001; Boomershine 1994; Bauckham 2006: 264–357, especially the attention he draws to the function of memory of other texts in the process of composition; Byrskog 2000; for liturgy in the early church see Bradshaw 1992; 2009; for the Passion Narratives as the earliest Christian liturgy see Trocmé 1983: 49–92; for OT appropriation in the patristics see Norris 1991; Albl 1999.

[100] For a similar approach regarding Paul and Romans see Wagner 2002: 20–8, to whom I am indebted.

[101] More specific assumptions about the composition of the letter will be highlighted at various points in this book. For example, in Chapter 3 I will discuss the exploitation of textual variants for theological and rhetorical purposes, and in Chapters 4 and 6 I will underscore my assumption that the OT is being interpreted within the framework of Jewish Restoration eschatology, and in Chapter 6 I will develop my view regarding the literary integrity, the structure and the strategy of 1 Peter.

[102] Especially given the conclusions of Jobes (2006: 332).

tradition with the MT and the Targum for Zechariah, noting significant differences when necessary.[103]

1.3.3   The aim and structure of the book

The aim of this study is to discern what has shaped the theology of Christian suffering that is developed in 1 Peter. I will argue that the eschatological programme of Zechariah 9–14, read through the lens of the gospel concerning Jesus Christ, undergirds, animates and constrains the logic of Peter's eschatological programme, and thus his conclusions regarding Christian suffering.

My argument will unfold in five movements. First, in Chapter 2 I will detail the eschatological programme of Zechariah 9–14 and then analyze how this programme was received in the Jewish Second Temple period and in the NT. In this chapter I seek to establish the availability of Zechariah 9–14 and some ways in which Zechariah 9–14 was appropriated during the period in which 1 Peter was composed. Second, in Chapter 3, I will argue that the shepherd imagery of 1 Pet. 2.25 is best understood within the milieu of the Passion Narratives tradition, and that it alludes to the eschatological programme of Zechariah 9–14. Third, in Chapter 4 I seek to show that the fiery trials imagery found in 1 Pet. 1.6–7 and 1 Pet. 4.12 is distinct from that which we find in Graeco-Roman and OT wisdom sources, and that it shares exclusive parallels with some unique features of the eschatological programme of Zechariah 9–14. In Chapter 5, I will highlight ways in which Zechariah 9–14 offers a more satisfying explanation for the modification of Isa. 11.2 in 1 Pet. 4.14, the transition from 4.12–19 to 5.1–4, why Peter has oriented his letter with the term διασπορά and why he has described his addressees as οἶκος τοῦ θεοῦ. Finally, in Chapter 6, I will seek to trace the structure and the argumentative strategy of 1 Peter, highlighting in particular the prominent role that eschatology plays in Peter's efforts to persuade and encourage his addressees. From there I will identify the substructure of 1 Peter's eschatological programme, showing ways in which it has generated, animated and constrained the logic of Peter's discourse.

---

[103] For more see Chapter 2.

2

THE ESCHATOLOGICAL PROGRAMME OF
ZECHARIAH 9–14 AND ITS RECEPTION

The thesis of this study is that Zechariah 9–14 functions as the substructure for 1 Peter's eschatological programme[1] and thus informs Peter's
theology of Christian suffering.[2] In order to advance this proposal it is
first necessary to examine the contents of Zechariah 9–14. In this chapter
I will focus on the literary shape of these six chapters in their final form,
drawing particular attention to the distinctive eschatological restoration
programme. Such an examination will not only enable us better to ascertain the text-plot of Zechariah 9–14 and familiarize ourselves with its
principal themes, but also better enable us to discuss possible allusions
in 1 Peter in Chapters 3, 4 and 5 of this study.

After analyzing the content of Zechariah 9–14, I will survey its reception in Second Temple Judaism and early Christianity, demonstrating
its availability (and prominently so), and thus the historical plausibility of the present thesis, while also revealing some of the ways that
Zechariah 9–14 has been interpreted and appropriated for theological
reflection.

2.1   The eschatological programme of Zechariah 9–14

2.1.1   Introduction

Before I survey the content of Zechariah 9–14, a few words must be said
regarding my handling of the text. Much of modern historical-critical
scholarship has tended to emphasize the composite nature of the book of
Zechariah, which is widely regarded as consisting of at least two separate
prophetic works (Zechariah 1–8 and Zechariah 9–14) each containing

---

[1] By 'eschatological programme' I mean the way in which a given text describes how
and when God will bring his will to consummation.
[2] See §1.3.1 for my definition of 'substructure'.

layers of a variety of traditions and written in distinct historical settings.[3] Although there may be compelling reasons for such a conclusion, this is not why I have narrowed my examination to Zechariah 9–14.[4] Instead, I have focused our attention on the second half of Zechariah because, as will be demonstrated in §2.2.2 and following, there is every indication that it was understood to be a coherent unit at the time of the composition of 1 Peter, which presented an eschatological schema that offered insight into the manner in which YHWH was to restore his people. In other words, it is likely that Peter (and other early Christians) would have read Zechariah 9–14 as a coherent unit.

Given what many believe to be the composite nature of Zechariah 9–14, some might question whether it is advisable or even possible to ascertain cohesion within these six chapters. This can be turned on its head, however. If Zechariah 9–14 is made up of a variety of disparate traditions, the fact that they have been gathered together and arranged as they now are would seem to suggest that someone has appropriated them precisely in order to communicate a coherent message. This would compel us, then, to attempt to discern its coherence.[5] Furthermore, I can point to at least three features of Zechariah 9–14 that provide warrant for the kind of study I offer in this chapter. First, as Carol Meyers and Eric Meyers, and also Paul Lamarche have demonstrated, Zechariah 9–14 bears witness to an 'innertextuality' (both lexically as well as thematically) that suggests these chapters are intended to be read together in their final form.[6] Second, there is an intertextuality phenomenon in which

---

[3] Regarding the task of discovering the historical and social setting of Zechariah 9–14, Childs (1979: 481) comments that 'the inability of critical research to establish a convincing case for one period is further evidence that the present canonical text has been dislocated from its original moorings. Elements of historical detail have been retained which in spite of their ambiguity and even incongruity the biblical author has used faithfully to testify to an *eschatological pattern* of divine judgment'. Italics mine. See also Childs 1979: 474–86; Meyers and Meyers 1993: 15, 28. See Conrad 1999, and Redditt 1989, 1995, 2008: 315–75 for canonical approaches to reading Zechariah 9–14.

[4] Childs (1979: 485) comments that '[t]he referential reading of Zechariah which assumes that its text can only be illuminated when it is properly correlated with the historical moment from which it emerged has been an utter disaster for exegesis'.

[5] In keeping with the conclusions of discourse analysis, I assume that '[t]he natural effort of hearers and readers alike is to attribute relevance and coherence to the text they encounter until they are forced not to' (Brown and Yule 1983: 66).

[6] By 'innertextuality' Meyers and Meyers (1993: 33–4; see also Chart 7 on pp. 36–7) mean 'the way various thematic and lexical features of the text cohere'. Lamarche (1961) has argued for a complex chiastic structure in Zechariah 9–14, which has been followed by Joyce Baldwin (1972). Although many scholars have regarded Lamarche's study as overworked, most nevertheless consider that many of his observations about the coherence

disparate sections of Zechariah 9–14 draw upon similar prophetic texts – most notably Jeremiah 23, Ezekiel 34 and Isaiah 40–66.[7] This suggests that the author or redactor of Zechariah 9–14 is intentionally constructing an eschatological programme that builds upon these earlier programmes. Finally, as I have already mentioned and as will be further developed, we have clear evidence that contemporaneous with the composition of 1 Peter, some early Christians read Zechariah 9–14 as a coherent unit that prefigured the last week of Jesus' life. (I will also suggest that Peter regards Zechariah 9–14 as pointing beyond the last week of Jesus' life, offering warrant for Christian suffering until the return of Jesus.) Thus, in seeking to discern the coherence of these six chapters I will be reading Zechariah 9–14 in a manner that is in keeping with the way that many early Christians (such as Peter) would have read it.[8]

In tracing out the eschatological programme of Zechariah 9–14 I will use the Hebrew text as the starting point;[9] my study, however, will also include a comparison of the Hebrew text with the Septuagint[10] and the Aramaic Targum[11] when necessary, especially when there is a variant which affects the text-plot. As I have revealed in Chapter 1, it is my assumption that there were likely a variety of modes in which texts were appropriated, and that if alternate translations were

---

of Zechariah 9–14 are a valuable contribution. See also Hanson 1975: 286–354; Butterworth 1992: 166–212; Larkin 1994.

[7] Delcor 1951; Lamarche 1961: 124–47; Mason 1973, 1977: 79–82; Black 1990: 48–52; Meyers and Meyers 1993: 35–45; Larkin 1994; Mitchell 1997: 146–53. Childs (1979: 482–83) notes the following parallels between Zechariah 1–8 and 9–14: (a) a new Jerusalem without walls, which is specially protected by YHWH (Zech. 2.5/9.8; 14.11); (b) the promise of a return to paradisal fertility (Zech. 8.2/14.8); (c) the affirmation of the ancient covenant formula (Zech. 8.8/13.9); (d) divine judgment against the nations (Zech. 2.1; 1.18/14.6); (e) the conversion of the nations, and universal worship of YHWH (Zech. 2.25; 2.11; 8.20–2/14.6–21); (f) the collection of the exiles (Zech. 8.7/10.9–12); (g) a new age that results in a change in cultic rites (Zech. 8.8ff./14.20); (h) the outpouring of God's spirit which evokes transformation (Zech. 4.6/12.10); (i) cleansing of those who swear falsely in God's name (Zech. 5.4/13.3); and (j) a messianic figure who triumphs, not by might, but in humility (Zech. 3.8; 4.6/9.6–16). I would add to this list stone imagery which is integrally connected to messianic restoration (Zech. 3.9; 4.9/10.4).

[8] See note 5 concerning coherence and discourse analysis.

[9] When I refer to the Hebrew text, or the MT, the Codex Leningradensis in the standard edition of *Biblica Hebraica Stuttgartensia* is meant unless otherwise specified. See Meyers and Meyers (1993: 50–1) regarding the textual reliability of the MT.

[10] From this point on the term Septuagint refers to the best critically reconstructed Greek text available of the given OT book under examination, which in the case of the Twelve Prophets is J. Zielger's *Duodecim prophetae* (2nd edn; Septuaginta 13; Göttingen: Vandenhoeck & Ruprecht, 1984). The terms OG, LXX and Septuagint will be used in a synonymous fashion.

[11] Cathcart and Gordon 1989.

available, Peter would have consulted them and exploited the variants for theological and rhetorical purposes. An exploration of the variant translations will reveal ways in which Zechariah 9–14 was being read. Additionally, such an examination will also enable us to ascertain whether 1 Peter was dependent upon a particular translation of Zechariah 9–14.

2.1.2   An analysis of Zechariah 9–14

Zechariah 9–14 is characterized by two prominent features, which I will underscore in this section. First, these six chapters offer a comprehensive eschatological programme,[12] which has been demonstrated in detail by Mark Black and David Mitchell.[13] I have benefitted from both of their studies, and reliance upon them will be duly noted. Second, Zechariah 9–14 is characterized by a pervasive engagement with earlier prophetic material, so much so that Meyers and Meyers have commented: 'It may not be an exaggeration to suggest that Zechariah 9–14 surpasses any other biblical work in the way it draws from existing tradition [sic].'[14] Coggins goes so far as to regard Zechariah 9–14 as 'the beginnings of a biblical commentary, applying to the contemporary situation the warnings against false shepherds which are found particularly in Jeremiah 23 and Ezekiel 34'.[15] These intertextual features will be underscored in due course in order to understand better the eschatological programme of Zechariah 9–14.

---

[12] Dodd (1952: 64) suggested that Zechariah 9–14 made up part of a larger body of texts which formed the narrative substructure of New Testament theology. Regarding Zechariah 9–14, he commented that 'while its component visions are not easy to bring into a consistent scheme . . . it can be understood as setting forth a whole eschatological programme, many elements of which have been taken up in the New Testament'.

[13] Black (1990); Mitchell (1997). I wish to highlight the fact that each scholar seeks to do different things with his analysis of the eschatological programme in Zechariah 9–14. Black's thesis was explicitly designed to test Dodd's assertion that Zechariah 9–14 forms part of the narrative substructure of the Passion Narratives, which he affirms in his conclusion (Black 1990: 243). Mitchell, on the other hand, sought to demonstrate parallels between the eschatological programme of Zechariah 9–14 and the Psalms of Asaph, the Songs of Ascents and the 'Royal Psalms'. In the course of his study he argues compellingly (1997: 131–65) that Zechariah 9–14 is the most comprehensive eschatological programme offered in the Jewish scriptures (and that Zechariah 9–14 further develops the programmes of Joel and Ezekiel).

[14] Meyers and Meyers 1993: 35; see also Mason 1973: 21–8, 1977: 79–82; Black 1990: 49–53; Meyers and Meyers 1993: 35–45; Larkin 1994; Duguid 1995: 266. Regarding the tendency of post-exilic prophets to reuse earlier prophetic material see Fishbane 1985: 558–605.

[15] R. J. Coggins 1987: 71.

We turn now to an analysis of Zechariah 9–14, which I will argue presents an eschatological programme that is revealed in progressive steps in the two oracles of Zechariah 9–14, though not in a strictly linear fashion.[16]

2.1.2.1 Zechariah 9.1–17

The opening section (9.1–17) of the first oracle functions paradigmatically as a miniature of what will be developed in more detail in 10.1–14.21,[17] and introduces the predominant theme of Zechariah 9–14, YHWH's intention to restore his people. This restoration is initially depicted in terms of a journey in which YHWH, like an invading king, travels from Syria south along the Mediterranean coast disempowering all of Israel's political threats. According to the prophet, YHWH's campaign will culminate in Zion, where he will guard his 'house' (בֵּיתִי), which will never again be harassed or oppressed (9.8).

This initial picture of Israel's restoration is further enhanced in 9.9–10, but with several significant and perhaps unexpected turns. Zech. 9.9 picks up the journey motif that was initiated in 9.1–8: Zion is exhorted to rejoice, for 'Behold, your king comes to you' (9.9).[18] However, as the coming king is described it becomes surprisingly apparent that he is not YHWH (as the narrative would lead one to imagine), but rather a human agent. While the human royal figure goes unnamed in the passage, there are several factors that suggest that this human agent is to be understood as a scion of David. Consideration should be given first to the ideological background of this text, especially given the fact that Zechariah is known to be dependent upon earlier prophet material (especially Jeremiah, Ezekiel and Isaiah): in exilic and post-exilic Judaism there was a widespread expectation of a royal Davidic figure who would be an integral part of the national and spiritual restoration of Israel. This ideology, rooted in the unwavering belief that YHWH would remain faithful to his covenant with David and the perpetual reign of his house (2 Sam. 7.11–16;

---

[16] It is widely regarded that, literarily, Zechariah 9–14 consists of two oracles, 9–11 and 12–14. Regarding the second oracle (12–14), Childs (1979: 481) notes that 'there is some sense of progression of thought in the sequence of oracles which moves from judgment, through salvation, to the new Jerusalem, but is not a closely-knit logical one. Rather, there is much repetition and overlapping of associated traditional motifs to form a rich mosaic which depicts the end time'. As I describe this unfolding eschatological programme, it is important to stress that I do not pretend to offer the definitive reading of Zechariah 9–14, but one that is nevertheless plausible.

[17] Mitchell 1997: 141.

[18] All English Bible citations are taken from the NRSV unless otherwise noted.

cf. Isa. 9.7; Pss. 18.50; 89.4,29–37; 132.11–12), finds expression in several texts in which the future Davidic ruler is described as either a branch of David (Isa. 11.1; Jer. 23.5; 33.15) or a shepherd (Ezek. 34.23–4; 37.24).[19] Significantly, branch and shepherd are two designations used in Zechariah to describe YHWH's future ruler (Zech. 3.8; 6.12; 13.7), which suggest that envisioning a Davidic royal figure in 9.9 is reading with the grain of the text.

Zecharian scholars have pointed to a number of allusions in the passage that are intended to point to either David or to promises of a future Davidic ruler. The reference to the Jebusites in Zech. 9.7 is likely intended to draw readers to Zion's founding event, when king David marched into Jerusalem, defeated and incorporated the Jebusites and established the capital of the united kingdom.[20] That the coming king is described as 'righteous and having salvation/saved' (צַדִּיק וְנוֹשָׁע) may also suggest that a Davidic figure is in view. In Jer. 23.5, YHWH declares that he will raise up for David a righteous (צֶדֶק) branch who will restore righteousness in Israel (see also Jer. 33.15; cf. Zech. 3.8; 6.12).[21] Meyers and Meyers have noted that this term not only indicates the coming king's moral quality but also his legitimacy as heir to the throne.[22] This notion of a double meaning of 'righteous' (צַדִּיק) is strengthened by the second term used to describe the coming king, נוֹשָׁע,[23] which is best translated as 'saved' or 'delivered'.[24] The Greek, Aramaic and Latin translations (as well as many English translations) obscure the Hebrew reading, rendering the Hebrew Niphil into an active voice (the one who saves, redeemer, and saviour, respectively). These two terms in the Hebrew (righteous and saved), however, seem to point to a coming king whose legitimacy is questioned, but who is ultimately vindicated (or saved) by YHWH. As we will see, this interpretation certainly fits with the larger text-plot of Zechariah 9–14. It also parallels David's own ascent to the throne, as well as the depiction of the future Davidic king found in the Psalms – who maintains his righteousness while suffering ill-treatment, and is then vindicated and enthroned by YHWH (cf. Pss. 22–4).

---

[19] See Collins 1995; Laato 1997; Horbury 2003; Tromp 2001: 179–201. This Davidic messiah ideology is intensified in the later part of Second Temple Judaism in such texts as *Pss. Sol.* 17–18, 4 Ezra 12.31–2; T. Jth. 24.1–5; 1QM; 4Q Isa.ᵃ; 4Q Flor.; 4Qp Bless.; 4Q Testim.; 4Qp Gen.ᵃ; 4QMᵍ.

[20] Meyers and Meyers 1993: 168; Baldwin 1972: 161.

[21] Meyers and Meyers 1993: 127; Ollenburger 1996: 807.

[22] See Meyers and Meyers 1993: 126 for a full discussion. See also Ollenburger 1996: 807.

[23] The Niphil of יָשַׁע.

[24] Lamarche 1961: 43; Meyers and Meyers 1993: 126; Duguid 1995: 267. See Num. 10.9; Deut. 33.29; 2 Sam. 22.4; Isa. 45.22; Jer. 30.7; Ps. 33.16.

This 'righteous and saved' king is further described as 'humble' and riding into Jerusalem on an ass (Zech. 9.9). Mason notes the peculiarity of the epithet 'humble' (עָנִי) to describe a royal figure, and from that observation argues that the term is intended to allude to the wrongful affliction of the righteous sufferer of Isaiah's servant songs.[25] Although not all have been convinced of this reading, there does seem to be a growing acknowledgment that there are resonances between Zech. 9.9 and Isaiah's servant songs.[26] Lamarche has noted several conceptual parallels between Isaiah 42 and Zech. 9.9–11. In both contexts the figure is righteous, releases captives from the pit or dungeon, establishes universal peace and is connected with a covenant.[27]

Finally, the most conclusive indication that the coming righteous and saved king is a Davidide can be found in Zech. 9.10, which clearly draws (almost verbatim) on Ps. 72.8, a prayer for the future son of David – that he may have 'dominion from sea to sea, and from the River to the ends of the earth'.[28] Iain Duguid has noted an important distinction between Psalm 72 and its appropriation here in Zech. 9.10. Whereas in Psalm 72 it is the king who 'saves' (72.13) and issues forth the blessings of YHWH, in Zechariah 9 YHWH is the lone agent who defeats Israel's enemies (9.1–7) and protects his house (9.8).[29] It is here in this contrast that we find one further parallel that can be drawn to Solomon in Zechariah 9.10: 'Zion's coming king is like Solomon, a royal son of David, whose universal reign is without military power.'[30]

The basis for YHWH's restoration is given in Zech. 9.11: 'because of the blood of my covenant I will set your prisoners free from the waterless pit'. It is not entirely clear which covenant is in view. Apart from Zech.

---

[25] Mason 1973: 50. Mason (1973: 24) also notes that '[t]he three adjectives used to describe [the coming king] and his role, saddîq, nôsaʿ, and ʿanî', while all, in one form or another, descriptive of the king in Psalms are also used of the Servant of Second Isaiah (e.g. Isa 50:8; 49:6; 53:4)'.

[26] Meyers and Meyers (1993: 127–8) argue that 'humble' simply refers to the king's attitude towards YHWH. Additionally, they note (Meyers and Meyers 1993: 172) that

> [t]he royal figure himself must be saved ... like the second, third, or fourth generation captive community, he has been subjected innocently to the trials of exile and thus is a righteous individual to whom kingship belongs according to the eschatological ideal. In this sense, the images of humbleness and restoration associated with the royal figure of Zech 9:9 are like certain features of the servant motif of Second Isaiah.

[27] See Paul Lamarche 1961: 131–4.

[28] Mason 1977: 89; Meyers and Meyers 1993: 136–7; Ollenburger 1996: 807; Duguid 1995: 266–7.

[29] Duguid 1995: 267. Duguid also notes a contrast between Ps. 72.13, where the king 'saves', and Zech. 9.9, where the king is the object of YHWH's salvation.

[30] Ollenburger 1996: 808.

9.11, the phrase 'the blood of the covenant' appears only in Exodus 24, and may provide us with our best clue. In that context, the stipulations of YHWH's covenant have just been read to the people of Israel. The final stipulation (23.20–33) culminates with the promise to establish the Israelites in the land. The people respond to the covenant stipulations by declaring that they will obey all that is required of them. The ceremony culminates with Moses sprinkling 'the blood of the covenant' that YHWH made with Israel. Since restoration ideology is often characterized by a recapitulation of past events, this may well be the appeal in Zech. 9.11.

There is the possibility, however, that the covenant of Zech. 9.11 refers to the eternal covenant mentioned in Jer. 32.40, 50.5 and Ezek. 16.61 (again, two texts that Zechariah 9–14 frequently draws from), which is mentioned in the context of YHWH's declaration to restore Israel from exile. The two, of course, are not mutually exclusive, especially if Exodus 24 is being read typologically in reference to the second exodus imagery of Jeremiah and Ezekiel.

The covenantal language may also be another allusion to Isaiah 42, where the servant is said to be given as a covenant to the people in order to bring the prisoners out of the dungeon (42.6–7).[31] If this is the case, then the mention of blood may foreshadow the (sacrificial) death of YHWH's agent, which would align well with developments in the second oracle, especially Zech. 12.10 and 13.7.[32]

It appears that Isaiah might also stand behind two more images found in this section of Zechariah, both which point to exile. That the people are referred to as prisoners living in a pit without water underscores their status as exiles.[33] This again may reflect an intentional interaction between Zechariah 9–14 and Isaiah 40–66, a text in which the exiles are described as prisoners on three occasions (Isa. 42.7; 49.9; 61.1). That the readers are called to return (שׁוּבוּ) to their stronghold (i.e. Jerusalem) where they will receive their 'double portion' further reiterates that their restoration is near, and perhaps reflects yet another allusion to Isaiah 40–66.[34] In Isa. 40.2, YHWH comforts his exiled people with the news that their penalty has been paid for, and that they have received double for all their sins. A similar idea is echoed in Isa. 61.7, where restoration is described as a double portion.

Zech. 9.1–17 culminates by describing YHWH's coming restoration as 'salvation' (9.16; וְהוֹשִׁיעָם). This is followed by two clauses which provide further basis for YHWH's saving actions: (a) 'because they are the flock

---

[31] Mason 1977: 92.   [32] See §2.2.2.
[33] Meyers and Meyers 1993: 140.   [34] *Ibid.*: 143.

of his people', and (b) because 'like stones of his crown they will shine in his land'.[35]

The shepherd imagery of 9.16 likely points to the rich tradition in the exilic and post-exilic literature, which depicts Israel's predicament (exile) and YHWH's solution (restoration) with pastoral metaphors. YHWH, the good shepherd, will judge the bad shepherds (Israel's unfaithful leaders), regather the straying (exiled) sheep of Israel, renew his covenant and appoint for his people a new shepherd (king) from the house of David, who will bring about healing and restoration and usher in the new age (Jeremiah 23; 25; Ezekiel 34; 37). As will be developed, Zechariah 9–14 affirms this overarching schema of the shepherd tradition found in Jeremiah and Ezekiel, often echoing the language of the latter, but not without significant modifications.

The stone and crown imagery is more ambiguous, however, as is illustrated not only in the variety of proposals found in modern commentaries, but also in the translation of the passage in the LXX and the Targum. What makes an interpretation allusive, in part, is the variety of ways that 'stone' is used in Zechariah. In Zech. 3.9, YHWH's cleansing of the land is associated with an inscribed stone;[36] the 'top stone' of Zech. 4.7 symbolizes the completion of the temple project; in Zech. 10.4 YHWH declares that he will raise up a cornerstone; and in Zech. 12.3 YHWH declares that Jerusalem will become a heavy stone for the people. Mason has drawn a connection to the first half of Zechariah: 'Just as the "crown" in Zech. 6.14 was to be a memorial in the temple to ensure men that God's purpose would be completed, so people here are seen as testimonies to God's purposes.'[37] He also suggests that the imagery of Zech. 9.16 echoes Isa. 62.3.[38] There are some interesting parallels between Isaiah 62 and Zechariah 9.16. Both texts announce YHWH's restoration in terms of salvation (cf. Isa. 62.1). In Isaiah 62.3, the restored people are said to be a crown of beauty and a royal diadem in the hand of YHWH. And in Isa. 62.8, wine and grain are said to be restored to YHWH's people (cf. Zech. 9.17). Ollenburger has suggested that the reference to the stones glittering 'is a verbal form of the word "signal" (נוס) in Isa

[35] Sweeney 2000: 667.

[36] Brevard Childs (1979: 478) suggests that when read canonically 'Joshua's crowning now functions symbolically to foreshadow the coming of the future messianic figure of the "Branch".'

[37] Mason 1977: 95; see also Meyers and Meyers 1993: 158. Mason (1973: 86) suggests that the crown imagery is a reinterpretation of the promise made in proto-Zechariah: the community is to become what Joshua and Zerubbabel had been.

[38] Mason 1977: 95.

Table 2.1 *Restoration schema of Zechariah 9.1–17*

1. A Davidic king arrives in Zion.	2. Israel is ingathered and returns to the land.	3. Israel faces hostility from the nations, but is delivered by YHWH.	4. Israel worships YHWH in the land as his sheep and shining stones.

11:10–12, where the "root of Jesse" – like the Branch, and king in the line of David – will signal return from diaspora'.[39] In a similar fashion, people of YHWH shining in the land is a sign of redemption and return. Marvin Sweeney proposes that the stones/crown imagery calls upon the image of the stones that adorn the crown of the high priest (cf. Exod. 24.1–8; 28.36–8).[40] As can be seen in this survey, it is unclear whether the imagery is priestly, royal or is meant to relate to the temple. The Targum seems to understand it as priestly imagery, translating the phrase 'stones of the ephod'. The LXX appears to regard it as temple imagery, translating the phrase as 'holy stones' (λίθοι ἅγιοι). As is often the case in interpreting Zechariah 9–14, a definitive conclusion eludes us.

One final feature in this opening section of Zechariah 9–14 must be mentioned. In Zech. 9.10–15 the return or ingathering of Israel will involve hostility from the nations. What is significant about this passage is that it is YHWH, and not the king, who will engage in warfare and ultimately defeat Israel's enemies before she enjoys peace in the land.[41] Thus, the kind of restoration that is envisioned in Zech. 9.1–17 is not simply release from captivity, but also the defeat of Israel's enemies in Zion.

Given the paradigmatic function of this first unit of Zechariah 9–14, it is important to briefly highlight two of our findings before exploring the further development of these themes in Zechariah 10–14. First, much in keeping with Mitchell's assessment, I have demonstrated the restoration schema in Table 2.1.

As I suggested, there is an indication in Zech. 9.9–10 that this coming Davidic king will face hostility from his own people, and that his legitimacy as king will be challenged before he is 'saved' or vindicated by YHWH. Second, it is possible to perceive a variety of intertextual allusions in Zech. 9.1–17, most notably from Isaiah 40–66, but also from Jeremiah and Ezekiel. The ambiguity of many of the allusions in the passage have made it difficult to arrive at any definitive conclusions,

---

[39] Ollenburger 1996: 811.   [40] Sweeney 2000: 666.   [41] Mitchell 1997: 141.

which perhaps explains why Zechariah 9–14 was fertile ground for speculation and fresh interpretations, especially in the early Christian movement, which sought to both understand as well as to justify Jesus' last week.[42]

2.1.2.2   Zechariah 10.1–12

Zech. 10.1–12 makes up the second sub-unit of this first oracle and provides further details of YHWH's restoration programme. The passage begins with an admonition, which is then followed with an accusation. The admonition is to ask for rain from YHWH – instead of seeking provision, guidance and consolation from teraphim, diviners and false prophets (10.1–2). In keeping with what has been promised in Zech. 9.17, the emphasis in Zech. 10.1 is on the fact that it is YHWH alone who provides prosperity and fruitfulness in the land (cf. 9.17) – and therefore should alone be sought for guidance and provision. The accusation which follows gets to the heart of why Israel is in need of restoration: Israel's leaders, that is, her shepherds, have failed to seek YHWH and have instead deceived the people with lies and false consolation. This leadership crisis, according to Zech. 10.2, is the principal cause of Israel's national crisis – exile. Israel has been scattered (lit. 'set out'; נָסְעוּ)[43] like sheep (cf. 9.16) and afflicted (יַעֲנוּ; cf. with the coming king of 9.9) because they lack good shepherding.

Zech. 10.1–2 becomes a significant passage for understanding the diagnosis and the cure for Israel's predicament, as well as the language that is used in Zech. 10–13 to describe how YHWH intends to restore her: both idolatry as well as a lack of spiritual leadership have led to Israel's expulsion from the land as well as their failure to re-establish themselves as a nation now that some have returned.[44] This particular way of describing Israel's predicament (that is, with pastoral imagery) finds its antecedent in Ezekiel 34, which itself builds upon Jeremiah 23.[45] From Jeremiah's standpoint, for example, Israel's impending national crisis is credited to selfish and unrighteous leaders: YHWH's 'sheep'

---

[42] Cf. John Barton 1986: 193.

[43] The verb נָסַע is used often in Numbers and Deuteronomy to describe Israel as they journeyed in the wilderness (e.g. Num. 2.9; 10.2,34; 21.11; 33.1; Deut. 1.19), and is perhaps used here in order to draw parallels between exile and the wilderness experience of Israel's ancestors.

[44] The Targum seems to confirm this reading in a number of ways. First, it regards those who enquire of teraphim as 'worshippers of idols'. Second, it interprets the scattering of the flock as 'they went into exile'. And finally, it interprets shepherd to mean 'king'.

[45] Sweeney 2000: 668–71; Laniak 2006: 162–5.

have been dispersed for lack of good, caring 'shepherds' (Jer. 23.1–4; 25.34–8). According to Jeremiah, Israel will not forever be 'scattered'; instead, YHWH has promised to 'gather the remnant of his flock' out of all the countries where he has 'driven' them, and will bring them back to his 'fold' (Jer. 23.3; see also Jer. 31.10). This regathering of the 'sheep' will be done through a righteous branch of David, who will reign as king and execute justice (Jer. 23.5).

Like Jeremiah 23, Ezekiel 34 places the blame squarely on the shoulders of Israel's leaders, also by employing pastoral imagery (34.1–9). YHWH's 'flock' has been scattered because of selfish and harsh 'shepherds' who have failed to 'feed the sheep, strengthen the weak, heal the sick, bind up the injured, bring back the stray, and seek out the lost' (Ezek. 34.3–4).[46] For this reason, YHWH is against the 'shepherds'. Nevertheless, as the 'Good Shepherd', he promises to rescue his 'sheep' from being devoured by their leaders (34.10). Unlike the 'bad shepherds', he will search for his 'flock' (34.11); he will bring back the 'strays' (34.16). In addition to YHWH personally intervening, he also foretells of his plan to set up over the 'sheep' 'one shepherd', his servant David, who will give them the kind of leadership they need (34.23 and again in 37.24–5). All this is said to happen on the day when YHWH will vindicate his name, gather in his people from the nations, cleanse them from their idolatry, give them new hearts and put his spirit within them that they might walk in his statutes (Ezek. 36.25–7). A similar programme of cleansing is developed in Zech. 12.10–13.1, as we will explore.

Before moving to Zech. 10.3–11.3, it should be noted that there is an interesting and, as I will argue in Chapter 3, perhaps significant variant in Zech. 10.2 between the Hebrew and Greek versions. The MT reads: 'Therefore the people wander like sheep; they suffer for lack of a shepherd.'[47] The LXX rendition replaces the word shepherd with the word 'healing': 'because of this, they were driven away like sheep and were afflicted, since there was no healing'.[48] I am unaware of any manuscript evidence from either the Hebrew or the Greek texts which might explain how this alternative reading in the LXX tradition appeared.[49] It is possible that the initial LXX translator deliberately made the change (*al tiqré*) from shepherd to healing because he noted within

---

[46] Ezekiel 20 would suggest that idolatry is partially in view here.

[47] עַל־כֵּן נָסְעוּ כְמוֹ־צֹאן יַעֲנוּ כִּי־אֵין רֹעֶה.

[48] διὰ τοῦτο ἐξήρθησαν ὡς πρόβατα καὶ ἐκακώθησαν, διότι οὐκ ἦν ἴασις; Translation mine.

[49] With respect to other textual traditions, Targum Zech. 10.2 translates *shepherd* as *king* (Cathcart and Gordon 1989: 208); Aquila, Symmachus and Theodotion follow the MT.

the shepherd tradition the connection between a lack of healing and the absence of a good shepherd (Ezek. 34.4/Zech. 11.16).[50] Healing terminology is often, though not exclusively, used in the OT as a metaphor for forgiveness of sins and/or restoration from punishment, affliction or exile.[51]

In Zech. 10.3, YHWH reiterates sentiments found in Jeremiah 23 and Ezekiel 34: 'My anger is hot against the shepherds, and I will punish the leaders.' There appears to be in view here two levels of leadership that are being chided – the shepherds (הָרֹעִים; cf. Ezek. 34.1–16) and the he-goats (הָעַתּוּדִים; cf. Ezek. 34.17–24).[52] Zech. 10.3 indicates, then, the profundity of Israel's leadership crisis, and further points to the need for a complete leadership overhaul. The terminology used in Zech. 10.3 once again suggests parallels between Ezekiel 34 and Zechariah 9–14. The remainder of the passage concerns itself with a description of how YHWH intends to remedy Israel's predicament. First, a new leader will be appointed from 'out of' the house of Judah, described as both a 'cornerstone' (פִּנָּה) as well as a 'tent peg' (יָתֵד). Outside of Zechariah, פִּנָּה is often (though not exclusively) used as a term to refer to a leader of Israel (Judg. 20.2; 1 Sam. 14.38; Isa. 19.13). In the case of Isa. 28.16 and Ps. 118.22, it carries an eschatological significance, referring to YHWH's appointed agent who will bring about restoration.[53] It appears that the Targum has understood פִּנָּה in this latter sense, regarding the word as a reference to the coming king. 'Tent peg' may allude typologically to Eliakim (Isa. 22.20–3), who was variously described as (a) having authority over Jerusalem and the house of Judah, (b) having the keys to the house of David and (c) 'like a tent peg'.[54] The Targum seems to read 'tent peg' typologically as referring to 'the anointed one', or messiah. Curiously, the LXX renders Zech. 10.4 καὶ ἐξ αὐτοῦ ἐπέβλεψεν καὶ ἐξ

---

[50] See an example of *al tiqré* with the MT and the LXX in Instone-Brewer (1992: 178).

[51] LXX: Deut. 30.3–5; Jer. 3.22; 33.6; Isa. 30.26; 53.5; 57.18–19; 61.1; Hosea 14.4; Ps. 59.4; 102.3; 106.20; 146.3. For healing and national restoration outside of the OT see Jub. 23.29, T. Zeb. 9.8; 2 Bar. 73.2; 4 Ezra 13.50 and 4Q521. R. E. Clements (1998: 52) writes, '[t]he sufferings of Servant-Israel would be the offering by which the relationship of all the scattered nation with Yahweh would be renewed. Israel would once again be returned to the sphere of blessing and divine protection, which in its own sins had nullified in the past'.

[52] Duguid 1995: 270; Meyers and Meyers 1993: 196–7; 'Zechariah extends his criticism below royalty to the power brokers within the flock who shared the responsibility for the demise of Israel' (Laniak 2006: 165). It could be that the diviners, false prophets and those who seek teraphim fall into this latter category of 'he-goats'.

[53] Mason 1973: 114–15; Given the immediate context, the expectation of Zech. 9.9, and references in Zechariah 1–8, Meyers and Meyers suggest that פִּנָּה probably refers to an eschatological Davidide (1993: 2000), in keeping with Ps. 118.22.

[54] Meyers and Meyers 1993: 201; Duguid 1995: 271.

αὐτοῦ ἔταξεν, καὶ ἐξ αὐτοῦ τόξον ἐν θυμῷ, ἐξ αὐτοῦ ἐξελεύσεται πᾶς ὁ ἐξελαύνων ἐν τῷ αὐτῷ ('and from it [οἶκος] he gazed, and from it he commanded, and from it was a furious bow, from it all of those who march out with him [κύριος ὁ θεὸς ὁ παντοκράτωρ] will go forth').[55]

Many modern interpreters along with the LXX and the Targum understand the third term as a reference not to the coming ruler but instead to the military might that YHWH will provide.[56] Along with this military might, YHWH will provide overseers (lit. 'every overseer'; כָּל־נֹגֵשׂ), or a faithful second tier of leadership.[57] According to the Zechariah programme, in the new order there will no longer be self-serving under-shepherds who abuse YHWH's sheep (cf. Ezek. 34). Instead, YHWH's new leadership will serve the people in such a way as to bring about victory for the entire nation (10.5; cf. 9.11–13).[58]

Zech. 10.6–12 draws on two prominent restoration images in order to elaborate the deliverance that awaits Israel. In Zech. 10.6, the return of YHWH's compassion upon a people he once rejected recalls the promises of Hosea 2.[59] Here YHWH declares that though he has rejected his people because of their idolatry, he will nevertheless draw them out to the desert where he will have compassion on *Lo-ruhamah* ('no compassion'), and where he will declare 'You are my people' to *Lo-ammi* ('Not my people'; Hosea 2.23).

The second image found in Zech. 10.6–12 is that of a second exodus. Several scholars have noted the prominence of the second exodus tradition in such books as Jeremiah, Isaiah and Ezekiel. Many of the elements of that tradition appear in Zech. 10.6–12. First, there is the imagery of YHWH as the caring, intervening shepherd: 'I will whistle for them' (10.8; cf. Isa. 40.10–11; Jer. 23.2; Ezek. 34.11–16).[60] Second, both in the earlier prophetic material as well as here in Zechariah this shepherd imagery has been coupled with YHWH's ingathering of his flock, Israel: 'I will gather (קבץ) them in, for I have redeemed[61] them' (10.8; 10.10; cf. Isa. 40.10–11; Jer. 23.3; Ezek. 34.13).[62] This ingathering will result

---

[55] Translation mine.

[56] Mason 1973: 118–19; Meyers and Meyers 1993: 202; Duguid 1995: 272.

[57] Meyers and Meyers 1993: 203; Duguid 1995: 272.

[58] Mason 1977: 100; Meyers and Meyers 1993: 203–4.   [59] Sweeney 2000: 672–3.

[60] Laniak 2006: 165. Laniak's work highlights how shepherd imagery is part and parcel with the promises of a second exodus.

[61] As Laniak (2006: 166) has noted: 'Redemption (*pdh*) defines the original exodus (Deut. 7:8; Ps. 78:42; Mic. 6:4) and second exodus promises (Isa. 35.10=51:11).'

[62] Mitchell has shown that in the eschatological programmes of the prophets, קבץ is the preferred term to indicate YHWH's ingathering of Israel, while אסף is the word often used to describe the ingathering of the hostile nations against Israel (1997: 164).

in a return (שׁוּב) to the land, and by implication a return to YHWH (10.6,10; cf. Jer. 23.3; Ezek. 34.13). And third, Israel's redemption is described as a recapitulation of the first exodus: (a) they will be brought home from Egypt, and (b) they will pass over the sea of troubles; the depths of the Nile will be dried up.[63] Zech. 10.12 reiterates that YHWH will give strength to his people in order that they 'walk' in his ways (cf. 10.5,7). This promise of strength to walk might hint at a possible desert journey as a part of Zechariah's restoration programme, especially if read in light of the possible allusion to Hosea 2 in Zech. 10.6 (i.e. the ingathering of YHWH's people in the desert) and the second exodus allusions in Zech. 10.8–12. As Childs noted, what is interesting about the appropriation of second exodus imagery in Zechariah is that it no longer points to Babylonian liberation, but instead bears witness to a still-future referent.[64] As such, it reflects a shift in thinking, in which the second exodus is no longer thought of as being concomitant with return from Babylon.[65]

2.1.2.3 Zechariah 11.1–3

The 'call to lament' found in Zech. 11.1–3 functions as a transition passage. Enigmatically, both trees (cedar, cypress and oak) as well as shepherds are exhorted to wail, for fire and lions (respectively) are set to devour them. On the one hand, this passage has the potential to function as a sort of 'taunt song' that exults in the pending yet certain defeat of Israel's enemies (cf. Zechariah 9–10).[66] On the other hand, the arboreal, shepherd and lion metaphors can point to Israel, and may be intentionally ambiguous in order to also point to the pending judgment of Israel's own shepherds (cf. 10.3; 11.4–17).[67] For example, while the arboreal imagery of Zech. 11.1–2 is often used in prophetic literature to speak of the destruction of prideful, powerful nations (Isa. 2.6–21; 10.5–34; 14.3–23;

---

[63] Sweeney 2000: 675.   [64] Childs 1979: 483.

[65] Childs (1979: 484) argues that Zechariah 9–14 has been added to the prophetic book precisely in order to explain this period before the end.

[66] Mason 1977: 103. Trees often represent the pride of foreign kings (e.g. Ezek. 17.3; Amos 2.9; Judg. 9.15; 2 Kings 19.23; Isa. 2.13; 14.8; 37.24; 60.13; Jer. 22.20).

[67] Tigchelaar (1996: 94) argues that 11.1–3 (as well as 10.1–2) functions both as a conclusion to the preceding unit as well as an introduction to the following one. So also Mason 1977: 103. Ollenburger (1996: 817) suggests that the ambiguity serves to both celebrate YHWH's triumph announced in Zechariah 9–10, as well as to foreshadow the conflict in Zech. 11.4–17. Hanson (1975: 335) suggests that the prophetic genre of taunt against foreign nations is adopted here 'and given a double ironic twist to form a sharp barb directed against Israel's leaders'.

Jer. 21.11–14; 22.1–22), in Ezek. 17.3 the cedar of Lebanon is the king of Judah.[68] The principal point of the imagery is nevertheless clear: YHWH will destroy any haughty leader that stands in his way.

The final verse in this 'taunt song', Zech. 11.3, appears to be a conflation of three passages in Jeremiah. For example, in Jer. 25.36–8, YHWH also issues a call to lament for the shepherds:

> Hark! the cry of the shepherds, and the wail of the lords of the flock! For the LORD is despoiling their pasture, and the peaceful folds are devastated, because of the fierce anger of the LORD. Like a lion he has left his covert; for their land has become a waste.

In Jer. 49.19 and 50.44, YHWH is described as a lion coming up from 'the thickets of the Jordan' (cf. Zech. 11.3) who will clear out his pasture and appoint whomever he chooses as leader. The passage ends with the provocative taunt: Who is the shepherd who can stand before me? While Jer. 49.19 and 50.44 clearly speak of the defeat of Israel's enemies (Edom and Babylon respectively), in Jer. 25 Jerusalem and Judah are included in the list of nations that will be dethroned (25.18). The prophet's move away from lion (Jer. 25.38; 49.19; 50.44) to 'young lions' (Zech. 11.3) is also difficult to explain. It may be a reference to the house of Judah, and point to them being the ones who defeat the foreign rulers (cf. Zech. 9.13–15; 10.5), or as the Targum suggests, it may be yet another descriptor of lament of the shepherds.[69]

2.1.2.4   Zechariah 11.4–17

Zech. 11.4–17 is rightfully regarded as one of the most difficult passages to interpret in the Jewish scriptures, especially if one comes to these passages with the aim of trying to identify historical figures behind the prophet's symbolic actions.[70] Our aim as we analyze this passage is to trace the development of the eschatological programme of Zechariah 9–14. To that end, it seems that reading Zech. 11.4–17 as the shocking reversal of many of the promises found in the shepherd traditions of Jeremiah 23 and Ezekiel 34 proves to be most fruitful.[71]

---

[68]   Ollenburger 1996: 817; Sweeney 2000: 676.

[69]   Sweeney (2000: 676) notes that the roaring lion recalls the common association of the lion with the tribe of Judah and the house of David (Gen. 49.9; Amos 1.2; 1 Sam .17.34–6).

[70]   For example, there are over forty proposals for identifying the three shepherds in Zech. 11.8 (Mitchell 1912: 306).

[71]   So also Hanson 1975: 343–5; Mason 1977: 109; Meyers and Meyers 1993: 285; Duguid 1995: 272–4; Sweeney 2000: 677–83; Laniak 2006: 167.

Zech. 11.4–6 reiterates that YHWH will indeed punish the bad shepherds (cf. 10.3), who have had no compassion for the sheep, and instead have used them for profit. The following verses, however, add a crucial twist to the shepherd tradition and the restoration programme of Zechariah 9–14.[72] The prophet's symbolic actions indicate (in keeping with Ezek. 34.7–16 and Jer. 23.3–4) that YHWH will come to tend his 'flock doomed to slaughter' (Zech. 11.7). His coming will involve the removal of the wicked shepherds, that is, the upheaval of the present leadership system (Zech. 11.8). While affirming the unworthiness of the shepherds, it also becomes clear that the people themselves share responsibility for the deterioration of the community; they detest the good shepherd, and the good shepherd in turn loses patience with them (11.7–9). As a result, in what appears to be a reversal of Ezekiel 34/37, YHWH declares that he will no longer be their shepherd (11.9), culminating with the breaking of the two staffs, 'Favour' and 'Unity'.[73] In addition, instead of sending a good shepherd (Ezek. 34.23; 37.24), YHWH commissions a wicked shepherd who will not care for the sheep (11.16).[74] The first oracle ends with a final word of judgment over the bad shepherd, who will be struck by the sword, perhaps leaving the possibility for hope in restoration (11.17). As Duguid has argued, '[t]he last word is not judgment upon God's people but woe to the worthless shepherd (v 17), which brings with it at least the hope that a return to the promises of Ezek 34 and Jer 23 is possible'.[75]

At this point it is important to underscore that Zech. 11.4–17 has significantly altered the picture that has thus far been painted regarding Israel's restoration. Zechariah 9–10 has given the impression, much in keeping with Jeremiah 23 and Ezekiel 34, that the good shepherd would be welcomed by YHWH's people, and that his coming would bring immediate liberty, peace and prosperity. While Zech. 11.4–17 is not the easiest passage to understand, it is clear that the coming of the good shepherd will provoke enmity among those in Jerusalem and even more

---

[72] Mason (1977: 105) notes the pessimistic shift in tone in this section of Zechariah.

[73] The two staffs used by the prophet seem to be a deliberate borrowing from Ezek. 37.15–28. There the staffs symbolized YHWH's covenant with Israel and the unity of the two kingdoms (Duguid 1995: 273; Laniak 2006: 167). See also Hanson 1975: 343–5. Regarding the identity of the 'I' in Zech. 11.8–10, I follow Larkin who comments that 'the "I" of God and the "I" of the prophet are almost inextricable' (Larkin 1994: 128). Similarly, Sweeney notes that in Zech. 11.4–17 YHWH's communication is symbolized in the action of the prophet's symbolic performance (2000: 678).

[74] It is no coincidence that the characteristics of this newly commissioned bad shepherd parallel the characteristics of the shepherds who will be punished in Ezek. 34.16. See Meyers and Meyers 1993: 285; Duguid 1995: 273.

[75] Duguid 1995: 274.

upheaval before there is final restoration. As we will see, this theme, which is only hinted at here, will be further developed in the second oracle of Zechariah 9–14.

2.1.2.5   Zechariah 12.1–13.6

The opening of this second oracle of Zechariah 9–14 reiterates what has been mentioned in Zech. 11.4–17, namely that there will be a time of tumult before final restoration.[76] In keeping with the first oracle (cf. 9.1–8, 13–16; 10.5–7), Zech. 12.2–9 warns of an attack by the nations against Jerusalem. Zion, however, will be a 'cup of reeling' and a 'heavy stone' with respect to the nations (Zech. 12.2–3). Sweeney has suggested that the stone imagery is connected with the temple foundation mentioned in Zechariah 4. He argues that the temple, thus, functions as the agent of the incapacitation of the nations.[77] Many have also noted a connection with Isa. 28.16, where YHWH declares that he is laying a foundation stone in Zion, and concludes by remarking that the one who trusts will not panic (cf. Zech. 12.4).[78] Several obscure verses in Zechariah 12 (2,5–7) suggest that perhaps some among Judah will take part in the siege, or that there will be some sort of rivalry among the inhabitants of Judah.[79] Meyers and Meyers suggest that the 'cup of reeling' imagery (Zech. 12.2) has been adapted from Jer. 25.15–31. In that context, Judah and her king are included in judgment. They argue, however, that Zechariah 12 modifies Jeremiah 25 by making Jerusalem the cup that will mete out judgment against the nations.[80] Whatever the case may be, ultimately YHWH's care for Judah and Jerusalem is confirmed (Zech. 12.7), as well as YHWH's defeat of the hostile nations (Zech. 12.9).

The triumphant tone of the second oracle drastically changes, however, in Zech. 12.10–14: the house of David will be filled with remorse as they mourn for the mysterious 'pierced one' (12.10). Scholars have noted the

[76] 'There is a certain general development of theme in 12.1–13.6 which gives the section a basic unity' (Mason 1977: 113). The phrase 'on that day' is repeated ten times (Zech. 12.3,4,6,8 [2x], 9,11; 13.1,2,4) in this passage, which also seems to suggest that 12.1–13.6 is a unit, and which also points to the future orientation of the oracle.

[77] Sweeney 2000: 685; Meyers and Meyers (1993: 317) draw a line to the temple imagery in Zechariah 1–8.

[78] E.g. Mason 1977: 116.

[79] Some manuscripts of the LXX interpret these passages thus, as does the Targum: 'and even the people of the house of Judah shall the nations bring by force, in the siege, to Jerusalem' (Zech. 12.2; Cathcart and Gordon 1989). So also Sweeney 2000: 685.

[80] Meyers and Meyers 1993: 314; Mason (1977: 115) also does not think these passages include some of Judah in the siege against Jerusalem.

numerous difficulties in Zech. 12.10, reflected as well in the LXX and the Targum, which make identifying the figure a challenge. First, there is a question as to whom 'they' will look upon.[81] While some Hebrew manuscripts read, 'they will look upon *him* whom they have pierced', the original rendering was most likely 'they will look upon *me* whom they have pierced', a reading which is also confirmed by the LXX, Theodotion, the Targum, Syriac and the Vulgate.[82] Ollenburger has suggested that the phrase 'whom they have pierced' could be regarded as an accusative of respect, which would render the verse as follows: 'they will look upon me concerning the one whom they pierced'.[83]

The LXX and the Targum reveal further complications with Zech. 12.10. The LXX reads 'they will look to me because they [the enemies?] have danced triumphantly', whereas the Targum reads 'they will entreat me because they were exiled'. At issue here seems to be the translators' unwillingness, for whatever reason, to give a literal rendering of דקר (i.e. to pierce (with a sword or knife)).[84] While these readings (i.e. in the LXX and the Targum) seem to obscure a significant element in the text-plot of Zechariah's restoration programme, the latter part of Zech. 12.10 and Zech. 12.11 may help re-establish it to some degree. In Zech. 12.10b we read that 'they will mourn for *him*'. Who is it that is to be mourned? While Zech. 12.10 does not explicitly identify the person, there is reason to believe that it is a human, perhaps even a royal figure, that has been killed (i.e. pierced). In Zech. 12.10 the mourning is likened to losing an only child. In Zech. 12.11 the figure is likened to king Josiah, who was killed at Meggido by Pharaoh Neco, and whose death was mourned by Judah and Jerusalem (2 Chron. 35.22–4/2; Kings 23.28–30). As Mitchell has noted, '[l]ike Zechariah's figure, Josiah was pierced in battle and his death was followed soon after by national exile'.[85] The Targum appears to read Zech. 12.11 as an allusion to Josiah: 'the mourning in Jerusalem shall be as great as . . . the mourning for Josiah son of Amon whom

---

[81] For a comprehensive and up-to-date discussion of the textual problems surrounding Zech. 12.10 see Chapter 2 of Bynum 2009; see also Delcor 1951.

[82] While most manuscripts of Aquila and Symmachus confirm the MT, some extant fragments are ambiguous.

[83] Ollenburger 1996: 828.

[84] This can be seen also in Zech. 13.3, where רקד is softened in both the LXX and the Targum to 'bind' and 'to lay hold of' respectively. Elsewhere in the Hebrew bible דקר is translated as a literal, physical piercing (e.g. Num. 25.8; 1 Sam. 31.4).

[85] Mitchell 1997: 205 (see discussion of Zech. 13.7–9 below). Cathcart and Gordon (1989: 218) note that Strack-Billerbeck suggests a possible rendering of Zech. 12.10 to be 'they will entreat me for him on whose account they went into exile'. This might confirm Mitchell's observations regarding a second exile which is incurred by the death of the 'pierced one'.

Pharaoh the Lame killed in the valley of Megiddon'.[86] I concur with Mitchell, who argues that if a reference to Josiah is intended here, then the pierced one, 'by analogy, may be taken as an antitype of Josiah, that is, an eschatological Davidic king'.[87] This seems to be confirmed by the emphasis in this passage on the fact that it is the house of David that mourns (12.10,12), followed by the house of Nathan (12.12), the Levites (12.13) and all of the families who are left in Jerusalem (12.14).[88]

The sombre tone of Zech. 12.10–14 has been infused with hope in Zech. 13.1–6. Concomitant with the death of the pierced one is a 'day' in which a fountain will be poured upon the house of David and the inhabitants of Jerusalem to cleanse them from their sin and impurity (13.1). This cleansing will include the removal of false prophets in the land (13.2–5). Several scholars have found resonances here with Ezek. 36. Like Zech. 12.10–13.6, Ezek. 36.20–30 speaks of Israel's restoration in terms of a gathering and settling of YHWH's people in Jerusalem (36.24; cf. Zech. 9.1–17; 10.8–12), the cleansing with waters from idols (36.25), the giving of the spirit (36.26–7), and abundance in the land (36.30; cf. Zech. 9.17).[89] If this is the case, then once again we see that Zechariah has added to the Ezekiel programme a time of trouble, which is to include the death of a royal figure and a time of mourning.

2.1.2.6   Zechariah 13.7–9

Nearly every commentator agrees that Zech. 13.7–9, in its canonical position, functions as an interpretative guide to themes opaquely intimated in the earlier part of the oracle.[90] Exactly what it 'clarifies', however, has been the subject of extensive debate, which centres on the identity of the smitten shepherd of Zech. 13.7. Much like the perplexed eunuch in Acts 8.34 who was puzzled at the identity of the figure in Isa. 53.7–8, scholars query, 'About whom does the prophet say this?'

---

[86]   As does Mitchell 1997: 205, n. 23.
[87]   Mitchell 1997: 205. Ollenburger (1996: 829) argues that 'the comparisons suggest that the unidentified victim in v.10 had, or is given, royal status'.
[88]   This list may symbolically point to all segments of Jersusalem – royalty (house of David), the prophets (house of Nathan), the priests (Levites) and the population at large. See also Sweeney 2000: 691.
[89]   Delcor 1951: 386; Black 1990: 85; Ollenburger 1996: 831.
[90]   Many scholars since Ewald have argued that Zech. 13.7–9 was originally placed just after 11.4–17 (e.g. Mason 1977). While there may be merit to this proposal, as we have already stated, we are concerned with the final form, which is likely the best indication of how this material is to be interpreted. See Stephen Cook (1993) for a detailed discussion of Zech. 13.7–9 in its initial and final forms.

Although it is possible to understand the smitten shepherd to be either the bad shepherd of Zech. 11.15–17 or some historic figure like Cyrus,[91] there are compelling reasons to regard the figure as the good shepherd who was rejected and despised by his own people (cf. Zech. 11.4–14).[92] Zechariah's programme thus far has left the reader wondering (a) what happened to the good shepherd (11.4–15), (b) what the fate is of those who rejected the good shepherd and (c) who the pierced one of Zech. 12.10 is. Arguably, Zech. 13.7–9 has been placed here to clarify precisely these questions.[93] It is significant that the figure to be struck in 13.7 is qualified as YHWH's shepherd (*my* shepherd; רֹעִי), and is then further described as YHWH's compeer or associate (*my* associate; גֶּבֶר עֲמִיתִי).[94] Having already noted that the shepherd imagery of Zech. 11.7–14 is linked to the eschatological Davidic shepherd-king of Jeremiah 23 and Ezekiel 34, it would seem that the references to 'my shepherd' and 'the man who is my associate' point to the same divinely appointed Davidic figure, who is now set to receive a smiting blow that will cause the scattering of YHWH's sheep. With this linkage in place, it is not hard to see how Zech. 12.10–12 (with its mention of a mysterious 'pierced one' and its emphasis on the mourning in the house of David) could be understood as an oblique gesture pointing towards Zech. 13.7–9.

If read in its wider context, Zech. 13.7–9 can be understood as providing further details regarding not only the identity of the 'pierced one' (12.10) but also regarding the fate of those that have rejected the good shepherd (11.8–14), and details regarding what will happen to the house of David and the inhabitants of Israel. According to the prophet, the shepherd will be struck, the sheep will be scattered and YHWH will turn his hand against his 'little ones'. Two-thirds of the people in the land will be cut off and perish, and one-third will have to endure an unspecified period of 'fiery trials' intended to test their fidelity. The one-third that is put into the fiery trials will participate in the renewal of YHWH's covenant with his people, in which he will declare, 'They are my people' (Zech. 13.9; cf. Zech. 10.6 and Hosea 2.23; Ezek. 37.23).

There are several features of this passage that must be highlighted. First, Zech. 13.7–9 (read along with Zech. 14.1–2) suggests that there will be a severe time of trouble following the smiting of the shepherd, which will include an invasion and pillage of Jerusalem by the nations

---

[91]　E.g. Mason 1977: 111; Hanson 1975: 338; Redditt 1989: 634–5; Sweeney 2000: 696.
[92]　E.g. Cook 1993; Larkin 1994: 177.
[93]　So also Cook 1993: 460–3; Hanson 1975: 338.
[94]　See Mason (1973: 171–87), who regards these terms as ironic, and thus as a reference to the bad shepherd of 11.15–17.

(14.1–2), and a time of fiery trials that will test the remnant in preparation for YHWH's covenant renewal (13.8–9).[95] Mitchell has suggested that 13.7–14.2 has borrowed from Ezek. 20.34–8, a passage that also foresees a time of trouble prior to final restoration.[96] He notes that in Ezekiel 20 this period of trouble is described as an exile in 'the wilderness of the nations' (20.35). He also highlights the comparisons made between the first exodus wanderings and the 'second' exodus described in Ezek. 20.34–8, and the fact that the eschatological exodus serves the purpose of purifying Israel. Whether or not literary dependence can be proven, it does raise the question of whether the ensuing fiery trials described in Zech. 13.8–9 are meant to add texture to the second exodus motif of Zech. 10.6–12. In other words, are we now to understand the fiery trials of Zech. 13.7–9 as being a part of the second exodus journey mentioned earlier? There seem to be three indications that such a connection can be made: both Zech. 10.6 as well as Zech. 13.9 seem to allude to Hosea 2. We have already discussed the relationship between Hosea 2.23 and Zech. 10.6. The declaration 'They are my people' in Zech. 13.9 seems also to point to the climactic promise of YHWH's renewed favour.[97] As has been pointed out, in the context of Hosea 2, YHWH will allure his people out to the wilderness to make such a declaration (Hosea 2.16). Additionally, as we have seen, in Zech. 11.4–17 the covenant with YHWH and his people has been broken. It seems that Zech. 13.7 is indicating that this covenant will be renewed either during or after the period of fiery trials, which would then make it possible to understand the new exodus journey of 10.6–12 to also include this period of fiery trials. And finally, as I have already suggested, the strength promised for the second exodus journey in Zech. 10.12 is fitting for those who are soon to endure a period of fiery trials.

The second noteworthy feature of this passage is that, according to Zech. 13.8, the two-thirds that do not journey through the fiery trials will be 'cut off' and will subsequently 'perish'. As Meyers and Meyers have pointed out, 'the two-thirds no longer exist as part of Yahweh's people'.[98]

Third, it is unclear, at least in my view, whether the metallurgy imagery in Zech. 13.9 is intended to convey the notion of purification. A close reading of Zech. 13.9 in its context seems to suggest otherwise. First, according to Zech. 12.10–13.6, cleansing or purification comes as a result of the death of the 'pierced one' (12.10): 'on that day [i.e. the day

[95] Mitchell 1997: 210–12.   [96] *Ibid.*
[97] Mason (1973: 186), who notes the connection between Hosea 2 and the Exodus tradition; see also Mason 1977: 112; Meyers and Meyers 1993: 396–7.
[98] Meyers and Meyers 1993: 392. Cf. 1 Pet. 4.17–18.

the Davidide is pierced] a fountain shall be opened for the house of David and the inhabitants of Jerusalem, to cleanse them from sin and impurity' (13.1);[99] 'on that day' idolatry, unclean spirits and false prophets will be removed from the land (13.2–6). Second, the poetic parallelism of 13.9 suggests that the metallurgy imagery is principally there to emphasize that the time of trouble is a time for testing one's fidelity to YHWH. In the first stanza of the parallelism, the word which has the subject 'silver' and which is translated 'refine', צרף, in the Qal can mean either 'to smelt', 'to refine' or 'to test'.[100] In the second stanza of the parallelism, in which gold is the subject, the word בחן is used, which means 'to put to the test in order to judge quality', but not in a punitive sense.[101] Meyers and Meyers have pointed out that various grades of gold existed in the Ancient Near East (ANE). When gold was put to fire, it was usually not in order to purify it, but instead in order to ascertain its degree of purity, and thus its value.[102] The poetic parallelism of Zech. 13.9 suggests, then, that the metallurgy imagery is not being used as a metaphor for purification (as is the case in Ps. 66.10–11; Prov. 17.3; Jer. 9.6; Isa. 48.10 or Mal. 3.2), but instead has been appropriated in order to convey the notion of testing or evaluating, in the case of Zechariah 13, the fidelity of YHWH's remaining one-third. This usage of fire is not unique to the OT. In the book of Daniel, the faithfulness of Shadrach, Meshach and Abednego is proven through fire (Dan. 3.19–30), whereas the men who lifted them to the furnace were consumed.[103]

Fourth, Zech. 13.9 indicates that YHWH will place one-third in fire, and that they (not unlike Shadrach, Meshach and Abednego) will emerge from the testing. That is, there is a strong expression of optimism for those who have aligned themselves with the stricken shepherd; there is no sense that any of those who make the journey through the fiery trials will be destroyed.[104] The significance of this is found in the fact that 'on the other side of this convulsion [i.e. the time of trouble described as fiery trials] the nucleus of a new community will emerge'.[105]

---

[99] Mason (1973: 185) comments that '[t]he gift of water symbolizes God's cleansing of the community from a corrupt and tainted leadership'.
[100] Even Meyers and Meyers (1993: 394), who envision purification in this verse, acknowledge this.
[101] Meyers and Meyers 1993: 395. Cf. Jer. 12.3; Job 12.11; Ps. 95.9, where the word is used metaphorically to test the mind, heart or character of someone.
[102] Meyers and Meyers 1993: 395.
[103] Goldingay's (1989: 74) comment that '[t]he three have not been delivered from the fire, but they have been delivered in the fire' can also be applied to Zech. 13.9 and 1 Peter.
[104] See Mason (1973: 127–8), who highlights this feature of Zech. 13.7–9.
[105] Mason 1973: 130.

Finally, the most significant modification in the eschatological programme of Zechariah 9–14 is found here in Zech. 13.7–9: contrary to
what one might have been led to believe from the programmes of Jeremiah
and Ezekiel, the coming of the eschatological Davidic shepherd will not
immediately usher in a time of peace and prosperity. Instead, a time of
trouble, described as a period of fiery testing, will precede final deliverance. This has led some to draw connections between Zech. 13.7–9 and
the 'messianic woes' of Jewish restoration ideology in the second temple
period.[106]

2.1.2.7   Zechariah 14.1–21

As we have already hinted, Zech. 14.1–2 reveals that YHWH's final deliverance will be preceded by a time of trouble for Israel: the nations will
gather against Jerusalem and inflict considerable damage. It is possible
to understand these events of Zech. 14.1–2 to be contemporaneous with
the smiting of the shepherd – both cause the scattering of the sheep and
a period of fiery testing, and may even be the means by which YHWH
turns his hand on the 'little ones'. Zech. 14.3–21 makes it clear, however,
that the time of trouble will not be the end of Israel's story. YHWH
will intervene along with his 'holy ones', appearing first on the Mount
of Olives (14.4), to defeat the nations, secure Jerusalem and reign over
all the earth (14.4–15). Those among the nations who survive will, year
after year, join Israel in worshipping YHWH during the Feast of Booths
(Zech. 14.16). The oracle ends with there no longer being a distinction
between the sacred and the profane, and 'there shall no longer be traders
in the house of the Lord of hosts on that day' (Zech. 14.21).[107]

Many have noted the conspicuous absence of any human royal figure
in this final section of Zechariah: this might be intentional. It may be that
we are expected to draw connections to the surprising fusion of images
from Zech. 9.1–8 to Zech. 9.9–10, where YHWH's north–south royal
campaign is conflated with the coming of the 'righteous and saved' king.
It could also be that our author wants to emphasize YHWH as the principal
agent in the unfolding and ultimate culmination of the eschatological
programme. Additionally, Mitchell has convincingly argued that a royal

---

[106] Ackroyd (1962: 654–5) maintains that 'the picture [of Zech. 13.7–9] is one of
messianic woes ushering in the final age'. Similarly, R. C. Dentan (1956: 1,109) asserts
that 'the picture is that of "messianic woes"... in the dramatic scheme of late Jewish
eschatology'. From my survey of Messianic Woes studies in 1 Peter, it seems that Zechariah
9–14 has been almost entirely overlooked as a possible source (§4.1.3).

[107] The word כְּנַעֲנִי can be translated either 'trader' (so Targum) or 'Canaanite' (so LXX).

or 'messianic' figure 'may indeed be present in and with the person of YHWH descending upon the Mount of Olives and coming with his holy ones' (Zech. 14.4–5).[108] First, he notes that the Mount of Olives in particular was regarded as a place for messianic activity.[109] Second, he points out that the anthropomorphic imagery suggests human agency, since the text suggests that YHWH's feet will 'touch' the Mount.[110] And finally, he highlights several instances in Zechariah 9–14 where YHWH and the Davidic shepherd-king are conflated (Zech. 11.10, 12.8,10; 13.7), which has also been underscored in my survey. In light of all this, Mitchell queries: 'Could it be that the [human] king is unmentioned simply because his presence is implied in the Lord descending on the Mount of Olives, and that Zech. 14.4 is the apogee of this writer's high messianism?'[111]

2.1.3   The eschatological programme of Zechariah 9–14

In order to develop my hypothesis, it is necessary not only to trace out the eschatological programme of Zechariah 9–14, but also to draw out the texture of that programme – that is, to highlight the inner- and inter-textual allusions, and to observe how Zechariah builds on earlier programmes. Before we turn to the reception of Zechariah 9–14, I will tie together three important threads that have run through this survey. First, I will explore whether a Davidic eschatological figure can be discerned throughout Zechariah 9–14. Second, I will summarize the eschatological programme, noting its sequence and significant features. And finally, I will highlight the interface between Zechariah 9–14 and earlier prophetic material.

2.1.3.1   An afflicted eschatological Davidic shepherd-king in
Zechariah 9–14?

Although it is difficult (if not impossible) to arrive at any definitive conclusions regarding the figures spoken of in Zech. 9.9–10, 11.4–14,

---

[108] Mitchell 1997: 212.

[109] Here he notes texts like T. Naph. 5.1, Test. XII Part. and Acts 1.11, which all envision the Mount of Olives as the place where the messiah will appear. He also points to an account in Josephus, where a messianic group marched from the desert to the Mount in order to take over the city from the Romans. This would again suggest that it was regarded as a place of messianic import. See Mitchell 1997: 212–13 for the full discussion.

[110] Here Mitchell rightly notes that other anthropomorphisms in the Jewish scripture stress YHWH's majesty and immensity, but do not suggest his physical contact with earth (1997: 214).

[111] *Ibid.*

12.10 and 13.7, it is possible to discern two principal themes that unite them all. First, in every reference it is plausible to regard the figure as an eschatological Davidic king. In Zech. 9.9–10 I highlighted the prevalent ideological backdrop which existed in exilic and post-exilic Judaism – the widespread expectation of a royal Davidic figure who would be an integral part of the national and spiritual restoration of Israel. I also noted several allusions, which can be connected to either David or an eschatological Davidic figure: the reference to the Jebusites in 9.7, the description of the coming king as 'righteous and saved' and its relations to, for example, Pss. 22–4, and the near verbatim citation of Ps. 72.8, which is widely regarded as pointing to a future royal son of David. Additionally, I have demonstrated a strong link between the eschatological Davidic shepherd traditions of Jeremiah 23 and Ezekiel 34, even if in a reworked fashion, and the shepherd of 11.7–14. Regarding the figure mentioned in Zech. 12.10, I noted the emphasis in 12.8–12 on the mourning that will take place 'in the house of David', how the death of the 'pierced one' might be related typologically to king Josiah, and how Zech. 12.10–13.1 parallels the eschatological programme of Ezekiel 36, where the eschatological Davidic king is the central figure. And finally, I have argued that, given YHWH's close association with the shepherd figure in Zech. 13.7, it is possible to understand him as the good shepherd of Zech. 11.7–17 (and Jeremiah 23/Ezekiel 34). I also suggested that Zech. 13.7–9 was placed where it is in its final form precisely in order to bring clarity to the figures mentioned in 11.7–14 and 12.10. With this in mind, it seems reasonable to suggest that, according to Zechariah 9–14, and in keeping with the shepherd traditions of Jeremiah and Ezekiel, an eschatological Davidic shepherd-king features integrally in YHWH's restoration of Israel.[112]

But that is not all we can say about this eschatological Davidic shepherd-king. In a reversal of previous developments of the shepherd tradition, the coming eschatological Davidic shepherd-king will have his legitimacy questioned, and then be afflicted (9.9–10); he will be rejected by Israel's leaders and despised by his own people (11.8–14); he will be pierced and mourned (12.10–14); and he will be smitten by YHWH

---

[112] Similarly, Ollenburger (1996: 742) has argued that 'Second Zechariah expects a future royal figure in the line of David' and that 'the motif of sheep and shepherds' provides the continuity in Zech. 9–14 (*ibid.*: 741). Meyers and Meyers (1993: 169) maintain that '[t]he depiction of a royal figure in 9:9 is more than a mere calling forth of a familiar theme. It is a statement of ideology that lies at the very core of the message of Second Zechariah . . . The figure described is none other than a king, in biblical terms most surely a Davidic descendant'. So also Lamarche 1961; Black 1990; Duguid 1995; Mitchell 1997; and Chae 2006.

(Zech. 13.7). But he will also be vindicated, or 'saved' (9.9), and will (somehow) live to manifest YHWH's presence in the destruction of the nations, establishing YHWH's universal reign (14.3–21).

2.1.3.2 A summary of the eschatological programme of Zechariah 9–14

In my analysis of Zechariah 9–14 I have highlighted the way in which the eschatological programme unfolds.[113] I have shown that the programme is not presented in a clean linear sequence of events. Instead, following Zech. 9.1–17, each section builds on earlier material, offering elaboration on things previously hinted at, while also hinting at further developments that will be elaborated in subsequent material. So for example, in 9.1–17 we get the big picture of YHWH's return to Zion, and his defeat of the nations; we are told that a Davidic king will be appointed over Israel, and there are hints that this king's legitimacy will be questioned and that he will eventually be 'saved' or vindicated. We also learn that Israel, like (straying) sheep, will be gathered and returned to Jerusalem to worship YHWH and shine as stones in an abundant land.

Zech. 10.1–12 reiterates the basic scheme of Zech. 9.1–17, but frames the ingathering and return with two images – the Good Shepherd caring for his flock, and a new exodus (echoing Hosea 2 and the new exodus traditions of Jeremiah, Isaiah and Ezekiel). It is within this framework that YHWH announces that he will restore the leadership in Israel by appointing a 'stone' or 'tent peg', along with a second tier of faithful leaders, suggesting also that strength will be required for the new exodus/wilderness journey.

Zech. 11.1–3 functions as the bridge between these two elaborations of the eschatological programme, affirming YHWH's defeat of the nations, but also hinting at a time of trouble for Israel. This time of trouble is adumbrated in 11.4–17, where we learn that the arrival of the shepherd will not usher in immediate peace and prosperity. Instead, the leaders and the people will reject YHWH's appointed king, YHWH's covenant will be broken and Israel will once again find itself under a wicked shepherd.

Zech. 12.1–13.6 seems to give more details about this time of trouble. First, it is announced that the nations will gather together in hostility against Jerusalem. But, Jerusalem will be like a heavy stone that incapacitates her enemies. The triumphalism is subdued, however, in the

---

[113] I am indebted to Mitchell (1997: 142) for this fundamental observation about Zechariah 9–14, even if, in the end, we differ on how the programme develops.

Table 2.2 *The eschatological programme of Zechariah 9–14*

1. Ingathering and return of Israel to Jerusalem.	2. The coming of Israel's eschatological Davidic shepherd-king.	3. A time of trouble for Israel: (a) the king is killed; (b) Israel is scattered; (c) the remnant pass through fiery trials (linked with a second exodus journey); (d) the nations gather against Israel.	4. The remnant of Israel is regathered; YHWH renews his covenant; and the nations are defeated.	5. Israel's remnant, along with the survivors of the nations, worship YHWH and celebrate his universal reign.

announcement that a member of the house of David will be pierced, and all of Israel will mourn. The death of this Davidide, however, will be followed by spiritual renewal – the cleansing from idolatry and false prophecy.

Zech. 13.7–14.2 further develops Israel's time of trouble. The mysterious identity of the pierced one (12.10) is linked with the good shepherd of 11.7–14 and the smitten shepherd (13.7). His death will lead to a new scattering of Israel, and a period of fiery trials in which the remnant will call on the name of YHWH, to which he will respond with the words 'You are my people.' Zech. 14.3–21, however, reaffirms that YHWH and his shepherd-king will eventually secure Jerusalem and reign over all the earth. Table 2.2, then, illustrates the eschatological programme as it has been elaborated since 9.1–17.

Along with the above narrative, I would also highlight the following features included in the restoration programme:

(1)   YHWH's newly appointed leader is described as a 'cornerstone' or 'tent peg' (10.4).

(2)   A restored second tier leadership is a sign of the new age (10.4; 13.1–6; 14.5).

(3)   YHWH's declaration 'They are my people' is made in the new exodus (10.6–12)/after the piercing of the shepherd (during or after the fiery trials; 13.7–9).

(4)   The rightly functioning 'house of David' is restored (12.3; 14.16–21).

(5)   YHWH's people are described as sheep and precious stones (9.17; 10.3).

(6)   The spirit is poured upon the house of David/God (12.8–10).

Table 2.3 *Parallels between Zechariah and Isaiah*

Description	Zechariah	Isaiah
1. Arrival is announced with a divine oracle[a]	9.9	62.11
2. Righteous	9.9	42.6; 53.11
3. Humble or afflicted	9.9	42.2
4. Come to restore Israel	9.10–12	49.5–6
5. Releases captives from the pit or dungeon	9.11–12	42.7; 49.9; 61.1
6. Associated with a covenant	9.11	42.9; 49.8
7. Released captives receive a double portion	9.12	61.7
8. Gathers the scattered people of Israel	9.12	49.5–6
9. Associated with shepherd imagery	11.4–14; 13.7	53.6–7
10. Laboured in vain	11.4–9	49.4
11. Despised by the people	11.8	53.3
12. Smitten, pierced or slain	13.7; 12.10	53.4,5,8,12
13. Suffered in keeping with the will of YHWH	13.7	53.6,10
14. Mourned by people after death	12.10–14	53.4–12
15. Death has atoning qualities	12.10–13.1	53.5–12
16. Redemption as a second exodus journey	10.8–12	63.11–12

[a] Hanson 1975: 321; Mitchell 1997: 209.

2.1.3.3 *Zechariah 9–14 and earlier prophetic material*

As I have noted in my analysis of Zechariah 9–14, several allusions to Isaiah 40–66 can be discerned throughout the two oracles.[114] While direct dependence upon Isaiah is difficult to establish, commentators have nevertheless found several points of resonance between the two, as is detailed in Table 2.3.[115]

Zechariah's pervasive interaction with Ezekiel 34 (which itself builds upon Jeremiah 23) and Isaiah 40–66 has led some to suggest that these two books have shaped Zechariah's eschatological programme. Black, for example, has argued that '[t]he unique picture which has emerged may well be the result of the combination of the future Davidic leader from Ezekiel (and elsewhere) with the servant of Isaiah. Yahweh's representative in Zechariah 9–14 may be understood as the future Davidic leader who brings great blessings and rules over the nations in peace; yet he is

---

[114] So Lamarche 1961: 124–47; Ackroyd 1962: 654; Hanson 1975: 404–7; Mason 1977: 88, 119; Black 1990: 85–7; Mitchell 1997: 207–8.
[115] Black 1990: 87; Mitchell 1997: 208–9.

rejected and afflicted and through suffering leads the people to repentance and salvation.'[116] It should come as no surprise, then, if we discover that subsequent interpreters of Zechariah 9–14 find corroboration in Isaiah.

2.2   The reception of Zechariah 9–14

In this section I will examine the reception of Zechariah 9–14 in Jewish Second Temple Literature and the New Testament.[117] In particular, I will analyze a number of texts that scholars have suggested parallel the eschatological programme of Zechariah 9–14 to determine whether there is in fact dependence and/or derivation. In this endeavour, explicit citations, possible allusions and shared eschatological patterns will be considered. Additionally, I will seek to ascertain whether Zechariah 9–14 was available prior to and contemporaneous with the composition of 1 Peter. Finally, I will seek to discern if there are any patterns of interpretation that emerge, especially regarding the eschatological programme.

2.2.1   The reception of Zechariah 9–14 in Jewish Second Temple Literature

2.2.1.1   Daniel 9.24–7

I begin our examination with Dan. 9.24–7, a passage which Mitchell has suggested shares several parallels with features found in the eschatological programme of Zechariah 9–14.[118] Central to Dan. 9.24–7 is Israel's resurgence after exile, epitomized in the rebuilding of the temple and the community (9.25).[119] According to Dan. 9.25, this rebuilding will take place in a 'time of trouble', during which there will appear an 'anointed one' who will eventually be cut off.[120] The death of this 'anointed one' will be followed by a foreign invasion that will ultimately destroy the city

---

[116]   Black 1990: 88.
[117]   An examination of the reception of Zechariah 9–14 in the Rabbinic sources falls beyond the scope of this study. For a thorough study of this see Black 1990: 105–57.
[118]   Mitchell 1997: 218.
[119]   In accordance with the argumentation of Childs (1979: 611–13), it is likely that Daniel 9 was written some time in the late second century BCE; see also Collins 1984b: 36 and Goldingay 1989: xxxvi. Although there is a wide variety of proposals regarding the historical setting and date of Zechariah 9–14 (ranging from the eighth century BCE to the fourth century BCE), all of the available theories would place Daniel after Zechariah 9–14 with respect to date of composition.
[120]   For a discussion on the *mashiah* being Jewish and not foreign see Goldingay 1989: 262.

(i.e. Jerusalem) and the sanctuary (Dan. 9.26). Our author underscores that this time of destruction has been decreed, and that it will result in Israel's restoration. Dan. 9.27, for example, states that the desolation will take place 'until the decreed end is poured out upon the desolator'. And Dan. 9.24 notes that all of this will occur in order to put an end to sin, to atone for iniquity and to bring everlasting righteousness. Although Dan. 9.24–7 shares a similar pattern with the eschatological programme of Zechariah 9–14, it is nevertheless difficult (if not impossible) adequately to establish dependence one way or the other, not least since shared patterns are not sufficient in and of themselves to adjudicate whether one text has drawn from the other.

2.2.1.2 The Sibylline Oracles

According to Mitchell, Books 2 and 3 of the Sibylline Oracles also portray similar eschatological patterns to those found in Zechariah 9–14.[121] In Sib. Ora. 2.154–76, a passage that describes the events that will occur in the 'last generation' (2.160), Mitchell notes the following pattern:[122] (1) the ingathering of Israel (2.170); (2) a 'plundering' and 'a terrible wrath' against the Hebrews, which suggests the invasion of foreign powers (2.165,169); (3) 'the confusion of holy and faithful men', which may be an indication that there was some debate regarding legitimacy in leadership (2.169); (4) and finally, the destruction of the nations and their subjugation to 'faithful chosen Hebrews' (2.173–5). Mitchell then compares this schema from Book 2 with the eschatological programme in Book 3 (Sib. Ora. 3.652–723), in which God sends a king who will bring abundant peace to Jerusalem and the earth (3.652–60).[123] Hostile kings, however, will align themselves against this king and surround the city (3.660–8). It appears that God will not allow the enemies to destroy the city or the temple, however; and he will ultimately defeat the enemies (3.671), and bring salvation to the elect, who presumably are Israelites (3.702–30). One further parallel that Mitchell could have drawn out more emphatically was the significant manner in which the eschatological programme culminates (3.710–30) – with the nations joining the Israelites in worshipping the Most High God (cf. Zech. 14.16–21).

---

[121] All English quotations of the Sibylline Oracles come from Charlesworth 1983: Vol. 1.

[122] Mitchell 1997: 219.

[123] Mitchell (1997: 221) argues that this king is envisioned to be an Israelite messiah. In so doing, he does not adequately interact with the consensus position that the king in view was a Ptolemaic king (see the following paragraph).

While there are indeed similar patterns between Sib. Ora. 2.154–76 and Sib. Ora. 3.652–723, there is a significant difference that has not been allowed for in Mitchell's study. Whereas Book 2 envisions a plurality of Hebrew leaders who will usher in peace, the programme in Book 3, *pace* Mitchell, foresees, as Collins convincingly has argued, a Ptolemaic king (i.e. 'God will send a king from the sun'; 3.652) to be the agent that will bring peace and prosperity.[124] If Book 3 was written in Egypt within a Jewish community,[125] as many scholars contend, then this may explain, in part, why Book 3 stands in remarkable contrast to Book 2 regarding the identity, and indeed the ethnicity, of God's redeeming agent. This either means that both programmes are drawing from different sources, or that both authors are interpreting the same source in an incompatible manner (something entirely possible when reading Zechariah 9–14). There is some indication that the author of Book 3, if in fact he is appropriating from Zechariah 9–14, is more flexible when seeking to actualize the Zecharian programme. If we are right to assume that Sib. Ora. 3.652–723 has been influenced by Zechariah 9–14 in some way, and that Book 3 envisions a Ptolemaic king as the redeemer figure, then Sib. Ora. 3.544 also seems to demonstrate yet again the tendency to actualize the text. In its context, the oracle is announcing the impending demise of Greece (3.520–44) in terms that echo Zech. 13.8–9: 'the one who created heaven and earth will set down much lamented fire on the earth. One third of all mankind will survive' (3.542–4). If this saying is intentionally alluding to Zech. 13.8–9, it appears that our author has not only altered the location of the fire (i.e. from Jerusalem to Greece), but also the objects of the fire (i.e. Greeks instead of Israelites).[126]

2.2.1.3 Josephus

In *Jewish Wars* 6.109–10, Josephus may demonstrate a similar exegetical move. In this passage, Josephus exhorts his fellow Israelites to embrace the Roman occupation of their land, and does so by appealing to 'that oracle' (6.109) which was soon to be fulfilled upon 'this miserable city'.

[124] Collins 1993: 40–2; Collins 1984b: 354, 356, esp. n.17.
[125] All indications are that the earliest traditions of Book 2 come from Phrygia (Collins 1984b: 332).
[126] The reference to Zech. 9.9 in Sib. Ora. 8.430 has not been considered in this section since Book 8 is most certainly a Christian document. Similarly, 4 Ezra 16.73, which some have suggested alludes to Zechariah 13.8–9, has been excluded since it is very likely a Christian emendation (especially given the likely allusions to Revelation) written after the destruction of the temple (Davila 2005a: 137).

According to Josephus, the oracle foresaw that Jerusalem would be taken 'when somebody will begin the slaughter of his own countrymen' (6.110; cf. LXX Zech. 13.7). He further describes the destruction to come upon Jerusalem in terms that echo Zech. 13.9: 'it is God himself who is bringing on this fire, to purge that city and temple *by means of the Romans*, and is going to pluck up this city, which is full of your pollutions' (6.110; italics mine). Josephus' description fits closely with the developments of Zech. 13.7–9 and its environs (13.1–14.2), especially if he was reading from the LXX, which speaks of Israel's 'shepherds' being struck by a sword (which might correspond with the slaughter of the countrymen, though the Greek is distinct in both passages). This event would eventually bring cleansing from sin upon the land, but not before a foreign attack. If Josephus is alluding to Zech. 13.7–14.2, it is clear that he regards the Romans as the foreign nation that God will use to cleanse his people and their land of their corruption.[127] This interpretation would run contrary to the programme of Zechariah 9–14 for two reasons. First, purgation is said to come as a result of the death of the pierced one from the house of David (12.8–13.2). And second, as I demonstrated in §2.1.2.6, the fire imagery of Zech. 13.7–9 refers more to the notion of testing the fidelity of YHWH's people rather than to the idea of purgation.

2.2.1.4   The testament of the Twelve Patriarchs

Two passages from the *Testaments of the Twelve Patriarchs* share parallel features with the eschatological programme of Zechariah 9–14.[128] Both the *Testament of Judah* as well as the *Testament of Dan* describe a time of trouble prior to God's rout of the nations, which will be followed by Israel's restoration and God's universal rule in which the nations

---

[127]   See also Josephus *Jewish Wars* 4.386–8 for another possible allusion to Zech. 12–14 in which Josephus suggests that Rome is on God's side. For the possible but unlikely allusions to Zech. 14.4 through the interpretive tradition that links the Mount of Olives with messianic activity, see *Jewish Wars* 2.261–3 and *Jewish Antiquities* 20.170 (Black 1990: 144–5).

[128]   There is still considerable debate as to whether the *Testament of the Twelve Patriarchs* is a Jewish document with Christian emendations, and, if so, where such emendations occur (e.g. H. C. Kee in Charlesworth 1983: 775–80), or whether it is a Christian document which draws on Jewish sources (e.g. de Jonge 1975: 193–246). In the case of the *Testament of Judah* and the *Testament of Dan*, it is difficult to adjudicate whether the specific passages under examination are Christian interpolations. If Collins (1984b: 325–56) is correct ('There is no doubt that the *Test. 12 Patr.* are Christian in their final form, and so constitute evidence for Christianity in the second or early third century'), then our examination here may simply highlight the reception of Zechariah 9–14 in early Christianity after the composition of the Gospels.

gather to worship.[129] In the *Testament of Judah* 22–5, the time of trouble, precipitated by Israel's idolatry and licentiousness (cf. Zech. 10.1–2) will be initiated when the kingship of the house of David is interrupted by foreign invasion (22.2). This time of trouble will be devastating (23.1–4), and is described as yet another captivity or exile for Israel (23.5). The tribulation will end, however, when a new king from Judah arises, who is characterized as one who walks in gentleness and righteousness (24.1–2; cf. Zech. 9.9–10).[130] Concomitant with his arrival will be the pouring out of God's spirit upon Israel (24.2–3; cf. Zech. 12.10–13.1). Additionally, this coming king is described as the shoot (24.4; cf. Zech. 3.8; 6.12; Isa. 11.1) and the fountain of life (24.5; cf. Zech. 13.1), who will not only rule over the nations, but also because of whom all the nations will worship God (22.3; 24.6; cf. Zech. 14.16–21). The *Testament of Dan* also predicts a time of trouble for Israel after their return from Babylon, which is also precipitated by wickedness (5.1–7). As a result of their sin, Israel will be led off to captivity again (5.7). Nevertheless, there will arise from the tribe of Judah 'the Lord's salvation', which likely refers to a Davidic messiah figure (5.10), who is later described as lowly and humble (6.10; cf. Zech. 9.9). This figure's coming will bring the release of the captives (5.11,13; cf. Zech. 9.11–12), and the establishment of a New Jerusalem, which will never again suffer desolation (5.12–13).

2.2.1.5   *The* Psalms of Solomon

One might expect to find features of Zechariah 9–14 in the *Psalms of Solomon* (especially Chapter 17), given that they both share a number of common themes, such as: (a) the return and restoration of Israel; (b) a time of trouble prior to the establishment of God's kingdom, which involves the despoilment of David's throne on account of 'sinners'; (c) the defeat of the nations; (d) a future Davidic king to rule over Israel and the nations; and (e) the future Davidic king described in terms of shepherd imagery.[131] And yet, upon closer examination, the *Psalms of Solomon* does not appear to be interacting with Zechariah 9–14.[132] The time of trouble, for instance, does not point to a decreed future event (like the one described in Zechariah 11–13), but instead is a reference

---

[129]   Mitchell 1997: 222–3.

[130]   Black (1990: 99) suggests that this is an allusion that 'probably points to a messianic understanding of Zech. 9.9–10'.

[131]   *Psalms of Solomon* was most likely composed in the middle of the first century BCE (Wright 2007: 640–1), especially given the likely reference to Pompey.

[132]   *Pace* Mitchell 1997: 223–4.

to the past and present illegitimate rule of the Hasmoneans (i.e. 'sinners'; 17.5–7a), and then the Romans (17.7b–15; Pompey's invasion in 63 BCE) respectively. Similarly, the wilderness/exile described in *Ps. Sol.* 17.17–18 is not that which is envisioned in the Zechariah programme, but instead is the result of the Roman invasion. Additionally, it is difficult to discern any Zecharian influence in the eschatological features of *Psalm of Solomon 17* (i.e. the emergence of a Davidic king who will gather in and shepherd Israel, and defeat the nations), which are more likely derived from Psalm 2, Isaiah 11 and 49, and Ezekiel 34 and 37, as has been pointed out by a number of scholars.[133]

2.2.1.6   *The* Dream Visions *(1 Enoch 83–90)*

First Enoch 83–90 (also known as the *Dream Visions*) consists of two visions – the first concerning the flood (83–4), and the second, known as the *Animal Vision* (85–90), which spans from creation to the restoration.[134] According to Nickelsburg, the *Animal Vision* divides history into three eras.[135] Within the second era (89.9–90.27), which begins with the renewal of creation after the flood and culminates with cosmic judgment against disobedient angels and unfaithful Israelites, Nickelsburg has observed a 'peculiar blend' of images which he links to a conflation of Ezekiel 34 and Zechariah 11.[136] The imagery concerns shepherds who, in response to Israel's long history of repeated apostasy, have been commissioned by God (89.59), the 'Lord of the sheep' (89.58), to destroy the flock. In the course of the vision, it becomes apparent that these shepherds have disobeyed God because 'they took and killed more than I [God] commanded them' (90.23). As a result, these shepherds, along with the disobedient sheep, were judged, thrown into an abyss full of fire, and burned (90.24–7). The sheep that remained were gathered to the Lord of the sheep, who 'rejoiced greatly because they were all good and had returned to the house' (90.33–4), that is, the newly constructed Jerusalem (90.28). Nickelsburg has rightly argued that the biblical basis for the Lord

---

[133] See, e.g. Chae 2006: 115–25; Willitts 2007a: 81–5. Black has unconvincingly suggested (1990: 103) that *Ps. Sol.* 17.32–5 (which 'describes the messiah as a king who is righteous and peaceful, repudiating the horse, rider, and bow') likely alludes to Zech. 9.9, and is evidence of a messianic reading of that passage in Jerusalem in the mid-first century BCE.

[134] The titles and translation of the *Dream Visions* are from Nickelsburg and VanderKam 2004, which is based on Nickelsburg's Hermeneia commentary on 1 Enoch. I follow Nickelsburg (2001: 360–1), who argues that the *Animal Vision* was likely composed between 165 and 163 BCE.

[135] Nickelsburg 2001: 354–5.   [136] Nickelsburg 2001: 355, 390–1.

of the sheep handing his flock over to worthless, disobedient shepherds, who in turn will be judged for their wickedness, is most likely derived from Zech. 11.15–17.[137] But this biblical tradition has been altered in a significant fashion, and for reasons that are not clear: whereas in Zech. 11.15–17 the shepherds are Israel's human leaders, in the *Animal Vision*, the shepherds are heavenly angels.[138] What has not been explored, to my knowledge, is the possibility that the images of the shepherds being cast into fire along with the disobedient sheep, and the remnant sheep being gathered to the Lord in the new Jerusalem, have their antecedents in Zech. 13.7–9 and its wider context. If this is indeed the case, then it would indicate that the author of the *Animal Vision* regards both the shepherd of Zech. 11.15–17 and the shepherd of 13.7 as wicked.

2.2.1.7   The Dead Sea Scrolls

I conclude our survey of the reception of Zechariah 9–14 in Jewish Second Temple Literature with an examination of the Damascus Document (CD), which offers the only explicit reference to Zech. 13.7 in the extant literature of the Second Temple period. CD[b] 19.5–11 reads as follows:[139]

> [5] But (over) all those who despise the precepts [6] and the ordinances, may be emptied over them the punishment of the wicked, when God visits the earth, [7] when there comes the word which is written by the hand of the prophet Zechariah: 'Wake up, sword, against [8] my shepherd, and against the male who is my companion – oracle of God – strike the shepherd, and the flock may scatter, [9] and I shall turn my hand against the little ones' [Zech. 13.7]. Those who revere him are 'the poor ones of the flock' [Zech. 11.7,11]. [10] These shall escape in the age of the visitation; but those that remain shall be delivered up to the sword when there comes the Messiah [11] of Aaron and Israel.[140]

As many scholars have noted, the purpose of this passage is to admonish the members of the community to remain faithful; this is done, in part, by interpreting events that have occurred in light of events that are

---

[137]   Here I would concur with Chae (2006: 105–6), who nuances Nickelsburg's proposal by arguing that 89.59–90.39 is a midrash on Zechariah 11–13, which itself modifies the shepherd tradition of Ezekiel 34.

[138]   Nickelsburg 2001: 390.

[139]   The title and translation of the Damascus Document, unless otherwise noted, are from Martínez and Tigchelaar 2000.

[140]   There is some debate among CD scholars whether CD[b] is the original copy.

soon to come. For our purposes, there are three features of this unfolding programme that will be highlighted from this passage. First, the CD envisions an eschatological programme that includes a period of trouble for Israel. This time of trouble has already been initiated by the epoch-marking death of the shepherd.[141] Not unlike the debate among Zecharian scholars regarding the identity of the shepherds in Zechariah 11 and 13, Qumran interpreters do not agree with respect to the identity of the shepherd figure in this passage. Three options are most frequently suggested: (1) the shepherd is the leader of the enemies of the Qumran community;[142] (2) the shepherd represents the Hellenizing aristocracy in Jerusalem;[143] or (3) the shepherd is a reference to the Teacher of Righteousness.[144] The subsequent references in CD^b 19.9–10 would seem to suggest that the shepherd was at least a part of the Damascus community (thus nullifying options 1 and 2): the 'poor ones of the flock' are said to escape the time of trouble because of their reverence for the struck shepherd, who, in keeping with Zechariah 13.7, is regarded as YHWH's companion.[145] While it is not clear whether the shepherd is a reference to the Teacher of Righteousness, it is quite clear that the shepherd is not understood to be the messiah, since it is the death of this shepherd that precedes the coming of the messiah (CD^b 19.10).

Second, according to CD^b 19.9–10 a remnant of Israel would be protected during the 'age of wrath' (CD^b 20.15–16), which is the time subsequent to the shepherd's death and prior to the coming of the messiah.[146] This remnant is referred to as 'the little ones' and 'the poor ones of the flock'. The first epithet, 'the little ones', is clearly derived from Zech. 13.7. While its usage in the MT seems to refer to those who will face YHWH's judgment, in CD^b 19.9 it has been interpreted as an indication of YHWH's hand of protection on the remnant.[147] The second reference, 'the poor ones of the flock', seems to have been formed from Zech. 11.7 (or 11.11).[148] It appears that these two passages, Zech. 11.4–14 and

---

[141] Mitchell 1997: 229; Pitre 2005: 465.   [142] Betz 1960: 178–9; Knibb 1987: 59.
[143] Rabinowitz 1954: 27–8.
[144] Rabinowitz 1954: 31; Davies 1983: 119–25; Mitchell 1997: 228–31.
[145] Mitchell 1997: 229.   [146] See Willitts 2006 on the remnant in the Dead Sea Scrolls.
[147] So also Knibb 1987: 59.
[148] Wacholder (2007: 254) argues that the allusion is to Zech. 11.7, while Knibb (1987: 59–60) and Campbell (1995: 159), following many others, contend that it is from Zech. 11.11. Both Zechariah passages contain the same phrase (הַצֹּאן עֲנִיֵּי); I would argue that an allusion to Zech. 11.7 makes a link with 13.7 more natural, especially if one regards the shepherd figure of CD^b to be a member of the Qumran community. 4Q163 21.7 also features an allusion to Zech. 11.11, which is referenced in connection with the Teacher of Righteousness and his followers.

Zech. 13.7–9, have been intentionally drawn together, in part, because
of pesher-logic – that is, both passages are linked via their shared shepherd imagery.[149] But perhaps more significantly, these two passages have
been brought together because they both have been interpreted as referring to a shepherd appointed by YHWH, who is rejected by his people,
and whose death brings about a period of judgment for those who have
failed to respond to YHWH's plans. Additionally, it should be mentioned
that these shepherds both are regarded as good, and that Zech. 11.4–14
and Zech. 13.7–9 are interpreted as referring to the same eschatological
sequence.

The last feature to highlight is the manner in which the final period of
tribulation (that is, the time subsequent to the death of the shepherd in
which the remnant is protected by the hand of YHWH) is described in
CD[b] – as a second exodus:[150]

> [13] . . . And from the day [14] of the gathering in of the unique
> teacher, until the end of all the men of war who are turned back
> [15] with the man of lies, there shall be forty years. And in this
> age the wrath [16] of God will be kindled against Israel.
>
> (CD[b] 20.13–16)

The passage goes on to describe this second exodus as a time of testing, in
which the just and the wicked will be distinguished (CD[b] 20.20–1), until
the salvation and justice are revealed. It is perhaps significant that within
the context of second exodus imagery, the author of CD[b] alludes to Hosea
3.4, a passage that is linked to yet another depiction of a second exodus
journey prior to restoration – Hosea 2.14–23. As has been underscored,
Zech. 10.6–12 and Zech. 13.7–9 make similar links with Hosea and the
second exodus.

The eschatological vision of CD[b] 19–20, then, seems to parallel, and
is perhaps even undergirded by, a particular reading of the eschatological
programme of Zechariah 9–14. Israel has been gathered to the shepherd;
the shepherd has been struck; the sheep have once again been scattered,
and yet the faithful remnant are now protected by YHWH as they endure
'forty years' of testing prior to the coming of the messiah; YHWH will
establish a universal reign. It is, then, not impossible to surmise that the
Qumran community regarded themselves as living in the last days of the
Zecharian programme.[151]

[149] Campbell 1995: 159.   [150] So also Mitchell 1997: 229; Pitre 2005: 465.
[151] Mitchell 1997: 232. There may be one other possible allusion to Zechariah 9–14
in the Dead Sea Scrolls. In 1QM 12.1,4,7 the 'holy ones' who accompany God to battle

2.2.1.8   Conclusions regarding the reception of Zechariah 9–14 in Jewish Second Temple Literature

Although several texts in the Second Temple period appear to share similar eschatological patterns with the eschatological programme of Zechariah 9–14, in some cases I was unable to determine whether these texts were in fact dependent upon Zechariah 9–14 (e.g. Dan. 9.24–7; Sib. Ora. 2). However, I am inclined to regard Zechariah 9–14 as the likeliest origin of these programmes since (a) 'the Zecharian programme is without parallel in the Bible for scale, scope, and detail', and since (b) the texts under examination were all most likely composed after Zechariah 9–14.[152] Other texts that were surveyed (e.g. Sib. Ora. 3; Josephus *JW* 6), if they did in fact draw from Zechariah 9–14, have altered the referentiality of key passages in order to speak to contemporary needs. We have also observed that while some texts read Zechariah 11 and 13 together as referring to the same feature of the eschatological sequence, they differ as to whether they regard the shepherd(s) to be wicked or good (*Animal Vision* and CD respectively). More importantly, although the survey does suggest that Zechariah 9–14 was available prior to the first century CE, for the most part there was no consistent pattern for how the eschatological programme of Zechariah 9–14 was interpreted or appropriated, and no one seems to be reading the programme holistically. For example, none of the texts regards Zech. 9.9, 11.4–14, 12.10 and 13.7 to refer to the same individual, though it may be that several features of Zechariah 9–14 have undergirded the eschatological programmes of the *Testament of Judah* and CD.

2.2.2   The reception of Zechariah 9–14 in the Passion Narratives

Many scholars agree that a Passion Narrative tradition emerged early on in order to come to terms with Jesus' tragic death.[153] Joel Marcus, for

---

rebellion on earth may point to the 'holy ones' referenced in Zech. 14.5, though in that context it seems more likely that the passages were pointing to human figures, whereas in 1QM the 'holy ones' are angels.

[152]   Mitchell 1997: 242.

[153]   The Passion Narrative tradition includes a pre-Markan Passion Narrative, the canonical Gospel accounts and the Gospel of Peter. Following the work of Myllykoski (1991: 191–2) and Reinbold (1994: 192–3), I agree that the Passion Narrative tradition likely began with Jesus' entry into Jerusalem. For this reason I have set the boundaries of the Gospel Passion Narratives to begin with Matthew 21, Mark 11 and Luke 19.28. Most scholars consider the Passion Narratives to terminate with Jesus' burial (Matthew 27, Mark 15 and Luke 23). John's Passion Narrative material is more difficult to determine, but is most likely found throughout John 10–19. For the early emergence of the Passion Narratives see

example, writes:

> From a very early stage of its existence, the church would have required an explanation for the fact that Jesus, whom it proclaimed to be the Messiah, the expected King of Israel, had finished his life on a Roman cross, abandoned by his followers. Messiahs were not supposed to end up like this . . . but were to overthrow the yoke of pagan oppression through the power of God and to lead Israel to national liberation and world rulership as well as spiritual rejuvenation . . . The best way of doing this would have been to compose a narrative showing that Jesus' suffering and death were in line with the hints that God had squirreled away in the only scriptures the earliest church possessed, namely the sacred writings of Israel.[154]

Much attention has been directed towards the influence that Isaiah, Daniel 7 and the Psalms have on the theology of the Passion Narratives. There is perhaps less awareness regarding the extent to which Zechariah 9–14 also served as one of the primary sources for the Evangelists and the early church as they interpreted the significance of Jesus' unjust suffering, death and resurrection.[155]

The prominence of Zechariah 9–14 in the Passion Narratives can be illustrated most immediately by Table 2.4, which indicates citations and allusions to Zechariah 9–14 in the Passion Narratives.[156]

As can be seen, each of the four Evangelists points to Zech. 9.9–10 in orienting their account of Jesus' last week prior to his crucifixion:[157]

J. B. Green 1988: 164–74; for a pre-Markan Passion Narrative originating in Jerusalem see Theissen 2004: 166–99 and Bauckham 2006: 183–201; see also Soards 1994 for evidence of a pre-Markan Passion Narrative. Cf. Crossan 1988.

[154] Marcus 1995: 205–6.

[155] This in spite of several fine studies such as Dodd 1952: 64–7; C. F. Evans 1954; Bruce 1961: 336–53, 1968: Chapter 8; B. Lindars 1961: 110–34; France 1971: 103–10; Moo 1983: 173–224; Kim 1987: 134–48; Black 1990; Marcus 1995: 218–22; N. T. Wright 1996: 585–611; C. A. Evans 1999; Foster 2003: 65–85; Ham 2005; Porter with Boda 2005: 215–54; McAfee Moss 2008. Notably absent from Juel 1988 was a comprehensive discussion of Zechariah 9–14 in the Passion Narratives.

[156] These citations and allusions to Zechariah 9–14 have been compiled from the studies of Dodd 1952: 64–6; Bruce 1968: 101–14; Moo 1983: 173–221; Black 1990 :158–232; Marcus 1992; and Ham 2005; the latter four have been given prominent consideration given that their studies were the most thorough. Not every suggested allusion has been included in Table 2.4, but only the ones that, in my view, have been judged to be either likely or probable. For a more detailed chart that classifies the citation techniques, see Moo 1983: 222.

[157] Black (1990: 161) notes that '[i]n each of the Gospels the account of the triumphal entry occupies an important structural position. It forms the introductory and beginning episode of the Passion Week'.

Table 2.4 *Zechariah 9–14 in the Passion Narratives*

Citations/allusions from Zechariah[a]	Matthew	Mark	Luke	John
Zech. 9.9	21.5	*11.1–10*	*19.29–40*	12.15
Zech. 9.11.	26.28	*14.24*		
Zech. 11.12–13	27.9–10 *26.15*			
Zech. 12.3			*21.24*	
Zech. 12.10–14	*24.30*		*23.27*	19.37
Zech. 13.1; 14.8				*19.34*
Zech. 13.7–9	26.31–2 *26.56*	*14.27–8*		*16.32–3* *10.11,15,17*
Zech. 14.3–5,9	25.31 *26.30* *27.51b–3*	*11.23* *13.1–13* *14.25*		
Zech. 14.7	*24.36*			
Zech. 14.21	*21.12–13*	*11.15–17*		*2.16*

[a] All non-italicized references are citations. Allusions that are very likely or probable are italicized.

It is well outside the scope of this study to analyze the development of a pre-Markan Passion Narrative in the Synoptic Gospels, John and the Gospel of Peter. Instead, I seek to show the manner in which Zechariah 9–14 was appropriated in the Passion Narrative tradition, focusing in particular on Matthew, Mark and John, who each frame Jesus' entry into Jerusalem and his subsequent death with references to Zechariah 9–14.[158] The conclusions of this analysis will serve to illuminate my examination of 1 Peter, demonstrating points of continuity and discontinuity with respect to the way in which Zechariah 9–14 is read.

2.2.2.1 Zechariah 9–14 in Mark's Passion Narrative

The Markan account of Jesus' passion is probably the most primitive of the four Gospels,[159] and its appropriation of the OT is characterized by echoes and allusions rather than explicit citations.[160] In fact, the reference

---

[158] That Luke minimizes Zechariah 9–14 in his presentation of the Passion Narrative is intriguing, but an exploration of this falls beyond the scope of the present study. See Black 1990: 172–6, 236.

[159] I begin with Mark based on my assumption that it was the source for both Matthew and Luke. For a recent and comprehensive argument for Markan priority see Goodacre 2002.

[160] Marcus 1992: 153.

to Zech. 13.7 in Mark 14.27 is the only biblical quotation in the Passion Narrative introduced with a citation formula. This suggests that perhaps Mark assumed that his readers would have sufficient knowledge of the scriptures he alluded to and that they would be capable of making the appropriate connections to his narrative, and/or that, following Dodd (and more recently Black), Zechariah 9–14 was early on a recognized source of *testimonia* that explained the circumstances surrounding Jesus' death.[161]

Mark's use of Zechariah 9–14 is especially concentrated in three pericopes: 11.1–10 (Jesus' procession into Jerusalem), 14.22–5 (the institution of the Lord's Supper) and 14.26–31 (where Jesus predicts his death and the scattering of his disciples). In orienting his account, Mark alludes to Zech. 9.9–10 (Mark 11.1–10) in describing Jesus' entry into Jerusalem. That this is an intentional allusion is widely acknowledged, and seems clear enough given that in both Mark as well as the precursor text a royal figure rides into Jerusalem on a donkey while the people rejoice. That Jesus is portrayed (and understood) as a royal figure is clear from the Davidic acclamation from Psalm 118 (Mark 11.9–10; see §2.1.2.1 for the Davidic allusion in Zech. 9.9–10). It is notable that the Markan account, wherein Jesus commissions two of his disciples to acquire a donkey, portrays Jesus as self-consciously orchestrating the entry on a colt in a manner that is in keeping with Zech. 9.9–10.[162] This may be one of four indications in Mark's Passion Narrative that Jesus' own vocation was shaped by Zechariah 9–14. Some scholars, for instance, have suggested that in the following pericope (Mark 11.15–19), Jesus, in prohibiting anyone from bringing anything into the temple, is intentionally acting out the eschatological vision of Zech. 14.20–1, which states that 'there shall no longer be traders in the house of the LORD of hosts on that day'.[163]

A third possible indication that Jesus understood his vocation in terms of Zechariah 9–14 may be found in Mark 14.22–5. In passing the cup to his disciples, the Markan Jesus declares that 'This is my blood of the

---

[161] One might postulate that Mark, unaware of the Zecharian allusion, simply replicated the material that was handed to him (provided that we agree that there was a pre-Markan Passion Narrative). Black (1990: 158–232), however, has demonstrated that this postulation is very unlikely. Regarding the *testimonia* theory, see Dodd 1952, which should not be confused with the notion of *testimonia* books (Rendel Harris, and more recently Albl 1999).

[162] So also Black 1990: 167; Evans 1999: 375–88; France 2002: 434.

[163] Jeremias 1958: 65–70; Roth 1960: 174–81; Chilton 1992: 135–6; Marcus 1992: 160; Grant 1948: 300; Evans 1999: 383. Both Chilton and Evans have highlighted similar actions on the part of religious leaders.

covenant' (τοῦτό ἐστιν τὸ αἷμά μου τῆς διαθήκης). Many scholars regard this as an allusion to Exod. 24.8 ('See the blood of the covenant that the LORD has made with you'), but not without hinting at the possibility of an allusion to Zech. 9.11 instead.[164] As I have already suggested in §2.1.2.1, it is very likely that Zech. 9.11 is itself alluding to Exod. 24.8, describing YHWH's coming restoration in terms of a second exodus. I also noted that Zech. 9.11–12 appear to interact with second exodus themes found in Isa. 42.7 and 61.1. There may be a similar Zechariah–Isaiah interplay here in Mark 14.26, where 'my blood of the covenant' (Zech. 9.11) is 'poured out for many' (Isa. 53.12: 'he poured out himself to death . . . he bore the sin of many').[165] Given the redemptive and eschatological outlook of the pericope and the proposed precursor text (i.e. Zech. 9.11), the fact that the Markan Jesus has already alluded to Zech. 9.9–10, and that he understands his death in terms of Zech. 13.7 (Mark 14.27), an allusion to Zech. 9.11 seems more likely.[166] Marcus has perceived one further allusion to Zechariah in Mark 14.25: he argues that the phrase 'on that day' points to YHWH's future universal reign described in Zech. 14.9, noting that 'the Zecharian verse is one of only two Old Testament passages that link the phrase "on that day" with the establishment of God's eschatological kingship (cf. Mic 4:6)'.[167] His observation can be strengthened by pointing out that in the second oracle of Zechariah 9–14 (i.e. chaps. 12–14) the phrase 'on that day' appears fifteen times, and functions as an *inclusio* with references in 12.3 and 14.21 (where it is the very last phrase of the oracle). The reference to the fruit of the vine on 'that day' in the kingdom of God may also point to Zech. 9.17, which, as we noted, has a paradigmatic function for Zechariah 9–14, and expresses the culmination of YHWH's restoration.

The most explicit reference to Zechariah is found in Mark 14.27, where the Markan Jesus depicts his death and the disciples' flight as being in keeping with Zech. 13.7: 'You will all become deserters; for it is written, "I will strike the shepherd, and the sheep will be scattered".' Any definitive conclusion regarding the textual tradition that the Markan Jesus cites is elusive. At the very least, it seems quite clear that it does not come from the LXX, since the earliest LXX witnesses, shepherds are the object of the blow (τοὺς ποιμένας) rather than just one shepherd (τὸν ποιμένα). Additionally, in the OG the imperative is a second person

---

[164] E.g. France 2002: 570.
[165] Jeremias 1977: 291; Marcus 1992: 163; Watts 1997: 354–62; France 2002: 570–1.
[166] So Lindars 1961: 132–3; Black 1990: 182–3; Marcus 1992: 157.
[167] Marcus 1992: 156–7.

plural (πατάξατε).[168] In the Hebrew text, on the other hand, YHWH commands the sword to strike 'my shepherd'.[169] The Markan (as well as the Matthean and Johannine) appropriation of Zech. 13.7, in which only one shepherd is struck, then, would seem to be dependent upon the Hebrew rather than the LXX text-plot.[170] The modification from 'strike' to 'I will strike' (πατάξω) can be explained on the grounds that the Markan Jesus wanted to make clear that his death was in keeping with God's intentions, and was therefore not a tragic, unforeseen accident.[171] Brant Pitre has rightly linked Mark 14.27 with the prior material of Mark 13: 'Jesus not only went out to the eschatologically charged site of the Mount of Olives, where the prophet Zechariah had said the Great Tribulation would take place [14.1–5]; he also openly declared that he as messianic "shepherd" must be "struck down", and that his "sheep" (the disciples) would be scattered in the time of testing.'[172] In other words, Jesus understood (or is at least portrayed to have understood) his death as that which would initiate the tribulation period described in Mark 13.

In summary, some of the most essential elements of Mark's Passion Narrative – Jesus' entry into Jerusalem as the rightful king (Mark 11.1–10/Zech. 9.9–10), his prediction (Mark 14.27/Zech. 13.7) and explanation of his death (Mark 14.22–5/Zech. 9.11 and Mark 14.27/Zech. 13.7), the tribulation period following his death (Mark 13; 14.27/Zech. 13.7–14.5) and his temple actions (Mark 11.15–17/Zech. 14.21) – gain their significance from and are said to be in keeping with the eschatological programme of Zechariah 9–14. Additionally, it becomes clear that Mark regards the two figures of Zech. 9.9 (Mark 11.1–10) and 13.7 (Mark 14.27) to refer to the same person, a royal, messianic figure (in contrast to CD[b] 19.8), and that these two Zechariah figures point to Jesus. I have also highlighted that Jesus was portrayed as self-consciously acting on the basis of Zechariah 9–14, and this portrayal is perhaps founded on Jesus' own teaching. If Jesus did in fact understand and explain his vocation in

---

[168] -ξον AQS[c]LC.

[169] Although חֶרֶב is a feminine noun, it is personified in masculine terms with the imperative ה.

[170] For the best discussion regarding the textual issues see Willitts 2007a: 139–52.

[171] France (2002: 575, n.73) argues that 'Mark's indicative is best explained not as a variant text but as a grammatical adaptation necessitated by the abbreviated quotation, which does not include the explicit mention of the "sword" in the opening line of the oracle, to which the command is addressed.' This would not exclude what we have argued.

[172] Pitre 2005: 514. For the full argument see pp. 455–507. Jeremias 1977: 501 made a similar connection between 14.27–29 and Zech. 13.7–9, but did not credit this to Jesus' own teaching.

terms of the oracles found in Zechariah 9–14, this may explain why the early church was drawn to these six chapters in seeking to both understand as well as justify his death.

2.2.2.2 Zechariah 9–14 in Matthew's Passion Narrative

If we are right to assume Markan priority, then Matthew has included most of the material in Mark's Passion Narrative that in one way or another points to Zechariah 9–14: (1) Jesus' entry into Jerusalem (Matt. 21.5/Zech. 9.9; (2) his actions in the temple (Matt. 21.12–15/Zech. 14.21); (3) the prediction of Jesus' death and the disciples' desertion (Matt. 26.31–2/Zech. 13.7); and (4) the eschatologically pregnant reference to 'that day' (Matt. 24.36/Zech. 14.7).[173] Matthew, however, does not include this material unconsciously, or without his own redactional shaping.

Matthew's account of Jesus' entry into Jerusalem, for example, turns Mark's allusion to Zech. 9.9–10 into a fulfilment quotation (Matt. 21.4–5):

> 4 τοῦτο δὲ γέγονεν ἵνα πληρωθῇ τὸ ῥηθὲν
> διὰ τοῦ προφήτου λέγοντος·
> 5 εἴπατε τῇ θυγατρὶ Σιών·
> ἰδοὺ ὁ βασιλεύς σου ἔρχεταί σοι
> πραῢς καὶ ἐπιβεβηκὼς ἐπὶ ὄνον
> καὶ ἐπὶ πῶλον υἱὸν ὑποζυγίου.

The citation is both a conflation as well as an abbreviation of two texts.[174] The initial part of the citation comes directly from LXX Isa. 62.11: εἴπατε τῇ θυγατρὶ Σιων. The second part of the citation comes from two clauses in Zech. 9.9. The phrase ἰδοὺ ὁ βασιλεύς σου ἔρχεταί σοι appears to come directly from the LXX, while πραῢς καὶ ἐπιβεβηκὼς ἐπὶ ὄνον καὶ ἐπὶ πῶλον υἱὸν ὑποζυγίου appears to be a literal translation of the MT.[175] It appears that there are at least two features that have drawn these two passages together. First, both texts are oracular in nature, announcing YHWH's coming restoration. As we saw in our analysis of Zechariah 9–14, the restoration expectations of Isaiah 40–66 are regularly read together with the eschatological programme of Zechariah. Second, it

---

[173] Hagner 1993: 716; Ham 2005: 94–8.
[174] For a detailed analysis see Ham 2005: 21–3.
[175] See Ham 2005: 22; Hagner 1993: 594. The LXX reads: πραῢς καὶ ἐπιβεβηκὼς ἐπὶ ὑποζύγιον καὶ πῶλον νέον.

appears that the catchwords 'come' and 'save' have been instrumental in bringing these particular phrases together:

Isa. 62.11

אִמְרוּ לְבַת־צִיּוֹן הִנֵּה יִשְׁעֵךְ בָּא הִנֵּה שְׂכָרוֹ אִתּוֹ וּפְעֻלָּתוֹ לְפָנָיו
Εἴπατε τῇ θυγατρὶ Σιων Ἰδού σοι ὁ σωτὴρ παραγίνεται
ἔχων τὸν ἑαυτοῦ μισθὸν καὶ τὸ ἔργον πρὸ προσώπου αὐτοῦ

Zech. 9.9

הִנֵּה מַלְכֵּךְ יָבוֹא לָךְ צַדִּיק וְנוֹשָׁע הוּא
ἰδοὺ ὁ βασιλεύς σου ἔρχεταί σοι, δίκαιος καὶ σῴζων αὐτός

If it is the MT that has fostered this *gezerah shavah* (which seems most likely), and if Matthew understood וְנוֹשָׁע to be a Niphil (i.e. being saved or vindicated), then the evangelist may have intended to foreshadow that the coming king would also be a suffering and vindicated king. Along with the explicit reference to Zech. 9.9, Matthew also adds to the account of Jesus' entry into Jerusalem (1) a more literal fulfilment of Zech. 9.9 by noting that Jesus acquired a donkey and a colt (Matt. 21.2/Zech. 9.9),[176] and (2) an explicit reference to Jesus as the son of David.

Along with reworked Zecharian material from Mark, Matthew (Matt. 27.9–10) also adds an explicit (and modified) citation from Zech. 11.12–13 ('thirty pieces of silver') in order to give scriptural warrant for Judas' betrayal and the rejection of Jesus by the Jewish leaders.[177] Dodd has suggested that the inclusion of this event within the narrative, which would otherwise seem like an insignificant happening, indicates that 'the whole passage of Zechariah [9–14] was already recognized as a source of testimonies'.[178] This explicit citation is foreshadowed with an allusion to it in Matt. 26.15. It is also possible that Matt. 25.31 in mentioning the 'holy angels' who would come at the eschaton with the Son of Man alludes to Zech. 14.5.[179] And finally, the Matthean Jesus' reference to 'all the tribes of the earth' who will 'mourn' when they 'see' the Son of Man is likely intended to draw together Zech. 12.10–14 ('they shall mourn for him' . . . 'every tribe') and Daniel 7. If this is the case, Jesus is

[176] See Black 1990: 170–1; Ham 2005: 22–3.
[177] For a full discussion of this citation, which is attributed to Jeremiah, see Black 1990: 202–12; Ham 2005: 47–69. See also earlier proposals by Dodd 1952: 64; Bruce 1968: 108–10.
[178] Dodd 1952: 65; Bruce 1968: 109.
[179] Ham 2005: 98–9. See also Chae 2006: 335.

now not only linked to the royal king of Zech. 9.9 and the slain shepherd of Zech. 13.7, but also the pierced one of Zech. 12.10.[180]

Taken as a whole, Matthew's dependence upon Zechariah 9–14 is integral for explaining the significance of the essential events of Jesus' passion. In summarizing his analysis of Matthew's Passion Narrative, Ham has rightly noted the pervasive influence of Zechariah 9–14:

> Three times the Gospel of Matthew cites [21.5; 26.31; 27.9–10] from the prophetic book Zechariah. Between the first and last of these citations, Matthew alludes to Zechariah eight times [23.35; 24.30; 24.23; 24.36; 25.31; 26.15; 16.28; 26.56].[181] In addition, Matthew uses themes prominent in Zechariah in the portrayal of Jesus' ministry, death and eschatological reign. Collectively, these citations, allusions and thematic emphases indicate coherence between the theology of Matthew and the theology of Zechariah ... The messianic vision found in the prophetic oracles of Zechariah includes the restoration of the humble Davidic king, the smiting of the divinely appointed shepherd, the creation of a renewed remnant, and the worship of Yahweh by all the nations. Matthew finds this prophetic presentation particularly compelling for his own representation of Jesus as the fulfillment of Zechariah's shepherd-king.[182]

2.2.2.3 Zechariah 9–14 in John's Passion Narrative

The Fourth Gospel's appropriation of Zech. 9.9 (John 12.15), which may be independent of the Synoptic tradition, is nevertheless similar to that of Matthew in that it conflates two texts:[183]

μὴ φοβοῦ, θυγάτηρ Σιών·
ἰδοὺ ὁ βασιλεύς σου ἔρχεται,
καθήμενος ἐπὶ πῶλον ὄνου

---

[180] See Black 1990: 218–20; Ham 2005: 94–8 for the variety of parallels between Matt. 24.30 and Zech. 12.10–14, and for a suggestion that this may be yet another example of Matthew elaborating what he perceived to be an allusion to Zechariah in Mark 13.26.

[181] I have not included all of his proposed allusions in my survey.

[182] Ham 2005: 126. Earlier in his study, Ham notes that '[e]ven though Ezekiel 34 has provided many of the concepts and images used in Mathew's shepherd metaphor, it cannot...account for this new development based upon Zech 13.7: before the scattered sheep are gathered, Jesus the shepherd, struck by God, dies' (*ibid.*: 118–19).

[183] For a comprehensive study on the relationship between John and the Synoptic Gospels see Smith 1992 and Reinbold 1994. Following Bauckham (1998: 147–71), although John was likely not dependent upon Mark (so also Reinbold 1994), he likely did expect his readers to be familiar with it.

It is difficult to adjudicate whether the first phrase of line one, μὴ φοβοῦ, is an allusion to Zeph. 3.16[184] or Isa. 40.9,[185] or whether it is nothing more than a stock idiom. If the citation is a conflation with Isa. 40.9, it would be another example of Zechariah 9–14 being read in harmony with the eschatological hopes of Isaiah 40–66, and perhaps would reflect a wider exegetical tradition.

The second half of line one, and all of line two follow both the MT as well as the LXX. The final line does not follow either the MT or the LXX very closely, and may be the author's attempt to make sense of the donkey/colt reference in the MT. One important distinction in John's account of Jesus' entry into Jerusalem is that, whereas the Markan Jesus orchestrates the entry on a donkey, and in response is showered with Davidic acclamations from the crowd, in John Jesus 'finds' a donkey in response to the crowd's Davidic acclamations, perhaps in an effort to emphasize that his messiahship is in keeping with Zechariah's account – humble, and being saved/vindicated.[186] This might be one more example of an evangelist intending to show that Jesus' vocation was self-consciously understood in terms of Zechariah 9–14.[187]

Additionally, whereas Matthew and Mark frame Jesus' entry into Jerusalem on a donkey/colt (Matt. 21.5/Mark 11.1–10) and the time just before his betrayal in the garden (Matt. 26.31/Mark 14.27) with Zech. 9.9 and Zech. 13.7 respectively, John only alludes to Zech. 13.7 (16.32), and instead ends his Zecharian frame with Jesus' crucifixion (John 19.36–7), writing:

> These things occurred so that the scripture might be fulfilled, 'None of his bones shall be broken'. And again another passage of scripture says, 'They will look on the one whom they have pierced' (ὄψονται εἰς ὃν ἐξεκέντησαν).[188]

There is some debate regarding the initial allusion found in 19.36. Many scholars regard it to be a reference to the paschal lamb mentioned in either

---

[184] E.g. Brown (1966: 458), who suggests Zeph. 3.16 since the wider context of the passages seeks to assure Israel that the king is in her midst.

[185] E.g. Barrett (1962: 348), who opts for Isaiah since the phrase occurs a number of times in Chapters 40–66, but also notes the possibility of an allusion to Zeph. 3.16.

[186] Black 1990: 77–8.

[187] For Luke's depiction of the triumphal entry see Black 1990: 172–6. Since Luke's Gospel interacts very little with Zechariah, an analysis of his portrayal has been omitted for this study.

[188] See the section on Zechariah 9–14 in Revelation for a discussion of the textual tradition of Zech. 12.10.

Exod. 12.46 or Num. 9.12.[189] The Passover is certainly an important theme for John, and he goes to full measures to make sure the reader picks up the connection between Jesus' death and the Passover. For example, in 19.14 he mentions that it was the eve of Passover and repeats it again in 19.31. John adds to this the fact that it was around noon when Jesus was sentenced, significant perhaps because it coincides with the time when the paschal lamb was to be slaughtered; the mention of hyssop in 19.29 may also have been included in order to make Passover connections.[190] These nuanced comments by John, coupled with John the Baptist's announcement in 1.29 – 'Behold the Lamb of God' – have led many to conclude that this first OT citation in John 19.36 is intended to present Jesus as the Passover Lamb, slaughtered to take away the sins of God's people.[191] Some, however, have suggested that John 19.36 (ὀστοῦν οὐ συντριβήσεται αὐτοῦ) refers to the Righteous Sufferer of LXX Ps. 33.21 (34.20) (κύριος φυλάσσει πάντα τὰ ὀστᾶ αὐτῶν, ἓν ἐξ αὐτῶν οὐ συντριβήσεται), whose unjust treatment is vindicated by God. It has also been posited that both images – the paschal lamb and the Righteous Sufferer – are intentionally being conflated.[192]

There is, however, no doubt that the second OT citation (19.37) is from Zech. 12.10. John has been preparing his readers for this move. Earlier in 19.34 he mentions that one of the soldiers pierced Jesus' side, and then, as if to grasp the weight of this event (because it fulfils Zech. 12.10), he follows the comment up with 'He who saw this has testified so that you also may believe. His testimony is true, and he knows that he tells the truth' (19.35). John's emphasis on the veracity of this event may be another indication that Zechariah 9–14 was already a recognized source of *testimonia* at the time of composition.[193] The piercing of Jesus is described in details that seem to echo Zech. 13.1 ('On that day there

---

[189] See, e.g. Longenecker 1995: 434–40. There is some question as to the exact reference of ὀστοῦν οὐ συντριβήσεται αὐτοῦ in Verse 36 since the citation does not correspond exactly to any of the proposed options.

[190] I am indebted to Brown (1966: 953) for these observations.

[191] Some scholars, however, are convinced that instead of the paschal lamb (Exod. 12.46/Num. 9.12), the citation is actually referring to the Righteous Sufferer of Ps. 34.20 (LXX 33.21: κύριος φυλάσσει πάντα τὰ ὀστᾶ αὐτῶν, ἓν αὐτῶν οὐ συντριβήσεται) whose unjust treatment is vindicated by God. Beasely-Murray notes that Barrett, Schnackenburg and Lindars think John had both typologies in mind (Beasely-Murray 1999: 355). Lincoln (2005: 482) mentions that Jub. 49.13 combines images from the Passover and the Righteous Sufferer.

[192] Beasely-Murray (1999: 355), for example, notes that Barrett, Schnackenburg and Lindars posit that John had both typologies in mind. Jub. 49.13 combines images from the Passover and the Righteous Sufferer (Lincoln 2005: 482).

[193] Bauckham 1993: 318–21; Dodd 1952: 64–7.

shall be a fountain opened . . . to cleanse them from their sin') and Zech.
14.8 ('On that day living waters shall flow out from Jerusalem'), which
suggests that John expects his readers to make connections in Zechariah
which go beyond his citation of Zech. 12.10.[194]

Some scholars have proposed that John's citation of Zech. 12.10,
understood in its wider context (i.e. the slain shepherd of Zech. 13.7),
is also meant to allude back to Jesus' 'good shepherd' discourse in
John 10.[195] There Jesus twice refers to himself as the good shepherd
(10.11,14) and thrice declares that he will lay down his life for his sheep
(10.11,15,17). While many scholars have suggested that the notion of a
good shepherd laying down his life for his sheep is a conflation of ideas
found in Ezekiel 34 and Isaiah 53, a much simpler solution would be
to regard it as an allusion to Zech. 11/13.[196] First, unlike Ezekiel 34,
Zech. 11.4–14 and Zech. 13.7 both speak of a shepherd being killed
for the sake of YHWH's people and in keeping with his eschatological
programme of restoration. Second, like the account in John 10, both a
good and faithful shepherd, as well as a faithless and wicked shepherd,
appear in Zech. 11.4–17. Third, as Schnackenburg has pointed out, both
Zechariah (13.7) as well as John (10.12; 16.32) speak of sheep being
scattered upon the death of the shepherd.[197] If we are right that John
10 is dependent upon both Zech. 11.4–17 as well as Zech. 13.7 for its
theme, then both shepherd figures (Zech. 11/13) are regarded as one and
the same person – which I suggested as a possible and perhaps even
likely scenario in my analysis of Zechariah 9–14. Additionally, if John
had some awareness of the Synoptic traditions, John 10 may be an elaboration of the Zech. 13.7 citation found in Mark and Matthew, and may
explain why the Fourth Evangelist chose to frame his Passion Narrative
with Zech. 12.10 rather than Zech. 13.7 as the other two evangelists
did.[198]

In any case, in John 19.36–7, we have a conflation of two (possibly
three) OT citations that create two (possibly three) significant images of
Jesus. He is the slain paschal lamb (and perhaps the Righteous Sufferer)
who is also the pierced shepherd-king.[199]

[194] Moo 1983: 217–21.   [195] Lincoln 2005: 482; Beasley-Murray 1999: 355.
[196] Black 1990: 198–9.   [197] Schnackenburg 1990: 295.
[198] See Bauckham 1998: 147–71, who argues that John was written for readers of Mark.
[199] If we allow for the first OT citation in John 19.36 to be a conflation of the paschal
lamb and the Righteous Sufferer, then, as Beasley-Murray (1999: 355) has written, John
may well be saying that 'Jesus in his death brings to fulfillment the significance of the
Passover and the eschatological hope of a second Exodus. He also fulfills the role of the
Righteous Man who suffers but is under the care of God.'

2.2.2.4 Conclusions regarding the reception of Zechariah 9–14 in the Passion Narratives

Since several studies already have analyzed thoroughly the use of Zechariah 9–14 in the Passion Narratives, I have found it unnecessary to do the same.[200] I have, instead, highlighted some of the most essential features of Zechariah's reception, which will now allow me to make the following conclusions. First, the appropriation of Zechariah 9–14 in the Passion Narratives demonstrates that it was not only available for reflection and consultation around the time in which 1 Peter was written, but that is was also a prominent source in early Christianity for explaining how Jesus' rejection, suffering and death as messiah were according to the scriptures.[201] As Black has suggested, there are several reasons why Zechariah 9–14 was susceptible to such a reading: it had an eschatological outlook with messianic overtones that include Davidic traditions, shepherd imagery and royal imagery; and the oracles themselves are obscure enough to encourage speculation and creative readings of the text.[202] It is possible, though difficult to prove, that Jesus himself (and not just the Evangelists) drew from Zechariah 9–14 in order to understand his own vocation, and perhaps the unfolding events of the last week of his life prior to the crucifixion.[203]

Second, there are a number of events and details in the Passion Narratives which are integrally related to Zechariah 9–14.[204] The triumphal entry (Mark 11.1–11; Matt. 21.5; Luke 19.29–40; John 12.15/Zech. 9.9–10), the thirty silver pieces, Judas' betrayal and the rejection of Jesus by the Jewish leaders (Matt. 27.9–10; 26.15–Zech. 11.12–13), the prediction of Jesus' death (Mark 14.27–8; Matt. 26.31–2; John 10.11,15,17–Zech. 13.7), the prediction of the disciples' desertion (Mark 14.27–8; Matt. 26.31–2; John 16.32–3–Zech. 13.7–9), the piercing of Jesus' side (John 19.34–7–Zech. 12.10), the mourning at the crucifixion (Luke 23.27–Zech. 12.11–14), the flowing of living waters (i.e. forgiveness of sins; John 19.34–Zech. 13.1; 14.8) and Jesus' actions in the temple (Mark 11.15–17; Matt. 21.12–13; John 2.16) all find scriptural antecedents in Zechariah 9–14. As Black has suggested, 'Zechariah seems to have provided the stimulus for many of the traditions. Furthermore, the early Christians may have discovered within Zech.

---

[200] Most notably Moo 1983; Black 1990; and Ham 2005.
[201] Black 1990: 242–3.   [202] Black 1990: 242.
[203] Black (1990: 238–45) has argued that it was the early church, after Jesus' death, that discovered the fittingness of Zechariah 9–14 in explaining Jesus' rejection and death.
[204] Dodd 1952: 64–7; Black 1990: 158–232; 237–8.

9–14 a narrative sequence upon which they drew in shaping the Passion Narratives.'[205]

Third, although each Evangelist looked to Zechariah 9–14 in order to explain and provide scriptural warrant for the events surrounding the death of Jesus, they each did so in slightly different ways.[206] There was not, in other words, a monolithic approach to interpreting Zechariah 9–14. What they shared in common, however, was the tendency to read Zechariah 9–14 as a foundational narrative that offered an eschatological programme. Each Evangelist, however, connected different dots in that narrative. Mark, for example, connected the figures of Zech. 9.9 and 13.7 to Jesus' entry into Jerusalem and his betrayal and death. Matthew and John went one step further and interpreted the figures of Zech. 9.9, 12.10 and 13.7 as representing the same figure in the narrative of Zechariah 9–14; this figure, they argue, points to Jesus.[207] Such a reading of 9.9, 12.10 and 13.7 likely demonstrates dependence upon the Hebrew text-plot, since it would be difficult (though not impossible) to arrive at such a conclusion by reading the LXX or the Targum of Zechariah.

Fourth, all indications are that the early church perceived in Zechariah 9–14 an eschatological programme that included the advent of the mes-siah on a donkey, his betrayal and rejection, his tragic death, the scattering of his followers, a tribulation period prior to restoration, and cleansing from sin that would enable Israel's restoration.[208]

Fifth, Zechariah 9–14 was read alongside several other OT passages – most notably Isaiah 40–66, the Psalms and Daniel. Thus, although the eschatological programme of Zechariah 9–14 is foundational to the Pas-sion Narratives, it did not exclude and in fact appeared to encourage input from other relevant passages in the OT. Together then, Zechariah 9–14 and other key OT passages provided mutual interpretation of Jesus' suffering and death.

Finally, in the Passion Narratives shepherd imagery, and especially the designation of Jesus as the Shepherd, is integrally related to the eschatological programme of Zechariah 9–14.

Given the familiarity of these Passion Narratives in the early church,[209] and the variety of ways in which Zechariah is appropriated by these narratives, it is likely that (a) many early Christians were familiar with

---

[205] Black 1990: 8.

[206] In my view, this point is not emphasized enough in the studies of Dodd 1952; Bruce 1968; and Black 1990. They, instead, tend to present an aggregate reading of Zechariah 9–14 based upon all of the constituent parts found in Matthew, Mark, Luke and John (e.g. Black's (2008: 98) comment that 'the early church read Zech 9–14 as a whole').

[207] Moo 1983: 173.   [208] Dodd 1952: 64–7; Black 1990: 239; Mitchell 1997: 237.

[209] Here I concur with J. B. Green 1992a: 157–217.

the contents of Zechariah 9–14, perhaps even viewing it as a source of *testimonia*; (b) that many would readily hear allusions to Zechariah 9–14 when they were made;[210] (c) that some early Christian teachers (like Peter) would look to Zechariah 9–14 as an aid in explaining the meaning of Christ's suffering and death; and (d) that those familiar with the Passion Narratives might be inclined to associate shepherd imagery with the eschatological programme of Zechariah 9–14. It may also be the case that the manner in which the early church read Zechariah 9–14 was itself shaped by the way in which Zechariah 9–14 was appropriated in the Passion Narratives. In other words, it is possible that the Passion Narrative tradition influenced how early Christians interpreted Zechariah 9–14.

2.2.3   The reception of Zechariah 9–14 in Revelation

Marko Jauhiainen's *The Use of Zechariah in Revelation* is presently the most comprehensive analysis of the reception of Zechariah in Revelation.[211] One of the more intriguing conclusions of his study is that Revelation alludes more often to Zechariah 1–8 than to Zechariah 9–14. In fact, according to Jauhiainen, there are only two places where an allusion to Zechariah 9–14 can be discerned with certainty (Rev. 1.7/Zech. 12.10; Rev. 22.3/Zech. 14.1–19).[212] Additionally, he has discerned a number of possible allusions or simple allusions at various places in Revelation which all point to features found in Zech. 14.1–21 (7.1–17; 11.15; 16.19; 19.14,19; 21.25; 22.15).[213] According to Jauhiainen, the multiple allusions to Zech. 14.1–21 are intended to function as signs which point to the imminent and/or consummated restoration of YHWH's people, which include: YHWH's universal reign (11.15; 19.6); the realization of YHWH's kingship (11.15; 19.6); the absence of night (21.25; 22.5); living waters that flow from the New Jerusalem (22.1); and the absence of the ban of destruction, or the purity of God's people (22.3).[214]

---

[210] See Thompson's helpful study on early epistolary usage of the Jesus Tradition, which includes the Passion Narratives (1991: 37–63). Thompson concludes his survey of the usage of Jesus Tradition in non-Pauline epistles and the Early Church Fathers by noting that 'the readers' knowledge of JT was assumed as fundamental to their Christian instruction' (*ibid.*: 63).

[211] Jauhiainen 2005.

[212] Jauhiainen (*ibid.*: 29–32), following Ben-Porat, defines an allusion as the activation of two texts (see *ibid.*: 29–30 for full discussion).

[213] For Jauhiainen (*ibid.*: 30), a simple allusion is 'a hint to a known fact'. 'While its actualization depends on the application of information outside of the alluding text to the context, the process remains within the framework of the alluding text.' For a summary of his results on Zechariah 9–14 in Revelations see *ibid.*: 130.

[214] *Ibid.*: 146–7, 153.

Jauhiainen argues that the most significant allusion to Zechariah in all of Revelation, however, is found in Rev. 1.7, 'where it functions as a literary sign and an interpretative key, among other things evoking Zechariah's eschatological framework and suggesting the imminence of the promised and long-awaited restoration.[215]

It is difficult to determine, however, if Rev. 1.7 is in fact alluding directly to Zech. 12.10 (and conflating that with Daniel 7). For instance, Matt. 24.30, John 19.37 and Rev. 1.7 curiously all use the verb ὁράω instead of the verb ἐπιβλέπω, which is the OG rendering, in order to describe the action of looking upon the pierced one. This discrepancy has led many to argue that a well-known *testimonium* circulated in the early church in a fixed textual form.[216] Norman Perrin has suggested that this *testimonium* was based, in part, on the desire to exploit a word-play: ἐπιβλέπω was exchanged for ὁράω (ὄψονται) in order to create the parallel with κόψονται.[217] A rigid application of the *testimonium* theory, however, is unable to explain why Matthew has omitted the mention of piercing but has included the phrase 'all of the tribes of the earth will mourn', why the mourning of all tribes has been omitted from John 19.37 and why Rev. 1.7 has included both the piercing as well as the mourning of the tribes. In our view, there are two possible explanations for what we see in Rev. 1.7. First, it is possible that what Matthew, John and Revelation indicate is an exegetical practice in the early church, rather than a fixed textual form, in which Zech. 12.10 and Daniel 7 are (creatively) read together in order to understand the identity of Jesus and the unfolding of God's restoration. Second, it could be that the author of Revelation's understanding of Zech. 12.10 has been shaped by Matt. 24.30 and John 19.37, and that Rev. 1.7 is intended to invoke not only Zech. 12.10 and Daniel 7, but more immediately Jesus as he is presented in the Passion Narratives of Matthew and John.[218] Do we have any evidence that such an appropriation is possible or intended? Jauhiainen has pointed to Matt. 24.3 as a possible clue.[219] There the disciples of Jesus ask for a sign that would point to his coming and the end of the age. According to the

---

[215] *Ibid.*: 153. For Jauhiainen (*ibid.*: 142–3), Rev. 1.7 'gains extra significance from its placement immediately after the epistolary opening and the doxology, for in ancient documents the first sentence or first paragraph would often give important information regarding the subject of the document'.

[216] Perrin 1965: 153–5; Bauckham 1993: 320; Albl 1999.   [217] Perrin 1965: 153.

[218] Jauhiainen (2005: 143) similarly argues that the allusion 'activates the eschatological framework of the three primary narratives that were available to the early church regarding the final events: Zechariah's version, Daniel's version, and Jesus' version'. These two options are not mutually exclusive.

[219] *Ibid.*: 143.

Matthean Jesus, the sign of the end of the tribulation and the culmination of God's restoration will be the Son of Man coming on the clouds and all the tribes of the earth mourning (Matt. 24.30). As Jauhiainen suggests, the reference to this sign at the opening of Revelation orients the readers to the main theme of the letter: 'the close of the age is at hand – now is the time for the final tribulation and the following deliverance and restoration of God's people'.[220]

I note, then, one similarity and one difference between the appropriation of Zechariah 9–14 in the Passion Narratives and Revelation. The similarity lies in the fact that both the Gospels as well as Revelation have drawn on Zechariah 9–14 in order to confirm the imminence and consummation of the restoration of God's people; that is, both look to Zechariah in order to understand the unfolding of God's eschatological programme. In the Passion Narratives, however, Zechariah 9–14 is appropriated almost exclusively in order to understand the events leading up to the death of Jesus and how they could be a part of God's plan of restoration, whereas in Revelation Zechariah is seen to speak beyond the death of Jesus, to the culmination of restoration, that is, to things that have yet to come. Thus, the argument that I am making about the influence of Zechariah 9–14 on the eschatological programme of 1 Peter is strengthened by what seems to be the case with Revelation.

2.3   Conclusion

I have argued that Zechariah 9–14 progressively reveals a complex eschatological programme that infuses and reworks earlier material from Ezekiel and Isaiah, and ultimately promises restoration for YHWH's people through the agency of the eschatological Davidic shepherd. Central to Zechariah's programme is the revelation that this eschatological Davidic shepherd will not usher in immediate peace and prosperity. Instead, he will be rejected and killed; and his death will initiate a time of trouble for all of Israel, in which the remnant will be protected by YHWH as they endure fiery trials that will bring purity in preparation for YHWH's universal reign.

While the reception of Zechariah 9–14 in the Jewish Second Temple period was sparse, there was enough evidence to suggest that it was known and available for theological reflection, though without any uniform approach for interpreting and appropriating the eschatological programme. In contrast, in early Christianity, Zechariah 9–14 was a

[220] *Ibid.*: 143–4.

prominent and integral source for explaining how Jesus' rejection, suffering and death as messiah were in keeping with the scriptures (the Passion Narratives) and for indicating signs which pointed to the imminent and consummated restoration of YHWH's people (Revelation).

We are now well prepared to examine whether Zechariah 9–14 has shaped the eschatological programme of 1 Peter.

3

FIRST PETER 2.25 AND ZECHARIAH'S SHEPHERD-KING

In keeping with my outline (§1.3.3), in the following three chapters I will argue that 1 Peter alludes to material in Zechariah 9–14. More specifically, I will analyze the shepherd imagery of 1 Pet. 2.25 (Chapter 3) and 5.2–4 (Chapter 5) and the fiery trials imagery of 1.6 and 4.12 (Chapter 4) and argue that Zechariah 9–14 is the most plausible explanation for this imagery. In Chapter 6 I will seek to demonstrate how the conclusions that I have reached in Chapters 3, 4 and 5 can be understood in relation to the argumentative strategy of 1 Peter. Ultimately, I will propose that the eschatological programme of Zechariah 9–14 generates and undergirds the theology of Christian suffering as well as the eschatological outlook of 1 Peter.

In this chapter, then, I begin with an analysis of the shepherd imagery of 1 Pet. 2.25. Primopetrine scholars have long considered 1 Pet. 2.21–5 to be one of the most significant passages for understanding the letter as a whole. Some have gone as far as regarding it as 'the heart of 1 Peter's Christology',[1] and the place 'where all the literary characteristics of the letter converge'.[2]

The passage begins by exhorting Christians[3] to endure unjust suffering, since 'Christ also suffered for you' (2.21). This exhortation is followed by an appropriation of Isaiah 53, which is used to present Jesus' innocent suffering and subsequent death (2.22–3) both as an example to follow and as a means of 'healing' (2.24). It culminates with a description of the Anatolian Christians as straying sheep who have now been

---

[1] Jobes 2005: 192.
[2] '[D]onde todas las características literarias de la carta convergen' (Cervantes Gabarrón 1991a: 108). Brox (1986: 128) similarly posits, 'Darüber hinaus liegt darin [1 Pet. 2.18–25] die Logik der Theologie des ganzen Briefes, nicht nur der Sklaven-Paränese'.
[3] Although the passage specifically addresses slaves, most commentators agree with John Elliott (2000: 542), who writes that 'this passage has in view not simply servants/slaves but the entire community. The former are held up here as paradigmatic of the condition and vocation of the brotherhood as a whole'. See also Brox 1986: 128; Michaels 1988: 135; Achtemeier 1996: 192; Campbell 1998: 143; Jobes 2005: 187.

Table 3.1   Subdivisions of 1 Pet. 2.21–5

21a	εἰς τοῦτο γὰρ ἐκλήθητε,
	ὅτι καὶ Χριστὸς ἔπαθεν ὑπὲρ ὑμῶν
	ὑμῖν ὑπολιμπάνων ὑπογραμμὸν
b	ἵνα ἐπακολουθήσητε τοῖς ἴχνεσιν αὐτοῦ,
22	ὃς ἁμαρτίαν οὐκ ἐποίησεν
	οὐδὲ εὑρέθη δόλος ἐν τῷ στόματι αὐτοῦ,
23a	ὃς λοιδορούμενος οὐκ ἀντελοιδόρει,
	πάσχων οὐκ ἠπείλει,
b	παρεδίδου δὲ τῷ κρίνοντι δικαίως·
24a	ὃς τὰς ἁμαρτίας ἡμῶν αὐτὸς ἀνήνεγκεν
	ἐν τῷ σώματι αὐτοῦ ἐπὶ τὸ ξύλον,
b	ἵνα ταῖς ἁμαρτίαις ἀπογενόμενοι
	τῇ δικαιοσύνῃ ζήσωμεν,
c	οὗ τῷ μώλωπι ἰάθητε.
25a	ἦτε γὰρ ὡς πρόβατα πλανώμενοι,
b	ἀλλὰ ἐπεστράφητε νῦν ἐπὶ τὸν ποιμένα
	καὶ ἐπίσκοπον τῶν ψυχῶν ὑμῶν.

returned[4] to the shepherd and overseer of their souls (2.25). Primopetrine scholars have long considered 1 Pet. 2.21–5 (see Table 3.1 for the subdivisions of this passage) to be one of the most significant passages for understanding the letter as a whole.

Scholarly enquiry of this passage has almost exclusively focused on issues pertaining to the appropriation of Isaiah 53 and its relation to Jesus.[5] Although there is certainly warrant for this fruitful line of research, other important features in the passage have been neglected. In particular, there has been very little attention given to the shepherd imagery found in 2.25, and even less reflection as to why this imagery has been combined with the Suffering Servant of Isaiah 53 (1 Pet. 2.22–4).[6]

In this chapter, I will give special attention to ascertaining the logic that has brought together Isaiah 53 and the reference that straying sheep have being returned to the shepherd and overseer of souls. In other words, why has 2.22–5a been combined with 1 Pet. 2.25b?

---

[4] See the discussion below for translating ἐπεστράφητε as a passive rather than a middle deponent.

[5] This includes such debates as whether an early Christian hymn stands behind the appropriation of Isaiah 53, whether the passage promotes a theory of substitutionary atonement and which text form of Isaiah the author was using.

[6] Bosetti 1990 and Cervantes Gabarrón 1991b are notable exceptions to this trend; however, Cervantes Gabarón's work has been strongly influenced by the conclusions of Bosetti.

3.1 Recent proposals regarding the shepherd imagery of 1 Peter 2.25

Those few who have put forth an account of how 1 Pet. 2.22–4 and 2.25 relate to one another, broadly speaking, can be placed in one of two lines of interpretation. Goppelt and Michaels represent what I will call the 'conversion approach'.[7] The proponents of this approach contend that the two aorist verbs ἰάθητε and ἐπεστράφητε point us to the logic that connects 2.24 and 2.25, though there is some discrepancy in explaining how this linking occurs. Goppelt, for example, suggests that the two verbs are brought together through the aid of an early Christian tradition that developed from Isa. 6.10 (ἐπιστρέψωσιν καὶ ἰάσομαι αὐτούς), which is reflected in Mark 4.12, Matt. 13.15, John 12.40 and Acts 28.27.[8] Accordingly, we are to suppose that the author of 1 Peter, upon reading Isa. 53.5 (τῷ μώλωπι αὐτοῦ ἡμεῖς ἰάθημεν), was drawn to and appropriated this early Christian tradition (and not Isa. 6.10), which in turn led him to write that the straying sheep (Isa. 53.6) 'have turned' (ἐπεστράφητε) to the shepherd.[9] The foundational assumption which allows for such an interplay between Isa. 53.5 and the early Christian tradition is the conclusion that ἐπεστράφητε is a deponent verb ('have turned', rather than 'have been returned') that is to be understood, therefore, as a reference to conversion, presumably to Jesus. Goppelt, however, fails to justify this assumption, which will be critiqued in due course.[10] In the end, Goppelt suggests that the title 'shepherd' is ancillary to the main point of the passage – an add-on, perhaps, that provides poetic symmetry with the 'sheep' metaphor?[11]

[7] Other less developed proponents of this view are Reicke 1964: 99; Spicq 1966: 113; Kelly 1969: 124; Best 1971: 123; Brox 1986: 139; Achtemeier 1996: 204–5.

[8] Goppelt 1993: 215. Achtemeier (1996: 204) agrees that it is possible that Isa. 6.10 was the impetus for connecting the two verses. I would point out that neither Mark 4.12 (μήποτε ἐπιστρέψωσιν καὶ ἀφεθῇ αὐτοῖς) nor John 12.40 (στραφῶσιν, καὶ ἰάσομαι αὐτούς) contains both coordinating verbs ἰάομαι and ἐπιστρέφω.

[9] Goppelt (1993: 215) is adamant that it is the early Christian tradition and not Isa. 6.10 that has been impetus for this exegetical move: 'The connection of the two verbs in v. 24c and v.25 corresponds to a commonly used early Christian tradition ... But 1 Peter appropriates not this [Isa. 6.10], but the early Christian tradition that developed from it.'

[10] 'Healing from sinning is interpreted as ... a turning ... to the shepherd Christ' (Goppelt 1993: 215).

[11] He only addresses the shepherd imagery in four sentences, mentioning that shepherd imagery is common in the OT, that Jesus' ministry was likened to the shepherd's work of finding the lost sheep, and that 1 Peter appropriates early Christian developments of this OT imagery, but he does not develop this thought in detail or explain how this fits with the Isa. 6.10 tradition (Goppelt 1993: 215).

Michaels, who is hesitant to adopt Goppelt's proposal regarding the early Christian tradition based on Isa. 6.10, instead nuances the argument by positing that the logic of the passage is explained in light of one of the predominant themes of 1 Pet. 2.21–5 – conversion.[12] He notes that ἰάθητε and ἐπεστράφητε, along with ἐκλήθητε (2.21), refer to the recipients' conversion, which for him is the point which begins and ends 1 Pet. 2.21–5.[13] Reading 1 Pet. 2.21–5 in this manner, Michaels concludes that 2.25 'defines what Peter means (and what he thinks Isaiah means) by healing': 'Like Isaiah before him, Peter uses physical healing as a metaphor for religious conversion.'[14] The sheep metaphor appears to have wandered incidentally into the passage because 'we all like sheep have gone astray', found in Isa. 53.6, is a convenient way of describing the readers' lives before turning (conversion) to Jesus. Like Goppelt, Michaels (in his 1 Peter commentary anyway) is unable to explain why Peter has referred to Jesus as the shepherd, admitting that

> [t]he transition between vv 21–25a and this last clause of chapter 2 is rather abrupt. Christ was last mentioned as wounded and carrying sins to the cross after much abuse, while the readers of the epistle were compared to a scattered flock of sheep. Now suddenly the sheep are back together, with Christ (very much alive) as the Shepherd who reunites them.[15]

However, in an article written in 2004, Michaels amends his earlier proposal by offering a new way of explaining the 'shepherd' reference in 1 Pet. 2.25, arguing that Mark's Passion Narrative has played a role:

> At the end of Mark . . . the disciples, and Peter in particular, were to be told that Jesus would fulfil his promise to lead them into Galilee (Mark 14:28), where Peter and his companions 'will see him' (Mark 16:7). That promise had been given in a framework of Jesus as 'shepherd' to his disciples, on the basis of Zech 13:7, 'I will strike the shepherd and the sheep will be scattered' (Mark 14:27), to which Jesus had added, 'but after I am raised

---

[12] Michaels 1988: 150.

[13] *Ibid.*: 137, 142, and especially 149 where he writes, 'His purpose is to bring the exhortation back to the point at which it began, the conversion of his Gentile readers, represented by the ἐκλήθητε of 2.21a, and in this way to set the stage for v 25'.

[14] Michaels 1988: 149–50. Achtemeier takes a similar line, arguing that the logical connection between 2.24 and 2.25 is that both verses refer to conversion (Achtemeier 1996: 204–5).

[15] Michaels 1988: 151. Achtemeier offers no explanation for the shepherd imagery except to state that the shepherd refers to Jesus and not God (Achtemeier 1996: 204).

up I will lead you into Galilee.' To 'lead' them, or 'go before' them (προάγειν), was a word appropriate to a shepherd leading his sheep to new pastures. In 1 Peter, Jesus as 'shepherd' evokes for Peter his resurrection.[16]

The term 'shepherd', then, is intended to point to the resurrected Jesus, to whom the straying sheep have converted. Regardless of whether the scenario that Michaels lays out is historically plausible or not, the point I want to make is that this recent amendment still does not explain the logic of linking Isaiah 53 with the shepherd metaphor; it offers an explanation of what 'shepherd' refers to (i.e. the resurrected Jesus), but it does not explain why a healing wound, straying sheep and the shepherd have all been brought together.

Elena Bosetti, John Elliott, Mark Dubis and Karen Jobes represent a second line of interpretation, which I will call the 'restoration approach'. The proponents of this approach argue that the theme of restoration is the link between Isaiah 53 and the shepherd imagery of 2.25, pointing in particular to the shepherd tradition of Ezekiel 34. Bosetti's monograph, *Il Pastore: Cristo e la Chiesa Nella Prima Lettera di Pietro*, is without question the most comprehensive of the four, entirely dedicated to understanding the use of pastoral imagery in 1 Peter (i.e. 1 Pet. 2.25 and 5.1–4).[17] She regards the 'conversion approach' to be an inadequate explanation of the logic of 1 Pet. 2.24–5 principally on the grounds that 1 Peter reverses the order of Isa. 6.10 (cf. Deut. 30.2–3; Isa. 19.22; Jer. 3.22) and its tradents (i.e. Matt. 13.14–15; John 12.40; Acts 28.26–7). In other words, whereas 1 Peter speaks of healing and *then* turning, in these precursor texts healing is a consequence or condition of having already turned to the Lord.[18] She further argues that Isaiah 53 itself contradicts the 'conversion approach', since there healing is the end of the salvation process.[19] Whether this is an adequate critique of the 'conversion approach' is debatable. For example, Bosetti has not considered the fact that even though 'healing' comes before 'turning to the shepherd' at the level of presentation, that is, 2.24 comes before 2.25, it is nevertheless possible to read the passage in such a way that 2.25 happens *before* 2.24: the wounds of Jesus bring healing precisely because (γάρ; 'prior action') 'you have turned to the shepherd and overseer of

---

[16] Michaels 2004: 393; see also 389–90. For Michaels' argument for Petrine authorship see Michaels 1988: lv–lxvii.
[17] Bosetti 1990. Unfortunately her work has been ignored almost completely in the English-speaking world of 1 Peter scholarship. Elliott (2000: 539) is a notable exception.
[18] Bosetti 1990: 125–8.   [19] *Ibid.*: 128.

your souls'. Additionally, in Isaiah 53 healing is not the end of the process of salvation, but rather the entry point into the benefits of YHWH's restoration. Regardless, her rejection of the 'conversion approach' leads Bosetti to propose that the logical connection in 1 Pet. 2.24–5 is not ἰάομαι/ἐπιστρέφω, but rather πλανάομαι/ἐπιστρέφω. Drawing upon texts such as Jeremiah 23, Ezekiel 34 and Zechariah 10, Bosetti traces a tradition within the prophets (one which I have already highlighted in Chapter 2) in which YHWH's exiled people are frequently described as 'straying sheep' who lack a shepherd, and in which the restoration of YHWH's exiled people is portrayed in terms of being gathered (συνάγω) and returned (ἐπιστρέφω) to Jerusalem.[20] In particular, she points to Ezekiel 34 as the point of reference for 1 Pet. 2.25, noting two places within the chapter that explain why the straying sheep of Isaiah 53 (1 Pet. 2.24) have been linked with the shepherd and overseer in 1 Pet. 2.25. The first link is found in Ezek. 34.16 (τὸ πλανώμενον ἐπιστρέψω), where YHWH is the agent who promises to return straying sheep. This, in Bosetti's view, corresponds to the 'theological passive' ἐπεστράφητε of 1 Pet. 2.25: the agent who has returned the recipients to the shepherd is God, who, while he is unmentioned in the passage, is present nonetheless.[21] The second link is found in Ezek. 34.23–4, a text in which YHWH announces that his restoration will include the appointing of a shepherd, 'my servant David' (דָּוִד עַבְדִּי/τὸν δοῦλόν μου Δαυιδ), and which explains why the author of 1 Peter is able to describe the straying sheep as being returned to a person (namely the shepherd), rather than the more characteristic return to a place (i.e. Jerusalem).[22] For Bosetti, then, 1 Pet. 2.21–5 is a conflation of two prophetic formulations of restoration – the Suffering Servant of Isaiah 53 and the Davidic shepherd of Ezekiel 34.

Elliott has proposed the same conflation of OT sources in 2.25 (apparently independent of Bosetti), noting a number of verbal parallels:

> The verb *epestraphēte*... and the image of the return of straying sheep do not occur in Isa 53. It appears to be derived from Ezekiel (34.4–11, 16), where mention is made of sheep (*probata*, 34.5, 6, 8, 10, 11), straying (*planōmenon*, 34.4), return (*apostrephō*, 34.4, 6, 10); *epistrephō*, 34.16 [God's returning the strayed sheep]; and *episkeptō*, 34.11 (the verb related to the noun *episkopos*... in 1 Peter).[23]

---

[20] *Ibid.*: 128–42.   [21] *Ibid.*: 122.   [22] *Ibid.*: 133.

[23] Elliott 2000: 537. It is not clear whether Elliott has been influenced by Bosetti, though he does demonstrate an awareness of her work (Elliott 2000: 538).

Like Bosetti, he notes that '[t]he straying, scattering, and return of God's sheep eventually became one of several metaphors for the final gathering and salvation of God's scattered people'.[24] Additionally, he points out that the imagery of Israel as straying sheep is found not only in the OT, but also in the Gospels (Mark 6.34/Matt. 9.36; 10.6; 15.24) and in the mouth of Jesus, who citing Zech. 13.7 explains his disciples' desertion in terms of sheep being scattered.[25] Unfortunately, Elliott does not develop these observations any further, leaving the reader with two lingering questions: (1) Why has Isaiah 53 been conflated with Ezekiel 34? (2) What is the significance of this conflation?

Jobes, also working independently of Bosetti, likewise suggests that 2.25 alludes to Ezekiel 34.[26] She writes, '[e]lements of this passage in Ezekiel [34.11–13] correlate so well with elements of 1 Peter that it is tempting to conclude that Peter deliberately alludes to Ezekiel here [2.25] and elsewhere in his letter'.[27] She further adds that '[t]he motif of scattered Christians (cf. 1.1), converted from the Gentiles (cf. 1.2), who were sought after by the Shepherd and who have returned to the *episkopos* of their souls (2.25), aptly echoes Ezekiel's prophecy'.[28] Unfortunately, like Elliott, she does not develop this line of thought any further in her commentary.

Dubis links the apparent allusion to Ezekiel 34 in 2.25 with the larger motif of restoration from exile found in 1 Peter.[29] He also provides a rationale for why Peter would be reading Ezekiel alongside Isaiah – they both share the theme of restoration from exile. He writes, 'the Ezekiel

---

[24] Elliott 2000: 538. He notes the following texts in support of this comment: Ezek. 11.14–21; 20.34; 28.25; 34.11–16, 28–31; Zech. 10.1–2; Mic. 2.12; 5.3–4; Sir. 36.11; *Pss. Sol.* 8.28; 17.28; 2 Macc. 1.24–9; 2.18.

[25] Elliott 2000: 537.

[26] Jobes 2005: 198. According to Jobes, the shepherd imagery appears as a by-product. 'The thought in Is 53.5 that the wounds of the Suffering Servant heal is followed in 53.6 by the statement "We all have wandered like sheep . . .". Peter picks up the same imagery in the same sequence'.

[27] Jobes 2005: 198. The 'elsewhere' she is referring to is 1 Pet. 5.1–4 (*ibid.*: 304).

[28] *Ibid.*:199.

[29] Dubis 2002: 46:

> One will only properly understand 1 Peter's theology of suffering if one sets it within the broader framework of his exile/restoration metaphor. Indeed the suffering/glory pattern in 1 Peter (1.11; 4.13; 5.1, 10) is essentially an exile/restoration pattern. First Peter portrays the suffering of the readers as exilic suffering, and portrays future glory as the glory of Israel's anticipated eschatological restoration . . .

For the full argumentation see Dubis 2002: 46–58; see also Deterding 1981 for a development of exodus motifs in 1 Peter.

34 background of 1 Peter 2.25 highlights 1 Peter's restoration-from-exile motif... God has regathered the flock of Israel, and has established his faithful Davidic shepherd over them. The restoration of the OT prophets is thus underway.'[30]

3.2   A critique of the two approaches

Before I put forth my own proposal to explain the logic that brings together Isaiah 53 and the shepherd imagery of 2.25, I will offer some critiques of these two lines of interpretation as they presently stand, which ultimately make them either implausible or unsatisfying explanations respectively.

If the 'conversion approach' were the best option for understanding the relationship between 2.24 and 2.25, we would have to conclude that scholars have rightly paid little attention to the shepherd imagery, which would seem to be rather incidental to the main thrust of the passage. There are, however, certain features of this proposal which are implausible. First, all indications are that ἐπεστράφητε is best translated with the passive voice ('have been returned') rather than as a passive deponent ('have turned'), which is what Goppelt and Michaels have done.[31] While it is true that the aorist passive of ἐπιστρέφω can be deponent, this is rare in the New Testament. Outside of 1 Pet. 2.25, ἐπιστρέφω appears thirty-five times in the NT; only four times in a passive construction (Matt. 10.13; Mark 5.30; 8.33; John 21.20).[32] In none of these four cases does the passive construction convey the idea of conversion. Conversely, we do have cases in the NT where ἐπιστρέφω does mean 'to turn' in the sense of convert; in every case the verb appears with the active construction (e.g. Acts 3.19; 11.21; 14.15; 15.19; 26.18; 1 Thess. 1.9).[33] Additionally, in the texts that Goppelt points to as the likely impetus for the appropriation of the verb ἐπιστρέφω in 1 Pet. 2.25 (e.g. Matt. 13.15; Mark 4.12; and Acts 28.27) the active construct (i.e. non-deponent) is used. There is no evidence in the NT, outside of the debatable instance in 1 Pet. 2.25, where ἐπιστρέφω in the passive is meant to convey the idea of turning in the sense of conversion. This in no way makes a deponent reading impossible; however,

---

[30] Dubis 2002: 58.

[31] Bosetti 1990: 132; Achtemeier 1996: 204; Elliott 2000: 539; Dubis 2002: 57.

[32] It appears that ἐπιστρέφω is deponent most often when it occurs as an aorist passive participle – e.g. Exod. 7.23; Num. 23.5; Deut. 1.24; Mark 5.30; 8.33; John 21.20; Barn. 4.8; Herm. 12.4.6.

[33] Of particular note is Acts 11.21, ὁ πιστεύσας ἐπέστρεψεν ἐπὶ τὸν κύριον, which, like 1 Pet. 2.25, uses the preposition ἐπί with the personal object.

the lexical evidence of the NT coupled with what appears to be an intentional pattern of aorist passive verbs (2.21 ἐκλήθητε, 2.24 ἰάθητε, 2.25 ἐπεστράφητε) and the fact that in the LXX prophetic material ἐπιστρέφω is the verb often used in reference to YHWH's activity of returning his straying sheep (e.g. Ezek. 34.16) or exiled people (e.g. Zech. 10.10) make it highly improbable that ἐπεστράφητε should be translated 'have turned' in the sense of conversion.[34] This, in turn, would make it improbable that the early Christian tradition based on Isa. 6.10 is the source (and logic) that connects 2.24 (ἰάθητε) and 2.25 (ἐπεστράφητε), and calls into question the notion that healing is synonymous with religious conversion, in part because both Goppelt as well as Michaels argue that ἐπεστράφητε and ἰάθητε mutually interpret each other. In fact, as Elliott has argued, one can just as easily argue that it is healing which provides the means for conversion, rather than the two being synonymous.[35] What is more, while healing is at times a metaphor to describe conversion, it is also used in the OT (LXX) as a metaphor that refers to forgiveness of sins and/or restoration from punishment, affliction or exile.[36] As will be highlighted in greater detail below, this sense of healing seems to fit better within the context of Isaiah 53. It also complements the restoration theme that is developed throughout 1 Peter, which will also be detailed in due course.[37] In conclusion, the 'conversion approach' of Goppelt and Michaels does not adequately explain the relationship between 1 Pet. 2.24 and 2.25. We must, then, find a better solution, while also being open to the possibility that the shepherd imagery is more significant than we have been led to believe.

Bosetti *et al.* have helpfully anchored the analysis of 1 Pet. 2.21–5 within the wider theme of Jewish restoration eschatology, and have rightly pointed to the shepherd tradition of the prophets as a way to explain the

---

[34] In the LXX, for example, there are several cases of ἐπιστρέφω appearing in the passive construct but carrying an active or middle voice (e.g. Exod. 16.10; 34.31 ('to turn around'); 2 Kings 1.5 (to return from a journey); Deut. 30.2; Isa. 45.22; 55.7 ('to repent or re-establish relationship with someone')). When it is used metaphorically, this is almost always in the sense of repentance or as a way of describing forgiveness of sins rather than referring to conversion.

[35] Elliott 2000: 532: 'Through his own upright behavior (vv 22–23) and vicarious suffering (v 24), Christ has made possible the believers' renunciation of wrongdoing and their living for doing what is right'. First Peter 2.24b–c, then, is there to explain 'the effect of Christ's vicarious suffering and crucifixion: the transfer of human sins upon him and the consequence thereof; namely, liberation from the compulsion to do what is wrong and empowerment to live justly'.

[36] See e.g. LXX Deut. 30.3–5; Jer. 33.6; Isa. 30.26; 53.5; 57.18–19; 61.1; Pss. 59.4; 102.3; 106.20; 146.3; Hosea 6.1; 7.1; 14.4.

[37] Furnish 1975; Deterding 1981; Dubis 2002: 46–62.

logic behind the conflation of imagery. None of the proponents of the 'restoration approach', however, has adequately analyzed the shepherd tradition.[38] In particular, Bosetti, who offers the most comprehensive account, has failed to recognize the way in which the shepherd tradition of Ezekiel 34 has been significantly reworked in Zechariah 9–14, or how the Zechariah 9–14 tradition has been picked up in parts of the NT. Instead, her study focused in an atomistic fashion on words and phrases in the shepherd tradition that share parallels with 1 Pet. 2.24–5. Additionally, none of the proponents of the 'restoration approach' offers a sufficient rationale for why Peter would be reading Isaiah 53 together with Ezekiel 34 – an exegetical move that is not found elsewhere in the NT. Finally, no one advocating the 'restoration approach' has given serious consideration to similar verbal parallels found in Zechariah 10 – a text of particular significance since (a) it is widely agreed that Zechariah 9–14 interacts with and even reworks the shepherd tradition of Ezekiel 34, and (b) it is where the eschatological programme of Zechariah 9–14 begins to develop this reworked tradition of Ezekiel 34.[39] For example, an analysis of all three texts – Ezekiel 34, Zechariah 10 and 1 Pet. 2.25 – reveals that they all share the words πρόβατα, ἐπιστρέφω, ποιμήν and cognates of ἐπίσκοπος.[40] The only verbal parallel present in Ezekiel 34 and 1 Pet. 2.24–5 but lacking in Zechariah 10 is the verb πλανάω. There is, however, a similar connotation in Zech. 10.2 where the sheep are described as 'wandering' or 'cast out' (נָסְעוּ/ἐξήρθησαν).[41] It is inadequate, therefore, to establish a link between 1 Pet. 2.25 and Ezekiel 34 or Zechariah 10 respectively based solely on the presence of verbal parallels.

In what remains of this chapter, I will argue that it is more plausible that 1 Pet. 2.24–5 conflates Isaiah 53 with the shepherd tradition of Zechariah 9–14. The argument will develop in three movements. First, I will seek

---

[38] This is certainly understandable in the case of Elliott, Jobes and Dubis, since it was not the aim of their studies.

[39] Coggins regards the shepherd theme in Zechariah 9–14 as 'the beginnings of a tradition of biblical commentary, applying to the contemporary situation (whatever that may have been) the warnings against false shepherds which are found particularly in Jeremiah 25 and Ezekiel 34' (Coggins 1987: 71); Meyers and Meyers 1993: 35–45; Duguid 1995 Larkin 1994: 266, 272–5; Tigchelaar 1996; Laniak 2006: 162. In an otherwise comprehensive study of shepherd imagery in 1 Peter, Bosetti (1990: 118–52) notably fails to trace the progress of the shepherd tradition through to Zechariah 9–14.

[40] Additionally, given the proliferation of shepherd imagery in Zech. 10.8–12, YHWH is to be conceived as the ποιμήν.

[41] In other words, 'straying' (πλανάω) sheep and a 'wandering' (נָסַע) or 'cast out' (ἐξαίρω) flock in their respective contexts refer to YHWH's people in exile. As Gordon has noted, Targum Zechariah 10.2 makes the theme of exile more explicit, most notably by replacing 'they are afflicted' with 'they went into exile' (Cathcart and Gordon 1989: 208).

to build on the notion that 1 Pet. 2.21–5 is an example of early Christian 'pesher' on the passion of Jesus, making Zechariah 9–14 a more likely source than Ezekiel 34.[42] Second, I will examine the title 'shepherd' within the context of Israelite tradition and the ANE, and in light of the exegetical activity of 1 Pet. 2.21–5. My analysis will suggest that at the very least, the shared theme of restoration through YHWH's afflicted agent serves as the link between Isaiah 53 and Zechariah 9–14. I will further suggest that Peter, employing the exegetical technique *gezerah shavah*, may have linked LXX[43] Isa. 53.5–6 with LXX Zech. 10.2 via the catchwords ὡς πρόβατα and ἰάθημεν/ἴασις, so that the two texts and their wider text-plots mutually interpret each other.

3.3   First Peter 2.21–5: a passion 'pesher'?

A number of 1 Peter scholars have noted that the letter exhibits 'pesher-like' activity at various places.[44] Some have suggested that 1 Pet. 2.21–5 is one such example of an early Christian midrashic reflection on Isaiah 53.[45] In this section, I wish to expand on this proposal by first noting that (1) 1 Pet. 2.21 ('because Christ also suffered on your behalf', ὅτι καὶ Χριστὸς ἔπαθεν ὑπὲρ ὑμῶν) functions as the theme verse for the 'midrashic' activity (2.21–5) and that (2) the OT citations and commentary that follow it (2.22–5) serve to develop this primary theme. Richard Bauckham has demonstrated a similar exegetical technique in 1 Pet. 2.4–10, where 'vv. 4–5 briefly state the theme which is then both supported and expanded by OT citations and their interpretation in vv. 6–10'.[46]

---

[42]   See below for a discussion of the term *midrash*. I use the term *pesher* here because it is the way others have described the author's exegetical practice. This terminology will be critiqued at the end of this section. Additionally, I wish to point out that 1 Pet. 2.21–5 will be analyzed within its larger literary context in Chapter 6. Finally, I do not find warrant in the notion that 1 Pet. 2.22–4 is an early Christian hymn for the reasons laid out in Elliott 2000: 548–50.

[43]   From this point on, the term LXX refers to the critically reconstructed text of the *Septuaginta*. I acknowledge that the Greek OT was in a state of flux in the first century. The *Septuaginta* offers a working hypothesis for what Peter and the Anatolian Christians were likely reading, one that will be maintained unless there is good reason to adopt another reading. It should be noted that in a recent survey regarding the Septuagint textual tradition in 1 Peter, Jobes concluded: 'The author of 1 Peter seems to be . . . familiar with a Greek form that is . . . the same as the critically-reconstructed Septuagint text' (Jobes 2006: 332).

[44]   Bauckham 1988; Schutter (1989: 85–179) highlights 1 Pet. 1.22–2.3; 2.4–10; 2.21–5 in particular.

[45]   Michaels (1988: 136–7) uses the term Christian midrash, while Schutter (1989: 138–44, 168, 170) prefers 'pesher-like hermeneutic'.

[46]   Bauckham 1988: 310. Elliott 1966: 156–9; 1981: 167–70; 200–37.

This could also be compared to 1 Pet. 3.18 (ὅτι καὶ Χριστὸς ἅπαξ περὶ ἁμαρτιῶν ἔπαθεν), which appears to be the theme verse for 1 Pet. 3.19–22. The phrase Χριστὸς ἔπαθεν ὑπὲρ ὑμῶν (2.21) echoes several similar passages in the Pauline corpus (most notably 1 Cor. 15.3, but also Rom. 5.6,8 and 2 Cor. 5.14) that are considered to be either kerygmatic/creedal formulations or catechetical summaries regarding the significance of Jesus' death – the only difference being that in 1 Pet. 2.21 ἔπαθεν has been substituted for ἀπέθανεν.[47] In 1 Cor. 15.3, Paul himself identifies the phrase as a part of a tradition that has been 'handed down' to him, which may indicate that it is one of the earliest Christian traditions. Peter's deliberate choice of ἔπαθεν in 1 Pet. 2.21 instead of the more common traditional formulation of ἀπέθανεν found in 1 Cor. 15.3 and elsewhere can be explained on the grounds that he wanted to connect the traditional creedal formulation/catechetical summary to his prominent usage of the theme of suffering throughout the letter,[48] suffering which entails more than just Jesus' death (see 1 Pet. 4.1–2).[49] Barth Campbell has aptly demonstrated that the concept of suffering in 1 Peter may include but is not synonymous with (or limited to) death, but instead consists of a variety of forms of social ostracism within an honour-shame society.[50] Regarding the suffering of Jesus, Cervantes Gabarrón has noted that 'the use of this verb [πάσχω] in relation to Christ... is found also in the Synoptics, Acts, [and] Hebrews, and refers to the passion and death of Christ, considered as a whole, as one event, but at the same time highlights the sufferings that preceded the death of Jesus'.[51] In Peter's scope, then, was the entire narrative surrounding his death – his unjust trial, how

---

[47] Cf. Schutter 1989: 63; see also Conzelmann 1975: 251. Fee writes, 'it is generally agreed that... Paul is repeating a very early creedal formulation that was common to the entire church' (Fee 1987: 718). For more on 1 Cor. 15.3 as a catechetical summary, see Peter Stuhlmacher 1968: 266–82.

[48] The verb πάσχω appears twelve times in the letter (2.19,20,21,23; 3.14,17,18; 4.1 (bis), 15,19; 5.10). The cognate noun, πάθημα, is used four times (1.11; 4.13; 5.1,9). The subject of the suffering is predominantly either Jesus or those who faithfully follow him.

[49] See Elliott 2000: 525. Some manuscripts have ἀπέθανεν instead of ἔπαθεν. It is likely that a scribe wrote ἀπέθανεν instead of the original ἔπαθεν because it was more in keeping with both the oral tradition and the early textual form found in 1 Cor. 15.3 and elsewhere. The fact that the two words look alike may have also influenced the scribe's reading. On this see also Achtemeier 1996: 189, n.10; Elliott 2000: 524; Feldmeier 2008: 166. For a similar textual variant in 1 Pet. 3.18 see Dalton 1965: 119–21.

[50] Campbell 1998: 32–5.

[51] Cervantes Gabarrón 1991a: 167; translation mine. He notes the following texts as significant: Luke 22.15; 24.26,46; Acts 1.3; 3.18; 17.3; Heb. 9.26; 13.12. Dalton (1965: 120) argues that πάσχω has acquired a technical meaning in the NT 'by which it refers to the sacrificial death of Christ' (cf. Luke 22.15; 24.26,46; Acts 1.3; 3.18; 17.3). This is, of course, not mutually exclusive of what Cervantes has argued.

First Peter 2.25 and Zechariah's shepherd-king 91

Table 3.2 The order of Isaiah 53 in 1 Pet. 2.22–5

1 Peter 2	Isaiah 53 citation/allusion
22 ὃς ἁμαρτίαν οὐκ ἐποίησεν οὐδὲ εὑρέθη δόλος ἐν τῷ στόματι αὐτοῦ,	53.9 ἀνομίαν οὐκ ἐποίησεν, οὐδὲ εὑρέθη δόλος ἐν τῷ στόματι αὐτοῦ
23a ὃς λοιδορούμενος οὐκ ἀντελοιδόρει, πάσχων οὐκ ἠπείλει,	
b παρεδίδου δὲ τῷ κρίνοντι δικαίως·	
24a ὃς τὰς ἁμαρτίας ἡμῶν αὐτὸς ἀνήνεγκεν ἐν τῷ σώματι αὐτοῦ ἐπὶ τὸ ξύλον,	53.4 οὗτος τὰς ἁμαρτίας ἡμῶν φέρει
b ἵνα ταῖς ἁμαρτίαις ἀπογενόμενοι τῇ δικαιοσύνῃ ζήσωμεν,	
c οὗ τῷ μώλωπι ἰάθητε	53.5 τῷ μώλωπι αὐτοῦ ἡμεῖς ἰάθημεν
25a ἦτε γὰρ ὡς πρόβατα πλανώμενοι,	53.6 πάντες ὡς πρόβατα ἐπλανήθημεν

he responded to this unjust treatment and his subsequent crucifixion. It may be significant that Mark's Gospel has Jesus foreshadowing his unjust trial and crucifixion with the words 'the Son of Man must undergo great suffering' (δεῖ τὸν υἱὸν τοῦ ἀνθρώπου πολλὰ παθεῖν; Mark 8.31).[52]

This initial appraisal of ἔπαθεν is strengthened when consideration is given to why the Isaiah 53 citations do not appear in 1 Peter in the same order in which they occur in Isaiah 53 (see Table 3.2).

In this regard, a number of scholars have rightfully proposed that Peter arranges Isaiah 53 in this fashion in order to 'reflect fundamental aspects of the Passion narrative'.[53] Feldmeier, for example, posits that 'the paraenesis [2.21–5] is tied to a remembrance of the Passion in which Jesus' behaviour in his Passion becomes a pattern for Christian life'.[54] More specifically, Goppelt suggests that ὃς λοιδορούμενος οὐκ

[52] This becomes even more significant if one accepts that Peter is the author of the letter and the tradition that Mark's Gospel is based upon Peter's preaching, or if, like Elliott, one thinks that the letter was written by a Petrine group of which Silvanus and Mark were members (Elliott 2000: 118–30). For a recent argument proposing a close relationship between Peter and Mark's Gospel see Bauckham 2006: 155–239.
[53] Goppelt 1993: 211. See also Schutter 1989: 140; Achtemeier 1993: 180; Jobes 2005: 194–5; Feldmeier 2008: 167, 173. In his study of the Passion Narratives Joel Green (1988: 181) points to 1 Tim. 6.13, Heb. 5.7, and 1 Pet. 2.23 as cases in which the passion story has been used to illustrate an ethical or theological point.
[54] Feldmeier 2008: 173.

ἀντελοιδόρει (2.23) 'summarizes the impression that the [Passion Narratives] themselves give, such as slander after the condemnation in the Sanhedrin (Mk. 14.65 par.), the ridicule by the guards (Mk. 15.17–20a par.), and the derision by the crucified thief (Mk. 15.29–32 par.)'.[55] Similarly, Achtemeier has suggested that 2.22–3 alludes to Jesus' trial, and 2.24 refers to the crucifixion of Jesus.[56] If we are right that Peter has intentionally arranged the Isaiah material in order to fit the pattern of Jesus' trial and death, this demonstrates, importantly, that our author had at least some basic knowledge of the Passion Narrative tradition, which would include Jesus' unjust treatment before his death and the way he responded to that treatment. Peter's comparison of Jesus to the unblemished lamb (1 Pet. 1.18–19) may also indicate an awareness of the Last Supper tradition and its interpretation of Jesus' death as a new Passover.[57] Unfortunately, we are unable to determine with certainty the extent to which his knowledge of the Passion Narrative conformed to that which we have in the canonical Gospels; nevertheless this at least demonstrates that it is plausible to place our author's exegetical work within the milieu of the Passion Narrative tradition, which, as I have demonstrated, drew upon Zechariah 9–14. Peter's use of the Passion Narrative tradition for his paraenetic purposes also suggests that he assumed his readers had knowledge of the basic contours of that narrative.[58]

It appears that the modified Isaiah 53 citation[59] in 1 Pet. 2.22 (Isa. 53.9) was selected not only because it corresponds to the way Jesus responded when falsely accused (as per the Passion Narrative tradition), but also because it conforms with the description of the Righteous Sufferer of LXX Ps. 33.14, which Peter would later appropriate in Chapter 3 in another paraenetic passage (3.10): καὶ χείλη τοῦ μὴ λαλῆσαι δόλον.[60] In other words, the two passages (i.e. Isa. 53.9 and Ps. 33.14) are appropriated both because they share the same word, δόλος, as well as because they share a similar concept (i.e. the blameless speech of the Righteous Sufferer), which was a common exegetical technique in both Jewish as well as the Graeco-Roman contexts.[61] This is significant for two

---

[55] Goppelt 1993: 211.   [56] Achtemeier 1993: 180.

[57] The proliferation of Passover imagery in John's Passion Narrative could also have influenced Peter on this point, if he in fact had access to it.

[58] This is strengthened if the Passion Narrative tradition was in fact regularly reflected upon in Sunday worship. (Cf. Trocmé 1983; 1 Cor. 11.23–5; 15).

[59] For more on the modifications of Isaiah 53 in 1 Pet. 2.22–4 (which is beyond the scope of this study) see Schutter 1989: 139–44; and Jobes 2005: 193–8.

[60] Bauckham 1988: 313.

[61] A similar parallel exists between 1 Pet. 2.23 (ὃς λοιδορούμενος οὐκ ἀντελοιδόρει) and 1 Pet. 3.9 (μὴ ἀποδιδόντες κακὸν ἀντὶ κακοῦ ἢ λοιδορίαν ἀντὶ λοιδορίας). For another example of OT passages being linked via catchwords, see 1 Pet. 2.4–8. See David Daube's

reasons. First, it further substantiates that Peter is applying 'pesher-like' techniques in an effort to elaborate the theme verse, 'Christ suffered on your behalf' (Χριστὸς ἔπαθεν ὑπὲρ ὑμῶν).[62] Second, it parallels a similar exegetical pattern in the Passion Narratives – the appropriation of Psalms of the Righteous Sufferer, often conflating them with other OT texts, in order to explain Jesus' death.[63]

If 1 Pet. 2.21 is an intentional modification of the more traditional kerygmatic/creedal formulation, this may explain why the reflection on the passion of Jesus begins with Isaiah 53. A number of scholars over the years have proposed that Isaiah 53 stands behind this early confession, although there is no consensus regarding the text (i.e. Greek, Hebrew, Aramaic) which informs the idea of vicarious death.[64] Farmer's point probably gets us to the heart of the issue: 'It is . . . conceptual kinship more than any particular verbal kinship which leads scholars to identify Isaiah 53 as the most important scripture referred to in this traditional formulation.'[65] Otfried Hofius has highlighted a number of parallels between Isaiah 53 and 1 Cor. 15.3–5, chief of which is the concept of one person taking the place of others.[66]

In summary, rather than being simply an example of Christian 'pesher-like' exegesis, I propose that 1 Pet. 2.21–5 is more specifically a *Passion* 'pesher', to use the terminology of others. Portions of Isaiah 53 have been selected and modified in order to pattern key aspects of the Passion Narrative tradition, all with the view of elaborating the main theme of the passage – 'Christ also suffered on your behalf.' Peter's paraenesis,

---

(1949 and 1977) seminal essays on the comparison between Jewish and Graeco-Roman rhetorical devices.

[62] As Bauckham (1988: 305, 311) has shown, a common 'pesher-like' technique was the modification of a text in order to fit the exegete's purposes. See also Instone-Brewer 1992.

[63] See §2.2.2.

[64] E.g. Conzelmann 1975: 251–5; Fee 1987: 722–5; Bellinger and Farmer 1998: 263; Otfried Hofius 2004: 177–80.

[65] Bellinger and Farmer 1998: 263. Fee posits that this interpretation of Isaiah 53 comes from Jesus' own interpretation at the Last Supper (1987: 724). Hofius 2004: 177–80.

[66] For the full argument see Hofius 2004: 177–80. He (*ibid.*: 177) argues that Χριστὸς ἀπέθανεν ὑπὲρ τῶν ἁμαρτιῶν ἡμῶν (1 Cor. 15.3) represents the linguistic variation of διὰ τὰς ἁμαρτίας ἡμῶν (Isa. 53.5). For additional parallels between 1 Cor. 15.3–5 and Isa. 53.5 see Hofius 2004: 177, n.57. Hofius (*ibid.*: 177, note 58) also cites Christian Wolff who remarks that '[o]nly this Old Testament passage [Isaiah 53] deals with dying for others'. I would want to nuance this statement by adding that only this OT passage deals with *one person* dying for others, since the sacrificial system was certainly an example of 'dying for others'. Additionally, it could be argued that Zech. 12.10/13.7 together with the surrounding imagery of cleansing from sin and renewal also teaches about one dying for others, and more specifically a shepherd/messiah dying for others.

then, draws upon both traditional kerygmatic (or catechetical) material as well as the Passion Narrative tradition, along with OT passages (i.e. Isa. 53/Ps. 34 (LXX 33)) that are associated with these traditions. But what are we to make of the shepherd imagery? How does it fit within this exegetical activity?

Given what we know about the aims of 1 Pet. 2.21–5, then, and the fact that Zechariah 9–14 (especially its eschatological programme and narrative pattern) was a significant text in the Passion Narrative tradition for explaining how the messiah's death was in keeping with God's plan of redemption, we have good reason to suspect, perhaps even expect, an allusion to Zechariah 9–14. In the final section (§3.4) I will consider whether there is, in fact, textual evidence for such an allusion.

Before moving to the final section, however, it is essential that I explain why I will not be using the terms 'pesher' or 'midrash' in describing the exegetical activity in this passage or elsewhere in 1 Peter.[67] First, Old Testament/Hebrew Bible scholars routinely have complained that NT scholarship often misconstrues what midrash and pesher actually are; two decades ago Philip Alexander, for instance, characteristically wrote that 'a survey of recent contributions to New Testament studies has forced me to conclude that the nature and function of midrash is often misunderstood by New Testament scholars, and as a result the term midrash is tending to generate more confusion than light'.[68] This may be the case, in part, because Old Testament/Hebrew Bible scholars themselves have been unable to come to a consensus regarding the nature and function of midrash. Even a cursory survey of the seminal works on midrashic exegesis reveals that there are at least as many points of departure as there are points of contact among the many proposals.[69] Given this confusion, I find that the terminology tends to distract rather than illuminate.

Second, scholars often speak of midrash (or pesher) as a uniquely Jewish hermeneutical approach in which an authoritative (or canonical) text is actualized in order to address the present needs of the community and/or to justify or base contemporary beliefs on those authoritative texts.[70] I find such a definition to be so broad that almost any text of the

---

[67] I am indebted to Chris Chandler, Kristin de Troyer and Patrick Egan for orienting me in the midrash literature, even if at times I do not follow their conclusions.

[68] Philip Alexander 1984: 1. I am indebted to Quarles (1998: 32–3) for this reference.

[69] See, e.g. Quarles 1998: 30–46, who engages Zeitlin 1953; Gertner 1962a; Wright 1966; Vermes 1970; Porton 1981; Neusner 1983; and Maccoby 1988. To that list I would add Fishbane 1985; Stemberger and Strack 1991; Instone-Brewer 1992.

[70] For midrash as a hermeneutical activity based upon an authoritative (or canonical text) see Zeitlin 1953: 25–29; Vermes 1970; Neusner 1983: xvi; Maccoby 1988: 22–3; Quarles 1998: 53. For midrash as an attempt to actualize the authoritative text see Doeve

NT (or just about any piece of extant literature from the Second Temple period) could be considered midrashic. In this regard, the terminology is unhelpful; it does not actually clarify anything that we do not already know.

Third, the term midrash (or pesher) often refers to particular Jewish exegetical techniques, often imagined to be unique to Judaism, used in the interpretative act.[71] Although I would wholeheartedly agree that an awareness of these Jewish interpretative techniques is essential for understanding many passages in the NT,[72] most of the techniques that are employed in the NT, such as *qal vahomer* (argumentation from the less significant to the more significant), *gezerah shavah* (the interpretation of a text in light of another text via a related word or phrase) and *heqesh* (the interpretation of two texts by means of a similar topic or concept),[73] are also common to interpretative traditions in the wider Graeco-Roman world.[74] In relation to this, I would want to stress, as Hays has, that it is not the techniques themselves that generate interpretation; instead the techniques 'provide a descriptive account of a repertoire of possible imaginative operations that can be performed on the text in the act of interpretation'.[75] Whether we are speaking of Paul, Peter, the Evangelists or the Qumran exegetes, each appropriates these interpretative techniques in relation to their own understanding of what God has done, is doing or will do in their midst – and its implications for their present circumstances.[76]

1954: 55–6; Gertner 1962a; Wright 1966: 122–4; 134–8; Quarles 1998: 46. Vermes (1970: 221) writes that in the Christian era '[t]he point of departure for exegesis is no longer the Torah itself, but contemporary customs and beliefs which the interpreter attempted to connect with scripture and to justify'.

[71] For an introduction to these techniques see Stemberger and Strack 1991: 15–30; Instone-Brewer 1992: 14–23; Evans 1992; Gertner 1962a. For the origin and history of middoth see Instone-Brewer (1992: 4–7); his own study demonstrates that many of the exegetical techniques mentioned in second-century CE literature are evidenced in pre-70 CE material. For a helpful survey of pesher practices in the Qumran communities and a critique of term pesher see Lim 1997: 123–39.

[72] This point is repeatedly stressed in Gertner 1962a.

[73] For examples see Ellis 1988: 700–5; Instone-Brewer 1992: 23–225. Gertner (1962a: 270) and Ellis (1988: 703) both demonstrate that midrashic techniques are evident within the Hebrew Bible and the Qumran material, and even in the translations of the Hebrew Bible into Aramaic and Greek. Ellis (1988: 703) further claims that midrashic interpretation was an established practice in first-century Judaism in the synagogue service (see Luke 4.16–30; Acts 13.16–41; Philo, *De. spec. leg* 2, 60–4) as well as the academy (see Acts 22.3).

[74] See Daube 1949; 1977. So also Hays 1989: 13; Lim 1997: 129.

[75] Hays 1989: 12.

[76] See, e.g. Ellis (1988: 704), who comments that 'NT midrash with its eschatological orientation applies the text theologically to some aspect of Jesus' life and ministry'; or 'the NT writers give primacy to Jesus and to the surrounding messianic events, or tradition of

Finally, I would echo the concern of Hays when he writes that 'the label midrash tends to bring the interpretative process to a halt, as though it had explained something, when in fact we should keep pressing for clarity: what poetic linkages of sound or imagery makes this sort of imaginative leap possible, what effects are produced in the argument by it'?[77] These are precisely the kinds of question I want to explore, especially in Chapter 6.

Having said all of this, I think it would be a case of 'throwing the baby out with the bathwater' if we did not enrich our understanding of the NT with studies that explore 'midrashic' or 'pesher-like exegesis', both in as well as outside of the NT, and I will draw on some of these studies in this chapter and in the rest of the book. Meir Gertner, for example, has drawn attention to an exegetical practice in the NT that he calls covert or invisible midrash, which he describes in the following manner:

> A religious idea or legal principle is midrashically interpreted into, or derived from, a given text; and this is done by means of various midrashic techniques. Yet none of them, neither the text nor the idea nor the technique, are named, defined or mentioned. This type of midrash is usually presented either in the form of a concise paraphrase [e.g. Luke 1.67–75; 1 Cor. 15.53–6] or of an expanded periphrastic composition [e.g. Epistle of James]. Its midrashic nature, therefore, is veiled and not easily recognized.[78]

Gertner points to four NT texts which he considers to exhibit prototypical (and yet distinct) examples of covert midrashic exegesis (Mark 4.1–20/21–5; Luke 1.67–75; 1 Cor. 15.53–6; The Epistle of James). He has chosen these for their apparent 'absence of logic and topical coherence between adjacent pronouncements or teachings'. He argues, however, that once these texts are read with an awareness of midrashic exegetical

events, and only then use OT texts to explain or illuminate them'. Or Timothy Lim (1997: 180–1), who writes:

> For the pesherists, God in his holy spirit has revealed his will to the members of the community through the words of various leaders, the most important of whom is the Teacher of Righteousness. It was to this priest that God made known all the mysteries of the biblical prophets, the vents of which apparently concern the destinies of the pious and wicked men during the end time. Paul too relied on revelation of God in Jesus Christ . . . who . . . removes the veil that obscures men's vision of the glory of God.

See also Hays (1983), who argues that the Christ story is what generates interpretation in Paul.
[77] Hays 1989: 14.   [78] Gertner 1962a: 268.

techniques, coherence or logic can be discerned.[79] He thus encourages NT scholars to look for 'midrashic ground structures' when coherence and logic of text appear to be elusive.[80]

In short, it is helpful to be aware of the variety of interpretative strategies that were available to NT writers, strategies which find expression not only in Judaism, but also in the wider Graeco-Roman world. In what remains of this chapter, I will follow the lead of Gertner and similarly argue that an awareness of what he calls covert (or invisible) midrash will help us to understand the logic of 1 Pet. 2.21–5; it will also enable us to 'hear' allusions to Zechariah 9–14 in 1 Pet. 2.25. But this study will not stop at explaining the logic of the passage; instead I will seek to explain what made the 'imaginative leap' possible and how this affects the overall argument of 1 Peter.

3.4   First Peter 2.25 and the shepherd-king of Zechariah 9–14

Thus far I have indicated features in 1 Pet. 2.21–5 that make conditions ideal for an allusion to Zechariah 9–14: the passage is a reflection on the modified creedal tradition – 'Christ suffered on your behalf'; and Isaiah 53 has been arranged in order to pattern Jesus' Passion, and in order to echo LXX Ps. 33.10 in 1 Pet. 3.10. Zechariah 9–14 would be a logical text to turn to in light of its prominence in the Passion Narrative tradition, and considering the fact that several early Christian authors drew upon it to make sense of Jesus' death. I have yet to indicate, however, whether there is indeed textual evidence of material from Zechariah 9–14. This, then, will be the objective of this final section.

I start with the title 'shepherd' (2.25): no Israelite leader (whether royal or priestly) ever bore this title in the literature that would later become known as the OT or Hebrew Bible.[81] This is remarkable given the fact that in the wider ANE over a period of several centuries contemporaneous with Israel's history 'shepherd' was a common title for both deities as well as kings. In Mesopotamia, for instance, Enlil, the high god, Utu, the sun god, and Marduk all bore the title of 'shepherd'.[82] Mesopotamian

---

[79] *Ibid.*: 291.

[80] Gertner's 'midrashic ground structure' comes close to the way that I am using the term substructure in my argumentation.

[81] Jeremias 1962: 487–8; Vancil 1992: 1,189; Brueggemann 1990: 119; Hunziker-Rodewald 2001: 46. In Isa. 44.28, the foreign king Cyrus is referred to as YHWH's 'shepherd' in the Hebrew Bible. Curiously, the LXX omits this.

[82] Pritchard 1969: 69, 71–2, 337; see also Jeremias 1962: 486–7; Vancil 1992: 1,188; Laniak 2006: 58–61.

kings Hammurabi, Nebuchadnezzar I and Lipit-Ishtar, to name only a few, were likewise all given the title of shepherd.[83] A similar trend is found in Egypt, where both deities as well as pharaohs bore the title 'shepherd'.[84] In the historical books of the OT and the Psalms, the title 'shepherd' is reserved for YHWH alone, and although Israelite leadership (most notably that of Moses and David) was periodically described with shepherding terminology, the title of shepherd seems to have been intentionally avoided.[85] In the prophetic material the term 'shepherd' has three distinct reference points which are all integrally connected to Israel's restoration from exile, often depicted in terms of a second exodus and accomplished in conjunction with the rule of a Davidic shepherd-king.[86] As I have already noted in Chapter 2, the prophets announce that (1) YHWH is the good shepherd[87] who will judge the (2) bad shepherds (unnamed and unfaithful Israelite leadership), regather the straying sheep of Israel, renew his covenant, and appoint for his people (3) a new shepherd (king) from the house of David, who will bring about healing and restoration, and usher in the new age of universal peace. As noted, the shepherd tradition of the prophets, with its eschatological framework, is first developed in Jeremiah 23, elaborated in Ezekiel 34[88] and then is significantly altered in Zechariah 9–14, where YHWH not only affirms the unworthiness of the 'bad shepherds', but also reveals that the people themselves share responsibility for the deterioration of the community (11.7–9). As I have argued, in what appears to be a reversal of the shepherd tradition of Jeremiah 23/Ezekiel 34, the coming of YHWH's appointed good shepherd does not bring immediate restoration and renewal; instead, the shepherd will be rejected by not only the leaders but also the people (11.4–14), and struck by a sword (13.7). His affliction will bring about a time of trouble that is described as 'fiery testing'. The remnant

---

[83] For a full list of Mesopotamian kings who were referred to as shepherds seek Laniak 2006: 257–9.

[84] *Ibid.*: 67–72.

[85] For references to YHWH as the shepherd of Israel see Gen. 48.15; 49.24; Pss. 23; 28.9; 74.1; 77.20; 78.52–5; 79.13; 80.1; 95.7. For shepherding terminology used to describe Moses' leadership see Ps. 77.20; Hosea 12.13; Laniak 2006: 87–93. For shepherding terminology to describe David's leadership see, e.g., 2 Sam. 7.8; Ps. 78.70–71; Willitts 2007a: 54–8; Laniak 2006: 98–114.

[86] For a full development of this see Laniak 2006: 115–70. For a full development of the Davidic shepherd-king tradition see Willitts 2007a: 58–67; Chae 2006: 32–94.

[87] For YHWH as shepherd in the prophetic material see Mic. 2.12–13; 4.6–8; 7.14–15; Isa. 40.10–11; 49.9–13; Jer. 23.2; 31.10; 50.19; Ezek. 34.31; implied in Zech. 9.16; 10.8–10.

[88] Echoes of the Jeremiah 23/Ezekiel 34 tradition can be found in Isa. 40.1–11 and Mic. 4.14–5.5.

'one-third' that makes it through the time of trouble will be re-established with YHWH through covenant renewal (13.8–9; cf. 1 Pet. 2.9–10), and will worship him in purity as a renewed 'house' (14.3–20; cf. 1 Pet. 2.4–5; 4.14–17). It is significant for our present study that although the DSS and *Psalm of Solomon* 17 pick up the eschatological Davidic shepherd-king motif, it is not developed along the lines of Zechariah 9–14 (i.e. they omit any notion of the rejection and death of the Davidic shepherd-king).[89] Instead, their emphasis is on 'the abiding hope for national restoration by YHWH through his Davidic king'.[90]

Why is this significant? In 1 Pet. 2.25, the title 'shepherd', which is clearly a reference to Jesus (see 1 Pet. 5.2–4),[91] emerges in a context in which the author is elaborating the theme verse 'Christ suffered on your behalf' (2.21), and is doing so with reference to the Passion Narrative tradition, aided by Isaiah 53 and its eschatological restoration overtones. Several conclusions that I have made thus far converge at this point. First, Zechariah 9–14 is unique within the shepherd tradition for contributing to the notion that the 'shepherd' must first suffer and die before restoration is accomplished. We can be quite certain, therefore, that the point of reference for 'shepherd' in 1 Pet. 2.25 is not the more general shepherd motif found in Jeremiah 23, Ezekiel 34 and *Psalm of Solomon* 17. Second, in the Passion Narrative tradition (Mark 14.27–8; Matt. 26.31–2) Jesus references Zech. 13.7 in order to explain his pending death. Third, as I have argued in Chapter 2, both in Zechariah 9–14 itself as well as within the Passion Narrative tradition, the eschatological programme of Zechariah 9–14 is developed with frequent reference to significant portions of Isaiah 40–66.

At this stage in the argument, I would suggest that it is very likely that Peter has culminated his reflection on the creedal formulation, 'Christ suffered on your behalf', by echoing Zech. 13.7–9 and its wider eschatological programme. To borrow from Gertner, he has covertly employed a midrashic technique known as *heqesh* – the bringing together of two texts by means of a common feature.[92] In this particular case, both Isaiah 53 as well as Zech. 13.7 develop the theme of restoration which comes through the suffering and death of YHWH's appointed agent. Zech. 13.7 contributes two additional points to Peter's exegesis that Isaiah 53 lacks.

---

[89] For the development of the Davidic shepherd-king motif in the DSS and Psalms of Solomon see Willitts 2007a: 72–90.

[90] Willitts 2007a: 90.

[91] *Pace* Osborne (1983: 403–5), who argues that the title refers to God. Almost no 1 Peter scholar has followed his proposal.

[92] Instone-Brewer 1992: 18. This technique, of course, is not unique to Jewish exegetes.

First, it gives scriptural warrant for *Christ* dying on behalf of YHWH's straying sheep. It is significant that the creedal formula does not simply read, Ἰησοῦς ἔπαθεν ὑπὲρ ὑμῶν, but instead Χριστός ἔπαθεν ὑπὲρ ὑμῶν. As I argued in Chapter 2, Zechariah 9–14 is appropriated in the Passion Narrative tradition in order to justify the necessity of the Christ's death, and how it is in keeping with YHWH's eschatological restoration plan. Second, an allusion to Zech. 13.7 and its wider context, especially 13.8–9, gives scriptural warrant not only for Christ's death, but also for why Christians must suffer as well, which is ultimately the point of 1 Pet. 2.20–5. According to Zech. 13.8–9, the death of the shepherd is precisely that which initiates a period of fiery trials which the remnant 'one-third' must pass through before they are to enjoy the full benefits of restoration. Again, although Isaiah 53 provides scriptural warrant for the 'healing' effect of Jesus' death, and reflects a pattern that corresponds to Jesus' passion, it does not provide a basis for why Christians must also suffer.

There are indications that perhaps an even more complex exegetical activity is being employed in this passage. Earlier the point was made that Ezekiel 34, Zechariah 10 and 1 Pet. 2.25 have various verbal parallels. LXX Zech. 10.2 has the advantage of providing an additional verbal parallel not found in Ezekiel 34, and one that Peter may have exploited. This additional verbal parallel comes from an intriguing variation between the Hebrew and Greek texts of Zech. 10.2. The Hebrew version reads: 'Therefore the people wander like sheep; they suffer for lack of a shepherd.'[93] The LXX rendition replaces the word 'shepherd' with the word 'healing': 'because of this, they were driven away like sheep and were afflicted, since there was no healing'[94] (see Greek text below). I am unaware of any manuscript evidence from either the Hebrew or the Greek texts which might explain how this alternative reading in the LXX tradition appeared.[95]

Whatever the case may be, Peter may have exploited this variation,[96] and employed the Jewish exegetical technique *gezerah*

---

[93] עַל־כֵּן נָסְעוּ כְמוֹ־צֹאן יַעֲנוּ כִּי־אֵין רֹעֶה.   [94] Translation mine.
[95] It is possible that the initial LXX translator deliberately made the change (*al tiqrê*) from shepherd to healing because he noted within the shepherd tradition the connection between lack of healing and the absence of a good shepherd (Ezek. 34.4/Zech. 11.16). See an example of this with the MT and the LXX in Instone-Brewer 1992: 178. I am indebted to Bauckham (1996: 161) for this helpful reference. In personal correspondence, Septuagint scholar Dr David Baer noted that it is also possible that the initial LXX translator simply made an error by reading the ע in רעה (shepherd) as a פ, and the ה as an א. This 'common transposition' would render רפא, or healing, instead of רעה.
[96] 'Jewish exegetes were accustomed to choosing among variants the reading which suited their interpretation or to exploiting more than one' (Bauckham 1996: 161).

Table 3.3 *Catchwords of Isaiah 53, Zechariah 10 and 1 Peter 2*

LXX Isa. 53.5–6	LXX Zech. 10.2
τῷ μώλωπι αὐτοῦ ἡμεῖς	διὰ τοῦτο ἐξήρθησαν ὡς πρόβατα καὶ
ἰάθημεν. πάντες ὡς πρόβατα	ἐκακώθησαν, διότι οὐκ ἦν <u>ἴασις</u>
ἐπλανήθημεν	

1 Pet. 2.24–5

²⁴ ὃς τὰς ἁμαρτίας ἡμῶν αὐτὸς ἀνήνεγκεν
ἐν τῷ σώματι αὐτοῦ ἐπὶ τὸ ξύλον,
ἵνα ταῖς ἁμαρτίαις ἀπογενόμενοι
τῇ δικαιοσύνῃ ζήσωμεν,
οὗ τῷ μώλωπι ἰάθητε.
²⁵ ἦτε γὰρ ὡς πρόβατα πλανώμενοι,
ἀλλὰ ἐπεστράφητε νῦν ἐπὶ τὸν ποιμένα
καὶ ἐπίσκοπον τῶν ψυχῶν ὑμῶν.

shavah[97] in order to draw together Isa. 53.5–6 and Zech. 10.2 and their wider text-plots via the catchwords ὡς πρόβατα and ἰάθημεν/ἴασις (see Table 3.3).

This sort of exegetical work is not uncharacteristic of Peter. Bauckham has demonstrated, for instance, that similar tendencies are evident in the stone imagery of 1 Pet. 2.4–10.[98]

That Peter links Zech. 10.2 with Isa. 53.5 via the cognates of healing (ἰάθημεν/ἴασις) becomes plausible when we consider the following feature of 1 Pet. 2.21–5: Peter's pattern prior to 2.24 has been to cite a modified verse from LXX Isaiah 53 and add to it a brief commentary describing how it relates to Jesus' unjust suffering and death (1 Pet. 2.22–3). In 2.24, Peter again cites a modified verse from Isaiah 53, this time from Isa. 53.5 ('by his wounds you were healed'; οὗ τῷ μώλωπι ἰάθητε). But here, instead of adding commentary, Peter initiates a new sentence (2.25) with γάρ, which 'links this verse [2.25] with the foregoing idea of healing'.[99] Consequently, Peter's final citation of Isa. 53.5 carries particular rhetorical weight since it encapsulates the effect of Jesus' unjust suffering and

⁹⁷ To be clear, I am following Instone-Brewer's taxonomy (1992: 18) and arguing for a type II *gezerah shavah*: 'the interpretation of one text in the light of another text to which it is related by a shared word or phrase'.
⁹⁸ Bauckham 1988: 309–12.
⁹⁹ Elliott 2000: 537; similarly Achtemeier (1996: 204) writes, 'γάρ indicates that the author sees v.25 as an explanation of the preceding clause'.

death as *healing*, but also because it calls for further commentary, which Peter provides with the shepherd imagery in 2.25.

LXX Zech. 10.2 is a fitting text, then, to link with Isa. 53.5 for two principal reasons. First, it is where we read that YHWH's people are in exile (and in need of restoration) because they lack *healing*. Second, as we have already seen, it is where a particularly important theme in Zechariah 9–14 begins to develop, namely, that YHWH will 'return his sheep' (Zech. 10.10) unexpectedly through the affliction of his chosen shepherd-king (Zech. 13.7–9).[100] Having already noted that 2.25 elaborates 2.24, two important points now become clear. First, Peter interprets healing in Isaiah 53 to include the idea of restoration. In so doing, he does not find himself to be out of step with the traditions from which he frequently draws. Healing terminology was often, though not exclusively, used in the OT as a metaphor for forgiveness of sins and/or restoration from punishment, affliction or exile (LXX: Deut. 30.3–5; Jer. 3.22; 33.6; Isa. 30.26; 53.5; 57.18–19; 61.1; Hosea 6.1; 7.1; 14.4; Pss. 59.4; 102.3; 106.20; 146.3).[101] With reference to Isaiah 53, R. E. Clements writes, '[t]he sufferings of Servant-Israel would be the offering by which the relationship of all the scattered nation with Yahweh would be renewed. Israel would once again be returned to the sphere of blessing and divine protection, which its own sins had nullified in the past.'[102] John Goldingay similarly comments that '[t]he passage [Isaiah 53] constitutes the prophet's final attempt to picture how the problem of Jacob-Israel rebellion is resolved. How does forgiveness and renewal come about?'[103] Second, what these two texts have in common (Isaiah 53 and Zechariah 9–14) is not simply the theme of restoration[104] but more specifically restoration which is accomplished *by the affliction of YHWH's chosen agent*. This also likely explains why Peter would want to link the two texts together with the phrase ὡς πρόβατα, since in the shepherd tradition straying, wandering or cast out 'sheep' are a metaphor for YHWH's people in need of restoration.

---

[100] The argument is strengthened by the fact that there is no other place in the LXX, apart from LXX Zech. 10.2, where πρόβατα and ἴασις are linked. What is more, LXX Ezek. 34.4 does not use ἰάομαι but rather σωματοποιέω.

[101] For healing and national restoration outside of the OT see Jub. 23.29, T. Zeb. 9.8; 2 Bar. 73.2; 4 Ezra 13.50 and 4Q521.

[102] Clements 1998: 52. In reference to Isaiah 53, Clements (*ibid.*: 54) further comments that 'God provides the very sin-offering by which Israel can be healed, cleansed, and forgiven'.

[103] Goldingay and Payne 2006: 283. For more on the relationship between healing and national restoration in Isaiah read Watts 1997: 170–7.

[104] *Pace* Bosetti, Elliott, Jobes, Dubis.

This proposal fits well with what David Instone-Brewer has concluded in his study on Jewish exegetical assumptions and techniques up to the time of the NT. He argues that the *gezerah shavah* technique intends to draw its readers to the passages that are being united, and certain themes or narratives of those passages are mutually to interpret one another.[105]

The deliberative manner in which this passage has been composed would seem to indicate that the shepherd imagery in 1 Pet. 2.25, far from being incidental (as some have suggested), was intentionally placed at the end in order to summarize Peter's main point. This intentionality is perhaps also reflected in an apparent *inclusio* (2.21 (following in his footsteps) and 2.25 (being returned to the Shepherd)), and in the fact that Peter picks up the shepherd motif again in 1 Pet. 5.1–4. As I will demonstrate in subsequent chapters, the shepherd imagery is part of a larger complex of images that are drawn from the eschatological programme of Zechariah 9–14.

3.5   Conclusion

In this chapter I have argued that the two extant proposals which try to explain the relationship between the 1 Pet. 2.21–5a and 2.25b are either implausible or incomplete. In particular, I noted how the 'restoration approach' has failed to consider how Zechariah 9–14 has significantly reworked earlier shepherd traditions of the prophets. In turn, I have proposed that Peter has drawn from two influential OT sources in order to elaborate the theme of 1 Pet. 2.21–5: 'Christ suffered on your behalf' (Χριστὸς ἔπαθεν ὑπὲρ ὑμῶν; 2.21). There is no question about the first OT source: Peter has carefully chosen portions of Isaiah 53 in order to pattern Jesus as he is portrayed in the Passion Narrative tradition. Regarding the second OT source, I have proposed that the best way to understand the shepherd imagery is as an allusion to the shepherd tradition of Zechariah 9–14. This approach is more satisfying than the 'restoration approach', which argues for a conflation between Isaiah 53 and Ezekiel 34, for at least four reasons: (1) Zechariah 9–14 was not just available for use, but was also an integral part of the Passion Narrative tradition. We do

---

[105] Instone-Brewer 1992. In her analysis of the OT in 1 Peter Jobes writes, 'The author of 1 Peter does not use Scripture quotations to proof-text. Instead, the way the quotations are used in 1 Peter involves an application of their original contexts as well ... This kind of use does not support the idea that the author got his quotations from a list of disjointed passages that circulated out of context' (Jobes 2006: 332).

not find a similar phenomenon with Ezekiel 34; (2) Isaiah 53 and the shepherd tradition of Zechariah 9–14 share a more specific conceptual link than do Ezekiel 34 and Isaiah 53 – restoration through the affliction of YHWH's chosen agent; (3) Zechariah 9–14 explains why Christians must also suffer, which is the main point of the passage; and finally, (4) Peter's selection of LXX Zech. 10.2, 'they were driven away like sheep and were afflicted, since there was no *healing*', best explains why Peter chose to culminate his appropriation of Isaiah 53 with 'by his wounds you have been *healed*' (οὗ τῷ μώλωπι ἰάθητε; 2.24) and to then link it with shepherd imagery.

The kind of exegetical activity that I have suggested in 1 Pet. 2.21–5 concords well with what others have noticed in 1 Peter. For example, William Schutter, in his comprehensive analysis of Primopetrine hermeneutics observes that '[n]othing is quite so significant as the variety of ways [that OT] materials have been handled'; Peter conflates OT texts, gathers OT texts around a single idea, assumes that readers will pick up on the wider text-plot cited and interacts with exegetical traditions in existence.[106] Both Bauckham as well as John Elliott have also demonstrated that in 1 Pet. 2.4–10 Peter not only creatively uses the OT but also builds on early Christian tradition in order to 'create a midrash specifically designed for its context'.[107] Similarly, Ceslas Spicq asserts that 1 Peter 'peut être caractérisée comme une "Épître de la Tradition"', drawing upon creedal formulas, Jesus' own teachings and midrash from the OT in order to craft his message.[108]

Given the importance of this passage, this initial proposal clears the way for a fresh assessment of the letter as a whole. For example, can Zechariah 9–14 explain the shepherd imagery in 1 Pet. 5.2–4? Is there evidence that Zechariah 9–14 undergirds the fiery trials and metal imagery of 1.6–7 and 4.12–13?[109] Is the shepherd imagery of 1 Peter related to the second exodus motif developed in 1 Pet. 1.3–2.10 (akin to the way the two images function in the prophetic traditions of the OT)? These questions will be explored in Chapters 4 and 5.

---

[106] Schutter 1989: 43.   [107] Bauckham 1988: 312; Elliott 1966: 16–49; 2000: 405–49.
[108] Spicq 1966: 15.
[109] Some scholars have noted verbal and conceptual parallels between Zech. 13.8–9 and 1 Pet. 1.6–7 and 4.12–13, but their initial observation has yet to be explored in detail (Dodd 1952: 66; Spicq 1966: 50; Kelly 1969: 54; Duguid 1995: 278; Achtemeier 1996: 103, 309; Elliott 2000: 341; Jobes 2005: 94).

4

FIRST PETER'S FIERY TRIALS AND THE ESCHATOLOGICAL PROGRAMME OF ZECHARIAH 9–14

Among the many concerns that Samuel Sandmel raised in his 1961 Society of Biblical Literature presidential address 'Parallelomania' was the tendency of biblical scholars to juxtapose, as he put it, 'mere excerpts' and note their similarities without performing a detailed study of their respective contexts: '[t]wo passages may sound the same in splendid isolation from their context, but when seen in context reflect difference rather than similarity'.[1]

Although identifying the source behind the fiery trials imagery of 1 Peter might have potential to shed light on why Christian suffering is regarded as a necessary (1.6) and expected (4.12) feature of following Jesus, seldom has the discussion moved beyond mentioning parallels between 1 Peter and, for example, a Graeco-Roman *topos* (e.g. Seneca's *On Prov.* 5.10), a Jewish wisdom saying (e.g. Sir. 2.1–6; Wis. 3.4–6; Prov. 17.3), a Jewish apocalyptic tradition (e.g. Messianic Woes) or an OT prophetic oracle (e.g. Mal. 3.2; Zech. 13.9).[2] This may be, in part, because no precursor text offers anything more than a few verbal parallels, which perhaps suggests that our author is not necessarily working from or alluding to any particular passage. Given the variety of proposals that have been put forth, which span the gamut of both Jewish as well as Graeco-Roman culture, one might conclude that the fiery trials imagery was so ubiquitous that the parallels between 1 Peter and any other source are essentially vacuous. That is always a possibility. But before arriving at such a conclusion, it would seem that due diligence would require a detailed study of the proposed parallel texts in their respective contexts.

---

[1] Sandmel 1962: 2. In this now famous address, Sandmel complained (1962: 1) that biblical scholarship had been infected with a disease that he termed parallelomania – the 'extravagance among scholars which first overdoes the supposed similarity in passages and then proceeds to describe source and derivation as if implying literary connection flowing in an inevitable or predetermined direction'.

[2] The noted exceptions to this being Sander 1966; Dubis 2002; Holloway 2002; and Johnson 1986, who all in their own way have sought to give a detailed examination of their proposed parallels.

In this chapter I will focus attention on the potential relationship between the fiery trials imagery of 1 Pet. 1.6–7; 4.12 and Zech. 13.8–9, which often has been hinted at in the literature, but in my view has yet to receive the full attention it deserves. Dodd, for example, in an effort to show that Zechariah 9–14 was a source of *testimonia* for New Testament theology, noted that Zech. 13.9 'seems to be echoed' in 1 Pet. 1.7 and 4.12.[3] John Elliott suggests that our author probably 'is drawing on biblical imagery as found in such texts as Zech 13.9'.[4] While he notes three verbal parallels in common with the two texts (πῦρ, δοκιμάζω, and χρυσίον), he also points to other texts such as Wis. 3.4–6, Sir. 2.1–9 and Mal. 3.2, which also share verbal parallels (though not the same ones) with 1 Pet. 1.6–7, perhaps leaving the impression that all of these precursor texts were using the fiery trials imagery in the same way, and that Zech. 13.9 is only one of many possible sources that make up a single widespread tradition. Like Dodd and Elliott, Dubis also has noted the verbal parallels (that Dodd has noted) between 1 Pet. 1.6–8 and Zech. 13.9, but seems to go one step further than both to say that 1 Peter alludes to Zechariah. However, rather than explore the apparent allusion and its possible bearing on the theology of suffering in 1 Peter, he instead insists that it is the 'messianic woes' that stand behind the δεῖ (or necessity) of 1 Pet. 1.6.[5] And finally, in a footnote buried in the middle of his published doctoral thesis, Troy Martin suggests that Zechariah 9–14

---

[3] Dodd (1952: 66):

> In the context the shepherd who is to be smitten is apparently a leader of Israel, whose death is followed by a drastic purge of the people, leaving only one-third to call upon the name of the Lord and to be accepted as His people. The language of verse 9, πυρώσω αὐτοὺς ὡς πυροῦται τὸ ἀργύριον καὶ δοκιμῶ αὐτοὺς ὡς δοκιμάζεται τὸ χρυσίον, seems to be echoed in 1 Pet. i.7, τὸ δοκίμιον ὑμῶν τῆς πίστεως πολυτιμότερον χρυσίου τοῦ ἀπολλυμένου διὰ πυρὸς δὲ δοκιμαζομένου (cf. also iv. 12, τῇ πυρώσει πρὸς πειρασμόν), and the conclusion, 'They shall invoke my name and I will hear them; I will say, It is my people; and they shall say, The Lord is my God', is closely similar to other Old Testament passages which are cited as *testimonia*.

[4] Elliott 2000: 341.
[5] Dubis 2002: 69.

> While 1 Peter no doubt considers such suffering as necessary because of scriptural warrant (1 Pet 1.6–8 alludes to Zech 13.9), the apocalyptic dimensions of δεῖ should not be ignored. The readers' sufferings are necessary because they are an inevitable aspect of God's eschatological plan. Since 1 Peter is apocalyptic in character, and since messianic woes are a necessary prelude to the end elsewhere in Jewish apocalyptic literature, it is this background of messianic woes that offers the best explanation as to why 1 Peter regards the readers' sufferings as 'necessary'.   (Dubis 2002: 69–70)

provides important background material for, among other texts, 1 Pet. 1.7 and 4.12.[6]

In light of these suggestions, it would seem that a closer examination of both texts (i.e. Zech. 13.8–9 and 1 Peter) is in order, one that moves beyond simply noting verbal parallels to include an exploration of the wider context of both the precursor text as well as the wider contours of 1 Peter. To begin, however, I will table a variety of proposals that regard a source other than Zechariah 9–14 as in some way standing behind the fiery trials imagery of 1 Peter, offering critiques when pertinent. I will then examine the fiery trials imagery in 1 Peter, placing it in its wider epistolary context, and noting ways in which it is subtle but nevertheless significantly different than the proposed precursor texts. Finally, I will relate my conclusions regarding the fiery trials imagery of 1 Peter to my examination of Zech. 13.8–9 and its wider context (Chapter Two), concluding that Zech. 13.8–9 is the most plausible source for the imagery in 1 Pet. 1.7 and 4.12.

4.1 A survey of the proposed sources behind 1 Peter's fiery trials imagery

As I have indicated briefly, Primopetrine scholars have suggested several sources behind the fiery trials/metal imagery of 1 Pet. 1.6–7/4.12–13. The proposed sources can be placed within four categories: Graeco-Roman backgrounds, Jewish wisdom traditions, Jewish apocalyptic traditions and OT prophetic traditions.[7]

4.1.1 Graeco-Roman backgrounds

There was a time when scholars regarded the fiery trials imagery of 1 Peter to be an allusion to Nero's persecution of Christians following a devastating fire in 64 CE that destroyed large portions of Rome.[8] According to Tacitus, it was suspected that Nero intentionally set the fire in order to make room for his garden. In an effort to relieve himself of any culpability, he gathered together a multitude of Christians and convicted them

---

[6] Martin 1992: 259, n.418. The other texts that he thinks are influenced by Zechariah 9–14 are 1 Pet 2:10, and 1 Pet 2:25, which 'alludes to ideas expressed in Zech 13:7–9'.

[7] With these four categories I do not wish to suggest that each is hermetically sealed off from the other. I acknowledge that there was fluidity between many of these categories (e.g. wisdom and apocalyptic; on this see Collins 1993; Macaskill 2007). I use these categories, then, as a heuristic aid.

[8] E.g. Selwyn 1958: 221; Leaney 1967: 65; Beare 1970: 188–90; Thurston 1974: 176.

of arson, making a spectacle of them in his garden and in the circus – crucifying some, covering others with animal skins and leaving them to be devoured by dogs, and burning the rest in order to illuminate the events 'when daylight had expired'.[9] Elliott, however, has demonstrated (along with numerous others) that this proposal is implausible for at least three reasons. First, Nero's 'fiery' persecutions were limited to Rome, whereas 1 Peter is written to Christians suffering 'fiery' trials throughout Asia Minor (1.1; 1.6) and beyond (5.9). Second, there was no official empire-wide Neronian policy against Christians.[10] Third, the suffering in 1 Peter, which is described as worldwide in scope (1 Pet. 5.9), is principally characterized as verbal abuse, slander and social ostracism, which probably was in keeping with what Peter Oakes has imaginatively described in his monograph on Philippians.[11] Elliott is right in underscoring that the '[d]etails of the situation point rather to social polarization and conflict which was local, disorganized and unofficial in character'.[12] Upon surveying recent scholarship on the subject, Elliott concludes that '[t]he attempt to link 1 Peter with putative Roman persecutions of Christianity ... has now been abandoned by the majority of recent commentators, who point rather to local harassment as the cause of the suffering mentioned in this letter'.[13] In spite of this consensus, there remains, often in popular works on 1 Peter, the notion that the fiery trials imagery refers to Neronian proscription that extends even to Asia Minor.[14]

Among the many possible sources that Karen Jobes has suggested for the fiery trials imagery in 1 Peter is Seneca's aphorism, *ignis aurum probat, miseria fortes viros* ('Fire tests gold, affliction strong men'; Seneca

---

[9] Tacitus, *Annals*, 15.43–4; see also Suetonius, *Nero* 16.2; Eusebius, *Hist. eccl.* 2.25.1–8.

[10] Elliott 2000: 98–9. Selwyn (1958: 221) makes the bizarre suggestion that we cannot rule out the possibility that 'Christians in Asia Minor may have suffered, like the Jews in modern Germany, from acts of deliberate incendiarism'. There is, however, no evidence that this took place in Asia Minor during the first century CE.

[11] Oakes 2001. See Horrell 2008: 54–5, who also notes correspondence between the suffering described in 1 Peter and that which Oakes imagines to have taken place in Philippi. To say that suffering in 1 Peter is 'principally characterized as verbal abuse, slander, and social ostracism' is not to suggest that 1 Peter does not allow for suffering which included physical abuse (e.g. 2.20), formal accusations (e.g. 3.15; 4.12–19) and perhaps even execution (e.g. 2.21–4). Bechtler's monograph (1998: 94–104) is helpful for understanding how the suffering as it is described in 1 Peter fits within the Graeco-Roman world of honour and shame. Another factor for many is that 1 Peter was written at a much later date, somewhere between 70 and 95 CE, which would of course make the Neronian allusions highly unlikely. See also Webb 2007: 88.

[12] Elliott 1992: 274.   [13] Elliott 2000: 100. Cf. Bechtler 1998: 19–20.

[14] E.g. Paul Barnett 2006: 303–304; *Holman Illustrated Study Bible* 2006: 1,805.

On Prov. 5.10).[15] At this stage in the argument, I will simply point out that (a) this aphorism emphasizes the character-forming benefits of adversity, that (b) it does not explain why suffering is a necessary (see 1 Pet. 1.5–7) part of a wider programme, and that (c) it is unclear whether this aphorism would have been available to the author or known by the readers. As I will demonstrate in due course, these three factors make it very unlikely that Seneca's aphorism was in view.

Paul Holloway has argued that 1 Pet. 4.12–5.11 is at its core a development of the Cyrenaic consolatory *topos, nihil inopinati accidisse* ('nothing unexpected has happened').[16] The Cyrenaics developed the *topos* as a strategy for aiding those who were already suffering the pain of unexpected calamity.[17] Although he does not deal directly with the fiery trials imagery of 1 Peter, his proposal, if it is correct, has the potential of undercutting Zech. 13.8–9 as the primary source behind this passage.

His argument develops in three movements. First, he describes the Cyrenaic *topos* and argues for its widespread usage in the Graeco-Roman period.[18] Second, he seeks to show evidence of the *topos* in Jewish (e.g. Philo, *De spec. leg.* 2.87) and Christian sources (1 Thess. 3.1–10; Phil. 1.28–30; John 16.1–4a).[19] Finally, he argues that '[t]he consolation of 1 Pet 4.12ff. takes as its point of departure the assurance that "[nothing] strange is happening"'.[20] Although I find his broader conclusion to be helpful, namely that 1 Pet. 4.12–17 is intended to offer consolation to the beleaguered Christians of Asia Minor, I find it difficult to conclude that 1 Pet. 4.12–17 is in any way based upon the Cyrenaic *topos*. First, there is the issue of availability. The NT examples that Holloway highlights (1 Thess. 3.1–10; Phil. 1.28–30; John 16.1–4a) can just as easily be explained as an extension of either the Jesus Tradition, in which suffering was seen to be an inevitable part of life for faithful Jesus followers (see Mark 13.9–13/Matt. 10.16–25/Luke 21.12–17; Mark 8.34/Matt. 10.38–29; Matt. 5.10–11; John 15.18–27), or as reminders of the still-unfolding eschatological programme initiated by Jesus' own suffering. Neither of these possibilities were explored adequately, calling into question whether the Cyrenaic *topos* was available and in view in these NT

---

[15] Jobes 2005: 94. Her other suggestions are Ps. 66.10; Prov. 17.3; 27.21; Zech. 13.9; Mal. 3.3; and Sir. 2.1–6.
[16] Holloway 2002.
[17] *Ibid.*: 436–7. The strategy was based upon their theories regarding pleasure and pain. The Cyrenaics also offered a pre-emptive strategy for suffering which involved contemplation of future evil (*ibid.*: 436).
[18] *Ibid.*: 434–8.   [19] *Ibid.*: 438–41.
[20] *Ibid.*: 444; for the fuller development of his statement see *ibid.*: 441–8.

examples. Second, although Holloway helpfully has demonstrated the ways in which apocalyptic traditions are used in 4.12–19 for consolation, further argumentation is needed in order to conclude that these consolatory strategies in fact derive from the Cyrenaic *topos*. Holloway admits as much in his conclusion: 'From the fact that apocalyptic consolation of 1.3–12 is used to support the philosophical consolation of 4.12–19, one might argue that the principal consolatory strategy of the letter derives from our topos – but this requires further study.'[21] It may well be the case that the consolatory strategy of 1 Pet. 4.12–19 is a part of the apocalyptic tradition itself, or that it is simply one more example of a prevalent rhetorical strategy within the wider Graeco-Roman world that is in no way unique to the Cyrenaics. In short, I find it difficult to draw a straight line from the Cyrenaic *topos* to 1 Pet. 4.12–19, not least because a more apparent explanation is found in the fact that 1 Pet. 4.12–19 is an extension of the eschatological programme introduced in 1.3–2.10, as Holloway himself has demonstrated.[22] In particular, I would point to 1 Pet. 1.6, where the 'fiery trials' are first mentioned as a *necessary* period within a wider eschatological sequence. It is for this reason, then, that Peter, returning to his opening comments (1.6), has assured his readers that nothing strange is happening to them (4.12) – since he has already told them that it was part of a wider schema.[23]

4.1.2   Wisdom traditions

Leonhard Goppelt represents the position of many Primopetrine scholars when he posits that 1 Pet. 1.6–7 'appropriates primarily an OT-Jewish and primitive Christian wisdom tradition' in order to make sense of Christian suffering.[24] Goppelt seeks to substantiate the claim by first noting that 'Jas 1:2f. has such close affinities to 1 Pet 1:6f. . . . that one must assume a common primitive Christian tradition behind them'.[25] He then asserts

---

[21] *Ibid.*: 448.   [22] *Ibid.*: 441, 442, 447.

[23] J. B. Green (2007a: 158) has also questioned Holloway's hypothesis, pointing out that '[w]hereas the Cyrenaics counted as wisdom the orientation of one's life in and for the present, 1 Peter – both in the letter as a whole, but also in this present word [4.12–19] of consolation – is manifestly future-oriented. The Cyrenaic emphasis on the pleasure of the moment stands in stark contrast with the eschatological edge of Peter's theology'. He goes on to add that 'the theological endorsements for relating suffering and joy, both present and future, are simply lacking in the larger Greco-Roman world apart from the resources specific to the Jewish tradition'.

[24] Goppelt 1993: 91. Similarly, Feldmeier (2008: 224) asserts that 1 Pet. 1.6–7 and 4.12 reflects a dependence upon the wisdom tradition in which suffering is compared to the melting of metal, and interpreted as the possibility of purification.

[25] Goppelt 1993: 91.

that Wis. 3.5 is the 'direct precursor of this primitive Christian tradition, which dominates in wisdom interpretation of suffering'.[26] In line with a number of scholars, Goppelt points to other passages such as Ps. 66.10, Prov. 17.3, 27.21 and Sir. 2.5, which compare trials to the testing of gold or silver, and which probably serve as the foundation for a particular way of interpreting suffering in Wisdom 3.[27]

There are a number of problems with Goppelt's proposal, however. First, as I will detail in §4.2, it is not at all certain whether James 1.2ff. and 1 Pet 1.6ff. do in fact draw from the same 'primitive Christian wisdom tradition'. For now I will simply point to Achtemeier, who has noted that although James 1.2–3 and 1 Pet. 1.6–7 share some verbal parallels, they also carry distinct meanings. For James, temptation brings about endurance, whereas in 1 Peter, temptation results in praise, glory and honour at Christ's return.[28] Second, although Wis. 3.5 shares a number of verbal parallels with 1 Pet. 1.6–7, as Sandmel has warned, this does not necessarily suggest literary or conceptual dependence. A brief analysis of Wis. 3.5, along with Sir. 2.5, another wisdom text that is often said to stand behind 1 Pet. 1.6–7, then, is in order.

4.1.2.1 Wisdom of Solomon

As can be seen in Table 4.1, 1 Pet. 1.6–7 and Wis. 3.4–6 share five verbal parallels (ὀλίγος, πειρασμός/πειράζω, χρυσίον/χρυσός, δοκιμάζω, εὑρίσκω), which could suggest some sort of dependence.[29]

---

[26] *Ibid.*: 91. Cf. Witherington 2007: 81.

[27] Goppelt 1993: 91; So also Achtemeier 1996: 20. Jth. 8.25–7 is sometimes included in the discussion, which seems odd since it affirms that YHWH 'has not tried us with fire'.

[28] Achtemeier 1996: 20.

[29] Although most scholars accept the Alexandrian provenance of Wisdom of Solomon, there is still considerable debate regarding its date of composition, with proposals ranging from 220 BCE to 100 CE. David Winston (1979: 20–5) has demonstrated that there are thirty-five words or phrases in Wisdom that are unattested in secular Greek before the first century CE. Additionally, a number of scholars have argued that the ruler cult described in Wis. 14.16–20, along with a detectible critique of the *pax Romana* in 14.22, coincide well with the development of the Roman imperial ideology from the time of Augustus and into the first century CE (Oesterley 1935: 207; Winston 1979: 21–2; Gilbert 1984: 312; Collins 2000: 195). Curiously, the Muratorian Fragment lists Wisdom of Solomon as belonging to the canonical New Testament writings. This, along with the aforementioned evidence regarding vocabulary and ideological critiques, perhaps suggests that Wisdom of Solomon may have been written roughly around the time that the canonical New Testament writings were being composed. Conservatively, then, I would suggest that Wisdom of Solomon was written sometime within the first half of the first century CE. If Romans does in fact demonstrate literary dependence on Wisdom of Solomon (which is still debated), then this would serve as our *terminus ad quem*. The Greek text of Wisdom of Solomon is taken from the Göttingen critical edition, *Sapientia Salomonis* (Ziegler 198).

Table 4.1 *Verbal parallels between 1 Pet. 1.6–7 and Wis. 3.4–6*

1 Pet. 1.6–7	Wis. 3.4–6
[6] ἐν ᾧ ἀγαλλιᾶσθε, <u>ὀλίγον</u> ἄρτι εἰ δέον [ἐστὶν] λυπηθέντες ἐν ποικίλοις <u>πειρασμοῖς</u>, [7] ἵνα τὸ δοκίμιον ὑμῶν τῆς πίστεως πολυτιμότερον <u>χρυσίου</u> τοῦ ἀπολλυμένου διὰ πυρὸς δὲ <u>δοκιμαζομένου</u>, εὑρεθῇ εἰς ἔπαινον καὶ δόξαν καὶ τιμὴν ἐν ἀποκαλύψει Ἰησοῦ Χριστοῦ·	[4] καὶ γὰρ ἐν ὄψει ἀνθρώπων ἐὰν κολασθῶσιν, ἡ ἐλπὶς αὐτῶν ἀθανασίας πλήρης, [5] καὶ <u>ὀλίγα</u> παιδευθέντες μεγάλα εὐεργετηθήσονται, ὅτι ὁ θεὸς <u>ἐπείρασεν</u> αὐτοὺς καὶ <u>εὗρεν</u> αὐτοὺς ἀξίους ἑαυτοῦ, [6] ὡς <u>χρυσὸν</u> ἐν χωνευτηρίῳ <u>ἐδοκίμασεν</u> αὐτοὺς καὶ ὡς ὁλοκάρπωμα θυσίας προσεδέξατο αὐτούς.

There is a case to be made for the influence of Wis. 3.5 on 1 Pet. 1.6–7 that extends beyond mere verbal parallels. One of the primary aims of Wisdom of Solomon (henceforth Wisdom) is to encourage the righteous to persevere in spite of adversity, especially the kind of adversity that comes as a result of competing socio-religio-political ideologies.[30] In this regard, both the aim and the context of Wisdom converge with the agenda and backdrop of 1 Peter, making it a plausible source for reflection. More specifically, however, Wisdom is concerned with demonstrating that the way of wisdom (i.e. loyal allegiance to YHWH, the god of Israel) is superior to the way of folly (i.e. embracing the ideologies of the dominant Alexandrian culture). In order to establish this, Wisdom explains that the righteous (i.e. those who trust and obey YHWH and seek to learn wisdom) will be rewarded with immortality after their death (e.g. 5.15–16), while the ungodly, who have oppressed the righteous and rebelled against the Lord, will 'vanish like a shadow' (5.9; 3.10–13; 5.1–14).[31] It is within this rudimentary framework of judgment and reward that Wisdom speaks of testing, which, as becomes apparent over the course of the book, serves at least two purposes. First, it reveals the character of a person (e.g. 1.3; 3.1–9). Second, in keeping with earlier wisdom traditions (e.g. Prov. 3.11–12; Sir. 2.1–5; 4.17–18), it serves to transform the character

---

[30] For the socio-religio-political context of Wisdom, see Winston 1979; Barclay 1996: 183, 191; Collins 2000: 201.

[31] Wisdom emphasizes that the ungodly are not only opposed to the righteous 'because [they] are inconvenient to us and oppose our actions' (2.12), but that they also 'test' the righteous to 'see what will happen to them' (2.17; cf. 2.19–20).

of those who seek to trust in the Lord, inculcating discipline, knowledge and wisdom.[32]

The particular argument of Wisdom 3 is concerned with showing that God in the past used the ungodly to discipline (παιδευθέντες) and test (ἐπείρασεν) the righteous who have already died, and that in the end he found them to be worthy of himself (3.5): 'like gold in the furnace he tried them' (ἐδοκίμασεν; 3.6). The stress of this passage, then, read within the wider framework of Wisdom, is that God in the past used the oppression of the ungodly to transform the character of the righteous, who having been purified, were then found to be worthy of reward.

4.1.2.2 Sirach

Although Sirach[33] is not entirely antagonistic towards the Hellenizing forces present in second-century BCE Palestine, there is clearly an awareness of the threat they pose for Hebrew traditions (see Sir. 36.1–22).[34] Sirach responds to these forces, in part, by offering 'a kind of handbook of moral behaviour or code of ethics that a Jew of the early second century B.C. was expected to observe'.[35] The primary theme of Sirach is wisdom, which is in its essence the fear of the Lord expressed in fidelity towards all of his commandments (Sir. 19.20; cf. Sir. 1.11–30).[36] The first chapter of Sirach extols the virtues and value of wisdom, which, if sought, will bring peace, health, joy and a long and prosperous life. Sir. 2.1–6 warns

---

[32] Kolarcik 1997: 469. According to Kolarcik, the transforming quality of testing is expressed with the metallurgy metaphor in 3.5, which is also found in Ps. 66.10; Prov. 17.3; 27.21; and Sir. 2.5, and the fact that the righteous are given the task of ruling and judging at the time of judgment (e.g. Wis. 3.7–8; 4.16).

[33] There is broad consensus that Sirach was written some time around 180 BCE (with proposals ranging between 196 and 175 BCE; e.g. Di Lella 1987: 10, 16; Crenshaw 1997: 611), and almost certainly before the Maccabean revolt in 167 BCE. As the prologue indicates, Sirach was originally written in Hebrew, most likely in Jerusalem (50.27). It was later translated into Greek by Ben Sira's grandson (*c.* 132 BCE) so that the Jewish diaspora community of Egypt could benefit from its wisdom and learning. Since there are no extant Hebrew manuscripts of Sir. 2.1–6 (see Beentjes 1997 for all extant Hebrew manuscripts), I was unable to compare the Greek with the Hebrew. The Syriac manuscript contains an additional phrase at the end of Sir. 2.5: 'In sickness and in poverty be confident in him'. This variant can perhaps be explained by the notion that Sirach was translated into Syriac by Ebionites (Di Lella 1987: 57). In the following section, the Greek text of Sirach is taken from the critical edition of Ziegler 1965.

[34] For the socio-religio-political context of Sirach see Metzger 1957: 81; Kraft and Nickelsburg 1986: 371–7; Di Lella 1987: 8–16.

[35] Di Lella 1987: 4.   [36] *Ibid.*: 76.

Table 4.2 Verbal parallels between 1 Pet. 1.6–7 and Sir. 2.1–6

1 Pet. 1.6–7	Sir. 2.1–6
⁶ ἐν ᾧ ἀγαλλιᾶσθε, ὀλίγον ἄρτι εἰ δέον [ἐστὶν] λυπηθέντες ἐν ποικίλοις <u>πειρασμοῖς</u>, ⁷ ἵνα τὸ δοκίμιον ὑμῶν τῆς πίστεως πολυτιμότερον <u>χρυσίου</u> τοῦ ἀπολλυμένου διὰ <u>πυρὸς</u> δὲ <u>δοκιμαζομένου</u>, εὑρεθῇ εἰς ἔπαινον καὶ δόξαν καὶ τιμὴν ἐν ἀποκαλύψει Ἰησοῦ Χριστοῦ	Τέκνον, εἰ προσέρχῃ δουλεύειν κυρίῳ, ἑτοίμασον τὴν ψυχήν σου εἰς <u>πειρασμόν</u>, ² εὔθυνον τὴν καρδίαν σου καὶ καρτέρησον καὶ μὴ σπεύσῃς ἐν καιρῷ ἐπαγωγῆς, ³ κολλήθητι αὐτῷ καὶ μὴ ἀποστῇς, ἵνα αὐξηθῇς ἐπ᾽ ἐσχάτων σου. ⁴ πᾶν, ὃ ἐὰν ἐπαχθῇ σοι, δέξαι καὶ ἐν ἀλλάγμασιν ταπεινώσεώς σου μακροθύμησον, ⁵ ὅτι ἐν <u>πυρὶ</u> <u>δοκιμάζεται χρυσὸς</u> καὶ ἄνθρωποι δεκτοὶ ἐν καμίνῳ ταπεινώσεως. ⁶ πίστευσον αὐτῷ, καὶ ἀντιλήμψεταί σου, εὔθυνον τὰς ὁδούς σου καὶ ἔλπισον ἐπ᾽ αὐτόν.

would-be disciples of wisdom[37] that the way will not be easy; the Lord will test his children in order to see whether or not their fear is genuine.[38] In keeping with Prov. 3.10–11, which some regard to be the background for Sir. 2.1–6, adversity is not a sign of punishment or of God's disfavour, but instead is a demonstration of God's discipline and love.[39] It is important to note that the warning regarding adversity (2.1–6) comes just after would-be disciples are warned of double-mindedness (1.28), hypocrisy (1.29) and pride (1.30). As Crenshaw has noted, the Lord uses adversity to unmask insincere commitments to wisdom (see 4.11–19).[40] Adversity, then, functions in a pedagogical fashion, both revealing inadequacies as well as training disciples to know what it means to fear the Lord.

This, then, is the context in which we find four verbal parallels between Sir. 2.1–6 and 1 Pet. 1.6–7: πειρασμός, πῦρ, χρυσίον/χρυσός, and δοκιμάζω (see Table 4.2).[41]

The primary exhortation of Sir. 2.1–6 is to remain faithful to the Lord in the midst of adversity ('cling to him' (2.3); 'trust in him' (2.6); 'hope in him'; 2.6) because just as gold is refined by fire, so too acceptable men (ἄνθρωποι δεκτοί) are refined in the furnace of humiliation (2.5). Testing

---

[37] The term τέκνον, which opens this chapter, is often the word used to address disciples of wisdom (Di Lella 1987: 150; e.g. 3.12,17; 4.1; 6.32; 10.28; 11.10; 14.11; 31.22; Prov. 2.1; 3.1,11).
[38] Di Lella 1987: 150. [39] Ibid.; Crenshaw 1997: 654. [40] Ibid.
[41] Jobes (2005: 95) suggests that Sir. 2.1–6 'is perhaps the closest lexical and conceptual parallel' to 1 Pet. 1.6–7.

(πειρασμός; 2.1), then, if endured with faithfulness, not only ascertains the authenticity of one's commitment to the Lord, but also serves to purify, even educate the one who wishes to follow the path of wisdom (see 4.11–19; 44.20). In short, Sir. 2.1–6 seeks to affirm the inherent educational and authenticating value of testing; it is a necessary part of the educational process for one who wishes to grow in the fear of the Lord.

4.1.2.3 Conclusions

Both Wisdom 3 as well as Sirach 2 offer several compelling verbal and conceptual parallels with 1 Peter. For example, they each place suffering within a rudimentary sequence of judgment and reward. And both note that one of the purposes of suffering is to evaluate the authenticity of one's faith. However, both texts also underscore the inherent goodness of suffering – because of its educational value, or its ability to transform one's character. The educational and transformational value of suffering appears to be a particular emphasis in wisdom traditions, as Goppelt rightly has noted.[42] Von Rad explains that in Israel's wisdom tradition suffering is to be interpreted as God secretly but clearly 'pursuing the task of training men'.[43] He further notes that the idea that God organizes a beneficent training of individuals, often described as a testing, is rare in the Old Testament, found principally in 'the wisdom teachers'. He adds that 'since they themselves were concerned with the training of men and thought so highly of its usefulness [i.e. suffering/testing], it is understandable that the idea of divine training or correction through suffering was particularly cultivated by them'.[44] 'If one speaks of training through suffering, one must ask what the aim of such training is.'[45] For von Rad, the training is intended to return disciples back to God and to the community that he has provided.[46] Training, then, according to Von Rad, 'presupposes that the life of the man in question was not in order'.[47]

It is precisely on this crucial point that 1 Peter diverges from wisdom traditions. For according to 1 Peter, the addressees suffer, not because they lack character or wisdom, or because their lives need to be put in order, or because they have strayed from the community of God – but rather because suffering, or testing, is simply part of a wider eschatological

---

[42] Goppelt 1993: 91.   [43] Von Rad 1972: 200.
[44] *Ibid.* He references the following verses: Prov. 4.12; 13.1; 13.24; 19.18; 23.13; 29.15,17; Sir. 2; 4.17; 18.13; 23.2; 31.10; 36.
[45] *Ibid.*: 201.   [46] *Ibid.*   [47] *Ibid.*

programme in which they find themselves. They suffer precisely because they are faithful to God. Said in another way, both Wisdom 3 as well as Sirach 2 offer no certainty regarding the character of the would-be disciple or the outcome of those who undergo testing: they may or may not have what it takes, as the trials will reveal. First Peter, on the other hand, demonstrates an unusual sense of optimism regarding those being tested: they will emerge from the trials, protected by God throughout (see 1.5–7; 4.17–19). As I will demonstrate in §4.2 and §4.3, both 1 Peter as well as Zech. 13.8–9 downplay the educational or purifying benefits of suffering, and instead regard them to be a necessary period within a large eschatological sequence of events. In light of this, when we compare Wisdom 3 and Sirach 2 to Zech. 13.8–9 and its wider context, their verbal and conceptual parallels do not offer compelling enough evidence to suggest that one or the other (or both) served as the source for the fiery trials imagery of 1 Pet. 1.6–7/4.12.

4.1.3   Jewish apocalyptic traditions

Why, according to 1 Peter, is suffering 'necessary' (1.6), something that Christians (4.17) should expect to encounter (1 Pet. 4.12)?

Mark Dubis has noted that '[t]he necessity of suffering in 1 Pet 1:6 finds strong resonance with the Jewish conception of messianic woes, that limited time of eschatological tribulation that early Jews regarded as a necessary preliminary to the age to come'.[48] In his 2002 monograph, *Messianic Woes in First Peter*, Dubis argues that since '1 Peter is apocalyptic in character, and since messianic woes are a necessary prelude to the end elsewhere in Jewish apocalyptic literature, it is this background of messianic woes that offers the best explanation as to *why* 1 Peter regards the readers' sufferings as "necessary"'.[49]

More recently, Robert Webb, in a 2007 essay entitled 'Intertexture and Rhetorical Strategy in First Peter's Apocalyptic Discourse', also has observed several parallels between certain aspects of the Messianic Woes[50] and, for example, 1 Pet. 1.5–7: salvation is 'ready' (1.5), suffering

---

[48] Dubis 2002: 69.   [49] *Ibid.*: 70. Italics added for emphasis.

[50] The term Messianic Woes will be described below by using the definitions of its proponents. While I do not think Messianic Woes is the best term for describing the period of tribulation often discussed in Jewish Second Temple Literature, and would prefer the term 'eschatological crisis', it is the preferred term of 1 Peter scholars. For further discussion regarding the terminology see Dubis (2002: 3–4) and Pitre (2005: 7–8, 29–31). Two caveats should be mentioned regarding my use of the term Messianic Woes. First, I will treat it as a proper noun, capitalizing both words. Second, since it represents a scholarly construct of a

'necessary', though only for a 'little while' (1.6) and trials are 'by fire' (1.7).[51] He concludes that '[w]hile the author appears to have no particular textual resource in mind, he is *drawing upon* intertextual resources of Jewish apocalyptic discourse probably filtered through early Christian use of the resources in oral tradition in their apocalyptic discourse that understood the faithful would undergo a period of suffering just prior to the coming of Christ at the eschaton'.[52]

Dubis and Webb represent the latest and most developed articulations of an increasing trend among Primopetrine scholars to argue that 1 Peter's theology of suffering can be *illuminated*[53] when analyzed against the backdrop of the Jewish concept of Messianic Woes.[54] For example, according to Dubis, Messianic Woes brings clarity to the principal theme of 1 Peter, restoration from exile:[55] 'the suffering/glory pattern in 1 Peter (1.11; 4.13; 5.1, 10) is essentially an exile/restoration pattern. First Peter portrays the suffering of the readers as exilic suffering, and portrays future glory as the glory of Israel's anticipated eschatological restoration.'[56] Thus, in Dubis' schema, suffering in 1 Peter is to be interpreted as the necessary transition period where God's people move from exile to the restoration.[57]

---

supposed body of knowledge, I will treat it as a singular proper noun, which means a third person singular verb will be used in conjunction with the noun.

[51] Webb 2007: 90.   [52] *Ibid.*: 90–1. Italics added for emphasis.

[53] It is not always clear how Messianic Woes 'illuminates' 1 Peter. Webb (*ibid.*: 97), for example, argues that reading 1 Pet. 1.3–12 in light of Messianic Woes yields significant new ways in which 1 Peter's readers should understand their situation: first, 'it gives new meaning to their persecution. By fulfilling part of the messianic woes it places their suffering within the plans and purposes of God (1.6; cf. 4.17)'; second, 'it also places limits on the persecution'; third, 'new meaning is also attached to their persecution elsewhere in 1 Peter through a knowledge that those causing their suffering will be judged' (e.g. 3.17; 4.17–18); and finally, 'a new understanding of persecution serves to motivate perseverance as a response to their suffering'. This seems to be an overstatement, however, since one could arrive at similar conclusions about suffering simply by reading the text of 1 Peter and without having knowledge of Messianic Woes.

[54] Brown 1855: 86; Scott 1905: 234–40; Selwyn 1958: 128, 136, 299–303; Sander 1966; Leaney 1967: 64; Kelly 1969: 193–4; Schelkle 1970: 126; Best 1971: 76, 78, 162–3, 175; Michaels 1988: 270; Schutter 1989: 106–10; Davids 1990: 171, n.18; Martin 1992: 65–8, 242–52; Elliott 2000: 775–6; Dubis 2002; Green 2007a: 153–4; Webb 2007: 72–98. For a variety of reasons Goppelt (1993: 311, 330), Achtemeier (1996: 110–11, 315 (n.143)) and Jobes (2005: 291–2) are not convinced that Messianic Woes illuminates 1 Peter's theology of suffering. For reasons unknown, Witherington (2007) does not interact with the Messianic Woes proposal at all. Four passages in particular have been identified as having been influenced by the Messianic Woes tradition – 1 Pet. 1.5–7,10–11; 4.12–19; 5.9 – but surprisingly almost no one has offered sufficient argumentation to confirm such claims.

[55] See particularly Chapters 3 and 6 in Dubis 2002.

[56] *Ibid.*: 46.   [57] *Ibid.*: 59–62; 118–29.

Joel Green, one of the most recent commentators on 1 Peter, has affirmed Dubis' analysis,[58] and similarly maintains that glory is linked with God's people being returned from exile, adding that 'Peter paints the suffering of Christians onto a larger canvas of the restoration of God's people.'[59] He further postulates that '[j]ust as the suffering of Christ was efficacious for liberation (1:2, 18–19; 2:21–25), so the suffering of believers is efficacious . . . the suffering of Christians is a participation in the messianic woes by which God inaugurates the age of salvation (4:12–19)'.[60]

While the recent explorations of Messianic Woes in 1 Peter have been very helpful in placing the letter (and suffering) within a Jewish restoration framework, and have highlighted the important and often neglected eschatological aspects of the letter, there remain, in my view, some ambiguities or lacunae with the approach as it now stands. In what follows, I wish to draw attention to some issues that, in my view, need to be either explored or further clarified. In particular, I will highlight (a) a lack of clarity with respect to literary sources and dependence, (b) the absence of parallels between the Messianic Woes and 1 Peter regarding suffering, (c) the failure to consider whether the Jesus Tradition influenced the theology of suffering in 1 Peter, and finally (d) the neglect of possible OT sources that may have shaped not only 1 Peter but also the Messianic Woes and the Jesus Tradition. In keeping with the outline, we now turn to address ambiguities in the Messianic Woes approach with respect to literary sources and dependence.

4.1.3.1   What do parallels mean? How do they illuminate?

In the argumentation, it is not always entirely clear whether 1 Peter merely parallels patterns also found in the Messianic Woes,[61] whether the author, having already established his theology of suffering, is merely using

---

[58]   Green 2007a: 153–4. 'Dubis has demonstrated that virtually every clause in [4.12–19] is susceptible to a reading that locates it within the Jewish and Early Christian traditions of the messianic woes' (*ibid.*: 154).

[59]   *Ibid.*: 153.   [60]   *Ibid.*: 227.

[61]   E.g. 'the necessity of suffering . . . *finds strong resonance* with the Jewish conception of messianic woes' (Dubis 2002: 69); 'the theology of suffering in 1 Peter *is best understood against the backdrop* of messianic woes'; '[i]t is this background that offers the most helpful *interpretive grid* for a proper interpretation of 1 Peter' (*ibid.*: 186; italics mine). It is unclear to me what is actually being argued here – that Messianic Woes helps us interpret, or that it has influenced the theology of 1 Peter?

the Messianic Woes material for rhetorical effects[62] or whether what is being argued is that Messianic Woes has actually shaped the author's understanding (or theology) of suffering.[63] If what is being argued is that 1 Peter is dependent upon the Messianic Woes, then this raises at least two issues that need to be addressed.

First, there need to be clear parameters for adjudicating dependency: observing parallels between 1 Peter and Messianic Woes does not necessarily give warrant to conclude that one was dependent upon the other.[64] For example, have we adequately ruled out the possibility that 1 Peter and the texts that are used to construct the concept of Messianic Woes are both drawing from and/or developing their thoughts from the same independent source?[65] Sandmel points out that many Second Temple texts share parallels precisely because they all are a part of post-Tanach Judaism: 'If, accordingly, all these writings are post-Tanach Judaism, then obviously the Tanach has some status and influence in all of them.'[66] As a result, one should expect certain parallels: 'Paul and the rabbis should overlap, and Paul and Philo and the Qumran writings and the rabbis should overlap. Accordingly, *even true parallels may be of no great significance in themselves.*'[67]

Second, there are several reasons to question whether Messianic Woes (at least in the way that Dubis and Webb have characterized it) was as widespread and available as is often suggested.[68] This can be illustrated by the fact that there remains no consensus regarding the texts which

---

[62] 'These external phenomena [oral-scribal, cultural, social and historical intertexture] become resources that the author can use in developing the text's rhetorical argument' (Webb 2007: 79). Similarly, Webb states that the author 'uses a variety of intertextual resources to advance his rhetorical purposes' (*ibid.*: 72), or that intertexture is 'concerned with how a text interacts with material outside of the text' (*ibid.*: 78).

[63] Is this what is meant when it is said that the author of 1 Peter is 'drawing upon' (Webb 2007: 91,94) or 'picking up' (*ibid.*: 90) or 'adapting from' the Messianic Woes?

[64] See Davila's 'The Perils of Parallels' for some helpful guidelines for adjudication, which is presently only available online at www.st-andrews.ac.uk/divinity/rt/dss/abstracts/parallels/. Accessed 28 August 2010.

[65] It could be argued, for example, that Zech. 13.7–9 has influenced *Ps. Sol.* 17.11–18, T. Mos. 9–1.7 and 1 Macc. 3.35.

[66] Sandmel 1962: 3.

[67] *Ibid.* Italics added for emphasis. E. P. Sanders similarly comments that '[p]arallels are often illuminating, as long as one does not jump from 'parallel' to 'influence' to 'identity of thought' (1977: 11). See also Donaldson 1983: 193–210.

[68] Martin (1992: 246) represents this tendency well, positing that '[t]he conception of Messianic woes as a period of suffering for God's people just prior to the final consummation was so *widespread* and *prevalent* that our author could include this belief in his eschatological perspective without laying out the entire apocalyptic scenario' (italics added for emphasis). See also Best 1971: 76; Michaels 1988: 270.

make up the Messianic Woes construct.[69] Additionally, as Dale Allison
has underscored in his study of what he refers to as the Great Tribulation,[70]
among the variety of texts which are appropriated in order to construct
the Messianic Woes there is no agreement as to (1) when the Messianic
Woes will come (have they already come, are they present at the time of
the writing of the text being examined or are they still to come?), (2) who
will suffer the woes (God's enemies, God's people, both?), (3) how long
the woes will last or (4) whether the messiah's advent is even connected
with the woes.[71] Allison concludes his study by noting that

> Not only is the idea of final tribulation not always present in
> documents heavily informed by eschatological teaching, but
> when it does appear it receives no standard interpretation: there
> was no fixed eschatological doctrine. *Scholarly treatments of
> the great tribulation in Jewish literature have not always made
> this sufficiently clear.*[72]

That Jesus' disciples and then the early church struggled to comprehend
both the fact that their messiah had to suffer as well as the fact that
Christians had to suffer subsequent to the messiah's coming seems to
speak quite definitively against a widespread notion of Messianic Woes.[73]
Additionally, given the diversity among the texts regarding the whos and
whens of the tribulation, it would seem to be prudent (and more accurate)
to claim a widespread notion of a tribulation period. This widespread
notion of a tribulation period should not, however, be conflated with one
particular expectation regarding the events surrounding the woes: we
cannot isolate one particular strand of woes thought, such as that God's
people will suffer prior to the coming of the messiah, and assume that
it had the same widespread availability of the more general notion of a
tribulation period. Any claim of this sort would need to be demonstrated
with further research. Since we do not have a uniform, coherent tradition regarding the tribulation period upon which to draw, then method-
ologically scholars should work to be more precise when they speak of
1 Peter 'drawing upon' or 'adapting from' the so-called Messianic Woes.
More specifically, the lack of uniformity within the literature should push
scholars to demonstrate specific *textual* parallels – that is, a detailed study

---

[69] So also Pitre 2005: 2, 4–5.   [70] Allison 1985: 5–25.
[71] *Ibid.*: 5–25; T. Mos., 1 Enoch 91.5–7 and Jubilees 23, for example, do not connect
any messianic figure to tribulation. It is not insignificant that the tribulation is sometimes
depicted as a two-stage process (1 Enoch 91.5–7).
[72] Allison 1985: 25. Italics added for emphasis.
[73] E.g. Luke 24.13–35. I am indebted to Dr Luke Tallon for this observation.

of the relationship, whether verbal or conceptual, between texts – rather than compare a text like 1 Peter to a scholarly construct. And even when we encounter a text that seems to share parallels with 1 Peter, a close examination of both texts is still required, as Sandmel has already warned us. For this reason, it seems insufficient to argue that 1 Peter 'appears to have no particular textual resource in mind' but rather 'is drawing upon intertextual resources of Jewish apocalyptic discourse that understood that the faithful would undergo a period of suffering prior to [sic] coming of Christ at the eschaton' or that '1 Peter's theology of suffering adapts the Jewish notion of messianic woes'.[74] Without demonstrating parallels between specific texts from the apocalyptic literature and 1 Peter, how can we be certain whether such notions regarding the tribulation are even available to our author?

4.1.3.2   How can we explain the lack of parallels with regard to suffering?

The characteristics of suffering in 1 Peter in no way parallel the characteristics of the woes described in the texts which are used to construct Messianic Woes. Whereas in 1 Peter the suffering is described as (1) verbal abuse (2.12; 3.9,12–17; 4.4,14), with one possible indication of physical abuse in the case of slaves (2.18–21), (2) as unjust treatment (2.20–1; 3.14; 4.1,13,16,19) and (3) as a result of a new way of life (1.13–18; 3.1–6; 4.2–4),[75] suffering in the texts which are used to construct Messianic Woes is characterized as catastrophic and unprecedented, and often justly meted out by either God or Satan.[76] For example, Dan. 12.1 speaks of 'a time of anguish, such as has never occurred since nations first came into existence'. *T.Mos.* 8.1 refers to the tribulation as 'punishment and wrath such as has never happened to them [the righteous] from the creation till that time when he stirs up against them a king'. 1QM 1.11–12 describes the woes as a 'day of calamity' that has never been experienced before. In the Epistle of Enoch (1 Enoch 91–107) the tribulation is construed as 'a great scourge' that will come from heaven as God's judgment (1 Enoch 91.7), which will be characterized by political upheaval, miscarriages,

---

[74] Webb 2007: 90–1; Dubis 2002: 72.

[75] Webb (2007: 88) helpfully points this out, commenting that what 1 Peter's addressees are experiencing is 'social persecution that has arisen as a result of changes in their social relationships due to their conversion to the Christian faith (e.g., 4.3–4)'.

[76] Dubis (2002: 36) summarizes the Jewish apocalyptic literature by noting that 'God is usually the author of the woes, but often Satan is the one who is viewed as responsible for the eschatological suffering'.

abortion (1 Enoch 99.4–5), drought, cold (1 Enoch 100.1–2 and 11–13), a flood of fire from which sinners will not be able to flee, earthquakes (1 Enoch 102.1–3) and the persecution and murder of the righteous (1 Enoch 103.15).[77] Curiously, we find none of this language in 1 Peter.[78] Instead, the suffering in 1 Peter is paradigmatically framed as fiery πειρασμοί.[79]

4.1.3.3   What about the Dominical Sayings regarding suffering?

One issue that neither Dubis nor Webb adequately assesses[80] is whether the necessity of suffering and the 'Messianic Woes' language of 1 Peter can, in fact, be directly traced to the Jesus Tradition.[81] As Brant Pitre has demonstrated in his *Jesus, the Tribulation, and the End of Exile*:

> Jesus taught that the tribulation had in some way begun with the death of John the Baptist . . . and that it was Jesus' own mission to set into motion the 'Great Tribulation' that would precede the coming of the Messiah and the restoration of Israel. In fact, he even taught that he would die in this tribulation, and that his death would function as an act of atonement that would bring about the End of the Exile, the return of the dispersed tribes from among the nations, and the coming of the kingdom of God.[82]

There are at least four references in 1 Peter that can be traced to the Dominical Sayings found in Matt. 5.10–42, and in each of these cases the wider context refers to the inevitability of suffering or persecution for followers of Jesus: (a) 1 Pet. 2.12/Matt. 5.16; (b) 1 Pet. 3.8–9/Matt. 5.38–42,44//Luke 6.22–8 (cf. 1 Cor. 4.12; Rom. 12.7,14; 1 Thess. 5.15); (c) 1 Pet. 3.13–17/Matt. 5.10–12; Luke 12.8–12; Luke 21.9–17//Mark

---

[77] Several scholarly surveys of the pertinent Messianic Woes texts reveal similar characteristics as those found in the Epistle of Enoch, making it a steady feature (Allison 1985: 5; Dubis 2002: 35; Webb 2007: 89, 94–5).

[78] Dubis unsuccessfully tries to argue that in 1 Pet. 4.12–19 there is mention of increased wickedness, the threat of apostasy, and Christian suffering as judgment from God.

[79] While Dubis does offer an extensive study of the word πειρασμός, he does not offer an explanation as to why the characteristic language of Messianic Woes has been left out.

[80] In speaking of 1 Pet. 1.3–12, Webb (2007: 90–1) does note that 'the author . . . is drawing upon intertextual resources . . . probably filtered through early Christian use of these resources', but does not explain why this particular tradition cannot be the actual source of the author's reflection and rhetoric.

[81] I am grateful to Michael Thompson and David Wenham, who offered this critique of my own proposal in an early draft of this chapter at the Tyndale Fellowship conference in 2008.

[82] Pitre 2005: 4.

13.9–13//Matt. 24.9–14; Matt. 5.39–42; (d) 1 Pet. 4.13–14/Matt. 5.11–17//Luke 6.22–3.[83] The appearance of these Dominical Sayings in 1 Peter begs the question: did the author of 1 Peter regard suffering as necessary (1.6) and as something that was to be expected (4.12) simply because this is what he learned from the Jesus Tradition? It would also seem to compel further investigation as to whether other portions of the Jesus Tradition have influenced the language and theology of 1 Peter. In Mark 13, for example, Jesus teaches about an unfolding scenario which will involve necessary suffering, tribulations that echo the messianic woes (wars, earthquakes and birth pangs), court appearances before synagogues and governors (see 1 Pet .3.14–16), and where he mentions that these tribulations will only be for a little while.[84] And in Luke 12.49–53, Jesus speaks of bringing a time of fire and division upon the earth where the fidelity of God's people will be tested (see 1 Pet. 1.7; 4.12).

4.1.3.4 Is the OT an insufficient source for 1 Peter's theology of suffering?

In my view, the most significant weakness of the Messianic Woes proposal as it now stands is the failure to explain why the OT has been bracketed out of the conversation by asserting (in the case of Dubis) that it offers insufficient parallels to certain features in 1 Peter's theology of suffering.

It is significant to observe how Dubis and Webb frame their investigations of Messianic Woes in 1 Peter. As a starting point, both labour diligently to establish that 1 Peter shares important characteristics with apocalyptic discourse of its time.[85] Both, for example, filter the letter through particular parts of the SBL Apocalypse Group's paradigm for determining whether a piece of literature should be considered an apocalypse.[86] And both arrive at similar conclusions: Dubis confirms

---

[83] Elliott (2000: 776) notes that the only three places where 'rejoice' is connected with suffering are in Col. 1.24, Matt. 5.11–12, and 1 Pet. 4.13–14. For more on the Jesus Tradition in 1 Peter see Gundry 1967: 336–50. For a critique of Gundry see Best 1970: 95–113.

[84] It could be significant (depending upon one's view of authorship of 1 Peter and the date of the Passion Narratives) that in the account given in Mark 13, Peter is said to be one of the recipients of Jesus' teachings.

[85] Michaels regards 1 Peter as an apocalyptic diaspora letter (1988: xlvi–xlix); Davids considers 1 Peter to be 'characterized by an eschatological, even an apocalyptic focus' (1990: 15; see 15–17 for his full discussion); see also Holdsworth 1980: 226–7; Goppelt argues against 1 Peter being apocalyptic (1993: 311–13).

[86] Collins 1979: 1–20.

that '1 Peter shows important ties to the thought-world of Jewish apocalyptic literature',[87] while Webb deduces that 'apocalyptic topoi are found throughout the letter'.[88]

Placing 1 Peter within this apocalyptic milieu gives warrant, in their mind, for an examination of potential parallels between Jewish apocalyptic material and 1 Peter, particularly with respect to the themes of suffering and eschatology. Dubis says as much, maintaining that 'the "apocalyptic" character of 1 Peter *justifies* a comparison of 1 Peter with other Jewish apocalyptic texts, and strengthens the likelihood that 1 Peter's eschatological constructs may be related to similar constructs (specifically, messianic woes) in other apocalyptic texts'.[89] For Webb, the fact that 1 Peter evidences apocalyptic discourse means that it will likely draw upon particular apocalyptic traditions, whether oral-scribal or cultural, regarding suffering and eschatology.[90] This assumption, namely that because 1 Peter is apocalyptic in character it will therefore likely draw on and adapt from Jewish apocalyptic material, leads Dubis and Webb to explore the fruitfulness of a very specific apocalyptic tradition, one, I would add, that is a scholarly construct.

But in situating the letter within an apocalyptic framework, and then immediately looking for parallels between 1 Peter and Jewish apocalyptic literature, it appears that both studies have overlooked possible OT sources which may supply an explanation for certain features in Peter's theology of suffering.[91] Dubis seems to have done this consciously:

> One important implication of the similarities between 1 Peter and apocalyptic literature is that, although the OT is highly influential upon 1 Peter, one cannot interpret 1 Peter against the backdrop of the OT alone. Simply put, *the OT offers insufficient parallels to certain features of 1 Peter's thought.*[92]

Despite claims to the contrary, Dubis offers no explanation as to why the OT is an insufficient source for explaining 1 Peter's theology of suffering

---

[87] Dubis 2002: 45.   [88] Webb 2007: 83.   [89] Dubis 2002: 2.

[90] Webb, drawing upon Vernon Robbins, argues that since 1 Peter evidences 'apocalyptic discourse', the topics of the letter are likely to be derived first and foremost from the literary genre of Jewish and Christian apocalypses (Webb 2007: 72–9).

[91] Dubis offers one paragraph (2002: 61) in addressing the influence of the OT on Messianic Woes, pointing to Amos 9.11–15; Isa. 4.2–6; Ezek. 20.33–8; Dan. 12. See also Dubis 2002: 84, where Zech. 13.8–9 and Mal. 3.2–3 are also mentioned. In note 52, Webb (2007: 89) suggests the texts that probably were the origin of Messianic Woes.

[92] Dubis 2002: 44. Italics mine.

in the context of apocalyptic discourse.[93] And while he seems to be aware of possible OT foundations in 1 Peter, for whatever reason he refuses to explore their potentiality.[94] Instead, he turns to apocalyptic literature, asserting that 'the necessity of suffering in 1 Peter possesses not only scriptural grounds, but also reflects an apocalyptic understanding of a certain chronology of eschatological events in which the messianic woes are a prelude to the end of time'.[95]

Such an omission is perplexing for at least four reasons. First, as Dubis has himself already mentioned, one of 1 Peter's dominant characteristics is its prolific use and dependence upon the OT. William Schutter, who to date has done the most comprehensive study of the OT in 1 Peter, comments: 'It is clear the letter fairly teems with OT references, approximately forty-six quotations and allusions in all, not counting iterative allusions that would greatly boost the total, or nearly one for every two verses.'[96] Given this characteristic, it seems that anyone proposing that 'the OT offers insufficient parallels to certain features of 1 Peter's thought' ought to at least attempt to justify the statement, especially regarding suffering and eschatology – two prominent features in the OT prophets and the Psalms. Second, 1 Peter is clearly dependent upon early Christian traditions, such as the so-called stone *testimonia* (Ps. 118.22 (Matt. 21.14; Acts 4.11)/Isa. 28.16 (Rom. 9.33)/Isa. 8.14 (Rom. 9.33)), and the Passion Narrative tradition (1 Pet. 2.21–5), which provide warrant from the OT for not only Jesus' suffering but also for Christian suffering, and often with an apocalyptic flavour. If the OT was not insufficient for explaining Jesus' suffering in these earlier traditions, why would it be insufficient for what Peter is trying to do? Third, in 1 Pet. 1.10–12, Peter seems to indicate that he draws from the OT prophets in order to understand, as he puts it, τὰ εἰς Χριστὸν παθήματα καὶ τὰς μετὰ ταῦτα δόξας, or 'the sufferings *until* the Christ and the glories after these things' (1 Pet. 1.11).[97] This seems to suggest that Peter is engaging the OT prophets with a view to understanding Christian suffering until the return

---

[93] Dubis successfully argues that 'apocalyptic extra-biblical' literature is essential to understanding parts of 1 Peter (i.e. 1 Pet. 3.18–22); I fully agree with him here. But this is not the same as demonstrating that the OT is inadequate in explaining the theology of suffering in 1 Peter (Dubis 2002: 44).

[94] For example, regarding 1 Pet. 1.6 he comments that the necessity for suffering is 'grounded in an understanding of certain OT texts that provided scriptural underpinning for the messianic woes concept' (Dubis 2002: 76). See also Dubis 2002: 61, 69, 84, 188.

[95] Dubis 2002: 76. This statement, of course, assumes that the two (scriptural ground and a chronology of eschatological events) are mutually exclusive.

[96] Schutter 1989: 43.

[97] See §6.1 for argumentation regarding this rendering of 1 Pet. 1.11.

of the messiah. And fourth, as I highlighted in the introduction to this chapter, a number of scholars have suggested that the fiery trials imagery of 1 Pet. 1.6–7 and 4.12–13 is derived from Zechariah 13.8–9. Even Dubis concedes that '1 Peter no doubt considers such suffering as necessary because of scriptural warrant', and then in an aside remarks that '1 Pet 1.6–8 alludes to Zech 13.9'; but the potential for this to have shaped 1 Peter's theology of suffering has not been followed up.

Even a cursory survey of Zechariah 9–14 illustrates the potential significance of such an omission. First, like the texts used to construct the concept of Messianic Woes, Zechariah 9–14 contains a number of apocalyptic features – many of the same features, in fact, which were highlighted by Dubis and Webb in their examinations. In keeping with the SBL Apocalypse Group paradigm, Zechariah 9–14 contains (a) prophecies in which past events are associated with eschatological salvation (e.g. Zech. 10.8–12; 12.10–13.1), (b) an eschatological crisis (e.g. Zech. 12.10–14.2), (c) judgment upon sinners (e.g. 11.1–3; 11.15–17; 13.8–9), (d) eschatological salvation (e.g. 9.1–17; 13.9; 14.3–21) and (e) depending upon how one regards the oracles, supernatural revelation (9.1; 12.1).[98] Given these characteristics and the methodology that has been employed by Dubis and Webb (i.e. comparing 1 Peter with Jewish apocalyptic literature), it would seem that Zechariah 9–14 should have been given further consideration. Second, Zechariah 9–14 not only contains apocalyptic features, but also offers a detailed eschatological programme that includes a concrete scriptural rationale for the death of the messiah (12.10; 13.7) and a necessary period of fiery trials for the faithful remnant (13.8–9; cf. 1 Pet. 1.7; 4.12) prior to final restoration. It may well be the case that Messianic Woes studies are simply picking up echoes and resonance of Zechariah 9–14 in Jewish Second Temple Literature. Third, as we have already seen, Zechariah 9–14 served as one of the primary sources for the Evangelists and the early church as they interpreted the significance of Jesus' unjust suffering, death and resurrection. It is likely, then, that Zechariah 9–14 was available to our author, and given the predominant theme of 1 Peter (suffering), a plausible source for reflection. Additionally,

---

[98] Regarding apocalyptic characteristics of Zechariah 9–14, Meyers and Meyers (1993: 50) have noted that '[i]n drawing upon the language and imagery of prophetic eschatology, they contribute to the transformation of that eschatology into the kind of apocalyptic literature that becomes characteristic of much of the late Second Temple'. The similarities between Zechariah 9–14 and apocalyptic literature have been extensively examined in the work of Hanson (1975: 280–401), Larkin (1994) and Tigchelaar (1996), and while their conclusions differ, they all nevertheless demonstrate what Meyers and Meyers have noted.

some scholars have suggested that Jesus' own expectation that he would die in the eschatological tribulation was influenced by Zechariah 13–14. Brant Pitre, for example, has argued that

> the evidence suggests that Jesus not only went out to the eschatologically charged site of the Mount of Olives, where the prophet Zechariah had said the Great Tribulation would take place; he also openly declared that he as messianic "shepherd" must be "struck down" in the tribulation, and that his "sheep" (the disciples) would be scattered in the time of testing.[99]

Even if one were to reject the idea that Zechariah 9–14 shaped Jesus' self-understanding, at the very least we can say that it shaped early Christian thought regarding the necessity of suffering.

4.1.3.5 Conclusions regarding the Messianic Woes in 1 Peter

To be clear, I have not denied that Peter affirms the necessity of a tribulation period which is initiated by the messiah and is preliminary to the age to come – the letter itself makes that claim. What I have questioned, however, is whether the Messianic Woes is the basis for such a belief in 1 Peter, first by indicating ambiguities with respect to sources and dependence; second by pointing out an absence of parallels between 1 Peter and Messianic Woes with respect to suffering; third by noting that Dominical Sayings may have had a hand in shaping 1 Peter's theology of suffering; and fourth by pointing out that the OT unduly has been omitted from the discussion. Until these issues are addressed in more detail, it would seem to me that we should be more cautious when we assert that 1 Peter envisions his readers as participating in the Messianic Woes, or that he portrays his readers as enduring exilic suffering. Additionally, I have hinted that Zechariah 9–14, a text which was available and prominent in the early church as a resource for explaining suffering, and which concretely develops the notion of a necessary period of fiery trials which follows the death of the messiah, upon further examination, may yield fruitful insights into the necessity and meaning of suffering in 1 Peter.

---

[99] Pitre 2005: 514. For the details of his argument see *ibid.*: 455–507. Jeremias (1977: 501) also noted parallels between Matt. 14.27–29 and Zech. 13.7–9, but did not credit this to Jesus' own understanding or teaching.

4.1.4   Old Testament prophetic traditions

Although Dennis Johnson's article 'Fire in God's House: Imagery from Malachi 3 in Peter's Theology of Suffering (1 Pet 4:12–19)' has not received much attention in 1 Peter scholarship, it is nevertheless important to engage with it given what I am proposing in this volume.[100] Johnson has argued that the fire imagery of 1 Pet. 4.12 and the judgment language in 1 Pet. 4.17 are derived from Malachi 3, a text which, in his view, undergirds the theology of the entire passage (i.e. 1 Pet. 4.12–19). His argument is founded upon two claims. First, Johnson argues that Peter (1 Pet. 1.6–7) employs metallurgy imagery in order to highlight the authenticating and purifying functions of suffering.[101] And second, he contends that Peter describes his readers as God's temple or sanctuary (οἶκος; 1 Pet. 2.4–8; 4.17), rejecting the proposal put forth by Elliott in which οἶκος is understood to be a reference to a household or family.[102] According to Johnson, these two themes (i.e. the purifying function of suffering and God's temple as a metaphor for God's people) converge in 1 Pet. 4.12–19 and Malachi 3, where according to both texts God comes to his temple in order to cleanse and judge (Mal. 3.2–3; 1 Pet. 4.12,14,17), where fiery trials, rather than being a sign of God's absence or punishment, are in fact an indication of his presence (Mal. 3.2–3; 1 Pet. 4.14) and where the process of judgment commences with 'the house of God' but then 'moves out to consume the godless and disobedient' (Mal. 3.5–6; 4.1; 1 Pet. 4.17–18).[103] From this, Johnson concludes that 1 Pet. 4.12–19 draws on Malachi 3 in order to present the church as the new temple of God and the presence of God 'as a refining fire'.[104]

In due course, I will offer an alternative reading of 4.12–19 that will challenge some of the claims that Johnson makes. Here, however, I wish to underscore four features of his argument that are problematic. First, as I have already indicated in response to the other proposals, it is questionable whether the metallurgy imagery in 1 Pet. 1.6–7; 4.12 is in fact principally being used to highlight the purifying virtues of suffering. If I am right, this would undercut one pillar of his argument. Second, and in a related manner, it is hard to understand why purification by fire, at least in the way that Johnson envisions it, would be a necessary and important theme in 1 Peter given the manner in which the readers are described: having returned to the shepherd (2.25), or having placed their faith and hope in God (1.21), they have been 'ransomed from the futile

---

[100] Johnson 1986.   [101] *Ibid.*: 287.   [102] *Ibid.*: 289, 291–3.
[103] *Ibid.*: 286–93.   [104] *Ibid.*: 293.

ways of their forefathers' (1.18), their souls have been purified (1.22), they have been born anew (1.3,23), they are now a 'holy nation', they have been healed so that they may die to sin and live for righteousness (2.24), they have clear consciences (3.16,21), they no longer join the Gentiles in licentious living (4.3) and they are a spiritual οἶκος and a holy priesthood capable (now) of offering spiritual sacrifices which are pleasing to God through Jesus Christ (2.5).[105] This description (especially 2.5) does not concord with Mal. 3.3, in which God manifests himself as a refining fire in order to purify the Levites *until* they are one day able to present offerings to YHWH in righteousness. Again, I underscore that in 1 Peter the 'priesthood' *already* is capable of presenting acceptable offerings, and yet the 'fire' still remains.

Third, it is unnecessary and incorrect to define οἶκος as exclusively either a temple/sanctuary, or a household/family. In 1 Pet. 2.4–10 we see the blending of metaphors: the people that are referred to as the οἶκος are also an ἱεράτευμα which 'offers' spiritual sacrifices. Syntactically, it is best to understand the phrase οἶκος πνευματικός (along with λίθοι ζῶντες) to be in apposition to αὐτοί in the main clause αὐτοί οἰκοδομεῖσθε, and to understand the clause εἰς ἱεράτευμα ἅγιον ἀνενέγκαι πνευματικὰς θυσίας εὐπροσδέκτους τῷ θεῷ διὰ 'Ιησοῦ Χριστοῦ as dependent upon the main clause. With this in view, the living stones that are being built are also those that offer the sacrifices, leaving room to understand οἶκος as both a reference to a people as well as a building – but not necessarily a temple. Therefore, even if Johnson were correct in asserting that in the LXX οἶκος never refers to a community or household when joined with the genitive θεοῦ, in the context of 1 Peter it is most likely being used in this way.[106] What is more, it appears that Johnson has overlooked one significant instance in the LXX where οἶκος θεοῦ is clearly a reference to a community – Zech. 12.8, where the ὁ οἶκος Δαυιδ is ὡς οἶκος θεοῦ. The significance of this will be explored in Chapter 5.

Finally, in 1 Peter fire is never equated with God's presence. Instead, the fire is likened to the 'various trials', the variety of ways in which the Anatolian Christians experience suffering (see 1.6–7; 4.12); nowhere is God made out to be the agent of such trials. If anything, reading 1 Peter as a whole leaves the impression that the agents of the fiery trials are principally those who ridicule and ostracize the Anatolian Christians

---

[105] Marius Reiser (1994: 175) helpfully points out that the texts that are often put forth as standing behind 1 Pet. 4.12–17 (e.g. Ezek. 9.6; Jer. 25.29) actually speak of a judgment that annihilates rather than one that purifies for the purpose of transformation.

[106] *Pace* Johnson 1986: 291.

(1 Pet. 2.12,20; 3.9,16; 4.4,14).[107] That God is present in the 'fiery' trials to comfort and strengthen, and that such trials are within the scope of God's foreknowledge and will (1.2; 4.19) is without question (see 1.5; 4.19; 5.7); but this is not to be confused with God's presence 'as fire'.

4.1.5   Conclusions

In §4.1 I have analyzed several proposed sources for the fiery trials imagery of 1 Peter. In each case I have highlighted parallels with features found in 1 Peter. However, I have also indicated a number of inadequacies that make each of the proposed sources problematic, and in some cases highly unlikely. This analysis, then, has provided added warrant for a detailed study of Zechariah 9–14 and the fiery trials of 1 Peter.

4.2   The fiery trials of 1 Peter in context

A close examination of 1 Pet. 1.6–7 and 4.12 and their wider contexts will reveal that the fiery trials imagery, although not entirely incompatible with the imagery found in Wis. 3.4–6, Sir. 2.1–8, Prov. 17.3; 27.2 and Seneca's *On Prov.* 5.10, is nevertheless being used differently. Two distinctions in particular will be highlighted in this section. First, in the proposed precursor texts that I have just surveyed, the principal emphasis of the metallurgy metaphor is either the pedagogical, character-forming value of suffering, or the purifying effects that suffering brings about; the stress, then, is on the inherent benefits of suffering. As we will see, while these aspects of suffering are not absolutely negated in 1 Peter, they are nevertheless not of primary import.[108] Second, with perhaps the exception of Mal. 3.2, the proposed precursor texts are *not* addressing the necessity of suffering as a part of a wider unfolding eschatological programme, which as we will see, is the case in both Zechariah 13.8–9 as well as 1 Peter.[109]

---

[107] 1 Pet. 5.8 may inculpate the devil, the roaring lion who seeks someone to devour, as the ultimate agent who animates the humans to antagonize Christians.

[108] For this reason, I think that James 1.2–4 and Rom. 5.1–5 are often erroneously compared to 1 Pet. 1.5–7.

[109] This is not to deny that Wis. 3.4–6 and Sir. 2.1–8 have eschatological references, but simply to point out that they are not offering an eschatological programme like 1 Peter or Zechariah 9–14, which includes suffering as a necessary/predicted component.

4.2.1   First Peter 1.6–7 in context

We turn, then, to an examination of the first appearance of the fiery trials imagery, which is embedded within a larger section that many regard as the letter's *exordium*/or blessing (1.3–12).[110] It appears that one of the principal functions of this particular *exordium* is to orient the readers, that is, to direct them to a proper understanding of their present circumstances – in light of the death (1.2) and resurrection (1.3) of Jesus Christ. More particularly, this section of the letter not only seeks to help the readers understand who they are now that they have professed allegiance to Jesus, but also to point out *where* they are with respect to God's unfolding eschatological programme.[111] Said in another way, the *exordium* seeks not only to address the question, Who are you? but also, *When* are you?[112]

This kind of theological-eschatological orientation that I am suggesting is hinted at in the letter prescript (1.1–2), where Peter identifies his readers with the initially perplexing epithet ἐκλεκτοί παρεπίδημοι (1.1). The meaning of this phrase, especially παρεπίδημος, has been the topic of debate for several decades now.[113] I contend that much of the discussion has revolved around word studies and socio-historical reconstructions that take us far from the actual argument of 1 Peter itself. For reasons that will become clear, I would suggest that the epithet is best understood as a shorthand for a predominant theme of 1 Peter,[114] which is initially developed in the *exordium* (1.3–12) and the first main section of the letter-body (1.13–2.10): followers of Jesus are the

---

[110] 'Rhetorically, vv.3–12 function for Peter's letter as the exordium, the purpose of which is to create a good atmosphere, preparing the audience to receive the instruction that will follow and introducing the main elements of the letter' (Green 2007a: 22). Lamau (1988: 110) writes: 'Ce passage forme une unité de sens, que ne relève pas de l'eulogie proprement dite . . . mais en constitue une sorte de base doctrinale tout en commandant la parénèse qui suit.' See also Thurén 1990: 90–1; Cervantes Gabarrón 1991a: 106; Tite 1997: 22. See §6.1 regarding the structure and strategy of 1 Peter. Achtemeier 1996: 90; Jobes 2005: 79; Witherington 2007: 73, who also references Cicero *De or.* 2.80.325; Quintilian *Inst.* 4.1.23–7).

[111] Witherington (2007: 75) remarks that '[t]his exordium signals that we are dealing with future-oriented rhetoric'.

[112] This point is drawn out nicely by Bechtler 1998: 126–35. My reading will seek to add dimension and texture to his descriptive account of what he refers to as the liminality of the 1 Peter addressees.

[113] E.g. Elliott 1981: 23–70; Chin 1991; Feldmeier 1992: 5–52; Bechtler 1998: 70–82; Seland 2005: 39–78; Horrell 2009: 187–91.

[114] Achtemeier (1996: 80): 'the opening two verses set the stage for what is to follow in the letter in terms of content and themes'. Rendtorff (1951: 18) rightly contended that 1.1–2 encapsulates the letter's entire thematic thrust; see also Tite 1997.

remnant sojourners of a second exodus, faithfully awaiting their prepared inheritance.[115]

The *exordium*, then, begins to put flesh on the epithet, first by highlighting all that awaits those who have been 'born-anew' through the resurrection of Jesus Christ from among the dead (1.3). They have a living hope (1.3), an incorruptible inheritance that is kept in heaven for them (1.4), a prepared salvation which is to be revealed in the last time (1.5) – in which they even now rejoice, and which is the *telos* of their faithfulness (1.9).[116] Peter emphasizes that the outworking of this eschatological salvation occupied the attention of and perplexed both the prophets (1.10–11) as well as the angels (1.12); but he also notes that the when and how have now been revealed in the proclamation of the gospel, which he curiously leaves undefined (1.11–12).[117]

These glimpses into the final stage of God's eschatological programme are balanced by a set of passages that address the trying circumstances of the letter's addressees, which, as we have already learned, principally consisted of verbal abuse and social ostracism. Those awaiting the incorruptible inheritance are in the meantime guarded by the power of God (τοὺς ἐν δυνάμει θεοῦ φρουρουμένους) *until* (εἰς) the 'last time' (1.5).[118] Here I will underscore that the language of 1.5 suggests a rudimentary

---

[115] Goppelt (1982: 152): 'Peter views the church as being on the march, like Israel in the wilderness.' Martin (1992: 152) writes, '[t]hey have embarked upon an eschatological journey that takes them from their new birth to the eschaton . . . the new birth has taken place in the past, and the reception of salvation in the eschaton remains in the future'. According to the prescript, their status as ἐκλεκτοὶ παρεπίδημοι is in keeping with the foreknowledge of God the Father (which I take to be a circumlocution for 'in keeping with the Scriptures'); they are enabled by the sanctifying power of the Spirit; and they have been granted this status because of the obedience and sacrificial death of Jesus.

[116] Michaels (1988: 27, 30) has argued that ἐν ᾧ in the phrase ἐν ᾧ ἀγαλλιᾶσθε is to be understood temporally (i.e. 'then'), and that ἀγαλλιᾶσθε, while it bears the inflection of a present tense verb, should be regarding as having a future sense. Grammatically, this is certainly possible. However, in the near context (1.8) 'rejoicing' is clearly an activity done in the present.

[117] For more see §6.1.

[118] As Horrell (1997) has demonstrated, it is difficult to adjudicate whether διὰ πίστεως (1.5) refers to God's faithfulness in sustaining Christians, or whether the faith (or faithfulness) of Christians is in view. It is possible, and perhaps likely, that both aspects are in view given that the letter stresses both the Christian duty to entrust themselves to God's protection (e.g. 4.19) as well as the fact that suffering is in keeping with the will of God (4.19). (Regarding the deliberate rhetorical strategy of ambiguity in 1 Peter see Thurén 1990.) However, I would argue that the stress in 1.5 is on the faithfulness of Christians, not least because the theme is repeated in 1.7, and again in 1.9 (κομιζόμενοι τὸ τέλος τῆς πίστεως [ὑμῶν] σωτηρίαν ψυχῶν). Furthermore, given the preponderance of temporal references in the passage, I would argue that διὰ is to be understood temporally such that the phrase could be translated 'throughout [the course of your] faithfulness' (BDAG: 222, A, 2).

sequence that involves a time of trouble that will require God's protection, and a prepared salvation (σωτηρίαν ἑτοίμην) that is to be revealed in the last time (ἐν καιρῷ ἐσχάτῳ). It also projects optimism – a stalwart confidence in God's sustaining power through the duration of this time of trouble until salvation is finally manifested. For this, the addressees can rejoice; but this is tempered by the reality that the road to their inheritance[119] will necessarily require, as our author puts it, ποικίλοι πειρασμοί (1.6).[120] Given the paradigmatic, orienting function of the *exordium*/blessing, it seems quite significant that their difficulties in the present are described as πειρασμοί instead of the more characteristic term we find in the letter, suffering (πάσχω and its cognates are used sixteen times in the letter).[121] At the very least, this suggests that our author wants his readers to interpret their suffering in a particular light. But, what does the term πειρασμός point to? Several scholars, drawing on Emilie Sander's work, have argued that πειρασμός should be understood as a technical term that refers to a necessary period of suffering for God's people prior to restoration or eschatological salvation.[122] While I am sympathetic to this idea, I will argue that πειρασμός in 1 Peter does not point to some supposedly widespread, scholarly construct known as

---

[119] For κληρονομία as a circumlocution for arriving and possessing the promised land see Num. 34.2; 36.2; Deut. 12.9; Josh. 1.15; 13.1; Judg. 2.6; 18.1; 21.23; 2 Chron. 6.27; 31.1; Pss. 134.12; 135.21,22; Jer. 2.7; 3.19; 16.18; Ezek. 11.15; 25.4, 10; Zech. 9.4; for the use of κληρονομία in conjunction with the promise of restoration see Isa. 49.8; Jer. 12.25; Pss. 2.8;67.10; 110.6; Ezek. 45.1. Elsewhere in the NT the term is used in association with salvation (Acts 7.5; 13.33; 20.32; Eph. 1.11,14; Col. 3.24) and the second exodus (Heb. 9.15; 11.8). Hebrews 3–4 is significant because there is a connection between suffering and the wilderness, but without the optimism that is offered in 1 Peter; see also Rev. 21.7–8; 12.1–8.

[120] Here (*pace* Feldmeier 2008:16, n.9) I would concur with Michaels (1988: 28), who contends that εἰ δέον 'should be read as a first class conditional clause, referring in this instance to what is actually the case: i.e., not "if need be" but "since it is necessary"'. So also Achtemeier 1996: 101.

[121] Similarly Goppelt (1993: 37) notes that '[t]his affliction is not characterized by the LXX technical term διωγμός ("persecution") ... not even in 3:14, where the pronouncement of blessing upon the "persecuted" is appropriated'. Goppelt goes on, however, to also reject the apocalyptic meaning of the word.

[122] Sander 1966. Dubis (2002: 86–95) connects the concept of testing (πειρασμός and πειράζω) with YHWH's testing of the Israelites in the wilderness (Exod. 15.25; 16.4; Deut. 8.2; 13.3). Pitre (2005: 148–53) has argued that the term πειρασμός found in Matt. 6.13//Luke 11.14 is best regarded as the time of eschatological tribulation, which is part of a wider programme that includes suffering for the messiah, but also for his followers (cf. Rev. 3.10). He also points to connections between πειρασμός and the exodus/wilderness tradition (Deut. 4.27–34; 7.19; 29.3) and how the first exodus 'testings' could serve as a prototype for a future time of tribulation (2005: 152). His reading differs from 1 Peter, because he contends that the πειρασμοί precede the New Exodus (Pitre 2005: 216).

Messianic Woes, but instead more specifically to the necessary fiery trials that are anticipated in Zech. 13.8–9.

The elaboration in 1.6–7 may offer further clues. Here, it is neither the process nor the inherent goodness of testing that is emphasized, but rather the certainty of the outcome. Syntactically, 1 Pet. 1.6–7 stresses that a variety of trials is *necessary* and that the addressees' proven faithfulness (τὸ δοκίμιον ὑμῶν τῆς πίστεως) will result in (ἵνα)[123] their eschatological praise, glory and honour (something they lack in the present social setting in which they are shamed for their allegiances) when Jesus Christ is revealed (1.7).[124] The metallurgy imagery is employed *not* in a comparative fashion that illustrates that just as gold is refined in fire so too the Anatolian Christians will be refined through adversity. Instead, the fiery trials imagery is used in a *contrastive* manner to affirm with certainty the outcome of the final stage of the eschatological programme for those who have aligned themselves with Jesus: gold *perishes* when tested through fire (χρυσίου τοῦ ἀπολλυμένου διὰ πυρὸς δὲ δοκιμαζομένου). But the Anatolian Christians, whose proven faithfulness is of greater worth than gold, on the other hand, will indeed pass through the fire and not perish. The fiery trials, then, are characterized as a necessary step towards the certain culmination of God's eschatological programme, which includes the survival of a thoroughly tested remnant people.

As the referential διό indicates, the first main section of the letter-body (1.13–2.10) seeks to further develop how the readers are to understand this necessary period of fiery πειρασμοί, primarily by appropriating imagery and texts which refer to either the exodus and wilderness journey, or the promised second exodus. In 1.13, for example, our author exhorts his readers to 'gird up the loins of their understanding' as they put their hope in the grace to be brought to them when Jesus Christ is revealed (1.13);[125]

---

123   BDAG: 476, 3.

124   The genitive τῆς πίστεως in the phrase τὸ δοκίμιον ὑμῶν τῆς πίστεως is best understood as an attributed genitive. As such, the head noun, τὸ δοκίμιον (understood as 'genuineness as result of a test' (BDAG: 256, 2)), functions as the adjective, and the genitive, τῆς πίστεως, syntactically speaking functions as the head noun; the phrase, then, should be translated 'proven faithfulness'. As Wallace (1996: 91) points out, this manner of construction is often used to emphasize the adjectival idea, which in the case of 1 Pet. 1.7 is to highlight with confidence the proven fidelity of the readers with respect to their allegiance to Jesus in the midst of trials. See also Michaels (1988: 7), who notes that 'the phrase τὸ δοκίμιον ὑμῶν τῆς πίστεως is duplicated in James in 1.3, but with a subtle difference in meaning. In James it refers to *a process*, but in Peter it is 'virtually equivalent to faith itself'. I would point out as well that in James the basis for rejoicing is in the inherent value of trials, which ultimately produce character. In 1 Peter, however, the basis for rejoicing is in the certainty of salvation for those who maintain faithfulness.

125   Cf. Exod. 12.11.

they are urged to conduct themselves with fear during the time of their *sojourning* (παροικία; 1.17), since they have been redeemed with the precious *blood of the lamb* who was without defect or blemish, namely Jesus (1.19).

Within this narrative, Peter draws attention to the admonition given to the original wilderness sojourners, in which they were urged to 'be holy in all you do' (1 Pet. 1.15). He follows this exhortation by quoting the often repeated refrain from Leviticus, a foundational wilderness text, 'be holy, for I am holy' (1 Pet. 1.16; Lev. 11.44,45; 19.2; 20.7).

Several other significant OT texts are drawn on in this first section of the letter-body, which confirm that our author understands his readers to be participating in a second exodus/wilderness journey. Their new birth (1.3,23) is said to be in keeping with the word that was announced in Isa. 40.6–8, a passage that many scholars have noted serves as the prologue to Isa. 40–55 and its programme of restoration, regularly described in terms of a second exodus.[126] This is followed by an allusion in 1 Pet. 2.3 to Ps. 34.8, 'taste and see that the Lord is good'. It is likely that Psalm 34 has become operative here and in 1 Pet. 3.10–12 because it models behaviour which is fitting for sojourning righteous sufferers who are facing opposition while they wait for the fullness of what YHWH has promised to come.[127] The variant reading in LXX Psalm 33 (MT 34) seems to confirm this: whereas the righteous sufferer in the Hebrew text is delivered from all his 'fears', in the Greek variant he exclaims, 'I sought the Lord, and he heard me and rescued me from all of my sojournings' (LXX Ps. 33.4; ἐξεζήτησα τὸν κύριον, καὶ ἐπήκουσέν μου καὶ ἐκ πασῶν τῶν παροικιῶν μου ἐρρύσατό με).[128]

The final two verses of this section bring the developing theme to a climax. In 1 Pet. 2.9, our author conflates terms which are derived from Exod. 19.5–6 and Isa. 43.20–1: 'you are a chosen people [Isa. 43.20], a royal priesthood [Exod. 19.6], a holy nation [Exod. 19.6], a people belonging to God [Exod. 19.5], that you may declare the praises of him [Isa. 43.21] who called you out of darkness into his wonderful light'. In the literary setting of Exod. 19.1–6, YHWH has gathered his freshly redeemed and newly formed people in the wilderness at the foot of Mount

---

[126] E.g. Westermann 2001: 33.

[127] For a comprehensive analysis of the use of Psalm 34 in 1 Peter see Woan 2004. For a brief summary of her analysis see Chapter 6, note 47.

[128] Woan (2004: 229) argues that the author of 1 Peter has chosen Psalm 34 because it 'contains many features that would make it an ideal scriptural source for imagery about a righteous sufferer'. One feature that Woan has neglected is the fact that the Greek version of the psalm is set in the context of a wilderness sojourn.

Sinai, and has commissioned them to be a nation of priests who have a communal vocation to reflect YHWH's character and will. It appears that our author's appropriation of Exod. 19.5–6, then, is intended to evoke in his readers the call of recapitulating the wilderness journey, this time in fidelity to YHWH.

This recapitulating call is confirmed by our author's use of Isaiah 43 in 1 Pet. 2.9, where he draws his readers, not to the first exodus, but rather to the promise of a second exodus developed throughout Isa. 40–55.[129] It is within this section of Isaiah 43, however, that the new exodus theme predominates: YHWH speaks of a new day to come, a restoration that is likened to Israel's redemption from Egypt; a restoration in which He will ransom His exiled people, renew His covenant with them, form them as a new people (cf. 1 Pet. 1.3,23) and make a way in the desert for their journey towards their inheritance (cf. 1 Pet. 1.4; κληρονομία). That Peter envisions his readers as already redeemed from exile is further confirmed by his allusion to Isa. 43.21 and 42.12 in the latter part of 1 Pet. 2.9 (ὅπως τὰς ἀρετὰς ἐξαγγείλητε τοῦ ἐκ σκότους ὑμᾶς καλέσαντος εἰς τὸ θαυμαστὸν αὐτοῦ φῶς). In the original literary context, these passages from Isaiah charge YHWH's people to proclaim his saving wonders once they have been redeemed from Babylonian exile.[130] The appropriation of Isa. 43.20–1 betrays that Peter understands this promised second exodus to have been actualized in Jesus, who, as we learn later in 1 Pet. 2.23–5, is not only the unblemished, slain lamb (1.18; 2.22–3), but also the pierced shepherd-king (2.25; 5.4), who has redeemed (healed) and gathered his scattered, straying sheep through his sacrificial death. Our author's appropriation of Isa. 43.20 may also shed light on his understanding of ἐκλεκτός in 1.1. It is likely that, in keeping with the usage in Isaiah 40–66, our author regards the 'elect' as the faithful remnant who are sustained by God as they journey in the second exodus (Isa. 41.8–9; 43.1–7; 44.1–2; 49.7; 65.8–9).[131]

First Pet. 2.10 concludes with an allusion to Hosea 2.23. This refrain from Hosea is the climax of a prophetic oracle in which YHWH declares that he will deliver Israel in spite of her idolatry and radical infidelity,

[129] Anderson 1962; Stuhmueller 1970: 59–98; Watts 1990; Westermann 2001: 127–9.

[130] In the LXX ἀρετή is used to speak of God's saving acts in the first exodus, and his future saving acts in the new exodus of Isaiah.

[131] Pitre (2005: 322–3) successfully argues that in Mark 13.20 ἐκλεκτός is to be understood as faithful remnant, and is connected with the Noachic remnant that was preserved in the flood. He also demonstrates that some in the second temple period (1 Enoch 93.8, Dead Sea Scrolls community) used the concept of election to refer to themselves as the eschatological remnant of YHWH (*ibid.*: 323–5).

alluring her to the wilderness where 'she will respond as in the days of her youth, as at the time when she came out of the land of Egypt' (Hosea 2.15). According to Hosea 2, it is here, in the desert, having been redeemed from Babylonian exile, where YHWH will proclaim that those who once were not a people are now a people of God; those who once had not received mercy have now received mercy.

This brief survey of 1 Peter 1.1–2.10 fills out, in my view, the picture Peter wishes to paint when he opens his letter with the epithet ἐκλεκτοὶ παρεπίδημοι. The term ἐκλεκτός reminds his readers that they are the faithful remnant of the new exodus, who are sustained by God until their prepared salvation is revealed.[132] That they are elect παρεπίδημοί reiterates that, for now, their faithfulness is to be expressed in the wilderness, where, like their sojourning predecessors, they will be tested until they reach their inheritance.[133]

Before we move on to discuss 1 Pet. 4.12 in its context I must point out that this analysis of 1 Pet. 1.1–2.10 challenges an increasingly prevalent view which contends that Peter regards his readers as still living in exile. Dubis, for example, argues that the suffering/glory motif of 1 Peter (1.11; 4.13; 5.1,10) is best understood in terms of exile and restoration respectively.[134] Accordingly, 1 Peter 'portrays the

---

[132] '1 Pet. is the only NT work in which ἐκλεκτός has from the very outset thematic significance. Here everything is worked out in terms of this controlling concept' (Schrenk, taken from Elliott 2000: 446).

[133] Laniak (2006: 225–9) develops a similar line of thought, concluding that 'Peter encourages these churches as 'aliens and sojourners', understanding their identity as God's renewed covenant community, freshly formed in a new wilderness of testing, and anticipating glory in their future home' (*ibid.*: 225). Justin Martyr, in a rather creative fashion, understood the final destination of Christians in a similar manner, though it is difficult to know whether he got this from 1 Peter:

> Why do you Trypho never inquire why the name Hosea, the son of Nun, which his father gave him, was changed to Jesus [=Joshua in Hebrew]? Especially since not only was his name changed, but also, after becoming Moses successor, he alone, of all his contemporaries who fled Egypt, led the rest of the people into the Holy Land. *And just as he, not Moses, conducted the people into the Holy Land and distributed it by lot among those who entered, so also will Jesus the Christ gather together the dispersed people and distribute the good land to each*, though not in the same manner.
> (Justin Martyr, *Dialogue with Trypho*, 113.3; italics mine)

'For, *Joshua gave them an inheritance for a time only*, since he was not Christ our God, nor the Son of God; but *Jesus, after the holy resurrection, will give us an inheritance for eternity . . . After his coming the Father will, through him, renew heaven and earth*' (Justin Martyr, Dialogue with Trypho 113.4; italics mine).

[134] Dubis 2002: 46. Andrew Mbuvi (2007: 28) contends that 'the idea of exile' is the controlling metaphor for 1 Peter (for full argument see *ibid.*[3]: 10–69); and Joel Green (2007a: 18) writes that '1 Peter invites a reading among those who are ready to embrace the

suffering of the readers as exilic suffering'.[135] How does he arrive at such a conclusion?

Drawing on James M. Scott and N. T. Wright, Dubis first asserts that most Jews living prior to and during the time of the composition of 1 Peter understood themselves to still be living in exile. He further contends that 1 Peter is seeking to address the question of when restoration from exile will occur.[136] He then points to passages such as 1 Pet. 1.1, 1.17, 2.11–12, in which we find the words παρεπίδημος, διασπορά, παροικία and πάροικος, and insists that these words refer to exile, yet without offering any sufficient argumentation for why this must necessarily be the case.[137] From there, Dubis tries to explain the 'apparent' (in his view) confusion in 1 Peter between references that appear to place the recipients in exile while other passages such as 1 Pet. 1.13–22, which as even he notes 'brim with allusions to the exodus', seem to place them in the new exodus.[138] How can they be in exile on the one hand, and in the new exodus on the other? Dubis offers two solutions. First, he explains that Peter got his cues from Isa. 52.4, where Israel's sojourn in Egypt is linked to deliverance from Babylonian exile. From this he concludes that 'modern readers should find no consternation in 1 Peter's oscillation between exile and exodus themes... Indeed, 1 Peter regards these two themes as complementary rather than antagonistic to one another.'[139] Second, he argues that Peter regarded Messianic Woes as the necessary transition from exile to restoration, in striking continuity with early Judaism.[140]

I have already highlighted some significant problems at the macro-level with respect to Dubis' construction of Messianic Woes in 1 Peter, in which I raise the issue of whether the concept of Messianic Woes is in fact as prevalent within Judaism as he (and others) would lead us to believe. Here, then, I briefly wish to underscore at least four problems with understanding suffering in 1 Peter as exilic suffering.

---

identity and status of exiles in the dispersion'. Achtemeier (1996: 80, n.16): 'Although there are echoes in 1 Peter of the exodus and the establishment of the covenant in the wilderness, the major prototype of the Christian community's experience in the world is here [1 Pet. 1.1] furnished by the exile.'

[135] Dubis 2002: 46.   [136] *Ibid.*: 46–7.

[137] *Ibid.*: 48. Similarly, Achtemeier (1996: 80–2) translates παρεπίδημος as 'exile', failing to connect the word to the wider themes of exodus/new exodus found in 1 Pet. 1.3–2.10. Instead, he comments (1996: 80) that 'the theme of exile, announced in the first verse, serves as an introduction to the larger section 1.3–2.10, and with the addition of πάροικοι in 2.11, continues to underline the discussion of 2.11–4.11'.

[138] Dubis 2002: 50.   [139] *Ibid.*: 51.

[140] *Ibid.*: 59–62. Dubis (*ibid.*: 61) notes how his conclusion compares with the finding of N. T. Wright (1996: 576–7).

First, our survey of 1 Pet. 1.1–2.10 has demonstrated that Peter is clearly affirming that restoration *has already occurred* in and through Jesus: they are a newly formed people (1.3,23), redeemed by the unblemished lamb (1.18–19), declared to be a people of God again (2.9–10), healed (2.24) and returned to the eschatological shepherd (2.25) – all images that come from the OT prophets and point to restoration. Even Dubis acknowledges this as he works through the appropriation of OT passages in the letter: 'restoration from exile has happened in Christ'.[141] Second, as several studies have indicated, παρεπίδημος, παροικία and πάροικος have a range of meanings which can just as easily refer to wilderness sojourning as to exile.[142] Given the predominant theme of exodus/second exodus in 1 Pet. 1.1–2.10, it would seem to me that asserting that these words refer to the exile rather than wilderness sojourning runs against the grain of the text, and would require special argumentation. Third, as Peter Ackroyd has concluded in his seminal study *Exile and Restoration* (1968),

> exile is not comparable with the period of the Exodus. For at no point in the Exodus narratives is it suggested that the people of Egypt were brought into subjection by reason of their own sinfulness . . . it is true that estimates of [exile] varied, but in general the concentration is on the punishment, acknowledged to be just, of the people's failure.[143]

And finally, the claim that 1 Peter picks up his cues from Isa. 52.4 is dependent upon a spurious allusion to Isaiah 53 in 1 Pet. 1.18 that is asserted but never demonstrated. Curiously, he acknowledges that in Isa. 52.4 παροικῆσαι can be translated 'to sojourn', but he is unwilling to translate its cognate, παροικία, in a similar fashion in 1 Pet. 1.17.[144] In a qualified sense, I would agree with Dubis that exile and exodus are complementary rather than antagonistic, but how we understand this is essential. They are complementary in the sense that return from exile *precedes* the wilderness sojourning, where there will be testing and suffering. But this does not mean that the wilderness sojourn should be understood equally as exilic suffering. Said in another way, exile and exodus/new exodus do not appear to be synonymous for Peter. Exile is in the past, where they previously were; 'new exodus/fiery trials' is their

---

[141] Dubis 2002: 48.
[142] Chin 1991; Feldmeier 1992: 5–52; Martin 1992: 188–200; Bechtler 1998: 70–82; Seland 2005: 39–78; Horrell 2009: 187–91.
[143] Ackroyd 1968: 239. Cf. Martin 1992: 144–61.   [144] Dubis 2002: 51.

present 'location'. The one issue, then, that still needs to be addressed is what we are to make of the term διασπορά, for it seems to be particularly linked to notions of exile.[145] In Chapter 5 I will argue that the term διασπορά has not been appropriated in order to shape the identity of the 1 Peter addressees – except to the extent that the addressees understand themselves no longer to be living in exile, 'scattered' and under God's wrath. But first, in keeping with my outline, an examination of 1 Pet. 4.12 is in order.

4.2.2   First Peter 4.12 in context

There was a time when 1 Pet. 4.12–19 was, for a variety of reasons, thought to be originally independent of 1 Pet. 1.1–4.11.[146] In particular, some scholars tried to argue that 2.11–4.11 was written to those who had yet to experience suffering, whereas 4.12–5.11 sought to address those who were presently undergoing acute persecution.[147] A number of recent studies, however, have for the most part put the partition and composite theories to rest, demonstrating an organic coherence between 1 Pet. 1.1–4.11 and 4.12–5.14.[148] Achtemeier, in his review of the discussion, comments that '[a]s a result of continuing work on the content and style of 1 Peter, the emerging scholarly consensus is that far from being a composite work, the letter must rather be seen as a literary unity'.[149]

The recent interest in Primopetrine studies with respect to the literary structure and rhetorical strategy of the letter has resulted in a number of scholars observing a dependent relationship between 1 Pet. 1.1–4.11 and 4.12–19.[150] This is clearly the case with respect to 1 Pet. 1.3–9 and

---

[145] Achtemeier (1996: 80, n.16), for example, argues that 'although there are echoes in 1 Peter of the exodus and the establishment of the covenant in the wilderness (e.g., 1:16, 19; 2:9) . . . the major prototype of the Christian community's experience in the world is here [1.1; διασπορά] furnished by the exile'.

[146] The partition and compilation theories regarding 1 Pet. 1.1–4.11 and 4.12–5.14 are legion. See, e.g., Perdelwitz 1911; Bornemann 1919; Streeter 1929: 129–34; Windisch 1951: 82; Cross 1954; Moule 1956; Boismard 1961; Reicke 1964: 74–5; Beare 1970: 25–8.

[147] E.g. Moule 1956.

[148] See, e.g., Michaels 1988: xxxiv–xl; 257–8; Schutter 1989: 19–31; Thurén 1990: 79–88; Martin 1992: 41–79; 240–2; Achtemeier 1996: 58–62; 304–5; Tite 1997; Elliott 2000: 20–83; 768–70; Jobes 2005: 53–6; 285–6.

[149] Achtemeier 1996: 61. For a concise summary of the composite theories see *ibid.*: 58–62.

[150] Elliott (2000: 770) contends that '1 Peter 4:12–19 recapitulates and expands on what has already been stated on the issue of suffering. This unit does not mark a caesura or break in the line of thought but a crescendo'. See also Michaels 1988: 258; Schutter 1989: 74–6; Bechtler 1998: 199.

1 Pet. 4.12–19, where in both passages we find a number of shared themes: fiery (πῦρ/πύρωσις) trials (πειρασμοί/πειρασμός) which are necessary/ to be expected (1.6–7/4.12); rejoicing (χαίρω; χαρά; ἀγαλλιάω) in the midst of suffering (1.6–8/4.13); the expected revelation (ἀποκάλυψις) of Jesus (1.7/4.13); salvation (σωτηρία/σῴζω) of ψυχαί in the appointed time (καιρός; 1.5,9/4.17–19); as well as confidence that the faithful, sustained by God, will survive the trials, which are a part of God's overall plan (1.5–7/4.19). These striking parallels have led a number of scholars to conclude that the fiery trials imagery which is appropriated in 4.12 intentionally builds upon the usage in 1.6–7. Elliott, for example, comments that '[s]ince our author has already used this metaphor in 1:6–7 in speaking of faith as more precious than "perishable gold tested by fire," this sense of *pyrōsis* is clearly implied here as well'.[151] Given the nature of an *exordium*, one would expect this to be the case (i.e. the repetition of themes in the body of the letter which were initiated in the *exordium*). But again we must ask, how is this imagery being used? Goppelt argues that the 'fiery ordeal' is to be interpreted 'as a "trial" that *purifies* faith under pain and strengthens it through preservation'.[152] But, as was the case in 1 Pet. 1.6, the notion of purification, while not entirely absent from 4.12, does not appear to be the primary aim of the fire imagery. Instead, similar to what we found in 1 Pet. 1.5–7, the emphasis in 4.12 is on the inevitability of the fiery testing, as well as its authenticating or verifying purpose: Ἀγαπητοί, μὴ ξενίζεσθε τῇ ἐν ὑμῖν πυρώσει πρὸς πειρασμὸν ὑμῖν γινομένῃ ὡς ξένου ὑμῖν συμβαίνοντος. With fresh expression, Peter here is reiterating what he has already stated in 1.5–7: they ought not to be surprised by the fiery testing which comes upon them because, as he has already said, it is a necessary part of a larger eschatological schema, which was hinted at in 1.5–9 and will be outlined in greater detail in 1 Pet. 4.17–19.[153] In keeping with the imagery of 1.7, what they are going through is described in terms of a process of fire (πύρωσις) which serves the primary purpose of testing or ascertaining (πρὸς πειρασμόν) the true extent of their faithfulness.[154] Instead of being

---

[151] Elliott 2000: 772. See also Michaels (1988: 258, 261), who argues that 4.12–13 looks back to being tested by fire, and to final joy in 1.6–8; Selwyn 1958: 221; Achtemeier 1996: 304–6; Dubis 2002: 79; Witherington 2007: 208; Feldmeier 2008: 224. Regarding the term πύρωσις, Emilie Sander (1966: 43–4) has argued that it was a technical term for the eschatological test which the 'elect' must undergo before final vindication.

[152] Goppelt 1993: 314. Emphasis mine.

[153] So also Goppelt 1993: 311. Cf. Michaels 1988: 260.

[154] *Pace* Goppelt (1993: 313), who asserts that πύρωσις ought to be understood as a 'purifying fire' in keeping with its usage in the wisdom traditions of LXX Ps. 65.10 and Prov. 27.21. I would point out that there are other ways to conceive of fire. For example, in

surprised, they are exhorted to rejoice (see 1.6–8) in as much as (καθό) they are partners in 'the "belonging to the messiah" sufferings' (τοῖς τοῦ Χριστοῦ παθήμασιν; 4.13).[155] Since this passage highlights suffering that is experienced particularly 'in the name of Christ' (εἰ ὀνειδίζεσθε ἐν ὀνόματι Χριστοῦ; 4.14),[156] or that is the result of being labelled a Χριστιανός (4.16), in corresponding fashion it seems best to interpret the phrase τοῖς τοῦ Χριστοῦ παθήμασιν (4.13) as the 'of the messiah' sufferings; that is, the sufferings which come from associating oneself with those who demonstrate loyal allegiance to the Christ.[157] This translation of 4.13, which coincides with the thrust of the passage, helps bring out the meaning of κοινωνέω, which is best understood in terms of being partners of or associating with a particular group. This reading also helps explain why those who partner in the 'of Christ' sufferings will rejoice in the revelation of his glory (4.13): those who align themselves now with the shamed Christ and his people, will find honour (i.e. glory) when the Christ is honoured at his return.[158] Additionally, this reading challenges

Daniel 3 fire does not have a purifying function, but instead demonstrates the authenticity of the faithfulness of Daniel's three friends.

[155] Pace Elliott (2000: 774), who translates καθό as 'since' or 'inasmuch as'. First Peter, and in particular 1.5–9, places an emphasis on the ongoing faithfulness of the believers in the face of testing, which will be rewarded with praise, honour and glory in due course. Therefore, it seems best to translate καθό in its more customary sense as a marker of degree (i.e. 'in so far as', or 'to the degree that'); BDAG: 493,2.

[156] Here I would agree with Achtemeier (1996: 308), who argues that the phrase ἐν ὀνόματι Χριστοῦ is probably to be construed as a dative of sphere. Accordingly, they are ridiculed for associating themselves with the name of Christ. See Goppelt (1993: 322–3), who suggests that ἐν ὀνόματι Χριστοῦ should be understood as synonymous with Χριστοῦ ἐστε (cf. Mark 9.41). Michaels (1988: 264) remarks that '[t]o suffer ridicule . . . for Christ's name was to suffer because of one's allegiance to Christ'. He nevertheless takes the phrase to be a dative of cause.

[157] Compare this with 1 Cor. 1.12 (λέγω δὲ τοῦτο ὅτι ἕκαστος ὑμῶν λέγει· ἐγὼ μέν εἰμι Παύλου, ἐγὼ δὲ Ἀπολλῶ, ἐγὼ δὲ Κηφᾶ, ἐγὼ δὲ Χριστοῦ) in which the genitive construction is used to express identification with a group who holds in high esteem a particular figure; associating with this group brought with it a certain perceived societal status. As such, the proper names represented the group with which these people associated. Achtemeier (1996: 324, n.47) suggests that τοῦ Χριστοῦ is an objective genitive that should be translated as 'what is suffered for Christ'. In the end, I want to stress that my reading of the genitive construction derives from the overall thrust of the passage (4.12–19), which, as Martin (1992: 256) has highlighted, 'is dominated by the description of the readers as partners in the sufferings of the Messiah'. In other words, they suffer because they have associated themselves with the messiah.

[158] Both Bechtler (1998) and Campbell (1998) are very helpful in demonstrating how the term 'glory' fits within the letter and within the honour and shame culture, in which 1 Peter was composed and read.

the suggestion that the phrase (τοῖς τοῦ Χριστοῦ παθήμασιν) is a kind of technical term to denote Messianic Woes.[159]

Two passages in 1 Pet. 4.12–19, each of which begins with ὅτι, provide justification for assertions made by Peter, and, as will be argued in Chapter 5, probably provide us with glimpses of the substructure of his theology of suffering. In 1 Pet. 4.14 Peter contends that when his readers are ridiculed 'in the name of Christ' then they are blessed, and further explains this assertion with a possible allusion to Isa. 11.2: ὅτι τὸ τῆς δόξης καὶ τὸ τοῦ θεοῦ πνεῦμα ἐφ' ὑμᾶς ἀναπαύεται.[160] If, as it appears to be the case, Isa. 11.2 is the precursor text in 1 Pet. 4.14, then there are three substantial modifications that have been made:

(1) ἀναπαύσεται (future, 'will rest') has been changed to ἀναπαύεται (present, 'rests').[161] Thus, that which was once regarded to be something that would happen in the future is now regarded as taking place in the present.

(2) The object upon which the Spirit will rest has been changed from ἐπ' αὐτὸν (singular) to ἐφ' ὑμᾶς (plural). In other words, the object is no longer exclusively the messianic 'shoot' or 'root' of Jesse (Isa. 11.1; a scion of David), but instead is now applied to the wider community which identifies with this eschatological Davidic figure.[162]

(3) The genitive τῆς δόξης has been added to the phrase πνεῦμα τοῦ θεοῦ, and the word order has been changed from πνεῦμα

---

[159] Dubis (2002: 101) asserts that the highly eschatological context of 4.13 and 'the apocalyptic flavor of 1 Peter' make a strong case for a messianic woes interpretation of this verse. Because Messianic Woes is a scholarly construct of a number of texts, for Dubis to be correct it would require that the readers were somehow aware of such a tradition. And yet, if that were the case, that is, if Messianic Woes was a well-known, widespread tradition, then why would Peter have to remind them twice (1.6; 4.12) to not be surprised at their suffering? See also Martin (1992: 243), who regards 1.11; 4.13; 5.1 and 5.9 all to be references to the Messianic Woes.

[160] See Achtemeier (1996: 307), who writes that '[t]he εἰ with which the sentence begins, combined with a verb in the indicative mood (ὀνειδίζεσθε), emphasizes the reality of the assumption that Christians will be reproached, and hence has the force not so much of "if" as of "when"'. See also Elliott (2000: 778), who suggests that if this remark is based on the dominical sayings of Jesus which are found in Matt. 5.11–12, then the temporal meaning (i.e. when) is more likely what the author had in view. See also Michaels 1988: 263; Selwyn 1958: 191.

[161] Neither the Hebrew nor the Greek manuscript traditions help to explain this change.

[162] See Gen. Rab. 2.3–4, QpIs^a 8–10 iii 11–25, *Ps. Sol* 17.32,37 and the Targum on Isaiah for messianic interpretations of this passage. For messianic interpretations of Isa. 11.2 in early Christianity see Rom. 15.12, 2 Thess. 2.8 and John 1.32.

τοῦ θεοῦ to τὸ τῆς δόξης καὶ τὸ τοῦ θεοῦ πνεῦμα. There is some debate as to whether the additional genitival phrase is intended to modify πνεῦμα (and if so how it functions in relation to the head noun),[163] or whether it is a substantivized genitival phrase that stands on its own and that points back to the glory mentioned in 1 Pet. 4.13 (ἐν τῇ ἀποκαλύψει τῆς δόξης αὐτοῦ).[164]

What is the basis for these changes?[165] That is, what has compelled Peter to make the imaginative connection between a community that is blessed since it is reviled, and the messianic promise of Isa. 11.2? Additionally, what has prompted our author to take a promise that was originally addressed to the messianic 'shoot' or 'branch' of Jesse (11.1), and apply it now to the messianic community?[166] And finally, why has our author added the genitival phrase τὸ τῆς δόξης to the mix?

Surprisingly, not many have endeavoured to explain why these changes have occurred. Those who do have generally pointed to the Jesus Tradition. Goppelt and Michaels, for instance, both suggest that Peter's insistence on the Spirit resting upon the persecuted community of the messiah has probably been generated from the traditions which are found in Mark 13.11, Luke 12.12 and Matt. 10.20 (i.e. 'When they bring you to trial and hand you over, do not worry beforehand about what you are to say; but say whatever is given you at that time, for it is not you who speak, but the Holy Spirit').[167] This suggestion appears to fit well with the context

---

[163] Michaels (1988: 64–5), for example, thinks the phrase τῆς δόξης both points to 4.13 as well as modifies πνεῦμα. He renders the phrase as follows: 'for the spirit of that glory (i.e. the eschatological glory of Christ mentioned in 4.13), even the spirit of God, is resting upon you'. Elliott (2000: 782) regards the two genitive phrases as a pleonastic hendiadys construction that is best translated as 'the divine spirit of glory'. Elliott adds that the addition of the phrase *glory* 'is consistent with the stress on *glory* in this section (4:13, 14, 16; cf. 4:11d) and throughout the letter and may also have been prompted by the desire to ground the addressees' honor (*makarioi*) explicitly in the honor of God, thus once again linking glory to suffering'.

[164] So Achtemeier (1996: 309), who concludes that such a rendering of the grammar would mean that the sufferers are blessed because they already have a share in the eschatological glory yet to be revealed. Selwyn (1958: 222–4) also regards it as a substantivized genitival phrase, and suggests that *glory* refers to the Shekinah (so also Mbuvi 2007).

[165] There is no evidence from the extant Hebrew or Greek manuscripts that would suggest these changes are due to a textual variant.

[166] To be clear, I recognize that there was a variety of messianic visions and expectations in the first century. I do think, however, that many of the messianic hopes revolved around a coming king, appointed by YHWH, and often (though not always) associated with the eschatological Davidic king. For more see Schürer 1973–87: 2.488–549; Neusner *et al.* 1987; and Wright 1992: 307–20.

[167] Michaels 1988: 264; see also Goppelt 1993: 324.

of 1 Pet. 4.12–19, in which some sort of courtroom arbitration is hinted at.[168] There are two critical problems with this proposal, however. First, this particular Jesus Tradition really says nothing about the Spirit resting upon the messianic community, but instead promises that the Spirit will empower God's people for testimony when they are brought to court.[169] Second, even if Goppelt and Michaels were correct, this still does not explain why Peter went from the Jesus Tradition to Isa. 11.2, or why the aforementioned changes have been made.

Joel Green, on the other hand, has argued that Peter broadens the meaning of Isa. 11.2 to include the messianic community because of Isa. 11.12, which conjoins the holy remnant of Israel as partakers of what is promised to the messiah in 11.1–2.[170] This is certainly a plausible thesis for some of the changes that have been made to Isa. 11.2, but it does not explain why our author has connected a ridiculed messianic community with the abiding presence of the Spirit in Isa. 11.2. Curiously, although Dubis points to Zech. 12.10 as a possible candidate for Peter's modification of Isa. 11.2, he, like Green, opts for Isaiah as the source, arguing that Isaiah oscillates between the Spirit poured out upon an individual and upon the nation as a whole.[171] In Chapter 5, I will suggest that the eschatological programme of Zechariah 9–14 provides a remarkable explanation, one that can better explain how Isaiah 11.2 has been linked with a persecuted messianic community.

The second ὅτι passage is found in 4.17, a verse that builds upon 4.15–16. There Peter exhorts his readers that when they suffer as Christians, they are not to be ashamed. This exhortation underscores once again that Peter regards shame, understood within the context of a Graeco-Roman honour-shame society, to be a legitimate mode of suffering – perhaps the primary mode of suffering for these Anatolian Christians.[172] Instead of being ashamed, Peter's readers are exhorted to 'glorify' God 'in this name', turning the honour-shame paradigm on its head. In justifying this exhortation, much like he did in 1.5–7, he reminds them of *when* they are: 'For the time has come for judgment to begin with the household of God' (ὅτι ὁ καιρὸς τοῦ ἄρξασθαι τὸ κρίμα ἀπὸ τοῦ οἴκου τοῦ θεοῦ).[173] Given the way that καιρός is used elsewhere in the letter (1.5; 1.11; 5.6),

---

[168] See Horrell 2007: 138–40.
[169] For a helpful critique of Beare's suggestion that this is a temporary Spirit-empowerment, see Dubis 2002: 125–7.
[170] Green 2007a: 152.
[171] Dubis 2002: 121–2. He points to passages such as Isa. 32.14–15; 44.2–3; and 59.21.
[172] Bechtler 1998: 94–105; Campbell 1998.
[173] Michaels 1988: 270; see also Achtemeier 1996: 315.

it appears that Peter has in mind a fixed time that is in keeping with a foreordained eschatological programme.[174] In other words, there is an appointed time for restoration and salvation (1.5; 5.6), as well as a time for κρίμα (4.17), which is all in keeping with what the 'Spirit of Christ' announced beforehand to the prophets (1.11).

It is important to underscore that κρίμα does not necessarily imply punitive retribution for wrong behaviour.[175] Although it does often carry overtones of punishment (e.g. Rom. 3.8; Gal. 5.10; 2 Pet. 2.3; Jude 4; and Rev. 17), in its broadest sense κρίμα refers to the process of rightly ascertaining whether someone is innocent or guilty, a procedure of fairly evaluating whether one has remained loyal or not. Given that Peter has paradigmatically described Christian suffering as πειρασμοί (1.6; 4.12), and given that suffering is framed within an honour-shame system which is determined by the group with whom one associates, this broader sense of κρίμα seems to be in view. In other words, as Green has pointed out, here in 1 Pet. 4.17 'to judge' means 'to evaluate', 'to discern' or 'to distinguish', instead of 'to condemn'.[176] With this in view, suffering 'in the name of Christ' here (as elsewhere in the letter) is not understood to be punishment from God, but instead is evidence of one's loyalty towards God and his Christ, a loyalty that will be rewarded in the last time (1.5–9; 5.4).[177] According to Peter, this sifting process begins with 'the house of God' and will be carried forward to the eschaton.[178]

Some have argued that LXX Ezek. 9.6 might stand behind 1 Pet. 4.17, based in part on two lexical features shared between the two texts: (a) the phrase ἄρξασθαι ἀπό, and (b) the word οἶκος.[179] Elliott and Jobes have responded aptly to this proposal principally by highlighting the fact that Ezek. 9.6 and its wider context (Ezekiel 8–11) envision the destruction of God's temple and the punishment of God's people for their failure to abide by his covenant.[180] As Elliott has retorted, if Peter

---

[174] See BDAG: 497, 2. See also Bechtler 1998: 127–35; Jobes 2005: 292.

[175] This point is often missed in exegetical analysis of 1 Pet. 4.17. See especially Dubis 2002: 142–6.

[176] Green 2007a: 155; see also Elliott 2000: 799. This is not to suggest that punitive judgment is entirely absent from text; those who in the end refuse to associate themselves with the Christ will, as 4.17b–18 indicates, be punished.

[177] *Pace* Dubis (2002: 163–7), who unduly regards the suffering as punitive in nature. His reading runs against the entire grain of 1 Peter, which in no way suggests that the addressees are suffering as a result of their own sins.

[178] Green 2007a: 155.

[179] E.g. Schutter 1989: 156–63; Michaels 1988: 271; Dubis 2002: 151–2.

[180] Elliott 2000: 798 (for the full rebuttal see *ibid.*: 798–900); Jobes 2005: 291–2. Jobes (*ibid.*: 292) interprets Zech. 13.9 to be speaking of punitive judgment against God's people as well, a view that will be challenged in §4.3.

did draw from Ezek. 9.6, he did so by making a point entirely different from that which is made in the proposed precursor text.[181] In light of this, it seems very unlikely that Ezek. 9.6 stands behind 1 Pet. 4.17. I would echo Elliott, then, who comments that '[t]wo linguistic similarities "begin from" and *oikos*, do not outweigh the differences between the two texts'.[182]

Those who consider Ezek. 9.6 as the precursor text for 1 Pet. 4.17 also regard the term οἶκος τοῦ θεοῦ to be a reference to the temple, and thus argue for temple imagery as the primary metaphor of this passage. It seems, however, that the letter itself has defined οἶκος τοῦ θεοῦ for us in a different sense. There are, for example, several features in the near context (i.e. 1 Pet. 4.12–19) that press us to understand οἶκος τοῦ θεοῦ to be a reference to a particular community of people who are associated with a royal figure (i.e. the Christ).[183] As I have already demonstrated, leading up to 4.17 the primary subject of the passage has been the community that associates itself with the Christ or messiah. They are variously described as those who partner in the 'belonging to the Christ' sufferings (4.13), those who are ridiculed 'in the name of Christ' (4.14), the messianic community upon which the Spirit rests (4.14) and χριστιανοί who glorify in 'this name' (4.16). It would seem, then, that the most natural reading of οἶκος τοῦ θεοῦ, given the immediate context, would be as yet another reference to the community that has associated itself with the messiah.[184] The phrase ἀφ' ἡμῶν, which appears in the latter half of 4.17, and which stands in apposition to ἀπὸ τοῦ οἴκου τοῦ θεοῦ seems to corroborate this interpretation.[185]

Additionally, this reading of οἶκος τοῦ θεοῦ in 4.17 is confirmed if we allow 1 Pet. 2.4–10 to inform our interpretation. As I have already noted, 1 Pet. 2.4–8 presents a mixed metaphorical description of the community that associates itself with the rejected cornerstone: they are living stones that are under construction, a spiritual house that now offers acceptable sacrifices to God through Jesus Christ (2.5). These images of the community that associates itself with the rejected Christ are then elaborated with terms derived from Exodus 19, Isaiah 43 and Hosea 2,

---

[181] Elliott 2000: 799. Elliott (*ibid.*: 799) has also pointed out that proponents of Ezek. 9.6 in 1 Pet. 4.17 have overlooked the fact that the term οἶκος is used in reference to both the temple and God's people (9.6,7,9). For a critique of Elliott see Dubis 2002: 152–3.

[182] Elliott 2000: 800.

[183] So also Hillyer 1969: 126, who argues that οἶκος refers to royal dynasty.

[184] In Chapter 5, I will analyze the term οἶκος in more detail, and argue that it is neither exclusively a reference to the temple, nor to a household or family, but instead conveys the idea of royal (i.e. messianic) lineage (see BDAG: 698, 3).

[185] Elliott 2000: 799.

which all refer in various ways to the people of God – a chosen race, a royal priesthood, a holy nation, God's own people, and those who have received mercy (2.9–10). At its core, then, οἶκος τοῦ θεοῦ is a community of people, a royal (messianic), priestly lineage, who have willingly associated themselves with Jesus, whom they regard as the Christ, in spite of the fact that such an association incurs shame and suffering from their compeers.[186] Their faithfulness in the face of this ridicule and shame is the beginning of the sifting process, the κρίμα, which serves to delineate the house (or people) of God from those who have chosen to reject Jesus as the messiah. Suffering, then, is not regarded to have an educational or purifying purpose, but instead proves that they are in fact remaining loyal to the Christ. That they are called a 'spiritual house' (οἶκος πνευματικός) in 1 Pet. 2.5 likely points cataphorically to 1 Pet. 4.14 and 17, where they are described as the messianic house of God upon which the Spirit now rests. Unless we read 1 Pet. 2.4–8 and 4.17 in this manner, I find it difficult to make sense of the letter, which on the one hand would be presenting the messianic community as a newly built and renewed temple which is presently offering pleasing spiritual sacrifices (2.4–8; i.e. the OT promises regarding the temple have been fulfilled) and which, on the other hand, needs to be judged and purified for its sins (4.17; i.e. the OT promises regarding the temple are yet to be fulfilled).[187]

Before I turn to 1 Pet. 5.1–4, I wish to underscore two additional features of 1 Pet. 4.17–19 that help demonstrate the eschatological pro-gramme that Peter develops. First, at the end of 4.17 Peter rhetorically asks, if the sifting process begins with us, what will be the end for those who do not obey the gospel of God? He then elaborates with a citation from LXX Prov. 11.31 in 1 Pet. 4.18: εἰ ὁ δίκαιος μόλις σώζεται, ὁ ἀσεβὴς καὶ ἁμαρτωλὸς ποῦ φανεῖται. With these two rhetorical questions, Peter wishes to highlight the fact that the suffering which the ungodly will experience (i.e. those who choose not to align themselves with God's Christ) will be worse than that which they (the readers) are presently experiencing. But that is not all these rhetorical questions reveal. Addi-tionally, they further betray the fact that Peter envisions a select group of people that will not align themselves with the Christ (see 1 Pet. 2.8 – 'They stumble because they disobey the word, as they were destined

---

[186] Similarly, in Heb. 3.6 being a member of God's οἶκος is contingent upon loyal allegiance to Christ.

[187] E.g. 'The context [i.e. priesthood, sacrifices] . . . suggests an intention to describe the Christian community in terms of a new temple' (Achtemeier 1996: 156).

to do'). This is accentuated by the question – where will the ungodly sinner *appear* (ποῦ φανεῖται;)? It is probably that Peter has appropriated this proverb in order to point to the absence of the ungodly sinner when salvation and restoration are revealed in their fullness. In other words, he envisions an eschatological programme that includes the destruction or removal of those who do not presently suffer ridicule 'in the name of Christ'. This same proverb also underscores a theme that has been emphasized in 4.12–19, namely that it is with difficulty (μόλις) that the righteous one is saved. As several commentators have pointed out, the term μόλις does not indicate that followers of Jesus are 'barely' or 'scarcely' saved, but rather that the path to salvation will be difficult in the face of harsh opposition.[188] Thus Elliott is right when he comments that

> [t]he notion of the difficulty of salvation, in the context of this letter, pertains to the fact that salvation is gained only in the course of human opposition and unjust suffering and hence requires constant vigilance, trust in God's supportive power, steadfastness in suffering, and perseverance in doing what is right according to the will of God (v 19). This difficulty, however, does not vitiate the fact that the righteous will indeed be saved if they remain faithful.[189]

The appropriation of this proverb once again points to the fiery trials being a unique period of time in which the faithfulness of God's people is being assayed. Additionally, the fact that Peter appropriates LXX Prov. 11.31 (i.e. 'the righteous one is saved with difficulty'), instead of the Hebrew version of the same text (i.e. the righteous one is repaid on the earth), perhaps is one further indication that he feels no restriction in exploiting the variant text that best suits his theological purposes (see 2.25 in Chapter 3 §3.4).[190]

Second, this passage (4.12–19) is brought to a resounding conclusion (ὥστε καί)[191] with an exhortation that restates the main points that Peter has been trying to make in 4.12–18:

(1) Those who have chosen to associate with the Christ are suffering in a manner that is in keeping with God's will (κατὰ

---

[188] Michaels 1988: 272; Achtemeier 1996: 317; Jobes 2005: 294.

[189] Elliott 2000: 803.

[190] As Achtemeier (1996: 317) points out, without the emendation of μόλις in the place of באָרֶץ, LXX Prov. 11.31 would not have been useful for the author. Incidentally, the Peshitta follows the LXX, while the Vulgate and the Targum follow the MT.

[191] Michaels 1988: 272; Achtemeier 1996: 317.

τὸ θέλημα τοῦ θεοῦ).[192] Their suffering is not accidental, or a sign of God's disfavour, or even for the purpose of purification. Instead, it is within the foreknowledge of God (1.2), part of a preordained eschatological programme (1.5–7), to which the prophets have testified beforehand (1.11).

(2) Those who suffer because they have associated themselves with the Christ ought to entrust themselves to the 'faithful creator' (πιστῷ κτίστῃ παρατιθέσθωσαν τὰς ψυχὰς αὐτῶν). This exhortation expresses confidence in the fact that God will bring these Anatolian χριστιανοί through the fiery trials (see 1.5–7). It also points back to 1 Pet. 2.23, where Jesus in his passion entrusted himself to 'the one who judges justly'. That God is referred to as the 'creator' (κτίστης) probably points to the fact that he has the appointed times in his hand.[193] That he is the 'faithful' creator indicates that he will be true to his promises. In light of this, the Anatolian Christians are called to remain faithful to the Christ as they continue in their 'good works' (ἐν ἀγαθοποιΐᾳ).[194]

Before I draw several conclusions regarding the analysis of the fiery trials in 1 Pet. 1.6–7 and 1 Pet. 4.12, I want to highlight two features in 1 Pet. 5.1–4, which will be developed in more detail in Chapter 5, that either confirm earlier exegetical moves that I have made, or point to the substructure of Peter's thought.

First, Peter exhorts elders to 'shepherd' the 'flock' of God under their care (ποιμάνατε τὸ ἐν ὑμῖν ποίμνιον τοῦ θεοῦ; 5.2). The manner in which they are called to exercise their leadership over God's flock is expressed in terms that seem to reverse the negative qualities of leadership that are expressed in Ezekiel 34 and Zechariah 11: not under compulsion (ἀναγκαστῶς); not for shameful gain (αἰσχροκερδῶς); not as lording it over them (μηδ᾽ ὡς κατακυριεύοντες τῶν κλήρων). But instead, they are

---

[192] This is not to be confused with the notion that God gets pleasure out of suffering, or that it is a part of His moral will.

[193] Green (2007a: 161) suggests that in using the term κτίστης 'Peter may be engaging in a soft polemic against Roman hegemony, embodied in Rome's rulers, who were acclaimed with the title of "founder" or "creator"'. A search on the Packard Humanities database of inscriptions indicates that κτίστης was a particularly preferred term used in honorary inscriptions in Asia Minor. Peter, then, is perhaps drawing on this term once again to turn the honour-shame system on its head.

[194] *Pace* Winter (1988) and Harland (2003), Peter appears to be using ἀγαθοποιΐα not to advocate assimilation to the civic honour system of the Roman empire, but rather ironically to point out that their faithfulness will indeed one day be regarded with honour by the true king, Jesus. See also Achtemeier 1996: 318.

to watch over the flock (ἐπισκοποῦντες) intentionally (ἑκουσίως) and wilfully (προθύμως), serving as models (τύποι).[195] It appears that Peter envisions the restoration of a second tier of leadership as a part of the eschatological programme (see 5.4, where Jesus is designated as the Chief Shepherd (ἀρχιποίμην), which probably points back to 1 Pet. 2.25). He concludes this exhortation by reminding the elders that their selfless leadership will gain for them 'an imperishable crown of glory' when the Chief Shepherd, Jesus (see 2.25), appears.

Second, Peter's self-identification as a fellow-elder and 'a witness of the sufferings of Christ' (μάρτυς τῶν τοῦ Χριστοῦ παθημάτων; 5.1) confirms my interpretation of 4.13 (i.e. τοῖς τοῦ Χριστοῦ παθήμασιν as the '"belonging to Christ" sufferings'). As many commentators have pointed out, according to the Jesus Tradition, Peter was not present to witness Jesus' crucifixion.[196] Therefore, in 5.1 Peter is not using the term μάρτυς, as it so often is used, in order to suggest that he was an eye-witness of Jesus' passion.[197] But neither is he *merely* declaring himself to be one who bears witness to the facts regarding Jesus' suffering, death and resurrection.[198] As Strathmann has argued, in 1 Pet. 5.1 the term has a 'unique and equivocal' usage, in which it is paralleled with Peter's partnership with glory: 'At first glance it might seem that Peter is here calling himself an eye-witness of the passion of Jesus... But the continuation ὁ καὶ τῆς μελλούσης ἀποκαλύπτεσθαι δόξης κοινωνός shows that the reference is to personal participation, including participation in Christ's sufferings, and not just to being there as an eye-witness.'[199] Thus, Peter here in 5.1, as he has elsewhere in the letter, is juxtaposing suffering with glory, both of which come from one's association or participation with Christ and his people. Jobes rightly underlines the main point of Peter's self-identification: 'The courageous act of leading the church in perilous times rather than renouncing Christ is itself a form of witness that Peter shares with the local church leadership... This construal of *martys* coheres well with the major theme of 1 Peter: all believers are called to suffer as necessary for their faithfulness to Christ.'[200] With the phrase μάρτυς τῶν τοῦ Χριστοῦ παθημάτων Peter is indicating that he too has been participating in the sufferings that come with associating oneself with the Christ and his people, and for that reason shares in the

---

[195] Elliott 2000: 822–33; Bosetti 1990: 208–16.
[196] E.g. Best 1971: 168; Brox 1986: 229; Davids 1990: 177; Elliott 2000: 819.
[197] Strathmann 1976: 489–94; Elliott 2000: 818–19.
[198] *Pace* Elliott 2000: 819.   [199] Strathmann 1976: 494.1   [200] Jobes 2005: 302.

glory (i.e. honour) that is soon to come, when Christ returns (see 1.5–7; 5.4).

4.2.3   Conclusions

In §4.2, I have tried to demonstrate that, according to Peter, there is a necessary time of trouble for faithful followers of Jesus that is part of an eschatological programme which has been initiated by the death and resurrection of Jesus, and that will reach its culmination when he returns (1.7,13; 5.4). This time of trouble is paradigmatically described as 'fiery trials' (1.6–7/4.12), which principally function not as a means of purification, but rather as a means of authenticating one's faithfulness to God and his Christ. I have also sought to show that, through a number of images and allusions, Peter likens these fiery trials to a second exodus journey (rather than exile), which the readers must pass through before they receive their inheritance (1.4). In my analysis of 1.6–7 and 4.12 in their wider epistolary context, I have indicated several other features of Peter's eschatological restoration programme:

(1)   The Spirit now rests upon the community that associates itself with the messiah, the Christ.

(2)   This Spirit-endowed messianic community is described as the 'house of God' (οἶκος τοῦ θεοῦ), which will be evaluated and delineated through the fiery trials of the second exodus.

(3)   There will be those that choose not to express loyal allegiance to the Christ; they will be destroyed, that is, they will not appear in the age of full restoration (4.17–18).

(4)   Those who entrust themselves to God can have confidence in the final outcome of the fiery trials; in spite of the difficulties that come with remaining faithful, God will bring his elect-sojourners through the fiery trials.

(5)   The final outcome of God's restoration is an occasion for great joy.

(6)   Suffering 'in the name of Christ' is in keeping with God's will, a part of his overarching plan.

(7)   There will be a restored second tier of leadership charged with the task of shepherding God's flock in a manner that is on the one hand contrary to Ezekiel 34 and Zechariah 11, and on the other hand epitomized by the Chief Shepherd (2.20–5; 5.4).

In the course of my analysis of the fiery trials in 1 Peter I have raised several questions that have yet to be answered. For example, what has compelled Peter to make the imaginative connection between a community that is blessed since it is reviled, and the messianic promise of Isa. 11.2? What has prompted Peter to take a promise that was originally addressed to the messianic 'shoot' or 'branch' of Jesse (11.1), and apply it now to the messianic community? Why has Peter added the genitival phrase τὸ τῆς δόξης to Isa. 11.2? And finally, how should we understand the term διασπορά in 1 Pet. 1.1 if Peter does not envision them to be living in exile any longer?

In Chapter 5 I will attempt to answer these questions by drawing on my analysis of Zechariah 9–14 and its reception in Chapter 2, and relating it to our findings in 1 Peter. Before I can do that, however, I must highlight several features of the fiery trials of Zechariah in context and relate them to my analysis of 1 Peter.

4.3   The fiery trials of Zechariah 13.9 in context

In Chapter 2 I showed how Zechariah 9–14 presents a progressive unfolding of YHWH's eschatological programme, which begins with an affirmation of restoration hopes found in Jeremiah and Ezekiel, and is similarly couched with shepherd imagery (see 9.17; 10.1–12; 11.1–3). YHWH will return to Zion, exiled Israel will return to the land and the hostile nations will be defeated (9.1–17). But gradually, the prophet begins to introduce a radical twist to the earlier prophetic material. Whereas the eschatological programme of Ezekiel 34–8 (which builds on Jeremiah 23) has given the impression that YHWH's eschatological Davidic shepherd will emerge and immediately usher in peace and prosperity, Zechariah instead points to a time of trouble for Israel, declaring that the leaders and the people will reject YHWH's appointed king, YHWH's covenant will be broken and Israel will once again find itself under a wicked shepherd (11.4–17). In keeping with the progressive unfolding of the eschatological programme, Zech. 12.1–13.6 provides further details about this time of trouble, indicating that a member of the house of David will be pierced, and that all of Israel will mourn. The death of this Davidide, however, will be followed by spiritual renewal: The spirit of YHWH will be poured out upon the house of David (which is also described as the house of God; Zech. 12.8), and the people will be cleansed from idolatry, unclean spirits and false prophets.

The unfolding of this time of trouble climaxes in Zech. 13.7–9 as more details are provided: a shepherd will be struck (13.7), the sheep, who had returned from exile, will again be scattered and then, according to the prophet, two-thirds of the people will be cut off and perish, that is, they will not have a share in YHWH's restored world. YHWH will place the remaining one-third into the fire, where, as I have argued, their faithfulness will be tested or ascertained as they experience hostility from both the nations as well as their own people (Zech. 13.7–14.5). With surprising optimism, the prophet declares that the remaining one-third will emerge from the fiery testing, calling upon YHWH's name. YHWH will respond with the covenantal refrain alluded to in Hosea 2 – 'They are my people.' The people will respond by confessing 'The LORD is our God.'

Much like the passages that we analyzed in 1 Peter, it appears that the metallurgy imagery in Zech. 13.9 is not appropriated in order to illustrate the purifying qualities of the fiery trials, nor in order to characterize the trials as having some sort of inherent goodness (i.e. because it produces character); instead, the principal focus of the passage is to underscore that a necessary, predetermined time of trouble will occur prior to the shepherd's return and YHWH's universal reign (14.3–21), and that YHWH's remnant (or elect) must pass through these fiery trials on their way to their inheritance.

In Chapter 2 I also have shown that there are indications that this period of fiery testing in Zech. 13.7–9 is linked to and elaborates earlier material in Zech. 10.6–12 which depicted YHWH's restoration in terms of a second exodus journey.[201] Both Zech. 10.6 as well as Zech. 13.9, for example, allude to Hosea 2.23, a text in which YHWH climactically announces that he will draw his remnant people out to the desert where he will have compassion on *Lo-ruhamah* ('not pitied'), and where he will declare 'You are my people' to *Lo-ammi* ('not my people'; Hosea 2.23).[202] Second, as we have seen, in Zech. 11.4–17 the covenant with YHWH and his people has been broken. It seems that Zech. 13.9 is indicating that this covenant will be renewed either during or after the period of fiery trials, which would then make it possible to understand the new exodus journey of 10.6–12 to also include this period of fiery trials. Third, the strength that YHWH promises to provide his remnant in their second exodus journey in Zech. 10.12 is a fitting foreshadowing of a time of trouble, which Zech. 13.8–9 depicts as fiery trials. Thus, it is possible to regard the second exodus journey of Zech. 10.6–12 and the fiery trials of 1 Peter to be referring to the same sequence within the eschatological programme of Zechariah 9–14.

---

[201] So also Mitchell 1997: 210, n.37.
[202] Mason 1977: 112. Meyers and Meyers 1993: 396–7.

4.4   Conclusion

In this chapter I have analyzed the fiery trials imagery of 1 Peter (1.7/4.12) and Zech. 13.8–9. A relationship between the two texts often has been hinted at in the secondary literature, but the discussion has never moved beyond noting a few parallel features. When the fiery trials imagery of 1 Peter is compared to Zech. 13.9 and the wider themes that are developed in each of those texts, five striking parallels emerge. First, in both texts, the fiery trials imagery is used with a strong emphasis on it being a necessary part of a larger sequence of events that must take place. Second, in both texts the fiery trials are likened to a second exodus journey. Third, both texts express confidence in the positive outcome of the fiery trials for the remnant or elect. Fourth, in both texts the fiery trials period follows the death of a shepherd figure, and is prior to eschatological salvation/consummation. And finally, and perhaps most significantly, both texts downplay the purifying, educational benefits of 'fiery trials', and instead highlight their authenticating purposes. These five features, which are unique to both texts, eliminate, in my view, the likelihood that Peter was drawing on such texts as Wisdom 3 or Sirach 2.

There are, however, three additional compelling reasons on the one hand to suppose a relationship between 1 Pet. 1.6–7/4.12 and Zech. 13.7–9, and on the other hand to reject the notion that 1 Peter's fiery trials imagery was dependent upon some other proposed source. First, Zechariah 9–14 provides a framework for understanding why the addressees are described as returned from exile on the one hand (see 2.25), while also being elect-sojourners of the διασπορά on the other hand (1.1). Second, Zechariah 9–14 offers a compelling explanation for why Peter has connected a persecuted community of God with the promise of the Spirit resting upon a messianic community, and why they are described as the 'house of God'. And third, Zechariah 9–14 provides a rationale for the logic that brings together 1 Pet. 4.12–17 and 5.1–4. These three claims will be explored in Chapter 5.

5

ECHOES OF ZECHARIAH 9–14 IN 1 PETER

In Chapter 4 I raised three questions that now must be answered. First, if the addressees of 1 Peter are located theologically/eschatologically in a second exodus, as I have argued, then what are we to make of the term διασπορά, which would seem to suggest otherwise? Second, is there a better explanation for the modifications that Peter has made to Isa. 11.2 in 1 Pet. 4.14? And third, what is the relationship between the fiery trials of 1 Pet. 4.12–19 and the exhortation to elders in 5.1–4? In responding to these questions, I will demonstrate that in each case the distinctive eschatological programme of Zechariah 9–14 provides a unique explanation, which further supports the thesis that it is functioning as the substructure for Peter's eschatological programme.

5.1   διασπορά as point of departure

In Chapter 4 I highlighted an apparent tension (or perhaps even confusion) that scholars have noted between exile and new exodus imagery in 1 Peter. Based upon an analysis of 1 Pet. 1.1–2.10, I argued that Peter interprets his readers' precarious situation as necessary wilderness trials that *follow* return from exile and *precede* full restoration, rather than as exilic suffering. Although a number of scholars have noted a proliferation of new exodus imagery in 1 Pet. 1.1–2.10, most nevertheless consider exile to be the predominant metaphor. Perhaps the principal reason for this conclusion is the term διασπορά in 1 Pet. 1.1, which seems to locate Peter's audience (whether theologically or geographically) in some sort of exilic state. In fact, it is the case that Peter's usage of διασπορά in the opening of the letter often carries more interpretative weight for understanding the controlling metaphor of the letter than the content that follows in 1 Pet. 1.2–2.10. Achtemeier, for example, suggests that '[a]lthough there are echoes in 1 Peter of the exodus and the establishment of the covenant in the wilderness, the major prototype of the Christian community's experience in the world is here [1.1; διασπορά] furnished by the exile'.[1]

However, even if we were to grant that διασπορά connotes in some way the idea of exile, this does not necessarily mean that the word has been chosen in order to describe the recipients' current location or status.[2] It is at least plausible that διασπορᾶς signals the status or place *from which* the addressees have been redeemed, as I will demonstrate below.

Most scholars argue (or assume without any argumentation) that διασ-πορᾶς is either an epexegetical or a partitive genitive, which in one way or another locates the addressees in the Diaspora. There is, however, one other possibility that has been entirely overlooked. On grammatical and literary contextual grounds, it may be more accurate to regard διασπορᾶς as an ablative genitive, which expresses the idea of separation. Even though the ablative genitive is rare in NT Greek, often replaced instead with the preposition ἀπό or ἐκ, it is indisputably appropriated twice in 1 Peter (1 Pet. 3.21 (σαρκὸς ἀπόθεσις ῥύπου) and also 1 Pet. 4.1 (πέπαυ-ται ἁμαρτίας)) in order to describe that from which the head noun and the verb (respectively) are separated. Daniel Wallace points out that ablative genitives are usually dependent upon verbs or nouns with verbal ideas that contain the notion of separation.[3] These verbal notions can be either static (in a state of separation) or progressive (in movement away from). In the case of 1 Pet. 1.1 (ἐκλεκτοῖς παρεπιδήμοις διασπορᾶς), following the argumentation of Jobes, I would maintain that both ἐκλεκτοί as well as παρεπίδημοι are substantival adjectives in apposition to one another.[4] I would further suggest that Peter had in mind something along the lines of 'elect-sojourner' rather than 'elect, sojourner . . . '.[5] As such, both substantival adjectives function as the head noun, and both contain verbal

---

[1] Achtemeier 1996: 80, n.16; see also Michaels 1988: xlv.

[2] In my view, it is not certain whether the term διασπορά can do all the theological work that some claim it does. John Barclay (1996) and more recently Philip Harland (2003) demonstrate that Jews living in the Diaspora accommodated and assimilated in varying degrees. In particular, Harland (2003: 213–38) has shown that there was a variety of positive interactions between Jews and their host cultures in Asia Minor. Thus, it is not necessarily accurate to assume the term διασπορά conjures up notions of social ostracism and cultural alienation. What is more, διασπορά often implies some sort of punishment or wrong-doing, something that 1 Peter does not suggest. Note, however, Feldmeier (1992: 39–74), who, drawing from Qumran sources and Philo, argues that the term διασπορά connotes the dual realities of election and ostracism.

[3] Wallace 1996: 107–8.

[4] Jobes 2005: 75; so also Green (2007a: 14), who states that 'both adjectives . . . are substantival, describing in complementary (if seemingly oxymoronic) ways the identity of the addressees'.

[5] Cf. Feldmeier 2008: 53.

ideas of separation (whether static or progressive). There is, therefore, not only precedent within 1 Peter itself but also syntactical warrant for an ablative reading of the genitive διασπορᾶς.

A survey of the way that διασπορά is used elsewhere in the NT and in the LXX strengthens the likelihood that an ablative genitive is in view. There are four occurrences in which an author addresses a group who is living in the διασπορά.[6] In every case, either εἰς or ἐν is appropriated in a locative manner. James 1.1, which is often compared with 1 Pet. 1.1, offers a striking example of this. There the author greets the twelve tribes, which constitutes the group being addressed, and locates them with the locative phrase ἐν τῇ διασπορᾷ. The only reference in the LXX in which διασπορά appears in the genitive case is Jth. 5.19, and this proves to be very illuminating for our discussion of 1 Pet. 1.1: καὶ νῦν ἐπιστρέψαντες ἐπὶ τὸν θεὸν αὐτῶν ἀνέβησαν ἐκ τῆς διασπορᾶς, οὗ διεσπάρησαν ἐκεῖ, καὶ κατέσχον τὴν Ιερουσαλημ. In this passage, the people's return to their God (ἐπιστρέψαντες ἐπὶ τὸν θεὸν αὐτῶν) is described in terms of a departure or separation from the Diaspora (ἀνέβησαν ἐκ τῆς διασπορᾶς), and is specified even more concretely as the possessing of Jerusalem (καὶ κατέσχον τὴν Ιερουσαλη), which is likely a synecdoche representing the possession of their promised inheritance. This pattern in Jth. 5.19 closely parallels the sequence of events that is described in 1 Peter – a return to God/the shepherd (1.21; 2.25), separation from exile/διασπορά (1.1; 2.11) and a journey towards the inheritance (1.3–2.10).[7]

In light of the above, the question must be (and is rarely) asked: Why would Peter choose the genitive construction of διασπορά in order to refer to the location (whether geographically or metaphorically) of his readers, rather than appropriating a locative preposition such as εἰς or ἐν, which appears to be the more customary usage? In my view, given the rudimentary narrative of the letter, and the syntactical analysis just advanced, it is at least plausible and perhaps even likely that Peter did not intend to locate his readers *in* the Diaspora, but instead wished to communicate separation from it.[8]

---

[6] James 1.1; Jer. 15.7; 41.17; Dan. 12.2.

[7] To be clear, I am not suggesting dependence on Jth. 5.19, but simply noting the parallels.

[8] In Chapter 4, I highlighted that Peter affirms that restoration *has already begun* in and through Jesus: the people are a newly formed people (1.3,23), redeemed by the unblemished lamb (1.18–19), declared to be a people of God again (2.9–10), healed (2.24), returned (ἐπεστράφητε) to the shepherd (2.25) and called to journey towards their inheritance (1.3–2.10).

This reading of διασπορᾶς in 1 Pet 1.1 may help make sense of an apparent tension between exile and second exodus imagery. It may well be the case that Peter is neither confused nor inconsistent. Instead, in keeping with one of the distinctive features of the eschatological programme of Zechariah 9–14, read through the lens of Jesus' death and resurrection, it may be that he understands fidelity to the Christ, the slain shepherd, to be both a return from exile (see Zech. 9–10; 1 Pet. 2.24–5) as well as the beginning of a wilderness journey characterized by fiery trials (see Zech. 10.8–12; 13.7–9; 1 Pet. 1.3–2.10; 4.12–17).[9]

If I am right on this matter, then διασπορά does not describe the addressees' present condition, nor is it the way they are to view their sufferings. In fact, it could be said that the addressees acquire the status of ἐκλεκτοί παρεπίδημοι precisely because in placing their faith and hope in the shepherd, God's flock has been gathered and returned (separated) from the διασπορά (2.24–5). They have been delivered from their exilic scattering and have been set on a wilderness journey, where their faithfulness will be tested along the way. As I demonstrated in Chapter 2, the OT prophetic material (especially Jeremiah 23, Isaiah 40 and Ezekiel 34, which is then reworked in Zechariah 9–14) frequently speaks of restoration as (a) scattered sheep being returned to the eschatological Davidic shepherd, and (b) a second exodus journey through the wilderness towards a renewed inheritance.[10] Thus, as scholars have suggested, the term διασπορά is theologically significant – but not necessarily in the way that has been imagined. It does not shape the identity of the 1 Peter addressees except to the extent that they understand that even though they are undergoing opposition from their compeers they are no longer to regard themselves as 'scattered' and under God's wrath; instead they have been returned to the Shepherd, who becomes not only the means for their redemption but also the pattern for what faithfulness looks like as they journey towards their inheritance (2.21–5). The hardships they face as newly formed followers of the Christ, then, are in no way to be regarded as a form of punishment (exile), but instead are concomitant with being in the wilderness, where God has regularly tested the fidelity of his newly formed people.

---

[9] It is noteworthy that other NT authors similarly develop an inaugurated eschatology that is described in terms of a second exodus and without the need to conflate it with notions of exile (e.g. Romans 5–8; Hebrews 3–4; Revelation 12).

[10] It should be noted here that the term διασπορά is related to the verb διασπείρω ('to scatter'), a verb which is commonly used in the OT to describe God's response (exile) to Israel's infidelity (e.g. Ps. 43.12; Ezek. 20.23; 34.5–6,12; 36.19; Jth. 5.19). See Laniak 2006: 94–170 on the conflation of new exodus and shepherd traditions in the OT.

In this opening line of the letter, then, the emphasis is not on the genitive διασπορᾶς (*pace* Martin) but rather on the phrase ἐκλεκτοί παρεπίδημοι. That is, the letter focuses not on their location or condition as exiles, but rather on the fact that no matter where they are located geographically in Asia Minor, they are in fact 'in Christ' (3.16; 5.10,14), ὁ ἐκλεκτός (2.4,6),[11] which means that they too are ἐκλεκτοί (see 2.9; 5.13) who are now on a journey (παρεπίδημοι) which will be patterned after their faithful slain shepherd (2.21–5). That Peter frames his letter in this way likely betrays early on in the letter his dependence upon the eschatological programme of Zechariah 9–14, and especially Zech. 13.7–9, as was developed in §2.1.2.6 and in Chapter 3. Said in another way, if we attune to the eschatological programme of Zechariah 9–14, it explains why Peter can describe his readers on the one hand as having been returned to the Shepherd (i.e. returned from exile; 2.25), while on the other hand as being elect-sojourners who are undergoing fiery wilderness trials.

There is one final plausible connection that can be made in the opening lines of 1 Peter with Zechariah 9–14, which would further strengthen this claim. As I argued in Chapter 2, the basis for YHWH's restoration pro-gramme is declared in Zech. 9.11: 'because of the blood of my covenant I will set your prisoners free from the waterless pit'. As I pointed out, it is not entirely clear what the author of Zechariah 9–14 envisions. It is possible that the covenantal language conflates imagery from Exod. 24.8 (the only other place in the OT that the phrase 'blood of my covenant' appears) and Isa. 42.6–7 (where 'the servant' is given as a covenant of/for the people in order to bring out prisoners from the dungeon), such that 'the blood of my covenant' mentioned in Zech. 9.11 is to be understood as a sacrificial death that initiates a new exodus like restoration.[12] Whether or not this is the case, within the literary context of Zechariah 9–14, it seems quite clear that 'the blood of my covenant' foreshadows and helps interpret the seemingly tragic death of YHWH's agent (12.10/13.7) as a sacrificial offering which renews the covenant and initiates restora-tion. This reading of Zech. 9.11 aligns well with developments in the second oracle (Zechariah 12–14), where the death of the pierced one (12.10)/slain shepherd (13.7) is described in terms that echo YHWH's promise to renew his covenant with an unfaithful, scattered people found in Ezekiel 36 and Hosea 2.[13]

---

[11] 'Peter works less to construct a perimeter as to define a center, and he does this by locating his audience geographically – not at the most basic level as persons of the diaspora, but rather as persons "in Christ"' (Green 2004: 289).

[12] Mason 1977: 92.   [13] See §2.1.2 for the development of these ideas.

It appears that Peter makes a similar move. In 1 Pet. 1.2, he amplifies the pregnant epithet ἐκλεκτοί παρεπίδημοι with three prepositional phrases. First, he underscores that their oxymoronic status as 'elect-sojourners' is in keeping with the foreknowledge of God the Father (κατὰ πρόγνωσιν θεοῦ πατρός). Here I follow Green, who suggests that Peter's point is that this divine choice and alien status 'are deeply rooted in God's purpose as this comes to expression in the Scriptures'.[14] In other words, this unique status that they have been given and which they must now live out is in keeping with what has been foretold by the prophets (see 1 Pet. 1.10–12). Peter's extensive dependence upon the OT throughout the letter would seem to underscore this reading of κατὰ πρόγνωσιν θεοῦ πατρός.[15] Second, the sanctifying activity of the Spirit (ἐν ἁγιασμῷ πνεύματος) is said to be the means by which the 'elect-sojourners' are empowered to live out their calling.[16] And finally, Peter culminates his amplification of ἐκλεκτοί παρεπίδημοι by declaring that Jesus Christ's obedience and sprinkling of blood cause this all to happen (εἰς ὑπακοὴν καὶ ῥαντισμὸν αἵματος Ἰησοῦ Χριστοῦ).[17] What is significant about this last prepositional phrase is that it frames Jesus' obedience as a covenantal/sacrificial offering that enables God's people to be restored again to their elect status.[18] This is precisely the point that Peter will make in two additional places in his letter, suggesting that 1 Pet. 1.2 foreshadows a theme that he will pick up again. First, in 1 Pet. 1.19 Jesus' 'precious blood' (τιμίῳ αἵματι) is likened to the Passover Lamb, which was YHWH's means of delivering his people out of Egypt and setting them on a wilderness journey to their promised inheritance. As I demonstrated in Chapter 4, this particular description of Jesus' death is surrounded by a number of allusions to either the first exodus (Lev. 11.44; 19.2; 20.7 in 1 Pet. 1.16; and Exod. 19.5–6 in 1 Pet. 2.9) or the second exodus promises in the OT prophetic material (Isa. 40.6–8 in 1 Pet. 2.24–5; Isa. 43.20–1 in 1 Pet. 2.10; and Hosea 2.25 in 1 Pet. 2.10). More

[14] Green 2007a: 19. [15] θεοῦ is to be taken as a subjective genitive.
[16] To be clear, ἐν expresses instrumentality or means, and πνεύματος is a subjective genitive and refers to the Holy Spirit.
[17] Thus, I regard the εἰς to be causal rather than telic (see Mantey 1951a, 1951b; Marcus 1952; Agnew 1983; Elliott 2000: 319; cf. Green 2007a: 20). For counter-arguments see Achtemeier 1996: 87; Jobes 2005: 71–2. Since in the two previous prepositional phrases the genitives are subjective, it seems most likely that Ἰησοῦ Χριστοῦ is best regarded as a subjective genitive as well. This reading alleviates the unnecessary and confusing fragmentation of ὑπακοὴν καὶ ῥαντισμὸν αἵματος. Taken together as the head nouns of the subjective genitive Ἰησοῦ Χριστοῦ, the phrase interprets Jesus' obedience (unto death) as sacrificial in character.
[18] See Exodus 24.1–8; Isa. 42.1–9.

significantly, however, in 1 Pet. 2.24–5 Jesus' death is described in terms of an offering upon a tree (ὃς τὰς ἁμαρτίας ἡμῶν αὐτὸς ἀνήνεγκεν ἐν τῷ σώματι αὐτοῦ ἐπὶ τὸ ξύλον) that heals (see §3.4 for healing as restoration from exile) and enables straying sheep to be returned to the shepherd. In Chapter 3, I demonstrated that this description of Jesus' death is constructed with conflated allusions to Isaiah 53 and the shepherd material in Zechariah 10–13. All this suggests that 1 Pet. 1.2 (εἰς ὑπακοὴν καὶ ῥαντισμὸν αἵματος Ἰησοῦ Χριστοῦ) is an early echo of Zechariah 9–14 that is then amplified in subsequent passages. Additionally, it supports my hypothesis that 1 Pet. 1.1 (ἐκλεκτοῖς παρεπιδήμοις διασπορᾶς) echoes and has been generated from the unique text-plot of Zechariah 9–14.

No doubt, one substantial objection to this reading of διασπορά in 1 Pet. 1.1 is the apparent exilic *inclusio* in 1 Pet. 5.13. Most scholars agree that these two references (1.1 and 5.13) are meant to frame the letter in such a way that it places all those involved, both the author as well as the addressees, in exile.[19] However, there are at least three alternative interpretative possibilities regarding 1 Pet. 5.13 which may indicate that an exilic *inclusio* may not be in view.

I would suggest that my analysis of the overarching message of 1 Peter holds enough weight at least to press us to reconsider whether the phrase Ἀσπάζεται ὑμᾶς ἡ ἐν Βαβυλῶνι συνεκλεκτή is in fact intended as a reference to exile. In other words, if we are to grant that Peter does not locate his readers in exile elsewhere in the letter, then this should encourage us to ask whether there is another way that Babylon could be appropriated, one that does not connote the idea of exile. Here I find the comments of Goppelt and Doering to be helpful – even if they ultimately maintain that 1 Pet. 5.13 is principally a reference to exile. Goppelt, for example, notes that

> [a]s early as the book of Daniel 'Babylon' had become a symbolic name for the world power that placed into conflict situations those who belonged to the people of God scattered throughout its realm as part of its society . . . 1 Peter was written . . . for Christians for whom Rome was not only the governmental authority . . . but also, in accord with Daniel, the eschatological world power.[20]

---

[19] E.g Michaels 1988: 311; Goppelt 1993: 374–5; Achtemeier 1996: 354; Elliott 2000: 133; Doering 2009: 229–36.
[20] Goppelt 1993: 374.

It is possible, therefore, that if Babylon is indeed an allusion to Rome, the point of the reference is to remind the readers of 1 Peter that this seemingly invincible, universal power, whose influence upon the world seems to negate the very claims that Peter is making in his letter (i.e. that restoration has begun in Jesus Christ), will in fact be judged and destroyed because it has oppressed the people of God and opposed God's ways. In other words, what lies behind the Babylon reference is a call to interpret Rome's rule as fleeting, its judgment and destruction as pending. Thus, as Goppelt has astutely noted, the name Babylon 'is not meant to conceal anything, but to open Christians' eyes';[21] and I would add in particular to open their eyes to the real nature of Rome's tenuous reign.[22] Doering advances a similar point: 'If Rome were indeed meant here [1 Pet. 5.13], it would be more likely a *qualification* of Rome as ultimately responsible for persecution and dispersion, than an oblique reference by code name.'[23] This leads to a second interpretative possibility, briefly explored below.

In order for 5.13 to form an exilic *inclusio* it is helpful if not necessary for Βαβυλών to be a reference to Rome.[24] However, several features in the letter make it uncertain that Rome is envisioned. For instance, although many scholars argue that Βαβυλών is a cryptic, subversive way of referring to Rome, and that this reference signals the place from which the letter is written, it is unclear, in my view, why such a cryptic reference would be necessary in a letter that advocates the honouring of the emperor (2.17) and which upholds Graeco-Roman household codes (2.13–20).[25] Additionally, one of the arguments for pseudepigraphical authorship of 1 Peter could be turned on its head. It is unlikely that Peter, the ascribed author of 1 Peter (1.1), who according to tradition died in Rome *c.* 65 CE, would have used the term Babylon to refer to Rome since we have no

---

[21] *Ibid.*: 375, n.36.

[22] The Book of Revelation appropriates apocalyptic imagery and refers to Rome as Babylon with a similar aim.

[23] Doering 2009: 233. The broad reference could be that Babylon points to the social alienation experienced by those that send greetings, but not necessarily because they viewed themselves as still being in exile.

[24] As I have just argued above, it is possible to maintain that Babylon refers to Rome without it denoting exile. However, in the secondary literature, the overwhelming majority of scholars make exilic connections when the term is understood in reference to Rome.

[25] Not every scholar who sees Babylon as an allusion to Rome thinks that Peter is using the term cryptically. For example, Achtemeier (1996: 354), who regards 1 Pet. 5.13 to be a reference to Rome, argues that the term Babylon has not been used to hide from Roman authorities, but rather to 'reaffirm the analogy of Christians living in the diaspora as exiles and aliens'. Doering (2009: 233) makes a similar point: 'the contemporary era of dispersion and Roman domination is seen through the lens of the Babylonian exile'.

extant evidence of this usage until after the temple was destroyed in 70 CE.[26] What, then, Babylon might refer to if not Rome is a question that falls outside the scope of this proposal, but is no doubt worthy of further consideration.

Third, if any *inclusio* is intended from the references of 1 Pet. 1.1 and 5.13, it is likely that the unifying feature is the notion of election.[27] Syntactically, and in keeping with the thrust of the letter, the emphasis in 5.13 is not on the location (Babylon), but rather that the community of Christ followers that sends the greeting is also *co-elect*, and likewise on the same eschatological journey. As I have shown in Chapter 4, Peter appropriates election imagery from Exodus 19 and Isaiah 43 to indicate that his readers *no longer are to regard themselves as being in exile*, but instead are participants in a new exodus journey.

5.2   Isaiah 11.2, οἶκος τοῦ θεοῦ and the text-plot of Zechariah 9–14

In Chapter 4 I argued that the term οἶκος τοῦ θεοῦ, read within its epistolary context, is primarily a reference to a royal house, that is, a people who have aligned themselves with God and his messiah. Peter further describes this house of God as (a) a *spiritual* house which offers acceptable sacrifices to God (οἶκος πνευματικός; 2.5)/the people upon whom the Spirit now rests (4.14), (b) living stones that are being built (2.5)/a house (of God) that is being examined (4.17) and (c) a people who, in keeping with God's will, face opposition because of their allegiance to the messiah (2.7–8/4.12–19) that is characterized as testing rather than purification. In this section I will argue that the impetus for this description of Christ followers comes from the eschatological programme of Zechariah 9–14. In order to do so, we must begin with a review of the eschatological programme as it was detailed in Chapter 2.

The first oracle (9.1–17) of Zechariah 9–14 functions paradigmatically as a miniature of what will be developed in more detail in 10.1–14.21, and introduces the predominant theme of Zechariah 9–14 – YHWH's intention to restore his people. In Zech. 9.8, this restoration is described in terms of YHWH coming as a conquering king to watch over his 'house' (בֵּיתִי/τῷ οἴκῳ μου). The parallel stanza of Zech. 9.8 suggests that 'house' refers to YHWH's people (עֲלֵיהֶם/ἐπ᾿ αὐτούς; cf. 9.14–15)

---

[26] For the extant usage of Babylon as a reference to Rome see the influential essay by Hunzinger 1965. For the most recent work on Peter's death in Rome see Bockmuehl 2007.
[27] So Fagbemi 2007: 66.

rather than the temple. In my analysis of Zech. 9.9–10, I underscored the sudden emergence of a divinely appointed human agent, who becomes integral to YHWH's restoration plans. Additionally, I demonstrated that there is warrant to regard this human agent as an eschatological Davidic figure, whose legitimacy as king would be questioned, and who would require vindication from YHWH. I highlighted that there was a prominent expectation within post-exilic Judaism for a royal eschatological Davidic figure that would emerge as an integral part of the national and spiritual restoration of Israel. This expectation was rooted in the covenant that YHWH made with David, in which he promised that David's 'house' (בֵּיתְךָ/οἶκος; 2 Sam. 7.11–16; cf. Isa. 9.7; Ps. 18.50; 89.4, 29–37; 132.11–12) would be established forever. This expectation of a perpetual reign for the house of David found expression in several texts in which the future Davidic ruler is described as either a branch of David (Isa. 11.1; Jer. 23.5; 33.15), or a shepherd (Ezek. 34.23–4; 37.24; see also *Pss. Sol.* 17–18). Significantly, branch and shepherd are two designations used in Zechariah to describe YHWH's future ruler (3.8; 6.12; 13.7). Finally, I highlighted that this opening oracle closes by indicating that the vindication of YHWH's king will bring forth the restoration of his people, who are climactically described as his flock and 'stones of a crown'/'holy stones' (אַבְנֵי־נֵזֶר/λίθοι ἅγιοι) in 9.16.

Stone imagery is picked up once again in Zech. 10.4, this time, however, in reference to a leader who will emerge from the house of Judah, and who, unlike the unfaithful shepherds of Israel's past (Ezekiel 34; Jeremiah 23), will faithfully lead YHWH's people. This leader is described as both a 'cornerstone' (פִּנָּה) as well as a 'tent peg' (יָתֵד). As I underscored, פִּנָּה is used in Isa. 28.16 and Ps. 118.22 with reference to an eschatological figure – YHWH's appointed agent who will bring about restoration.[28] 'Tent peg', I suggested, alludes typologically to an anointed figure that will have authority over Jerusalem and the house of Judah. This cornerstone/tent peg figure is linked to a second exodus in Zech. 10.6–12, in which YHWH's people will be gathered in the wilderness, the covenant will be renewed (along the lines of Hosea 2) and the people will be led to their inheritance.

As I have demonstrated, Zech. 11.4–17 significantly alters the picture that has thus far been painted regarding Israel's restoration. While Zechariah 9–10 has given the impression, much in keeping

---

[28] As highlighted in Chapter 2, the Targum also understood פִּנָּה as an eschatological royal figure.

with Jeremiah 23 and Ezekiel 34, that the good shepherd/cornerstone would immediately usher in liberty, peace and prosperity, Zech. 11.4–17 opaquely indicates that the good shepherd will be rejected, and will provoke enmity among those in Jerusalem before restoration is finalized.

Zech. 12.8–14 reveals and emphasizes that as YHWH's restoration unfolds, the house of David will be filled with remorse as they mourn for the death of the 'pierced one' (12.10; i.e. the eschatological Davidic king), and as a result will become like the 'house of God' (Zech. 12.8).

The sombre tone of Zech. 12.10–14 has been infused with hope in Zech. 13.1–6. Concomitant with the death of the pierced one is a 'day' in which a fountain will be poured upon the house of David to cleanse them from their sin and impurity (13.1). This fountain of cleansing resonates with the eschatological programme of Ezek. 36.20–30, in which the unclean spirit of the land (cf. Zech. 13.2) will be replaced with a spirit that cleanses the people of their idolatry (36.26–7; Zech. 13.1–2).

I argued that Zech. 13.7–9 provides further details regarding the identity of the 'pierced one' (12.10), the fate of those that have rejected the good shepherd (11.8–14) and what will happen to the house of David. According to Zech. 13.7, the shepherd will be struck, and the sheep will be scattered. In Zech. 13.8, two-thirds of the people in the land will be cut off and perish, and one-third, presumably those who identify with the pierced one, will have to endure an unspecified period of 'fiery trials' intended to test their fidelity to YHWH and his appointed agent. The one-third that is put into the fiery trials will participate in the renewal of YHWH's covenant with his people, in which he will declare, 'They are my people' (Zech. 13.9; cf. Zech. 10.6 and Hosea 2.23; Ezek. 37.23). As I argued, these ensuing fiery trials described in Zech. 13.8–9 add texture to the second exodus motif of Zech. 10.6–12: we now are to understand the fiery trials of Zech. 13.7–9 as being a part of the second exodus journey mentioned earlier in Zech. 10.6–12, a time, not of purification, but rather of testing. Zech. 13.9 highlights that the one-third that is placed in the fire will emerge from the testing, protected by YHWH – a renewed community will emerge from the fire.

The import of this section of Zechariah cannot be overstated. Contrary to what one might have been led to believe from the programmes of Jeremiah and Ezekiel, the coming of the eschatological Davidic shepherd will not immediately usher in a time of peace and prosperity. Instead, a time of trouble, described as a period of 'fiery testing', will precede final deliverance.

Zech. 14.3–21 makes it clear, however, that the time of trouble will not be the end of Israel's story. YHWH will intervene along with his 'holy ones', appearing first on the Mount of Olives (14.4), to defeat the nations, secure Jerusalem and reign over all the earth (14.4–15). Those among the nations who survive will, year after year, join Israel in worshipping YHWH. The eschatological programme of Zechariah 9–14 culminates in a very significant fashion, especially as it relates to our study of 1 Peter. The final vision that Zechariah casts before its readers is that of a holy house offering holy sacrifices to YHWH (14.21).

In our discussion of the alterations of Isa. 11.2 in 1 Pet. 4.14 I raised the following questions: What has led Peter to connect (a) a persecuted community of God with (b) the promise of the spirit resting upon a *messianic* community and (c) why is this messianic community described as the house of God? Additionally, what has compelled Peter to alter Isa. 11.2 from a text which originally spoke of a future day in which the spirit would rest upon the messianic 'shoot' to a text that now speaks of the spirit presently resting upon a persecuted community that is defined in terms of their steadfast allegiance to the Christ? In Chapter 4 I showed that there is no satisfactory explanation to date that can account for all of these features. In light of our review, I would argue that a more satisfying answer can be found in the eschatological programme of Zechariah 9–14, in which we find some unique parallels with 1 Peter: in both texts the community that aligns itself with God's royal figure is described as the house of God (Zech. 12.8/1 Pet. 4.17); (b) the royal/messianic agent is described variously as a slain shepherd (Zech. 13.7/1 Pet. 2.23–35), a stone (Zech. 10.3/1 Pet. 2.6–8) and the shoot of David (implied in Zechariah 9–14 from Zech. 3.8, 6.12 and in 1 Pet. 4.14 from Isa. 11.2); (c) the house of God will undergo a period of fiery trials that are likened to a wilderness/new exodus journey and that are designed to test fidelity towards God; (d) the spirit will be poured out/now rests upon the house of God; and (e) the house of God, that is, those who align themselves with the slain shepherd, are to be characterized by holiness, in which they offer acceptable sacrifices to God (Zech. 13.1–2; 14.21/1 Pet. 2.5). Simply put, there is no other place in Israel's scriptures where we find these particular parallels. In my view, the best explanation for these parallels, then, is that Zechariah 9–14 is working as the substructure for Peter's eschatological programme: read through the lens of Jesus' life, death and resurrection (something we know was done in the early church; see Chapter 2), it provides Peter with the impetus for imaginatively connecting a persecuted community with the future promise of the spirit which was to be poured out on the shoot of David (now realized in Jesus and his community of followers), and it explains why this community is referred to as the house of God.[29] If this is the correct reading of 4.14, that is, if the eschatological programme of Zechariah 9–14 undergirds Peter's alteration of Isa. 11.2, then the two ὅτι clauses in 4.14–19 (i.e. 4.14,17), which are both intended to provide scriptural justification for the corresponding exhortations, both betray Zecharian influence. As for why Peter would alter Isa. 11.2 instead of drawing attention to Zechariah 9–14, that important question will be addressed in Chapter 6.

If we allow for the possibility that the eschatological programme of Zechariah 9–14 may have shaped Peter's understanding of Christian suffering, then this might shed even more light on why he elected to use the term οἶκος in reference to a persecuted people who have aligned themselves with the Christ (2.5; 4.17). Primopetrine scholars have often noticed the conspicuous absence of the word ἐκκλησία in a letter that is keenly interested in identity and community formation. Elliott explains this absence in two moves. First, he argues that the bulk of the letter's addressees resided in rural areas, in which the term ἐκκλησία would be alien to their everyday experience.[30] Second, given the rural setting of the addressees, 1 Peter has adopted οἶκος terminology throughout the letter as a more contextually relevant strategy for dealing with social estrangement by showing their 'at-home-ness' in the family of God.[31] He notes that '[o]f the various ecclesial concepts employed in this letter, it is the symbolization of the community as the household of God that serves as the root metaphor and organizing ecclesial image in 1 Peter'.[32]

Recently, David Horrell has offered a fresh analysis of Elliott's description of the socio-economic situation of the 1 Peter addressees.[33] He underscores that Elliott's foundation for assembling a social profile is an (over) analysis of the terms πάροικος and παρεπίδημος, which, according to Elliott, provide clues to the social condition of the addressees.[34] As Horrell points out, Elliott concludes that the terms πάροικος and παρεπίδημος may indicate that the addressees were numbered among the rural populations, and that they were comprised of artisans, craftsmen, traders and merchants travelling through villages and towns respectively. Elliott suggests that if we combine these conclusions regarding πάροικος

[29] Although texts such as Ezekiel 36, Joel 2 and Isaiah 11 speak of the spirit coming upon God's people, none of these texts suggests that God's people will subsequently undergo persecution; Zechariah 9–14 is unique in this regard, and it is likely that Zechariah has modified these eschatological programmes with this unique feature.
[30] Elliott 1981: 62–3; 2000: 84–90.   [31] Elliott 1981: 165–266; 2000:105, 112–18.
[32] Elliott 2000: 113.   [33] Horrell 2009.   [34] *Ibid.*: 179–80, 187–91.

and παρεπίδημος with the limited urbanization of much of Asia Minor then it becomes likely that the letter is directed at a predominantly rural audience.

Horrell, however, argues convincingly that the terms πάροικος and παρεπίδημος do not offer a literal socio-economic description of the 1 Peter addressees, but instead (1) 'convey something about the character of their experience', and (2) 'express their alienation and estrangement in terms of Jewish tradition'.[35] He follows this critique of Elliott's proposal by pointing out that if the addressees are not literally πάροικοι, then there is little to support the claim that they were most likely rural dwellers.[36] We can also add to this that there is little to support the claim that οἶκος terminology has been appropriated instead of ἐκκλησία because it was a more effective way of constructing identity in a rural setting.

If οἶκος has not been appropriated in order to address the rural context of the addressees, then how can we explain its usage in place of the more common term ἐκκλησία? Here again I would suggest that the eschatological programme of Zechariah 9–14 may provide us with an answer. As I have highlighted in my review of the eschatological programme above, there is an *inclusio* in the Zecharian programme (i.e. Zechariah 9–14) built around the image of God's house. In Zechariah 9.8, YHWH announces that he is coming to his house, which, as we have seen, refers to his people. And in Zech. 14.20–1, the eschatological programme concludes with a rightly functioning house offering acceptable sacrifices in YHWH's house.[37] In between these two points, in a climactic episode of the programme, we see that those who have mourned the death of the 'pierced one' will be cleansed from their impurity, enabling them to be called both the house of David as well as the house of God (12.8–12). If I am right about the influence of Zechariah 9–14 thus far, then it is very likely that Peter has chosen the term οἶκος τοῦ θεοῦ rather than ἐκκλησία precisely in order to construct a community identity that echoes the Zecharian eschatological programme, which *uniquely* emphasizes that the true house of God is the house that faithfully aligns itself with the slain Davidic shepherd, and which *must* pass through fiery trials that are likened to a new wilderness journey before it experiences full restoration. In other words, Peter's appropriation of the phrase οἶκος τοῦ θεοῦ may actually be an attempt to connect

---

[35] *Ibid.*: 189.
[36] *Ibid.*: 190. See also his brief critique of the 'limited' urbanization of Asia Minor and the supposed rural metaphors in the letter.
[37] Zech.14.20–21 uses 'house' in a dual sense, as the people of God and as the temple.

his readers to a scriptural text-plot that supports precisely the point that he has been making in his letter, namely that their necessary (1.6) and to-be-expected (4.12) suffering is part of a wider eschatological programme.[38]

5.3 The restoration of under-shepherds and Zechariah 9–14

It appears that from the earliest stages of its reception, scribes and scholars have puzzled over the relationship between 1 Pet. 4.12–19 and 1 Pet. 5.1–5. Michaels notes that the manuscript variations for 1 Pet. 5.1 'reflect scribal questions about the connection of this statement [i.e. 5.1–5] with what immediately precedes [i.e. 4.12–19]'.[39] An analysis of the textual tradition of 1 Pet. 5.1 reveals that the majority of the later manuscripts substitute τούς for the inferential conjunction οὖν, which was most likely original to the text.[40] Michaels rightly concludes that '[t]he effect of the substitution is to eliminate the necessity of seeking any real connection to the preceding context'.[41]

Since the consensus position today is that οὖν was original to the text, many scholars have struggled to understand how these two passages are related; in other words, what is 5.1–5 inferring from 4.12–19? Green has suggested that 5.1–5 'particularizes 4:12–19 for relationships within the community of believers, drawing out inferences from the change of life-world documented in 4:12–19 for the particular sets of persons named in 5:1–5: elders, younger persons, and everyone'.[42]

Green's proposal, however, only partially explains the connection between the two passages; it describes epiphenomenally the relationship between the two texts. Why has Peter followed the exhortation in 4.12–19, in which he reminds his readers of to-be-expected trials that come to test fidelity, with an exhortation to the *elders* of the community to shepherd the flock of God, eagerly watching over them without selfish motives (5.2; ποιμάνατε τὸ ἐν ὑμῖν ποίμνιον τοῦ θεοῦ ἐπισκοποῦντες

---

[38] This may also help explain, in part, why Peter has applied Israel terminology to the church.

[39] Michaels 1988: 276.

[40] For a full discussion see Michaels 1988: 276; see also Elliott 2000: 811.

[41] Michaels 1988: 276.

[42] Green 2007a: 164. Achtemeier (1996: 321) proposes that the author is repeating a pattern in the letter in which a section deals with matters external to the community, and then is followed by a discussion of matters internal to the community: 4.1–6 (external); 4.7–11 (internal); 4.12–19 (external); 5.1–5 (internal). This distinction he makes between external and internal matters, however, is blurred throughout 1 Peter 4–5, which makes it hard to see the pattern that Achtemeier describes.

μὴ ἀναγκαστῶς ἀλλὰ ἑκουσίως κατὰ θεόν)? Michaels has suggested that
the occasion or 'excuse' for concentrating on elders 'may have been the
allusion in 1 Pet. 4.17 to Ezek. 9.6, which refers to the eschatological
judgment "from the house of God"'.[43] In his thinking, while appropriating Ezek. 9.6 to highlight the pending judgment upon God's temple,
Peter perhaps was influenced by the phrase that follows, which mentions the elders 'in front of the house'. This, however, is an unlikely
explanation since in the proposed precursor text the elders are among
the group that is set to be condemned and destroyed (see §4.2.2).[44]
There is, in other words, no basis in Ezek. 9.6 for the optimism that
is expressed in 1 Pet. 5.1–4, in which it is expected that faithful elders
will emerge in the fiery trials to shepherd God's flock. Elliott points us
in a more helpful direction, suggesting that 'the reference to "household of God", of which the elders and young persons were a logical
component', reflects 'the need for responsible leadership in the face of
suffering'.[45]

Troy Martin adds another layer to Elliott's observation, suggesting that
Zechariah 9–14 is the precursor text: '1 Peter's connection of the ideas of
God's flock being led by shepherds (5.1–5) and being tried by fire (4.12) is
paralleled by the collection of ideas in Deutero-Zechariah. This collection
of ideas provides part of the rationale for the connection of this subsec-
tion with the previous one.'[46] He supports this assertion by suggesting
that Zechariah 9–14 has shaped the letter elsewhere: 'Deutero-Zechariah
provides important background material for other notions expressed in
1 Peter. 1 Peter 1.7; 2.10; and 4.12 are paralleled by Zechariah 13.9.
1 Peter 2.25 alludes to ideas expressed in Zechariah 13.7–9.'[47] My analysis of the influence of Zechariah 9–14 on 1 Peter in Chapters 3 and 4
supports Martin's suggestions. And his case can be further strengthened
by noting one additional parallel between the two texts. In Chapter 4, I
argued that the eschatological programme of 1 Peter (especially 5.1–4)
includes the restoration of a second tier of leadership that will watch over
the flock of God in terms that are antithetical to the bad shepherds who
are chided in Ezekiel 34. This same theme is integral to the eschatological
programme of Zechariah 9–14.

In Chapter 2 I underscored that Zech. 10.1–5 is a significant passage
for understanding the diagnosis and the cure for Israel's predicament,
as well as the language that is used in Zech. 10–13 to describe how
YHWH intends to restore her: the people wander like sheep because

[43] Michaels 1988: 277; see also Jobes 2005: 300.   [44] See Elliott 2000: 812.
[45] *Ibid.*: 813.   [46] Martin 1992: 259.   [47] *Ibid.*: 259, n.418.

they lack shepherding (Zech. 10.2 (MT); LXX reads 'because they lack healing'). This particular way of describing Israel's predicament (i.e. with pastoral imagery) finds its antecedent in Ezekiel 34, which itself builds upon Jeremiah 23.[48] In both texts, Israel's crisis is credited to selfish and unrighteous leaders: YHWH's 'flock' has been scattered because the 'shepherds' have failed to 'feed the sheep, strengthen the weak, heal the sick, bind up the injured, bring back the stray, and seek out the lost' (Ezek. 34.3–4). For this reason, YHWH is against the 'shepherds' (Ezek. 34.10; Zech. 10.3). In addition to YHWH personally intervening, he also foretells of his plan to set up over the 'sheep' 'one shepherd', his servant David, who will give them the kind of leadership they need (34.23 and again in 37.24–5). All this is said to happen on the day when YHWH will vindicate his name, gather in his people from the nations, cleanse them from their idolatry, give them new hearts and put his spirit within them that they might walk in his statutes (Ezek. 36.25–7).

Zechariah 10–13 builds upon this programme in Ezekiel by complementing the one Davidic shepherd with a second tier of leadership. The 'cornerstone' (פִּנָּה) and 'tent peg' (יָתֵד) are accompanied by a group of leaders who are described as overseers in the MT (lit. 'every overseer'; כָּל־נוֹגֵשׂ).[49] According to the Zechariah programme, in the new order there will no longer be self-serving under-shepherds who abuse his sheep (see Ezek. 34). Instead, YHWH's new leadership will serve the people in such a way as to bring about victory for the entire nation (10.5; cf. 9.11–13).[50]

Zechariah scholar Paul Redditt highlights this (i.e. the restoration of leadership) as a major theme in Zechariah 9–14.[51] In particular, he points to Zech. 12.7–13.1, a passage that insists that restoration will only come about when the house of David becomes like the house of God (12.8).[52] As I have already noted above in §5.2 and in Chapter 2, this change comes about when the house of David mourns for the 'pierced one' and is cleansed from idolatry and impurity.

This major Zecharian theme, then, provides the distinctive link between 1 Pet. 4.12–19 and 1 Pet. 5.1–4. The house of God (4.17/Zech. 12.8),

---

48   Sweeney 2000: 668–71; Laniak 2006: 162–5.
49   Meyers and Meyers 1993: 203; Duguid 1995: 272.
50   Mason 1977: 100; Meyers and Meyers 1993: 203–4.
51   Redditt 2008: 338–9, 344.
52   Redditt (*ibid.*: 344) has also argued that Malachi was redacted in order to be read along with Zechariah 9–14 so as to 'stamp the Twelve with this word of caution: the promised restoration cannot come about until the leadership in Jerusalem repents and changes its ways'.

that is, those who have aligned themselves with the Christ (4.12–15), the pierced one (Zech. 12.10–13.1) and upon whom the Spirit now rests (4.14), is now, in keeping with the Zechariah programme, equipped with under-shepherds who will faithfully and selflessly lead God's people through the necessary fiery trials until the Chief Shepherd returns to reign (1 Pet. 5.4/Zech. 14.3–21). As Bosetti has pointed out, these elders are to pattern their leadership (ποιμάνατε; ἐπισκοποῦντες[53]) after the ποιμήν καὶ ἐπίσκοπος τῶν ψυχῶν ὑμῶν.[54] That Peter has included an exhortation to the νεώτεροι and to πάντες may also be a contextualized echo of the Zechariah programme, in which all the tribes and their wives are said to rightly align themselves with the pierced one and his appointed under-shepherds (Zech. 12.12–14).

5.4   Conclusion

In this chapter I have argued that the best way to read διασπορᾶς in 1 Pet. 1.1 is as an ablative genitive. An ablative reading is not only grammatically possible but also coheres with the overall narrative of 1 Peter, which describes its addressees as elect-sojourners who have returned to the shepherd and are now journeying through fiery trials towards their prepared inheritance. I have indicated that this distinctive description of the addressees is a unique feature of Zechariah 9–14 and is most likely an early indication of Peter's dependence upon its eschatological programme. Second, I argued that a number of unique features in the eschatological programme of Zechariah 9–14 explain Peter's modification of Isa. 11.2 in 1 Pet. 4.14 and his appropriation of the phrase οἶκος τοῦ θεοῦ in 4.17. Finally, I proposed that the unique emphasis in Zechariah 9–14 on the restoration of a second tier of leadership in 'the house of God' explains why Peter has moved from a discussion of the to-be-expected fiery trials to an exhortation to the elders to shepherd and oversee the flock through these wilderness testings.

This chapter, then, has helped to show the recurrence of Zecharian themes (echoes) outside of 1 Pet. 2.25 and 1 Pet. 1.6/4.12. What makes these proposed echoes significant is their distinctiveness, that is, they are unique to both Zechariah 9–14 as well as to 1 Peter. Additionally,

[53] Michaels (1988: 276) comments that '[t]he command to "watch over" (ἐπισκοποῦν-τες) the flock is omitted in certain MSS (including ℵ* and B) but is retained in the majority of MSS (including p[72] ℵ[2] A P Ψ the OL versions and g.). It is difficult to see why scribes would have added it if it were not original since the verse reads quite smoothly without it.'
[54] Bosetti 1990: 194.

the proposed echoes provide coherence to features of 1 Peter that are otherwise lacking. In Chapter 6, I turn to the task of drawing together all of the proposed allusions and echoes, to argue that Zechariah 9–14 functions as the substructure for the eschatological programme of 1 Peter.

6

ZECHARIAH 9–14 AS THE SUBSTRUCTURE OF 1 PETER'S ESCHATOLOGICAL PROGRAMME

To be clear, 1 Peter is not an exposition of Zechariah 9–14; Peter's aim is not principally that of shedding new light on a perplexing text. Rather, he is concerned with helping Anatolian Christians negotiate their allegiance to Jesus in a social context that, for a number of reasons, is antagonistic to such a commitment.[1] It is a letter written to encourage Christ followers to exegete their suffering and social alienation in light of Jesus' death and resurrection, to help them understand their new corporate identity 'in Christ' and to live accordingly.[2] It is with this end in view, I argue, that Peter draws upon Zechariah 9–14 – not merely in order to explain that according to the scriptures the Jewish messiah was to suffer and die (as is the case in the Gospels), but instead in order to make clear that *Christian* suffering is in keeping with God's will – for now.[3]

Thus far I have focused on selected passages in 1 Peter that, I have argued, are dependent upon and allude to material found in Zechariah

---

[1] Cf. Lohse (1954: 73), who comments that 'Der Brief wendet sich an Christen, die in Leiden und Anfechtung stehen. Sie darin zu stärken und zu trösten, ist die Absicht des Verfassers'. For the social and theological factors that contributed to the addressees' suffering see §4.1.1; See also Feldmeier 1992: 105–12; Bechtler 1998: 41–107; and Elliott 2000: 84–103 (though his rural audience hypothesis is quite problematic; see Martin 1992: 142–4; Horrell 2009: 187–91 for critique).

[2] Here I follow Campbell (1998), who has argued that rhetorically speaking 1 Peter is principally deliberative, seeking to inculcate new values and virtues in the readers (though note Thurén 1990, who argues that 1 Peter exhibits epideictic rhetoric designed to encourage believers to continue valuing that which they already know to be true). Dryden (2006) has helpfully highlighted that 1 Peter is not merely concerned with social identity per se, or even with merely helping his readers survive in the midst of suffering, but instead seeks to form moral character and active dependence upon God so that his readers might thrive in the midst of suffering (*ibid.*: 37–53). Unfortunately, Dryden unnecessarily limits the letter's character-formation strategy to individuals rather than focusing on the way in which the letter seeks to shape the community as a whole. For more see Elliott's critique of Dryden on this point (RBL 2009; available at www.bookreviews.org/pdf/7248_7887.pdf).

[3] See Bechtler 1998, Campbell 1998 and Elliott 2000, who each help root the addressees' situation and the rhetoric of 1 Peter within the honour and shame paradigm of the first century.

9–14. In some cases my analysis has included a discussion of the broader literary context of the letter; however, in order to appreciate the manner in which the Zecharian material shapes 1 Peter's eschatological programme it will now be necessary to survey the letter as whole. In what follows (§6.1), I will seek to trace the structure and the argumentative strategy of 1 Peter, highlighting in particular the prominent role that eschatology plays in Peter's efforts to persuade and encourage his addressees. From there I will identify the substructure of 1 Peter's eschatological programme (§6.2), which I will argue is generated from the distinct eschatological programme of Zechariah 9–14, read in light of the death and resurrection of Jesus.

6.1   The structure and argumentative strategy of 1 Peter[4]

In his monograph on the literary character of 1 Peter, Martin concludes that '[e]pistolary analysis reveals that 1 Peter exhibits the five basic parts of an ancient letter'.[5] These parts are as follows: (1) the prescript (1.1–2); (2) the blessing (1.3–12); (3) the letter-body (1.13–5.12); (4) the greeting (5.12–14a); and (5) the farewell (5.14b).[6] Although most Primopetrine scholars are in agreement with respect to the overall structure of the letter, there is some disagreement with regard to how the letter-body is best divided.[7] I have adopted the basic contours of Martin's overall

---

[4] In the first half of the twentieth century a number of scholars argued that 1 Peter was something other than a genuine letter (a baptismal homily (Perdelwitz 1911); a baptismal liturgy (Boismard 1961); liturgy for a baptismal paschal Eucharist (Cross 1954)). More recent studies, however, in a variety of ways have demonstrated that 1 Peter is best regarded as a genuine letter that was written in order to encourage its addressees (monographs: Schutter 1989; Thurén 1990; Martin 1992; Tite 1997; Bechtler 1998; Campbell 1998; Dryden 2006; commentaries: Michaels 1988; Goppelt 1993; Achtemeier 1996; Elliott 2000; Jobes 2005; Green 2007a). Michaels (1988: xlvi–xlix) and Elliott (2000: 12) have further suggested that 1 Peter is an 'apocalyptic diaspora letter', and Doering (2009) has put forth evidence that such a generic category likely existed when 1 Peter was composed. Although I do find the work of Michaels, Elliott and Doering to be helpful for understanding the generic qualities of 1 Peter, I nevertheless do not read 1.1 and 5.13 in the same manner, as has been seen.

[5] Martin 1992: 269.   [6] *Ibid.*: 269–70.

[7] Martin (*ibid.*: 135–267) for example parses the letter-body into three sections, which in his view correspond to three particular metaphor clusters: elect people of God (1.14–2.10); strangers and aliens (2.11–3.12); sufferers in the Diaspora (3.12–5.11). Campbell (1998: 58–198), drawing on classical rhetorical categories, divides the letter-body in the following manner: first *argumentatio* (1.13–2.10); second *argumentatio* (2.11–3.12); third *argumentatio* (3.13–4.11); *peroratio* (4.12–5.14). Campbell's outline of the letter-body has been modified by Witherington (2007: 49) to include five arguments: *proposito* (1.13–16); argument 1 (1.17–2.10); argument 2 (2.11–3.12); argument 3 (3.13–4.11); argument 4 (4.12–19); argument 5 (5.1–5); *peroratio* (5.6–9); doxology (5.10–11).

schema, but I have elected to divide the letter-body into the following three parts, for reasons that will become clear in my analysis: 1.13–2.10, 2.11–4.11 and 4.12–5.11; additionally, I have conflated the greeting and the farewell into one final unit.

In analyzing the argumentative strategy of 1 Peter, I am particularly interested in tracking the manner in which Peter seeks to accomplish his goal of helping his addressees cope with social alienation as a result of their allegiance to Jesus Christ. More specifically, I am interested in highlighting the principal exhortations of the letter along with the assumptions (narrative or otherwise) and proofs that are appropriated in order to make those exhortations persuasive.

6.1.1   The prescript: 1 Peter 1.1–2

The prescript (1.1–2), when read with a cognizance of the rest of the content of the letter, immediately begins to reveal an essential element of Peter's strategy for aiding the Anatolian Christians as they negotiate their existence in hostile environs. As I developed in Chapter 4, the epithet ἐκλεκτοί παρεπίδημοι stresses the liminality (or in betweenness) of Peter's readers, their paradoxical identity as elect-sojourners. According to Peter's reckoning, something has happened to the readers that has both put them in a favoured relationship with God as well as uprooted them socially and distanced them (theologically) from their diasporic status. Both Bechtler as well as Feldmeier have helpfully demonstrated that this liminality is not merely social, but is also foundationally undergirded by an assumed eschatological programme that has yet to come to fruition.[8] In Chapter 5 I argued that the three prepositional phrases (1.2) that modify the epithet ἐκλεκτοί παρεπίδημοι explain that the liminal status of the addressees is (a) in keeping with what God the father has revealed (i.e. foreknown in scripture), (b) enabled by the sanctifying, cleansing work of the Spirit and (c) inaugurated by the sacrificial obedience of Jesus Christ.[9] As I maintained in §5.1, these three prepositional phrases foreshadow subsequent material in 1 Peter that together outline in a rudimentary fashion the basic contours of the distinctive eschatological programme of Zechariah 9–14: YHWH's shepherd will suffer a death that will serve to cleanse 'the house of God' (upon whom the Spirit now rests; 4.14) and bring back the scattered sheep to God, while also placing them

---

[8] See Bechtler (1998: 126–35) on 'temporal liminality' in 1 Peter, as well as Feldmeier's (1992: 95–112) development of the concept of *Fremde* in the social context of 1 Peter.

[9] See §5.1 for my development of these three prepositional phrases.

in a period of fiery trials that they must endure until final consummation
(Zech. 12.8–12; 13.7–9/1 Pet. 1.5–7; 2.4–10; 2.21–5; 4.12–19).

6.1.2   The Blessing: 1 Peter 1.3–12

First Peter 1.3–12, often referred to as either the *exordium* or the blessing,
formally introduces this rudimentary eschatological programme, while
also pointing the readers to the major themes that will be developed
in the letter.[10] Here, Peter orients his readers to the situation they are
undergoing by reminding them of the future that awaits them. In keeping
with God's mercy and by means of Jesus' resurrection from the dead,
they have been born anew to (a) a living hope (1.3), (b) an imperishable,
uncorrupted and unfading inheritance (1.4) and (c) a salvation to be
revealed in the last time (1.5). Peter here has borrowed language from the
exodus tradition (inheritance; κληρονομία) and the prophets (salvation;
σωτηρία) in order to point his readers to a time when God will bring to
fruition his plan of redemption – a day which will mean vindication for
those who have aligned themselves with his Christ, and the establishment
of God's righteousness on earth (e.g. 2.12; 5.4).[11]

Although salvation is described as an outcome that is certain (i.e. it is
prepared (σωτηρίαν ἑτοίμην)), Peter explains that it will not be revealed

---

[10] For more on the function of the *exordium* see Tite 1997: 52; Thurén 1995: 90–1;
Campbell 1998: 33. Although I am not yet convinced that Peter consciously chose to
work with the standard Graeco-Roman rhetorical categories such as *exordium, narratio,
propositio* and *probatio*, I have no doubt that these rhetorical conventions had a shaping
effect, even if indirectly and/or subconsciously, in the way in which Peter presented his
material. Black (1995: 257), for example, suggests that although Jesus and the apostles
may not have received a formal education in rhetoric 'undeniably they were born into a
culture whose everyday modes of oral and written discourse were saturated with a rhetorical
tradition, which was mediated by . . . Caecilius, Cicero, and Quintilian'. Additionally, I find
that rhetorical studies in 1 Peter often help heuristically to organize the major sections of
the letter. At times, however, the material of the letter seems to be forced to fit with the
aims of particular rhetorical categories, as for example when it is claimed that our author
in the *exordium* is seeking to establish a positive ethos, or when the aim of 1 Pet. 1.3–12 is
to create attentiveness and goodwill among the readers (Campbell 1998: 33).

[11] For κληρονομία as a circumlocution for arriving in and possessing the promised land
see Num. 34.2; 36.2; Deut. 12.9; Josh. 1.15; 13.1; Judg. 2.6; 18.1; 21.23; 2 Chron. 6.27; 31.1;
Pss. 134.12; 135.21,22; Jer. 2.7; 3.19; 16.18; Ezek. 11.15; 25.4,10; Zech. 9.4; for the use of
κληρονομία in conjunction with the promise of restoration see Isa. 49.8; Jer. 12.25; Pss. 2.8;
67.10; 110.6; Ezek. 45.1. Elsewhere in the NT the term is connected with salvation (Acts 7.5;
13.33; 20.32; Eph. 1.11,14; Col. 3.24) and the second exodus (Heb. 9.15; 11.8), that is, that
which the people would acquire when the wilderness wandering is completed. Hebrews 3–4
is significant because there is a connection between suffering and the wilderness, but without
the optimism that is offered in 1 Peter. For the eschatological/restoration connotations of
σωτηρία see Isa. 45.17; 46.13; 49.6; 52.7,10; 63.8; Jer. 38.22; Pss. 17.51; 73.12; 117.14,21
28; 143.10.

(ἀποκαλυφθῆναι) until the last time (ἐν καιρῷ ἐσχάτῳ). In other words, Peter portrays his readers as living in a period of transition (inaugurated eschatology). And this transition period is characterized as a time in which faithful followers of the Christ must (δεῖ) pass through various trials (ποικίλοι πειρασμοί; 1.6), though not without God's protection (1.5). In 1.7 this transition period of various trials is further characterized as a time in which their proven faithfulness (τὸ δοκίμιον ὑμῶν τῆς πίστεως) will result in them being honoured at the revelation of Jesus Christ.[12] As I highlighted in Chapter 4, it is important to note that Peter's strategy for helping his readers rightly respond to trials is not, as is sometimes claimed, in conformity with a prevalent wisdom tradition that regarded suffering and trials as opportunities for improving one's character. Instead, the motivation for enduring trials is the certain outcome – eschatological salvation, an incorruptible inheritance for those who maintain faithfulness. As Peter states, 'your proven faithfulness is even more precious than gold, which perishes when tested in fire'. As I stressed in Chapter 4, Peter's confidence that his readers will indeed emerge from the fiery trials to be showered with future honour and praise parallels the distinct eschatological programme of Zech. 13.8–9. It is this eschatological perspective that undergirds the exhortations that will follow in the letter, and it functions as the lens through which the readers are to interpret their sufferings in the present. Now is their time to faithfully endure fiery trials; the *telos* (i.e. outcome) of their faithfulness to Jesus, whom they presently do not see, is the salvation of their souls (1.8–9).

Peter concludes this opening section of the letter (1.3–12) by reflecting on this salvation, drawing attention to the prophets, who diligently sought to understand the circumstances surrounding τὰ εἰς Χριστὸν παθήματα καὶ τὰς μετὰ ταῦτα δόξας (1.10–11).[13] Although many commentators interpret this phrase as a reference to Christ's sufferings (e.g. the sufferings destined for Christ), for the following reasons it seems more likely that the sufferings of Christ followers are in view.[14] First, there is the

[12] See §4.2.1 for my translation of τὸ δοκίμιον ὑμῶν τῆς πίστεως as 'proven faithfulness'.
[13] There is much debate regarding the best way to translate τίνα ἢ ποῖον καιρόν. The principal question is whether in 1 Pet. 1.11 τίνα is a personal pronoun (see Kilpatrick 1986: 91–2, who shows that in the rest of 1 Peter (3.13; 4.17; 5.8) and throughout the NT, τίς is a pronoun), or whether it is modifying καιρόν and being used somewhat redundantly with ποῖον. I follow both Michaels (1988: 41–3) and Jobes (2006: 101–2), who carefully conclude that the search of the prophets is not centred upon the person of the messiah, but rather the circumstances surrounding τὰ εἰς Χριστὸν παθήματα καὶ τὰς μετὰ ταῦτα δόξας, of which I have more to say in the remainder of this paragraph.
[14] Brown 1855: 86; Scott 1905: 234–40; Selwyn 1958: 136; Best 1971: 175; Michaels 1988: 270; Schutter 1989: 106–8; Martin 1992: 65–8, 242–52.

principal aim of the letter: whereas the Passion Narratives are primarily concerned with explaining why the Christ had to suffer and die and how that fits with what has been revealed in the scriptures, 1 Peter is primarily concerned with explaining why *Christian* suffering is necessary and to be expected in spite of the fact that, according to early Jesus followers, Jesus is the Lord's messiah.[15] In this regard, it is noteworthy that three key Christological passages in 1 Peter (1.18–19; 2.21–5; 3.18–22) do not seek to offer scriptural justification for the necessity of Jesus' death, but rather endeavour to explain the implications of Jesus' death for his followers.[16] The question that Peter appears to be addressing throughout the letter then is not *Who is to come?* or *What are the circumstances surrounding his coming?* but rather, *Why is there still suffering now that the Christ has come?* Second, as we have just seen, in this opening section of the letter Peter has explained that there is a necessary (if not also unanticipated) testing period, what he calls fiery trials, which must precede salvation. It would follow that this transition period in particular is what Peter refers to in 1.11 (i.e. τὰ εἰς Χριστὸν παθήματα καὶ τὰς μετὰ ταῦτα δόξας). Third, according to Peter, presently angels eagerly desire to know τὰ εἰς Χριστὸν παθήματα καὶ τὰς μετὰ ταῦτα δόξας.[17] It would seem quite unlikely that angels are still wondering about the circumstances surrounding Jesus' sufferings and the vindication he would enjoy after such things since this already seems to be a forgone conclusion (see 1 Pet. 3.18–22). Instead it makes more sense that they desire to watch the outworking of Christian suffering and the glories that will be experienced afterwards. Fourth, since the near context stresses the transition period prior to eschatological salvation, it makes more sense to read *both* prepositions in the phrase τὰ εἰς Χριστὸν παθήματα καὶ τὰς μετὰ ταῦτα δόξας as temporal in nature. In other words, that which the prophets are searching for pertains to the suffering *until* Christ (i.e. his second advent; 1.7; 2.12; 5.4) and the glories *after* these things (i.e. after the sufferings; cf. 1.5–7; 4.12–5.4). This reading has the added value of explaining why

---

[15] '[T]he Christians of Asia Minor . . . are suffering not only by reason of the absence of a tangible relationship [i.e. to Jesus, whom they 'do not see' (1 Pet. 1.8)] but also because of the seeming contradiction between the promise of renewal implied in the resurrection and the actual situation of trial and persecution in which they find themselves' (Hill 1982: 52). Brackets mine.

[16] Even the catena of stone passages in 1 Pet. 2.6–8 appear to function primarily in order to bolster the statement in 2.4–5, namely to show the connection between the precious stone and the living stones.

[17] I agree with Achtemeier (1996: 111) and Shimada (1981: 146–7), who argue that the things the prophets ministered (αὐτά) and into which the angels desired to look (ἃ) are τὰ εἰς Χριστὸν παθήματα καὶ τὰς μετὰ ταῦτα δόξας.

Peter chose the plural 'glories' (δόξας) instead of 'glory' – since what is in view is not the vindication of Jesus but rather the vindication of faithful Christians. One might object to this reading of 1.11 on the grounds that the prophets never envisioned a second coming of the messiah. This may be true, but Peter and many early Christians, who regarded the death, resurrection and ascension of Jesus to be the definitive revelation of God's dealing with humanity, were forced to read the prophets through a new lens, seeking to understand the witness of the Spirit of Christ (1.11) in a new light.[18]

Two principal points emerge from these last three verses of the *exordium*/blessing. First, 1 Pet. 1.10–12 stresses that Christians, in light of the gospel message, are in a privileged position to understand the outworking of God's restoration plan. Second, it appears that Peter looks to the prophets in order to explain both the necessity of Christian suffering until the Christ's return as well as the glories that are to be awarded to Christians after they endure such trials. While we cannot be certain, it could be that Peter here (1.10–11) reveals a key hermeneutical assumption: namely, that the prophets are to be read and interpreted in light of the life, death, resurrection, ascension and return of Jesus, and for the purpose of understanding what God's people can expect prior to his return.[19]

As one might expect (given the nature of a blessing/*exordium*), what emerges in this opening section of the letter is the primary strategy for helping Christians thrive in their present circumstances. Peter offers his readers a new interpretative framework for their experiences – they now 'participate in the epochal change that took place in Christ; their life is thereby defined as "eschatological" existence'.[20] It is this inaugurated eschatological perspective that will underpin the theological orientation and the exhortations that follow.[21]

---

[18] First Peter clearly envisions a second return of Jesus (e.g. 1.7; 2.12; 5.4), and this is in conformity with other witnesses in the apostolic age (e.g. Matt. 24.42–3; 25.13; 1 Thess. 1.10,19; Rev. 3.3; 16.15; 22.20). Additionally, there is evidence in Rev. 1.7 that Zech. 12.10 could be interpreted not only to refer to Christ's death but also to his second coming.

[19] Thus in contrast to Schutter's homiletic midrash hermeneutic (1989), I am suggesting that Peter's hermeneutic is essentially an ecclesio-centric approach which is informed by the Gospel. Cf. Hays' work with Paul (2005: 222): Paul was 'engaged in a hermeneutical project of re-presenting the Christ-story in relation to the needs of the church'.

[20] Feldmeier 2008: 95.

[21] Cf. Horrell 2008: 20. Similarly, Dryden (2006: 89) notes that '[t]he benediction of 1.3–12 is designed to map a narrative world that provides the readers a meta-history by which they can interpret their own life stories . . . provides them a hermeneutic for their suffering, as well as for the epistle's ethical instruction'.

6.1.3   First Peter 1.13–2.10

Given what Peter has developed thus far in the letter, it comes as no surprise that the first exhortation he offers to his readers is to 'hope completely in the grace to be brought to you when Jesus Christ is revealed' (1.13). As we saw in Chapter 4, what is significant about this exhortation is that it is accompanied with a number of exodus and new exodus references that together have the effect of placing the readers in a wilderness setting (theologically), even though the word 'wilderness' never appears in the entire letter. Echoing the narrative of the exodus, he calls them to 'gird up the loins' of their mind (1.13; cf. Exod. 12.11), that is, to understand *when* they are – in the transition period between redemption from exile and inheritance (1.1,3–7). He then exhorts his readers to be holy in all their conduct (cf. Exod. 19.5–6), and then offers as the scriptural basis for this exhortation a quotation from the exodus tradition ('Be holy since I am holy'; Lev. 11.44; 19.2; 20.7,26). Additionally, he stresses that his readers are to conduct themselves in keeping with *when they are* – in a time of sojourning (τὸν τῆς παροικίας ὑμῶν χρόνον; 1.17). According to Peter, this sojourn has been initiated by the sacrificial death of Jesus, which is likened to the Passover lamb (1.19) – who although he was foreknown before the foundation of the world has been manifested in these last times 'for your sake' (1.20). Much like he did in 1.3, Peter underscores that it is the resurrection of Jesus from among the dead that provides the basis for the hope that Peter has been developing (1.21).

The third exhortation of this passage, 'love one another earnestly from a pure heart' (1.22), is also undergirded with second exodus imagery. According to Peter, in keeping with what has been announced in Isa. 40.6–8, his readers have been born anew through the living word, which is equated to the gospel that has been preached to them (1.25). Isa. 40.6–8 is significant because it is the focal point of the prologue of Isaiah 40–55, in which YHWH announces his intentions to redeem his people from exile.[22] In Isaiah 43, a passage which is integral to the message of Isaiah 40–55, and which is cited later in 1 Pet. 2.9, YHWH announces (as a part of his 'word' or 'gospel') that he is about to do a new thing (43.19) – he is set to form a new people (43.1,7,15,21) and to make a way for them in the wilderness (43.19). This may help explain why Peter uses the unusual term ἀναγεννάω twice (1.3; 1.23) in order to describe those who have aligned themselves with Jesus Christ. In effect, Peter is maintaining that

---

[22] Anderson 1962; Stuhmueller 1970: 59–98; Watts 1990; Westermann 2001: 127–9; Jobes 2005: 126.

Jesus' sacrificial death (1.2; 1.19; 2.23–5) has actualized that which is spoken of in Isaiah 40–55: through Jesus, a new people has been formed (born anew), and God is making a way for them in the wilderness. In other words, once again Peter appears to be highlighting their present time as a wilderness sojourn.

The eschatological perspective necessary to live out their calling is again highlighted in 1 Pet. 2.1–3. Rather than being taken up with evil, deceit, hypocrisy, envy and malicious speech, which characterized the first wilderness sojourners (see Num. 11–12, 14, 16, 20–1; Ps. 106:24–5), Peter argues that 'if you have tasted that the Lord is good' (2.3), then the only natural response is to crave the unadulterated milk so that you can grow up to salvation.[23] This exhortation once again orients the readers by placing them in a transition period in which they are to be sustained by eschatological hope. Most scholars agree that the refrain 'if you have tasted that the Lord is good' is a modification of LXX Ps. 33.9 ('taste and see that the Lord is good'). The second colon of this verse reads: 'blessed is the man who hopes in him'. Thus, as Jobes has pointed out, tasting that the Lord is good 'is related to putting hope in him'. What is particularly significant about the LXX version of this psalm, as I have argued in Chapter 4, is that the context for deliverance is ἐκ πασῶν τῶν παροικιῶν, which fits with what Peter has been developing thus far in his letter.[24]

As Elliott has commented, 1 Pet. 2.4–10 'bring to a resounding climax the line of thought begun in 1:3'.[25] Here in these verses Peter seeks to orient his readers in relation to their allegiance with Jesus. He does this first in the theme verses (1 Pet. 2.4–5), where he makes it clear that the 'Lord' whom they have tasted to be good is none other than Jesus, the living stone (λίθος) – who was rejected by men but regarded as God's precious elect one (2.4). According to Peter, those who have aligned themselves with this living stone are likewise living stones (λίθοι ζῶντες). He amplifies this description by referring to his readers as a spiritual house (οἶκος πνευματικός) which is being built in order to be a holy priesthood that offers pleasing spiritual sacrifices to God through Jesus

---

[23] See Jobes (2002; 2005: 132–41), who argues convincingly that λογικός milk does not mean word-milk, but rather points to the milk that is true to the nature of the new eschatological reality established by the resurrection of Jesus Christ and into which Peter's readers have been reborn.
[24] Cf. Jobes 2005: 138–9. There is every reason to suggest that Peter had more than just LXX Ps. 33.9 in view since he again draws from other portions of the psalm (33.13–17) in 1 Pet. 3.10–12.
[25] Elliott 2000: 407.

Christ (2.5). These theme verses are then clarified and justified with six references to the OT, all of which appear to be dependent upon the LXX. The first three OT references (Isa. 28.16; LXX Ps. 117.22; Isa. 8.14), which each contain the catchword λίθος, elaborate the statement made about Jesus in 2.4. In 1 Pet. 2.6, Isa. 28.16 is drawn on both to confirm that Jesus is indeed the precious elect cornerstone (ἰδοὺ τίθημι ἐν Σιὼν λίθον ἀκρογωνιαῖον ἐκλεκτὸν ἔντιμον) as well as to remind the reader that whoever places trust in him (i.e. this precious elect cornerstone) will not be put to shame (likely a *litotes* to affirm the future glory associated with being aligned with Jesus (cf. 1 Pet 1.7; 5.4, 10)). The second and third OT citations are taken from LXX Ps. 117.22 and LXX Isa. 8.14, which assure the readers that Jesus' rejection by 'the builders' was in keeping with the foreknowledge of God, that is, part of his unfolding plan.[26]

The second half of the theme verse (2.5) is then elaborated in 1 Pet. 2.9–10 with three OT passages (Isa. 43.20; Exod. 19.6; Hosea 2.25) which are drawn on in order to shape further the identity and vocation of the community that has aligned itself with Jesus and also to orient them in their time of transition. At the surface, when these passages are woven together they unveil a special relationship between God and those who have placed their hope in Jesus. Their new status is described with familiar terms from Israel's tradition: they are an elect clan (Isa. 43:20), a priestly kingdom and a holy nation (Exod. 19.6), and a people (λαός) for God's possession (Exod. 19.5). Using the catchword λαός, Peter then links together portions of Isa. 43.21 and Hosea 2.25 to restate their vocation and affirm their special status: they have been made a people for God's possession 'in order to declare the mighty acts' (τὰς ἀρετάς; Isa. 43.21) of the one who has delivered them from darkness and into his marvellous light; they who were not a people have been made a people of God; they who did not receive mercy have received mercy from God (Hosea 2.25).

The catchword λαός can only partially explain why Isa. 43.21 has been linked with Exod. 19.6 and Hosea 2.25. Additionally, the *gezerah shavah* technique is unable fully to account for Peter's appropriation of Exod. 19.5 and Isa. 43.20. I argued in Chapter 4 that the primary link is not lexical but rather conceptual. All three texts are foundational passages in their respective literary contexts which point to the very theme that Peter has been developing in this section of his letter (esp. 1.3–7).

---

[26] See especially the final comments in 1 Pet. 2.8, οἳ προσκόπτουσιν τῷ λόγῳ ἀπειθοῦντες εἰς ὃ καὶ ἐτέθησαν.

In Exod. 19.5–6, for example, YHWH, in keeping with his covenant faithfulness, has redeemed his people from Egypt; as his newly formed people, his treasured possession, they have been given the vocation to be a priestly kingdom and a holy nation, who must live out their calling in the wilderness as they journey towards their inheritance. Similarly, Isa. 43.20–1 fits within a narrative in which YHWH promises to restore his people from exile. Significantly, Isaiah describes this restoration in terms that resonate with what Peter has been developing: YHWH will form his people for himself so that they might declare his praise (43.21), and he will guide and protect them in the wilderness as they journey towards their promised possession (43.13–20). Hosea 2 narrates a similar scenario: YHWH will gather his wayward, unfaithful people in the wilderness, where he will renew his covenant with them. Those who had previously been named *Lo-ammi*, not my people, will be called *Ammi*, my people (1.9; 2.1; 2.23(25)); those who had previously been named *Lo-ruhamah*, not pitied, will be called *Ruhamah*, pitied (1.6; 2.1; 2.23(25)). What is significant about the appropriation of these three passages, read within the larger context of 1 Pet. 1.3–2.10, is that Peter is declaring that the promises of restoration found in Isaiah 43 and Hosea 2 have now been actualized in the death and resurrection of Jesus, and that those who have been aligned to Jesus are encouraged to imagine their lives as a recapitulation of the first wilderness journey, this time in faithfulness.

One further point that must be highlighted is the fact that 1 Pet. 2.9–10 is intended to inform the way we are to understand the phrase οἶκος πνευματικός in 1 Pet. 2.5. As I developed in Chapter 4, the word οἶκος can be variously understood as either a house (i.e. a building, and as an extension, a temple), a household, a people or clan with a common descendent or a royal dynasty.[27] Since 2.9–10 has been added to elaborate 2.5, and since 2.9–10 contains six phrases which variously describe the readers as 'an elect people', 'a priestly kingdom', 'a holy nation', 'a people for God's possession', 'the people of God' and 'a people who has received mercy', it is likely best to interpret οἶκος (2.5) as primarily referring to either a people or clan with a common descendent (i.e. Jesus Christ), or as a royal dynasty (because of their alignment with Jesus the Christ (i.e. king)), rather than principally as a reference to a temple building. As I have shown in Chapters 4 and 5, when read along with 1 Pet. 4.12–19, and in light of the eschatological programme of Zechariah 9–14, this conclusion is further strengthened.

[27] BDAG: 698. See Hillyer 1969: 126, who argues that οἶκος refers to royal dynasty.

6.1.4   First Peter 2.11–4.11

Thus far in the letter (1.1–2.10) Peter has been principally occupied with the task of orienting his readers with respect to their identity, their vocation and their place within God's unfolding plan of restoration. He does this by declaring *who* they are (elect-sojourners, living stones, the house of God, etc.), *where* they are (a second exodus wilderness) and *when* they are (in the time of fiery trials prior to the time in which God will return to put all things right) as a result of the death and resurrection of Jesus Christ. In 1 Pet. 2.11–4.11, Peter moves from an elaborate discussion of the addressees' theological identity to a reflection on how this ought to affect the way they interact with their compeers, both Christian and otherwise, in this transition period. He begins with the theme verse for this section, 1 Pet. 2.11–12, in which he compactly summarizes what he has developed thus far:

> ¹¹ Ἀγαπητοί, παρακαλῶ ὡς παροίκους καὶ παρεπιδήμους ἀπέχ-
> εσθαι τῶν σαρκικῶν ἐπιθυμιῶν αἵτινες στρατεύονται κατὰ τῆς
> ψυχῆς· ¹² τὴν ἀναστροφὴν ὑμῶν ἐν τοῖς ἔθνεσιν ἔχοντες καλήν,
> ἵνα ἐν ᾧ καταλαλοῦσιν ὑμῶν ὡς κακοποιῶν ἐκ τῶν καλῶν ἔργων
> ἐποπτεύοντες δοξάσωσιν τὸν θεὸν ἐν ἡμέρᾳ ἐπισκοπῆς.

The principal exhortation, which is offered in 2.11, is to abstain from fleshly desires which wage war against the soul. The following verse appears to explain more specifically what Peter has in view: they are to maintain a good way of life among the Gentiles (τὴν ἀναστροφὴν ὑμῶν ἐν τοῖς ἔθνεσιν ἔχοντες καλήν) in the face of slander.²⁸ Here in 2.12, Peter simultaneously points backwards to the previous theme he has developed, reminding his readers that they have a new way of life (ἀναστροφή) as a result of what Jesus has accomplished in his death (1.15; note especially 1.17, where Peter frames this new ἀναστροφή in relation to their present sojourn), while also pointing forwards to an exhortation he will make in 3.8–12, where he will urge his readers not to retaliate when wrongfully slandered. Thus, the particular fleshly desire in view here is likely the impulse to offer a verbal riposte when one's honour has been challenged. As Peter will develop, Jesus (1 Pet. 2.21–3) becomes the paradigm for this new ἀναστροφή.

What is notable about this theme verse (for the purposes of the thesis I am putting forth) is that it emphatically reiterates their theological

---

²⁸ I take ἔχοντες to be a participle of means, further defining the main verbal clause παρακαλῶ ἀπέχεσθαι.

identity (aliens and sojourners) that Peter has just detailed in 1.1–2.10.[29] Thus, the basis for Peter's exhortation is the fact that they are a newly formed people who are on a journey towards their inheritance. Echoing 1 Pet. 1.5–8, their present conduct is to be informed by this eschatological reality: the salvation of their souls (σωτηρίαν ψυχῶν (1.9); cf. 2.12) depends upon their faithfulness (e.g. not responding to verbal slander in kind) in the midst of the fiery trials of this transition period (1.5–7; cf. 2.12). Green has helpfully observed that for Peter '[o]rienting one's life eschatologically is the means by which one creates distance from a life branded by the desires of this age'.[30] The result (ἵνα) of this new ἀναστροφή will be glorification when God appears (cf. 1 Pet. 1.5–7). In other words, the one who faithfully endures slander (which Peter envisions as being concomitant with aligning oneself with Jesus) will be vindicated when God is glorified at his return (2.12).

In what follows (1 Pet. 2.13–4.11), Peter begins to explain that his addressees' social/theological alienation, contrary to what might be expected, is not a licence to disengage from society. Instead, he urges his readers 'to submit to every human institution' (2.13).[31] He qualifies this exhortation with three phrases that connect his readers to what he has developed thus far in the letter and form the basis for their engagement with society: (1) on account of the Lord; (2) as free persons; (3) as slaves of God (2.13–16).[32] With these three qualifiers, Peter first reminds his readers that their true lord is no longer Caesar (and the concomitant way of life that such an allegiance requires) but rather Jesus, the Christ (2.3,13).[33] The final two phrases should be read within the context of the second exodus framework that Peter has been developing. Yes, the death of the Lamb has redeemed and set free those who have aligned themselves with Jesus (1.18–19), but just as was the case with the first exodus, this freedom is for the purpose of service to God and his creation. As Levenson has commented, '[t]he point of exodus is not freedom in the sense of self-determination, but *service*, the service of the loving, redeeming and delivering God of Israel, rather than the state and its proud

---

[29] I understand ὡς παροίκους καὶ παρεπιδήμους to be a hendiadys rather than an expression of two distinct groups of people.
[30] Green 2007a: 68.
[31] Green (*ibid.*: 73) argues that 'Peter's opening imperative ὑποτάγητε . . . is best understood as the negative of "withdraw" rather than an alternative to the exercise of power or rebelliousness. Finding and occupying responsibly one's place in society, not resignation, is more to the point.'
[32] So also *ibid.*: 74.
[33] Since in the near context 'lord' is a reference to Jesus (2.3), it seems most likely that Jesus rather than God (the Father) is in view.

king'.[34] Thus, their free status (ἐλεύθεροι) enables them to be slaves of God (θεοῦ δοῦλοι) in righteousness (2.16; cf. 2.24). Once again, we catch a glimpse of Peter's strategy, which is to root his readers' present comportment in the theological/eschatological reality that has been disclosed in 1.1–2.10. Subordination to every human institution, rather than being a form of cultural accommodation, is instead portrayed as a faithful expression of their vocation as the newly formed people of God.[35]

The catchphrases πάροικοι, παρεπίδημοι, ἐλεύθεροι and θεοῦ δοῦλοι, then, point the readers to the larger eschatological programme that Peter has been developing thus far, and serve to root their present conduct within that reality. Having established the theological/eschatological basis for their new way of life in this transition period, Peter proceeds with a number of exhortations directed first towards the wider audience (2.17), then to specific audience members (to slaves (2.18–20); to wives (3.1–6); to husbands (3.7)), then once again to the wider audience (3.8–17; 4.1–11). Strategically wedged within these exhortations are two Christological passages (2.21–5 and 3.18–22) which ultimately provide theological perspective not merely for understanding Christ's suffering and death, but more foundationally in order to make sense of Christian suffering, that is, suffering that is a direct result of aligning oneself with Jesus Christ.

First Pet. 2.17, then, reiterates the exhortation in 2.13, but with one bracing addition: the same honour that is owed to the king (i.e. emperor) is also owed to all people (πάντας τιμήσατε . . . τὸν βασιλέα τιμᾶτε). What is more, the Christian community and the God it worships are given special prominence, bracketed within the exhortation to honour all people and the king (τὴν ἀδελφότητα ἀγαπᾶτε, τὸν θεὸν φοβεῖσθε).

Peter then moves to address household slaves (οἰκέται), who are called to submit to their owners whether good or bad (2.18). This specific exhortation is followed by four γάρ clauses (2.19, 2.20, 2.21 and 2.25), each of which provides with increasing depth a theological rationale for the call to endure unjust suffering. First, Peter argues that when submission to one's master results in unjust suffering, if done precisely because of one's commitment to God (διὰ συνείδησιν θεοῦ) then this will be met with divine favour (χάρις).[36] He further reiterates that it is

---

[34] Levenson, J. D. 1991 'Exodus and Liberation' *HBT* 13: 134–74. Taken from Green 2007a: 74. See also Isa. 65.9, where the new exodus participants are described as slaves of God.

[35] *Pace* Balch 1981.

[36] In this particular instance χάρις is to be understood within the semantic domain of honour language rather than divine enabling grace. Cf. 1 Pet. 2.20. See also Achtemeier 1996: 196.

favourable in God's eyes (τοῦτο χάρις παρὰ θεῷ) to endure suffering for doing good rather than for some wrongdoing (2.20). But why is unjust suffering part of the Christian life? That is, why does fidelity to God result in unjust suffering?

In 1 Pet. 2.21 Peter digs deeper by responding to these questions with a third γάρ clause: 'For to this you were called' (εἰς τοῦτο γὰρ ἐκλήθητε). This is further explained (ὅτι) with the theme phrase for 1 Pet. 2.21–5: καὶ Χριστὸς ἔπαθεν ὑπὲρ ὑμῶν.[37] On the surface it appears that Peter's exposition regarding the suffering of Christ primarily functions as the paradigm for Christians to follow (ὑμῖν ὑπολιμπάνων ὑπογραμμὸν ἵνα ἐπακολουθήσητε τοῖς ἴχνεσιν αὐτοῦ; 2.21). For example, Peter initially highlights the fact that Jesus did not use retaliatory speech when reviled (2.22), but instead entrusted himself to the one who judges justly (2.23), implying that faithful Christians are to do the same (especially when read along with 1 Pet. 3.10–12). Although this is certainly one aspect of what Peter has in view, as I have demonstrated in Chapter 3, there is more going on in this passage than first meets the eye.

For instance, in 1 Pet. 2.24, Peter moves away from a reflection on the paradigmatic function of Jesus' suffering to address the atoning significance of his death. According to Peter, Jesus bore 'our' sins in his body when he died on the cross. This enables 'us' to die to sin and live to righteousness. He rearticulates this at the end of 1 Pet. 2.24 by stating that by his wounds 'you have been healed'.

This statement is followed with Peter's final γάρ clause (2.25); and here we strike theological bedrock. As I indicated in §3.4, Peter's pattern prior to 2.24 has been to cite a modified verse from LXX Isaiah 53 and add to it a brief commentary describing how it relates to Jesus' unjust suffering and death (1 Pet. 2.22–3). The effect of this has been to link Jesus' last week, his passion, with the Righteous Sufferer of Isaiah 53 and all of its theological implications (i.e. atonement for sins, restoration from exile, cleansing of the people of God, etc.) In 2.24, Peter again cites a modified verse from Isaiah 53, this time from Isa. 53.5 ('by his wounds you were healed'; οὗ τῷ μώλωπι ἰάθητε). But here, instead of adding commentary, Peter initiates a new sentence (γάρ; 2.25), which is intended to undergird all that he has been developing in this passage: 'For you were like sheep straying, but now you have been returned to the shepherd and overseer of your souls' (ἦτε γὰρ ὡς πρόβατα πλανώμενοι, ἀλλὰ ἐπεστράφητε νῦν

---

[37] See §3.3 for argumentation on this point.

190   The Eschatology of 1 Peter

ἐπὶ τὸν ποιμένα καὶ ἐπίσκοπον τῶν ψυχῶν ὑμῶν).[38] What does Jesus' suffering and death have to do with Christian suffering?

As I argued in §3.3 and 3.4, Peter has culminated his reflection on the creedal formulation, 'Christ suffered on your behalf', by covertly conflating Isaiah 53 and Zech. 13.7 and its wider eschatological programme in order to develop the theme of restoration which comes through the suffering and death of YHWH's appointed agent. In Chapter 2, I demonstrated that Zechariah 9–14 offers a unique twist to the shepherd tradition of the prophets: YHWH's agent, the appointed shepherd over God's people, will not immediately bring restoration. Instead, he will be rejected and suffer death (Zech. 11.4–17; 12.10). This death will initiate the gathering of God's scattered sheep (described also as healing; LXX Zech. 10.2); it will cleanse the 'house of God' from their sin (Zech. 12.8–13.2); but it will also bring about a transition period described in Zech. 13.8 as fiery trials, which are additionally likened to a new exodus (Zech. 10.8–12). In discerning Peter's allusion to Zech. 13.7 and its wider context in 1 Pet. 2.25, we see that he is providing scriptural warrant not only for Christ's death (as does Isaiah 53), but more to the point of the passage, he also explains why Christians must endure suffering.[39] Simply put, it is *when* they are.[40] With this in view, it appears that Peter interprets Isaiah 53 within the wider framework of the eschatological programme of Zechariah 9–14. As those who have been returned to the slain shepherd-king because of his sacrificial death, Peter's readers are now in the fiery trials where their fidelity to God will be tested while they undertake a new exodus journey towards their inheritance. That Jesus is characterized as the Shepherd and Overseer of their souls (τὸν ποιμένα καὶ ἐπίσκοπον τῶν ψυχῶν ὑμῶν) reminds them of the certain outcome of this journey (cf. 1 Pet. 1.5–7; Zech. 13.8–9; see also §4.2 and 4.3) in language that is borrowed from Zechariah 10, 11 and 13.[41]

Most commentators agree that even though 1 Pet. 2.21–5 falls within a passage specifically directed towards household slaves, Peter

[38] Translation mine in order to bring out the passive voice of ἐπεστράφητε.
[39] 'The elegance of Peter's reflections on Christ may blind us to the primary concern of this text. He is really not about christological reflection here but deploys christology in the service of his instruction about Christian life and witness in the world. This is christology in the service of ecclesiology' (Green 2007a: 83).
[40] We must recall that the unique contribution of Zechariah 9–14 is that it explains not only why the Christ must suffer but also why suffering is something to be expected for those who align themselves with Jesus.
[41] Reading this verse in light of Zech. 13.7–9 provides more texture to Jobes' (2005: 199) observation that 'walking in Jesus' footsteps, even through unjust suffering, is nevertheless the Shepherd's path of safety, protection, and deliverance'.

nevertheless has in view his entire audience (i.e. the 'house of God; 1 Pet. 2.5; 4.17). Elliott has helpfully suggested that the slaves 'are held up here as paradigmatic of the condition and vocation of the brotherhood as a whole'.[42] This seems to be the case since Peter previously refers to his entire audience as slaves of God (2.16), and since he draws on this passage in 1 Pet. 3.8–12 when addressing the entirety of his readership.

In 1 Pet. 3.1–7, Peter continues the instruction he began in 2.13 ('submit to all human institutions'). Here he highlights what this might look like in the context of marriage. What is underscored in his exhortation to both wives as well as husbands is what he has already said more generally in 1 Pet. 2.16: freedom that comes through Jesus' death and resurrection is for the service of God and others. Thus, in light of their new reality actualized through Jesus, husbands and wives are to find ways to serve their spouses with a way of life that is in keeping with their new identity. In keeping with his overall strategy, Peter reinforces his exhortation to the Christian spouses by reminding them of *when* they are. He does so, first, by drawing attention to Sarah, upholding her as the prototype for sojourning wives (see Gen. 12.11–20).[43] Secondly, he reminds Christian husbands that their believing wives are fellow-heirs of the grace which is come (see 1.3–8).

In 1 Pet. 3.8–17, Peter once again addresses his wider audience, underscoring the disposition that is in keeping with being the newly formed people of God (3.8; cf. 1.22). He follows this with a specific call not to retaliate when slandered, reminding them that they instead are to bless in order to receive a blessing (3.10). In addressing the way in which his readers are to respond to slander (1 Pet. 3.10–12), it is significant that Peter draws upon LXX Ps. 33.13–17.[44] As I highlighted in §3.3, LXX

---

[42] Elliott 2000: 542. See also Achtemeier 1996: 192; Michaels 1988: 135; Campbell 1998: 143; Jobes 2005: 187; Green 2007a: 78, 82.

[43] So also Green 2007a: 96–7.

[44] Woan (2004) argues that Psalm 34 makes a central contribution to the structure and the content of 1 Peter. For example, she notes that the quotation of Psalm 34 in 1 Pet. 3.10–12 both summarizes previous material in the letter and introduces material that will follow. With respect to the summarizing function of 1 Pet. 3.10–12, she highlights (*ibid.*: 223–4) the fact that a number of key words ('life', 'to see', 'evil', 'deceit', 'doing good', 'justly') are introduced throughout 1 Pet. 1.1–3.9 in the same order as they appear in 1 Pet. 3.10–12. Additionally, she notes (*ibid.*: 224) that 1 Pet. 2.11–20 is probably a development of the exhortation to 'seek peace and pursue it' in 1 Pet. 3.11, and that Psalm 34 is probably alluded to in 1 Pet. 2.1 and most certainly in 1 Pet. 2.3. With regard to the introductory function of 1 Pet. 3.10–11, Woan (*ibid.*: 224–5) underscores the significant degree of correspondence in vocabulary between 1 Pet. 3.10–12 and 1 Pet. 13–17, and argues (*ibid.*: 225) that the eschatological passages of 1 Pet. 4.7–11,13; 5.1,4,6 correspond to Ps. 34.10 ('those who desire life and desire to see good days . . . ').

Psalm 33 orients the psalmist in the midst of his 'sojournings' (33.5; ἐξεζήτησα τὸν κύριον, καὶ ἐπήκουσέν μου καὶ ἐκ πασῶν τῶν παροικιῶν μου ἐρρύσατό με).[45] Jobes has commented that the LXX translator, who is otherwise quite faithful to the Hebrew rendition of this psalm, has contextualized the text in order to address the needs of the Greek Jews living away from their homeland.[46] It appears that Peter, much in keeping with the LXX translator of Psalm 33, is also contextualizing the psalm. Accordingly, for Peter LXX Ps. 33.13–17 embodies the kind of ethic that is required for those who are presently sojourning in the wilderness awaiting their inheritance (note especially the pattern of 1 Pet. 3.10–11; 'Whoever desires to love life and see good days... let him... '). In other words, it appears that Peter has appropriated from LXX Psalm 33 not only because it contains the kind of ethic that he wants to put forth, and not only because embedded within the psalm is a pattern of righteous suffering and consequent vindication, but also (and perhaps more importantly) because it simultaneously reinforces the eschatological perspective he has so diligently developed thus far in the letter.[47] Said in another way, LXX Psalm 33 'bears witness to or exemplifies the fabula on which Peter builds his own narrative of faithful Christian existence', a narrative that includes a period of fiery trials prior to ultimate vindication.[48]

The latter content of LXX Psalm 33 (vv. 14–17) has clearly influenced Peter's statements in 1 Pet. 3.12–17. The exhortation to turn away from evil and to do good (3.11) is completed with the reminder that the Lord is against those who do evil. From here Peter raises the question – Who then is there to harm you if you are zealous to do good (3.13)? Surprisingly, however, Peter's response to the question is more nuanced than one might anticipate. He indicates that there may well be

---

[45] The Hebrew text reads 'he delivered me from all my fears'. In his study on the use of the OT for Christian ethics in 1 Peter, Green (1990) appears to miss the analogous sojourn setting shared by LXX Psalm 33 and 1 Peter. Woan (2004: 220) notes the difference between MT 34.5 and LXX 33.5 but does not associate the LXX variation with the sojourn motif of the eschatological programme of 1 Peter.

[46] Jobes 2005: 220. For more on the parallels between LXX Psalm 33 and 1 Peter see *ibid.*: 220–4.

[47] Thus, although I agree with Woan (2004: 229) when she argues that Psalm 34 has been chosen because it contains many features that would make it an ideal scriptural source for imagery about the righteous sufferer, I contend that the foundational feature is the sojourn setting and motif of the psalm (i.e. LXX Ps. 33.5), which parallels the eschatological programme of Zechariah 9–14.

[48] Green 2007a: 107, n.107. It should be noted that Green's notion of the fabula is limited to the rescue and vindication of the righteous sufferer and does not include the wilderness sojourn that I have put forth.

circumstances in which 'doing good'[49] will result in unjust suffering.[50] If this is the case, Peter urges his addressees to give a defence of the hope they have. This hope, which has been detailed in 1 Pet. 1.3–8, is linked to the Christ, who has paved the way for their salvation (3.15).[51] Peter concludes this section by once again orienting his readers with respect to the eschaton. First, in keeping with LXX Psalm 33, he reminds his readers that those who do evil will be put to shame (3.16). As was the case in 1 Pet. 2.6–8, this phrase points to the day in which God will justly judge all who oppose the messiah and his people.[52] Second, he reminds his readers that 'it is better' to suffer for doing good than for doing evil. Michaels has convincingly shown that there is a 'it is better' tradition both in the OT as well as in the NT 'which is characteristically used to set forth eschatological alternatives.' He adds that '[i]f 1 Pet 3:17 is read [in a manner consistent with this tradition], it yields a coherent meaning: it is "better" to suffer in this life at the hands of persecutors for doing good, than at God's hand on the "day of visitation" for doing wrong'.[53]

Peter's enigmatic reflection on Christ's proclamation to the spirits in prison (1 Pet. 3.18–22) serves to bolster this point.[54] Following the work of Dalton, most Primopetrine scholars now agree that this passage refers to the resurrected Christ's announcement of victory over evil as he ascended to sit at the right hand of God.[55] Read in this manner, 1 Pet. 3.18–22 emphatically affirms that all those who have placed their hope in Christ will indeed be secure in the eschaton, since not only sin (2.22–4) but also evil has been defeated (see especially 3.18: Jesus suffered death so that he might bring 'us' to God). It simultaneously reminds the addressees that they live in a transition period in which evil still yields power and influence.

---

[49] Broadly speaking, 'doing good', both in the context of 1 Peter as well as in Psalm 34, is maintaining fidelity to God in spite of what the wider culture might think about your actions. Thus, there are times when 'doing good' will not be met with resistance, while at other times 'doing good' will be perceived as evil-doing. See Michaels 1988: 191–2 for the development of this theme.

[50] Hence the optative case in 3.14 (εἰ καὶ πάσχοιτε διὰ δικαιοσύνην).

[51] Jobes 2005: 230.   [52] Michaels 1988: 191.

[53] *Ibid.*: 192. Elliott (2000: 635) helpfully notes that '[t]he qualification, *if this should be God's will*, refers to suffering *for doing what is right* and not simply suffering per se. The point is not that God wills suffering but that God wills doing what is right rather than doing what is wrong . . . even if and when this results in suffering'. Thus it is the transitional period, the fiery trials, that give opportunity for suffering for doing what is right.

[54] Hence the epexegetical ὅτι to begin the passage.

[55] See especially Dalton's (1965: 115) outline of the logic of 1 Pet. 3.18–22, which I follow.

Peter extends the implications of 1 Pet. 3.18–22, first by stating once again that Christ's suffering serves as a paradigm for Christians, who are urged to live no longer for human passions but rather for the will of God (1 Pet. 4.1–2; cf. 1 Pet. 2.11–12; 2.21–3). First Pet. 4.3–4 illustrates the kind of suffering that Peter has in view: verbal abuse that is the result of Christians no longer participating in the characteristic sinful behaviour of the Gentiles.[56] Secondly, yet again Peter points his addressees to the eschaton, when both the living as well as the dead will give an account of their lives and be judged accordingly (4.5). It is unlikely that the enigmatic reference in 1 Pet. 4.6, which states that the gospel was preached to the dead, is to be linked with 1 Pet. 3.19 (the spirits in prison);[57] neither is it to be understood as an opportunity for post-mortem repentance. Instead, it is more likely that Peter is referring to those who have heard the gospel and then died; they too will have to give an account.[58]

Given the way in which Peter has oriented his addressees in 1 Pet. 1.1–2.10 and the consistent references to the eschaton in 1 Pet. 2.11–4.6, it is no surprise that he brings the second section of his letter-body (2.11–4.11) to a conclusion by once again situating his readers' trying circumstances within an eschatological framework: 'The end of all things is near (Πάντων δὲ τὸ τέλος ἤγγικεν), therefore . . . ' (1 Pet. 4.7).[59] Although τέλος often carries the notion of cessation or termination, it is more likely, given what I have already outlined in the letter, that Peter has in view the goal or outcome of God's promised restoration initiated in the death and resurrection of Jesus Christ (e.g. 1.3–8; 1.20–1; 2.24–5).[60] This reading is strengthened by the verb ἤγγικεν, which in the perfect form likely stresses the 'now-but-not-yet' tension of God's restoration programme.[61] Here once again, Peter stresses that his readers are living in a transition period that will culminate with Christ's return (5.4), and that they are to live accordingly. Previously (2.11–4.6), the bulk of Peter's

---

[56] Although suffering in 1 Peter often is characterized in terms of verbal slander and social ostracism, the letter also suggests that suffering can take the form of physical abuse (e.g. 2.20), formal accusations (including public trials; e.g. 3.15; 4.12–17) and perhaps even legal punishment resulting in execution (e.g. 2.21–4). For the development of this more comprehensive view of suffering in 1 Peter than has typically been acknowledged, see Horrell 2007: 138–40; 2008: 54–9; Holloway 2009; for a comprehensive study of Roman attitudes towards Christians from Claudius to Hadrian see Cook 2010.

[57] Dalton 1965: 42–51; Michaels 1988: 237–8; Achtemeier 1996: 291; Elliott 2000: 730–1.

[58] See Jobes 2005: 272 for a full account of this interpretation. See also Horrell 2003.

[59] Jobes (2005: 274) notes that 1 Pet. 4.7 forms an *inclusio* with 1 Pet. 2.11–12, forming a well-defined, self-contained unit.

[60] Jobes 2005: 275; Green 2007a: 141.

[61] See also Mark 1.15; Matt. 4.17; 10.7; Luke 10.11; 21.8.

comments have been directed towards the way in which Christians are to engage with those outside of their community (with the exception of 1 Pet. 3.7–8). Here in 1 Pet. 4.8–11, he draws attention to the way in which Christians are to treat one another in this transition period. Green helpfully explains this new emphasis by commenting that Peter's 'eschatological compass . . . relativizes the claims of ultimacy voiced by present institutions and encourages social behaviors almost guaranteed to attract unwanted attention . . . [It] is incumbent on [Peter] that he lay out the character of the community and its practices that are faithful to that eschatological vision.'[62]

6.1.5   First Peter 4.12–5.11

The doxology in 1 Pet. 4.11 appears to indicate that the line of thought initiated in 2.11 is being drawn to a conclusion. Additionally, the vocative 'brethren' (ἀγαπητοί) in 1 Pet. 4.12 likely signals the beginning of a new section of the letter (cf. 2.11). This new section can be parsed further into three subsections: 4.12–19; 5.1–5; and 5.6–11.

Many scholars have noted the summative character of this final section of the letter-body. The most extreme example is Campbell, who argues that 1 Pet. 4.12 is the beginning of the peroration that extends to 5.14.[63] Witherington helpfully nuances Campbell's analysis, however, by pointing out that while 1 Pet. 4.12–5.11 does summarize previous material, it also contributes new arguments to the letter. He further explains that repetition and amplification are well-known aspects of Asiatic rhetoric, which better explain why themes are revisited in this final section and then further enhanced with new argumentation.[64] Michaels notes that 1 Pet. 4.12–19 echoes material in 1 Pet. 1.6–8 (e.g. necessary fiery trials; see also §4.2.2 for verbal parallels) and 1 Pet. 3.13–17 (e.g. personal security for those who maintain fidelity; blessedness of those who endure suffering; better to suffer now for doing good than to suffer later for doing evil now).[65] Feldmeier perhaps states it best, however, when he writes that 'the previous statements of the letter about suffering are tied up and taken further in order to take a position on this central problem of the letter with a thoroughness that has not yet been reached up to this point'.[66]

---

[62] Green 2007a: 142.   [63] Campbell 1998: 199–228.

[64] Witherington 2007: 208–9; see 39–51 for a more detailed explanation of the rhetoric of 1 Peter.

[65] Michaels 1988: 258.   [66] Feldmeier 2008: 223.

Accordingly, as I have already detailed in §4.2.2, 1 Pet. 4.12–
19 reminds the readers of a number of points already raised: (1) suffering
is to be expected; that is, it is inherent to those who have identified themselves with Jesus Christ (4.12; cf. 1.6); (2) suffering is to be interpreted as
fiery trials that serve the purpose of testing one's fidelity to Jesus Christ
(4.12; cf. 1.5–8); (3) those who participate in the 'belonging to Christ'
sufferings will receive glory at Christ's second coming (4.13; cf. 1.5–8;
2.19–20);[67] (4) there will be those that choose not to express loyal allegiance to the Christ; they will be destroyed, that is, they will not appear
in the age of full restoration (4.17–18; cf. 2.8); (5) those who entrust
themselves to God can have confidence in the final outcome of the fiery
trials; in spite of the difficulties that come with remaining faithful, God
will bring his elect-sojourners through the fiery trials (4.19; cf. 1.5–8);
(6) the final outcome of God's restoration is an occasion for great joy
(4.13; cf. 1.3–8); and (7) suffering 'in the name of Christ' is in keeping
with God's will, a part of his overarching plan (4.19; cf. 1.10–11; 2.15;
3.17).

Additionally, Peter amplifies two themes only hinted at earlier in the
letter: (1) the Spirit now rests upon the community that associates itself
with the messiah, the Christ (4.14; cf. 2.5; οἶκος πνευματικός); and (2)
this Spirit-endowed messianic community is described as the 'house of
God' (οἶκος τοῦ θεοῦ), which will be evaluated and delineated through
the fiery trials of the second exodus (4.17; cf. 2.5). As I argued in
Chapters 4 and 5, this section of 1 Peter (4.12–19) shares significant
parallels with several unique features of the eschatological programme
of Zechariah 9–14 and best explains Peter's appropriation of the phrase
οἶκος τοῦ θεοῦ and his modification of Isa. 11.2, such that he declares that
the Spirit now rests upon the messianic community rather than just the
messiah.[68]

One further unique feature of the eschatological programme of
Zechariah 9–14 best explains the logic which links 4.12–19 and 5.1–
5. As I argued in Chapter 5, Zechariah 9–14 emphasizes the restoration
of a second tier of leadership in 'the house of God' which will shepherd
and oversee God's flock through the fiery trials. Accordingly, Peter urges
the elders to 'shepherd' God's flock unselfishly (5.2–3), reminding them

[67] See §4.2.2 for why I read τοῖς τοῦ Χριστοῦ παθήμασιν as 'the "belonging to Christ"
sufferings'.
[68] Those significant parallels include (1) fiery trials which serve to test (rather than
purify) the remnant prior to full restoration (Zech. 13.8–9); (2) those who align themselves
with the slain shepherd are referred to as the 'house of God' (Zech. 12.8–10); and (3) the
Spirit will rest upon the house of God (Zech. 12.8–13.2).

that they are accountable to the Chief Shepherd, who will offer, upon his return, crowns of reward that will never fade (5.4).

Peter culminates his letter in 1 Pet. 5.6–11 by offering four summative exhortations which underscore and allude to a number of themes that he has developed throughout his letter. First, in light of all that Peter has written, he urges his addressees to humble themselves 'under the mighty hand of God' (τὴν κραταιὰν χεῖρα τοῦ θεοῦ). Jobes has helpfully observed that variations of the phrase τὴν κραταιὰν χεῖρα τοῦ θεοῦ appear in the exodus tradition and point to God's ability to deliver and preserve his people as they journey to their inheritance (LXX: Exod. 13.9; Deut. 3.24; 4.34; 5.15; 7.19; 9.26; 11.2).[69] He further reminds his addressees that an appointed time of exaltation awaits those who assume a posture of humility, and that God cares for them as they endure the fiery trials (5.6; cf. 1.5–7; 2.25). Second, he exhorts his readers to be sober-minded (5.8), which in the context of 1 Peter (1.13) means to be aware of where they are within God's unfolding restoration programme. Third, he warns them to be alert and on the lookout, because the chief slanderer, the devil, is seeking prey to devour (5.8).[70] Peter's attentiveness to the shepherd tradition of the prophets is reflected even in the description of the devil as a roaring lion, a term that is repeatedly appropriated in the tradition to refer to a predator of God's sheep (Isa. 31.4; 35.9; 38.13; Jer. 4.7; Ezek. 22.25; 32.2; Hosea 5.14). Peter's final exhortation is to resist the roaring lion by remaining steadfast in the faith (i.e. the confidence they have in God's restoration; 5.9), reminding them that the brother- and sisterhood in the entire world is undergoing similar sufferings. He concludes this final section of the body of the letter by reiterating that this time of suffering is but a transition period (ὀλίγον; cf. 1 Pet. 1.6), emphatically restating that the God who called you to his glory in Christ will 'restore, support, strengthen, and establish you' (5.11).[71]

6.1.6   The postscript: 1 Peter 5.12–14

Two references in the postscript point to the overall strategy employed in this letter. First, in mentioning 'the co-elect who is in Babylon', which

[69]   Jobes 2005: 311.

[70]   'The basic sense of διάβολος is "slanderer", a term particularly apt in a letter where the primary attack on Christians has been the slow-working malignancy of verbal abuse' (Green 2007a: 172).

[71]   Throughout 1 Peter 'glory' (δόξα) is a reference to the vindication that Christians will enjoy when Christ returns and God culminates his restoration programme (1.7; 4.13; 5.1,4). Cf. Jobes 2005: 312, 315.

is likely a reference to the church in Rome, Peter reminds his addressees that the community of Christ followers which sends the greeting is also *co-elect*, and likewise on the same eschatological journey (see 1.1–2; 1 Pet. 5.9). In referring to Rome as Babylon, Peter also reiterates that this seemingly invincible, universal power, whose influence upon the world seems to negate the very claims that Peter is making in his letter (i.e. that restoration has begun in Jesus Christ), will in fact be judged and destroyed because it has oppressed the people of God and opposed God's ways (all the more when read in light of 1 Pet. 5.10–11: 'He will restore, support, strengthen, and establish you. To Him be dominion forever and ever').

Secondly, the final phrase of the letter serves to recapitulate the essence of all that Peter has been saying: Εἰρήνη ὑμῖν πᾶσιν τοῖς ἐν Χριστῷ. For it is because of the sacrificial death of Jesus Christ that grace and peace are available (1.2). It is the Christ who has healed and returned the straying sheep (2.24–5); through Christ's resurrection the addressees have been born again to a living hope, an incorruptible inheritance and a prepared salvation (1.3–5), which await those who faithfully navigate the fiery trials on their way towards their inheritance – towards the peace that God has set forth to establish through his messiah, Jesus.

6.1.7   Preliminary conclusions regarding the structure and strategy of 1 Peter

Broadly speaking, Peter's argumentation unfolds in two moves. First, he orients his addressees theologically by offering an interpretative framework for making sense of the social alienation his addressees experience as a result of aligning themselves with Jesus Christ (1.1–2.10). This theological orientation encourages the addressees to interpret their experiences and understand their calling in relation to their place within the unfolding of God's restoration programme. In particular, Peter offers an implicit narrative through which his addressees are to view their lives: Jesus Christ has caused something to happen – as a result of his sacrificial death, the addressees have been relationally restored to God and presently are awaiting an inheritance, which will be awarded at the return of Jesus Christ. In the meantime, as the renewed people of God, they now find themselves living in a transition period characterized both as fiery trials in which their fidelity to God will be tested as well as a wilderness/second exodus journey towards their prepared inheritance. Peter's second move, broadly speaking, is to offer a variety of exhortations which instruct his addressees regarding how they are to live in light of this new theological orientation (2.11–5.14). As I indicated in my survey, these exhortations are undergirded with constant reference (in a variety of manners) to the theological orientation (including the implicit narrative) offered at the beginning of the letter.

But more can be said about Peter's strategy, and in particular the implicit narrative and its distinctive features which are embedded in the reflective discourse of the letter.

6.2 Identifying the substructure of 1 Peter's eschatological programme

Although it is clear that 1 Peter does not narrate a story per se, in recent years a number of scholars have argued (some more explicitly than others) that a narrative undergirds the theological orientation that Peter offers, particularly in 1 Pet. 1.3–2.10.[72] Martin, for example, argues that the entire letter of 1 Peter is organized around the controlling metaphor of Diaspora.[73] As Martin develops what he means by this, it becomes clear that he has in mind a rudimentary narrative:

> The author of 1 Peter has taken over this conception of Jewish Diaspora life in order to portray the Christian existence of his readers. They have embarked upon an eschatological journey that takes them from their new birth to the eschaton ... the new birth has taken place in the past, and the reception of salvation in the eschaton remains in the future. Between these two points lies the present journey in which the travelers encounter manifold temptations that engender grief... Their present time of testing is contrasted with their joyous arrival at their destination (1:7–9). Their destination has been studied by the Hebrew prophets of old (1:10). ... Clearly this blessing section indicates that the author of 1 Peter has taken over the conception of the Diaspora as a journey in order to describe the existence of his readers as the wandering people of God on an eschatological journey.[74]

---

[72] In the appendix of his commentary, Boring (1999: 183–201) offers one of the first and most explicit attempts to identify and analyze the narrative world projected in 1 Peter. In a subsequent work, Boring (2007) elaborates his narrative approach to 1 Peter, offering helpful definitions and methodological considerations.

[73] Martin 1992: 135–267. He parses out the controlling metaphor in the following manner: the elect household of God (1.14–2.10); aliens in the world (2.11–3.12); and Sufferers of the Dispersion (3.13–5.11).

[74] *Ibid.*: 152, 153–4.

Martin traces a narrative from new birth to an interim period of wandering which culminates in the eschaton, the consummation of God's restoration programme.

Bechtler also demonstrates that a foundational element of Peter's strategy for helping the addressees deal with their alienation and suffering is essentially narrative in character.[75] In particular, Bechtler reveals the manner in which Peter constructs a 'symbolic universe'[76] of temporal liminality:[77] '1 Peter presupposes a temporal context for Christian life that is liminal in the literal sense; the addressees are living in that ambiguous time between Christ's death and resurrection on the one hand and the imminent manifestation of the fullness of his glory on the other.'[78] He further comments that

> Christian life is thus an existence 'betwixt and between' history and the eschaton . . . the temporal context of Christian life is the end-before-the-end that was introduced in Christ's manifestation on earth and will be consummated at the revelation of his glory. First Peter's depiction of the temporal liminality of Christian life contains within it one very important element of the letter's total answer to the problem of suffering of its addressees. The duration of their suffering will be short; the imminent appearance of their salvation is beyond a doubt.[79]

Bechtler's narrative follows a similar line as Martin – new life as a result of placing faith in Jesus, a liminal period of suffering and testing, and the consummation of God's restoration programme at the return of Jesus Christ.

In his work on the paraenetic strategies of 1 Peter, Dryden is much more explicit about the narrative aspects within the letter:

> The author's aim in 1 Peter is to encourage young Anatolian churches to live out their beliefs in the midst of social hostility. He uses theology foremost as a tool to shape their way of looking at the world, and through this, their way of living in

---

[75] He does not, however, use the terminology 'narrative'.

[76] See Bechtler 1998: 23–40 for his development of 'symbolic universe'.

[77] '1 Peter's depiction of the temporal liminality of Christian existence provides part of the letter's answer' to their social liminality (*ibid.*: 126). To be clear, Bechtler does not grant Petrine authorship and would thus not attribute this strategy to the historical Peter.

[78] *Ibid.*: 126. For a full development see *ibid.*: 127–35.

[79] *Ibid.*: 134. Bechtler (*ibid.*: 135–78) argues that the second element in 1 Peter's strategy is what he calls 'metaphorical liminality', which I would argue is built foundationally upon the narrative temporal liminality he develops earlier. Thus, the two are inextricably linked together.

the world. He describes a universe that contextualizes and reinforces his agenda of moral transformation. Before giving them
moral instructions, he gives them a moral vision that places them
within a moral universe. He does this by depicting not simply
a theological worldview, but a *narrative* theological worldview.
He is not giving simply ontological statements about how the
world is, but weaving together a *story* of how the world is; and
this becomes the context for their own stories as individuals and
as a community. This is the sense in which the narrative world
of 1 Peter contextualizes the lives of the readers and their moral
choices. It places their lives within a story of the world conceived
on the largest possible canvas – a story of creation, fall, redemption, and consummation. What God is doing in their midst is
part of the grand narrative of his plan to redeem his creation and
a people for himself. Thus, the world is not spinning aimlessly,
but headed toward a goal. In this context, daily choices, as the
means by which they appropriate their salvation in the present,
take on truly cosmic significance.[80]

He further underscores that

the author only refers to key elements of the story of salvation
to evoke an entire narrative worldview that is familiar to both
author and readers. This sort of shorthand description of key elements is, as we have noted before, typical of paraenesis, where
only a few key points need to be reviewed and emphasized.
Thus, what we have access to in the epistle is that portion of
the entire presupposed narrative theological worldview that the
author found it useful to highlight. The author's goal is to be
relevant not comprehensive.[81]

This description comes very close to the language that I have employed in
Chapter 1 in order to describe what a substructure is and how it functions
in a letter: there is a foundational story known by both the author as well
as (at least some of) the readers, which is alluded to in the reflective
discourse, not in a comprehensive fashion, but enough so that the readers
are connected to the story.

Although my own reading of 1 Peter resonates with many of the
observations made by Martin, Bechtler and Dryden, I find each account
lacking in one or more significant manners. Martin, for example, constructs a narrative around the concept of Diaspora that is formed from a

---

[80] Dryden 2006: 64.   [81] *Ibid.*: 66.

number of references to texts that purportedly represent what Peter and his addressees understood about their diasporic status, and then compares this scholarly construct with 1 Peter. This composite construction is problematic, however, because we have no way of adjudicating whether Peter and/or his addressees had access to these texts or shared these peculiar notions of Diaspora (e.g. especially Diaspora as an eschatological journey). In other words, for Martin's reading to work we must assume that Peter and his addressees understood Diaspora precisely in the way that Martin has reconstructed it, and yet the availability of these texts and their ideas has never been sufficiently substantiated. Additionally, it is unclear whether the metaphor 'Diaspora' can actually bear all the exegetical weight that Martin places on it. For example, linking the motif of eschatological journey to the concept of Diaspora appears to broaden the concept of the latter such that it becomes unrecognizable. Furthermore, linking Christian suffering to Diaspora seems to go beyond what is described in the letter itself, in which suffering is integrally connected to one's allegiance to Christ and not to being in the Diaspora. What is more, in my own analysis of the letter, I have demonstrated that it is likely that Peter does not locate his addressees in the Diaspora (locative) but rather as having been redeemed from it (ablative).

Dryden's description of 1 Peter's 'story of salvation' or 'grand narrative' fails adequately to emphasize the prominence of liminality which emerges in the reflective discourse in a number of places (e.g. 1.5–7; 3.18–22; 4.12–19; 5.10).[82] And although Bechtler rightly emphasizes liminality as an integral feature of the narrative, he does not explore what may have generated this notion of Christian existence. The question thus becomes whether our author gives clues in the letter that might indicate the source from which he has constructed a narrative that includes an in between period prior to consummation (which he twice refers to as fiery trials for testing and links to a new exodus journey) and the imminent return of Christ.

My principal contention with the accounts of Bechtler and Dryden, however, is not that they are misguided, but rather that they are too generic: they describe in a one-dimensional fashion a narrative which has more texture and depth than they have indicated.[83] Defining the narrative within 1 Peter with generic terms like creation, fall, redemption

---

[82] The same can be said of Boring 2007.

[83] This also is a weakness of Boring's narrative approach (2007), especially when he argues that there is no story of Israel in 1 Peter, or that there is no direct sense that the Christian community is the continuation of the Old Testament story.

and consummation (as Dryden has) is akin to identifying the kingdom, and perhaps the phylum of a living creature but electing to say nothing about its class, order, family, genus or species when such an identification can be made. In particular, they have neglected to connect the narrative to its roots in Israel's scriptures, and more specifically to the prominent expectations of Jewish restoration eschatology – this in spite of the predominance of OT citations in the letter.[84] In this regard, the work of Mbuvi and Dubis can be commended. Each in his own way seeks to understand Peter's discourse within the narrative of exile and restoration; not without significant problems, however.

Although he does not state it explicitly, in his monograph *Temple, Exile and Identity in 1 Peter*, Mbuvi considers the exile and restoration of Israel to be the foundational narrative which undergirds the discourse of 1 Peter.[85] Mbuvi argues that an essential occurrence within the narrative of exile and restoration is the re-establishment of the temple.[86] Additionally, he contends that 'temple imagery undergirds the entire letter of 1 Peter'.[87] Two significant conclusions are drawn on the basis of these premises. First, Peter regards his addressees as none other than restored/new Israel: 'the eschatological "temple-community" envisioned in 1 Peter is understood to fulfil all Jewish eschatological expectations'.[88] Second, suffering, rather than being punishment in exile, is instead to be understood as the purging of God's house (read temple) in preparation for their heavenly inheritance.[89] With this, he implies that the notion of a transition or liminal period between exile and restoration is to be understood as a time of purification that is generated from the eschatological expectations of Jewish restoration eschatology (i.e. Jewish restoration expectations function as the substructure for Peter's theology of suffering).

---

[84] To be fair to both Bechtler and Dryden, this falls outside of the scope of their projects. My point is not to discredit their work, but rather show where their work, helpful as it is, can be taken further.

[85] Mbuvi (2007: 28) writes: 'the controlling metaphor of the letter should be the "idea of exile"'. What Mbuvi describes as 'background' (i.e. the exile and restoration of Israel) is actually a narrative that has a beginning (the election and creation of a people), a middle (exile) and an end (restoration).

[86] 'Restoration from exile was to be epitomized by the reestablishment of the temple and the cultus' (*ibid.*: 44).

[87] *Ibid.*: 71.   [88] *Ibid.*: 125.

[89] *Ibid.* Mbuvi further argues (*ibid.*: 125) that 'the temple imagery incorporates the concepts of exile, judgment and restoration'. Additionally, he contends (*ibid.*: 122) that 'suffering for being Christian is purificatory for 1 Peter and would deal with the sinful nature'.

Mbuvi's overall proposal, and in particular his explanation for suffering in a transition period prior to full restoration, is problematic, however, for at least three reasons. First, as I have demonstrated in Chapter 4, according to Peter the principal function of suffering is not purgation: instead, in both 1.5–7 and 4.12–17, suffering is for testing one's fidelity to God and his Christ. In this regard, Peter seems to be deliberately out of step with the eschatological expectations that Mbuvi highlights in Chapter 4 of his work.[90] Instead, Peter describes his readers as holy as a result of Jesus' sacrificial death (1.2; 2.9), equipped to offer holy sacrifices (2.5), 'healed' from sin (2.24) and anointed with the Spirit of glory (4.14). Second, Mbuvi likens the judgment mentioned in 1 Pet. 4.17 to that which is predicted in such texts as Ezek. 9.1–6, Mal. 3 and Zech. 13.7–9.[91] However, as I have demonstrated in Chapter 4, the judgment described in Ezek. 9.1–6/Mal. 3 is the punitive destruction of Israel's leaders and her temple;[92] the judgment mentioned in Zech. 13.7–9 on the other hand is in reference to the royal house of God/David (and not the temple; Zech. 12.8–12), and is a process of distinguishing between faithful and unfaithful members of that house, which is more in line with what Peter is describing in 1 Pet. 4.14–17. More importantly, however, Mbuvi is unconvincing in his claim that temple imagery undergirds the entire letter, in part because he unnecessarily limits *oikos* terminology (2.5; 4.17) to refer exclusively to the temple, and also (and perhaps more significantly) because he has not adequately explained how other imagery fits with the temple motif (most notably the shepherd imagery) nor sufficiently detailed how temple imagery fits with the rest of the letter. In the end, while Mbuvi's proposal helpfully places our reading of 1 Peter within the framework of Jewish restoration eschatology, it does not offer a satisfying explanation for Peter's notion of Christian suffering in the transition period prior to consummation.

If we were to follow Dubis' work to its logical conclusion, we would have to deduce that the Messianic Woes functions as the substructure of 1 Peter's eschatological programme:[93] it is the starting point for his appropriation of scripture, and generates a number of the key features found in 1 Peter, such as (1) the necessity of suffering (1.6; 4.12), (2) the 'Spirit of glory' and restoration (4.14), (3) lawlessness and apostasy during the Messianic Woes (4.15–16), (4) the beginning of judgment

---

[90]   *Ibid.*: 118–22.   [91]   *Ibid.*: 115–16, 119–20.

[92]   See Marius Reiser (1994: 175), who demonstrates that Ezek. 9.6 speaks of a judgment that annihilates rather than purifies unto transformation.

[93]   Dubis never uses the language of substructure in his monograph, but in actuality it is what he is arguing.

upon the people of God (4.17), (5) survivors of the eschatological trial
(4.18) and finally (5) the theme of entrusting oneself to God amidst the
eschatological trials.

I have already offered an extensive critique of Dubis' proposal at both
the micro- and macro-levels. Here, I will simply highlight that Dubis
unnecessarily has excluded the OT from consideration in his attempt to
understand the source that has generated Peter's theology of suffering. In
exchange he has proposed the scholarly construct of Messianic Woes. If
we are to accept Dubis' conclusion, then we are to imagine that Peter's
reflections regarding eschatology and Christian suffering were generated
from a narrative that has been constructed from a variety of texts whose
availability is uncertain at best. Additionally, we are to accept that the
narrative of Messianic Woes was widespread, even foundational, such
that Peter could merely allude to it. And yet, 1 Peter seems not to allow
for this to be the case since the addressees clearly have not anticipated
suffering as a part of their calling nor as part of God's restoration programme. In other words, if the narrative of Messianic Woes was in fact
widespread and available, then why is suffering because of one's allegiance to Jesus so unanticipated and in such dire need of justification and
explanation?

In my view, this is, in part, why the proposal I am putting forth is more
compelling. Zechariah 9–14 can account for all of the features that Dubis
highlights in his work on 1 Pet. 4.12–19 – and then some.[94] What is more,
we have solid evidence to affirm that Zechariah 9–14 was available to
Peter and known by (at least some of) the addressees.[95] In other words,
with my proposal we get a Messianic Woes type of narrative, but from an
available text rather than a scholarly construct. But I am running ahead
of the argument for the moment. I move now to address the substructure
of Peter's eschatological programme.

In Chapters 3, 4 and 5 I have argued that Peter alludes to the eschatological programme of Zechariah 9–14 in 1 Pet. 1.3–2.10, 2.21–5, and
4.12–5.4. Additionally, in Chapter 5 I have indicated a variety of echoes
of Zechariah 9–14 in such places as 1.1 (ἐκλεκτοῖς, παρεπιδήμοις, διασπορᾶς), 1.2 (as a foreshadowing of the Zechariah narrative) and 4.14
(Peter's modification of Isa. 11.2). In §6.1 I have shown that Peter's

---

[94] See especially Chapter 4. The 'then some' will be explored below.

[95] For the availability of Zechariah 9–14 see Chapter 2. In its reception, however,
Zechariah 9–14 was drawn on (especially in the Passion Narratives) in order to explain the
significance of Jesus' last week, including Jesus' entry into Jerusalem, his last supper and
his death. Peter, however, appropriates Zechariah 9–14 in a new fashion, namely, in order
to explain Christian suffering and the unfolding of God's restoration programme.

theological orientation (1.1–2.10) and his exhortations that follow (2.11–5.14) are rooted in a particular eschatological programme which undergirds the entire letter. In what follows I wish to draw out the implicit narrative that is embedded within the eschatological programme of 1 Peter, compare it to the rudimentary narrative of Zechariah 9–14, and then highlight a number of key features within 1 Peter's eschatological programme that parallel the distinctive programme of Zechariah 9–14.

Based upon my analysis of 1 Peter (§3.1–6.1), I have discerned the following implicit narrative embedded within the discourse of the letter:

(1)   Before the foundation of the world Jesus Christ was foreknown as the one through whom God would redeem and restore his people (1.20).

(2)   This redemption and restoration through Jesus was promised through the prophets (1.10–11; 2.6–7).

(3)   The suffering, humiliation, rejection and crucifixion of Jesus was in keeping with God's will (i.e. foreknown in the scriptures; 1 Pet. 2.7–8).

(4)   The resurrection of Jesus from the dead forms the basis for the consummation of God's restoration programme (1.3; 1.20; 3.18–22).

(5)   The death of Jesus atones for sin and cleanses the 'house of God', upon whom the Spirit now rests (1.2; 2.4–10; 2.23–4; 4.14).

(6)   The house of God/scattered sheep have been returned to the Shepherd, in keeping with the scriptures (2.24–5). This return to the Shepherd is also described as new birth, the reconstitution of God's people (1 Pet. 1.3,22; 1 Pet. 2.9–10).

(7)   Prior to the consummation of God's restoration programme, the returned sheep/house of God must pass through a period of fiery trials which are for the purpose of testing (judging) their fidelity to God (1.5–7; 4.12–19). These fiery trials are likened to a second exodus journey towards a kept inheritance (1.13–2.10).

(8)   God's restoration plan will culminate in the return (second coming) of the Chief Shepherd, Jesus Christ (5.4).

This implicit narrative in 1 Peter can now be compared with the rudimentary narrative of Zechariah 9–14 that I outlined in Chapter 2 (see Table 6.1).

What is most significant, perhaps even determinative, when the narrative of 1 Peter is compared to that of Zechariah 9–14 is that only 1 Peter and Zechariah 9–14 offer an eschatological programme that develops

Table 6.1 *The eschatological programme of Zechariah 9–14*

1. Ingathering and return of Israel to Jerusalem.	2. The coming of Israel's eschatological Davidic shepherd-king.	3. A time of trouble for Israel: (a) the king is killed; (b) Israel is scattered; (c) the remnant pass through fiery trials (likened to a second exodus journey); (d) the nations gather against Israel.	4. The remnant of Israel is regathered; YHWH renews his covenant; and the nations are defeated.	5. Israel's remnant, along with the survivors of the nations, worship YHWH and celebrate his universal reign.

the notion of a transition period subsequent to the coming of YHWH's redemptive agent and prior to consummation that is described both as a period of fiery trials as well as a second exodus journey.[96] In other words, Zechariah 9–14 offers the unique solution to the precise issue with which Peter and his addressees are struggling: if Jesus is in fact the Christ, the agent appointed to bring about restoration, then why are we suffering *after* his coming?

In keeping with the analysis that I offered in Chapters 3 to 6, I maintain that 1 Pet. 1.1–2.10 and 4.12–5.4 function as paraphrased expansions of the eschatological programme of Zechariah 9–14 (especially (3) of the eschatological programme of Zechariah 9–14), read in the light of Jesus' death and resurrection. If this is the case, then Peter would be in step with the interpretive tradition of the Passion Narratives, in which Jesus' last week was similarly understood in terms of the narrative and theological contours of Zechariah 9–14. This would suggest that for Peter, Zechariah 9–14 and the gospel concerning Jesus Christ both point to the same reality. Commenting more generally about Peter's approach to reading the Jewish scriptures, Joel Green posits that

[Peter's] hermeneutic is one that finds Christ and the scriptures of Israel as mutually informing. This is because they say the

[96] Isaiah 40–55, for example, cannot account for shepherd imagery in 1 Peter or the transition period of suffering which comes after the Suffering Servant has suffered and died and prior to consummation. And while Ezekiel shares the shepherd imagery that is found in both 1 Peter and Zechariah 9–14, as I have demonstrated in Chapter 2, Zechariah 9–14 develops the Ezekiel programme in a unique fashion, underscoring a transition period of fiery trials prior to consummation.

same thing, albeit in different theological idioms . . . The importance of Israel's Scripture is not worked out in terms of promise
and fulfilment, then, but simultaneity of substance and address.
This means that Peter finds an essential unity in the outworking
of God's purpose.[97]

Zechariah 9–14, read through the lens of Jesus Christ, then, becomes the
map for understanding the way to the promised inheritance.

But there is still more that can be said about the way in which Zechariah
9–14 is embedded within the discourse and the eschatological programme
of 1 Peter. In addition to sharing a similar unique narrative pattern, there
are a number of key themes and features of Peter's eschatological programme that are also found in the distinctive eschatological programme
of Zechariah 9–14:

(1)   The promised restoration of Israel (Zech. 9–10//1 Pet. 1.3–2.10;
       especially the ἀναγεννάω language in 1.3,23; and the appropri-
       ation of Isa. 43.21–2 and Hosea 2.25).[98]
(2)   A shepherd whose wounds bring about cleansing and restoration
       to a renewed house of God and the anointing of the Spirit (Zech.
       12.8–13.1,7–9//1 Pet. 2.23–5; 2.5; 4.17).
(3)   The ingathering of the scattered/straying sheep of Israel from
       exile (Zech. 9.16; 10:8–12//1 Peter 1.1; 2.24–5).
(4)   A transitional period following the piercing of the shepherd
       and prior to consummation, which is described as fiery trials
       that serve to test the fidelity of God's people (Zech. 13.8–9;
       10.6–12//1 Pet. 1.5–7; 4.12–19; 1 Pet. 1.3–2.10).
(5)   A second exodus journey which is linked to fiery trials that
       are intended to test the fidelity of God's people (Zech. 10.6–
       12/13.7–9//1 Pet. 1.3–2.10).
(6)   Metallurgy imagery that is used to describe trials in terms of an
       assaying/sifting process rather than as purgation (Zech. 13.7–
       9//1 Pet. 1.5–7).
(7)   The pouring out of the Spirit upon YHWH's royal house, those
       who have faithfully aligned themselves with his messiah (Zech.
       12.8–13.2//1 Pet. 4.14).
(8)   Renewed leadership as the sign of the new age – described with
       shepherd imagery (Zech. 10.2,8–12; 11–13//1 Pet. 2.25; 5.1–4).

[97] Green 2007a: 236.
[98] 'In 1 Peter, the language and hence the reality of Israel pass without remainder into
the language and hence the reality of the new people of God' (Achtemeier 1996: 69).

(9)   YHWH's declaration – 'You are my people' – to his ingathered/
        remnant sheep who are called to endure the fiery trials (Zech.
        13.7–9//1 Pet. 2.10).
(10)   A messiah figure who is referred to as a cornerstone (Zech. 10.4
        (esp. Targum)//1 Pet. 2.4–10).
(11)   A people aligned to the cornerstone who are described as pre-
        cious stones (Zech. 9.16//1 Pet. 2.5).
(12)   Optimism concerning those who have aligned themselves with
        God's appointed agent/shepherd; they will journey faithfully
        through the fiery trials/second exodus on to their salvation/
        inheritance/glory through God's enabling (Zech. 10.6–12; 13.7–
        9//1 Pet. 1.5–7; 4.12–19; 5.10).
(13)   God, through his agent, will restore a rightly functioning royal
        house/temple where acceptable offerings are presented to God
        (Zech. 14//1 Peter 2.4–10/2.23–4).

The distinctive narrative embedded within the discourse of 1 Peter along
with these thirteen themes strongly suggest that Peter's eschatological
programme has been generated from Zechariah 9–14. Something must
be made of the preponderance of parallels, and in my view the only
sufficient explanation is that Zechariah 9–14, read through the lens of the
death and resurrection of Jesus, has generated the eschatological outlook
that Peter presents in his letter. No doubt we can find some of the narrative
and its key features in a variety of texts in the OT and in Second Temple
Literature, but I am unaware of any two texts that share precisely these
parallels.

If my substructure proposal is on target, then how can we explain
the prevalence of OT passages in the letter which do not derive from
Zechariah 9–14? At first glance, Peter's appropriation of OT texts and
early Christian traditions can appear to be rather eclectic in nature. However, when we analyze Peter's appropriation in light of the substructure
proposal that I am offering there is more coherence than first meets the
eye. Assuming for the moment that my proposal is correct, it can be
argued that Peter has drawn on particular OT passages in order to support
and affirm the substructure provided by Zechariah 9–14. Said in another
way, Peter uses a variety of OT passages, and even sayings from the Jesus
Tradition (1 Pet. 2.11–12) and early Christian traditions (e.g. stone catena
in 1 Pet. 2.4–8) in order to fortify, explain, illustrate and corroborate the
very substructure that undergirds and generates his eschatological programme. In this regard, we could say that Zechariah 9–14 functions as
the frame upon which the bricks of OT citations and Christian traditions

have been laid. Additionally, Peter's fragmentary allusions and echoes derive coherence from their relation to the eschatological programme of Zechariah 9–14: they are allusive recollections of the foundational eschatological narrative. The eschatological programme of Zechariah 9–14 is thus a springboard for his understanding and presentation of the outworking of God's restoration, in which he feels the freedom to draw upon texts from the OT which concord with his reading of Zechariah 9–14.

For example, the stone catena in 1 Pet. 2.6–8 (Isa. 28.16; LXX Ps. 117.22; Isa. 8.14) further elaborates the narrative and several key themes of the eschatological programme of Zechariah 9–14: YHWH's appointment of a 'stone' (Zech. 10.4) who will bring about restoration;[99] the rejection of this stone by many, including Israel's leaders (Zech. 11.4–13.9); the suffering that comes with aligning one's self with the stone (Zech. 13.7–9); salvation that comes with aligning one's self with the chosen stone (Zech. 9.1–10.12; 13.7–14.21); and perhaps even the predicted destruction of two-thirds who will not choose to align themselves with YHWH's appointed redemptive agent (Zech. 13.8–9).

Peter's appropriation of Isa. 43.20–1 and Exod. 19.5–6 further develops the second exodus theme hinted at in Zech. 10.6–12, linking the wilderness journey, as Zechariah does, with the fiery trials described in 1 Pet. 1.5–7/4.12–19 (cf. Zech 10.6–12/13.7–9). Similarly, Peter's citation of Lev. 11.44/19.2 orients his addressees theologically in a recapitulation of the first exodus journey. Peter's citation of Isa. 40.6–8, with its wider reference to a promised second exodus, corroborates and fortifies this point. And Peter's usage of Hosea 1.6,9; 2.25 reiterates God's covenant renewal with his remnant people (Zech. 13.9).

Additionally, I have suggested that Peter was drawn to reflect upon LXX Psalm 33 not only because it offers an ethic for how to respond to ridicule and social alienation, but more precisely because it embodies the kind of ethic that is required for those who are presently sojourning in the wilderness awaiting their inheritance, and because it simultaneously reinforces the eschatological orientation he has so diligently developed in the letter.

Peter's appropriation of Isaiah 53 in 1 Pet. 2.21–5 is illuminating for what I am arguing here. I have shown that Isaiah 53 has been appropriated in order to reflect Jesus' passion, in order to interpret the significance of Jesus' death and in order to connect with Peter's reflections on

---

[99] See Kim (1987), who provocatively argues that Zechariah 9–14 is responsible for generating the stone tradition in the early church.

LXX Psalm 33 in 1 Pet. 3.10–12. However, as I have demonstrated in Chapter 4 and in §6.1, Isaiah 53 is brought into the larger narrative of Zechariah 9–14 by means of the covert midrash I have highlighted in 1 Pet. 2.24–5.

The substructure proposal that I offer is also able to explain the unusual modifications that Peter has made to Isa. 11.2 in 1 Pet. 4.14. In §5.2, I demonstrated how Zechariah 9–14 provides Peter with the impetus for imaginatively connecting a persecuted community with the future promise of the spirit which was to be poured out on the shoot of David (now realized in Jesus and his community of followers), while also explaining why this community is referred to as the house of God.[100]

One curious phenomenon that I underscored in Chapter 2 was that the author of Zechariah 9–14 frequently interacts with Isaiah 40–66, Ezekiel 34–7 and Hosea 1–2, incorporating those eschatological expectations into the reworked eschatological scenario which he puts forth that includes a unique period of fiery trials after the death of the shepherd and prior to consummation. I also showed that the Passion Narratives draw on Zechariah 9–14 as the schema for interpreting Jesus' last week, but also include allusions to, conflations of and citations from Isaiah and the Psalms (to name but two OT sources) in order to fill out and corroborate their interpretations.[101] Thus, what I am describing regarding 1 Peter is not out of step with the way in which Zechariah 9–14 and the Passion Narratives incorporate other OT passages.

It is extremely important to note once again that none of the OT texts that Peter cites or their wider text-plots offers the kind of eschatological programme that is embedded within the discourse of 1 Peter: there is, for example, no mention of a second exodus in Isaiah that follows the death of the Suffering Servant (Isaiah 53). Additionally, it is important to underscore that the OT texts that Peter appropriates are given a voice in their own right; they are not simply absorbed into the Zechariah schema:

---

[100] In §5.2 I showed that in both 1 Peter and Zechariah (a) the community that aligns themselves with God's royal figure is described as the house of God (Zech. 12.8/1 Pet. 4.17); (b) the royal/messianic agent is described variously as a slain shepherd (Zech. 13.7/1 Pet. 2.23–35), a stone (Zech. 10.3/1 Pet. 2.6–8) and the shoot of David (implied in Zechariah 9–14 from Zech. 3.8, 6.12 and in 1 Pet. 4.14 from Isa. 11.2); (c) the house of God will undergo a period of fiery trials that are likened to a wilderness/new exodus journey and that are designed to test fidelity towards God; (d) the spirit will be poured out/now rests upon the house of God; and (e) the house of God, that is, those who align themselves with the slain shepherd, are to be characterized by holiness, in which they offer acceptable sacrifices to God (Zech. 13.1–2; 14.21/1 Pet. 2.5). Simply put, there is no other place in Israel's scriptures where we find these particular parallels.

[101] See, e.g., Matt. 21.4–5 (Zech. 9.9 and Isa. 62.11), as well as John 19.36–7.

they contribute to and further develop Peter's reading of Zechariah 9–14 and his theological discourse.[102] This can be seen, for example, as Woan has demonstrated, by the way in which Psalm 34 contributes to the structure and the ethical content of 1 Peter; or in 1 Pet. 1.13–2.10, where Peter draws on a number of OT passages in order to further develop the second exodus theme in Zech. 10.6–12.[103] However, although these OT texts are given separate voices which help construct the theological orientation that Peter is developing, they are nevertheless generated from and to be interpreted in relation to the wider eschatological programme of Zechariah 9–14.

It must also be said that Peter is not simply trying to reduplicate the eschatological programme of Zechariah 9–14 in a wooden fashion, nor is he looking for a one-to-one correspondence. There are new features that Peter includes in his account. For example, central to Peter's eschatological programme is the resurrection of Jesus Christ – the basis for hope of salvation (1.3,21; 3.18–22). Additionally, Peter's eschatological programme features the return of the Chief Shepherd who comes to reward and presumably to reign (5.4; cf. 1.7; 2.12). And yet, there is no explicit mention of a resurrection or the return (second coming) of the shepherd in Zechariah 9–14, though Zech. 14.4 is suggestive.[104] Here is one example of the way in which the gospel of Jesus has had an effect on how Zechariah 9–14 is interpreted.[105] Finally, nowhere in Zechariah 9–14 is YHWH's shepherd ever referred to as a sacrificial/Passover lamb. And yet Peter has incorporated this description into his interpretation of Jesus' death (1 Pet. 1.18–19), mostly likely through the influence of Isaiah 53.

There also appear to be features of the eschatological programme of Zechariah 9–14 that have been omitted from Peter's discourse. It is particularly noteworthy that the violent imagery and tone of Zechariah 9 and 14, in which God's enemies (the nations who do not submit to God) are to be destroyed with fire and lethal military might, have not found their way into the discourse of 1 Peter. We find a similar omission in the way in which the Passion Narratives draw from Zechariah 9–14. Neither has the violent hostility of the nations been mentioned; instead

---

[102] This means that research on, for example, Peter's use of Isaiah or the wilderness tradition would be an appropriate study in and of itself.

[103] Woan 2004. For the ethical function of Psalm 34 in 1 Peter see Green 1990.

[104] See §2.1.2.7.

[105] As I demonstrated in Chapter 2, the more substantial way that the gospel has shaped how Zechariah 9–14 is read is to conflate the figures of 9.10, 11.4–17, 12.10 and 13.7, which, to my knowledge, was not done previously.

suffering is characterized for the most part as verbal abuse and social ostracism. Additionally, Peter has not incorporated the restoration of the land into his programme, instead speaking more generally in terms of 'salvation' and 'inheritance' but not offering much beyond that.[106] However, perhaps the most glaring omission, especially in light of what I have developed in §2.1.3.1, is any explicit mention of Jesus as the *Davidic* eschatological shepherd. This seems odd given Peter's emphasis on Jesus as the Christ, and in light of the Passion Narratives, which clearly affirm the Davidic roots of Jesus' messiahship.[107] There is, however, a sense in which David is nowhere mentioned and yet everywhere present in 1 Peter. Lurking behind the stone catena, for example, is Davidic kingship (LXX Ps. 118);[108] the 'shoot' of Isa. 11.2 has a tradition of being interpreted in line with the promise of a restored Davidic monarchy (not least as it is appropriated in Zech. 3.8 and 6.12);[109] prior to 1 Pet. 2.25 no Israelite leader ever bore the title 'shepherd', which was exclusively reserved for the eschatological Davidic king;[110] LXX Psalm 33 could be read with Davidic typology in view; and the 'house of God' language of 1 Peter, borrowed from Zech. 12.9–10, could be understood as a reference to the house of David, along the lines of 2 Sam. 7 and Psalm 2.[111] It is, however, beyond the scope of this volume to explore this any further.

What do we gain from the substructure proposal that I have put forth? First, we get a thicker description of the embedded narrative (and the eschatological programme) than has been noted by other scholars, one that is appropriately rooted in Israel's scriptures and the Jewish eschatological expectations which were prevalent at the time of composition. Second, my proposal brings coherence to the letter. The coherence that I offer, however, is different than the compositional and rhetorical approaches of Martin and Campbell (respectively). In my approach, coherence is discerned in relation to the substructure of Peter's eschatological programme, which is able to explain his seemingly eclectic appropriation of scripture and such apparently fragmented imagery as fiery trials, sheep

---

[106] Interestingly, Zechariah 9.1–16 epitomizes God's restoration programme as 'salvation' in 9.16.

[107] For example in the so-called triumphal entry pericope in the Passion Narratives of Mark (11.9–10), Matthew (21.9) and John (12.13), Zech. 9.9 is linked with Psalm 118 and Davidic acclamations.

[108] See p. 35, note 53 regarding the Davidic eschatological shepherd and Ps. 118. See also §2.1.2.2 and §5.2 for the interpretation of 'stone' and Psalm 118 with respect to the eschatological Davidic king.

[109] For the link between the Davidic covenant and the 'Branch' see 2 Sam. 7.11–16; Isa. 9.7; 11.1; Pss. 18.50; 89.4,29–37; 132.11–12; Jer 23.5; 33.15.

[110] See §3.4.   [111] See especially §5.2.

returning to the shepherd, house of God and second exodus.[112] Third, we get a Messianic Woes type scenario, but from an available text rather than a scholarly construct. And finally, and perhaps most importantly, we are able to discern that Peter's principal strategy for helping his addressees thrive in the midst of suffering and social alienation is to show them that what they are undergoing is κατά τάς γραφάς, and in particular κατά Ζαχαρίαν 9–14.

---

[112] In other words, instead of seeking to find a controlling metaphor in 1 Peter (e.g. Elliott, Martin and Mbuvi), perhaps it is more fruitful to think in terms of a governing eschatological substructure. It is perhaps no surprise that attuning to the narrative embedded within the discourse of 1 Peter yields a stronger sense of cohesion, since this was the objective of the narrative approach in Pauline studies (cf. Hays 1983: 1–31; Longenecker 2002: 3–11).

7

CONCLUSION

How can we know whether Zechariah 9–14 has served as the substructure of 1 Peter's eschatological programme and thus shaped Peter's theology of Christian suffering, especially when there is no explicit mention of this in the letter itself? The argument that I have presented is cumulative in nature. It begins with three assumptions about the way in which at least some of the authors of the NT went about constructing and communicating a distinctively Christian theology: first, that the Christ story (i.e. the gospel) and OT texts mutually generated theological understanding; second, that in the earliest constructions of Christian theology certain blocks of scripture, including Zechariah 9–14, were considered particularly relevant for explaining the significance and the implications of the Christ event; and finally, that reflective discourse, such as the kind we find in 1 Peter, can at times be governed by a foundational narrative that may find only allusive, fragmentary expression within the discourse itself.

With these assumptions in place, I proposed two phases of enquiry in order to identify whether a foundational narrative has shaped the reflective discourse of 1 Peter's eschatological programme. The aim of the first phase of enquiry (Chapters 2–5) was to identify allusions and echoes which point to a foundational narrative, and discern its general outline. The aim of the second phase of enquiry (Chapter 6) was to determine whether or how this foundational narrative undergirds, supports, animates, constrains the logic of and gives coherence to the argumentation in 1 Peter.

Since my hypothesis was that Zechariah 9–14 served as the foundational narrative for 1 Peter's eschatological programme, and given the complexities of this often enigmatic text, I elected to begin my investigation by first seeking to discern its outline and contours. Accordingly, in Chapter 2 I analyzed the eschatological programme of Zechariah 9–14 and surveyed its reception in Second Temple Literature and in the NT. Several significant points emerged from this analysis. First, I demonstrated that Zechariah 9–14 was available for appropriation during the period in which 1 Peter was composed. In particular, I noted that both the Gospels and Revelation drew upon Zechariah 9–14 in order to confirm the imminence and consummation of the restoration of God's people; that is, both the Passion Narrative tradition and Revelation looked to Zechariah in order to understand the unfolding of God's eschatological programme. In the Passion Narratives, however, Zechariah 9–14 was appropriated almost exclusively in order to understand the events leading up to the death of Jesus and how they could be a part of God's plan of restoration, whereas in Revelation Zechariah 9–14 was understood to speak beyond the death of Jesus, to the culmination of restoration; that is, to things that had yet to pass. Second, I noted that Zechariah 9–14 offers a unique twist to the exilic and post-exilic shepherd tradition of the OT prophets: in contrast to what one may have been led to believe from the programmes of Jeremiah 23 and Ezekiel 34, the coming of the good shepherd would not bring immediate restoration and renewal; instead, YHWH's shepherd would be struck by a sword, which would initiate a period of fiery testing for YHWH's remnant. Third, I demonstrated that the Passion Narratives, each in their own particular way, appropriated Zechariah 9–14 as the foundational narrative, in which the figures in Zech. 9.9, 12.10 and 13.7 were understood as references to Jesus. Finally, I highlighted that Zechariah 9–14 was read alongside other key OT passages (e.g. Isaiah and the Lament Psalms), which together provided mutual interpretation of Jesus' suffering and death.

In Chapter 3 I focused on the often neglected shepherd imagery in 1 Pet. 2.24–5, demonstrating that the extant proposals which try to explain the relationship between 1 Pet. 2.21–5a and 2.25b are either implausible or incomplete. In particular, I noted how the 'restoration approach' has failed to consider how Zechariah 9–14 has significantly reworked earlier shepherd traditions of the prophets. In turn, I argued that the best way to understand the shepherd imagery in 1 Pet. 2.24–5 was to read it within the milieu of the Passion Narrative tradition and as an allusion to the eschatological programme of Zechariah 9–14. My proposal, I argued, is more satisfying than the 'restoration approach', which suggests a conflation in 1 Pet. 2.24–5 between Isaiah 53 and Ezekiel 34, for at least four reasons: (1) Zechariah 9–14 was not just available for use, but also served as the foundational narrative in three of the Passion Narratives. We do not find a similar phenomenon with Ezekiel 34; (2) Isaiah 53 and the shepherd tradition of Zechariah 9–14 share a more specific conceptual link than do Ezekiel 34 and Isaiah 53 – restoration through the affliction of YHWH's chosen agent; (3) Zechariah 9–14 explains why Christians must also suffer (and in particular *after* the coming of God's shepherd), which is precisely the point that Peter wishes to make in 1 Pet. 2.21–5; (4) and finally, LXX Zech. 10.2 ('they were driven away like sheep and were afflicted, since there was no *healing*') best explains why Peter chose to culminate his appropriation of Isaiah 53 with 'by his wounds you have been *healed*' (οὗ τῷ μώλωπι ἰάθητε; 2.24) and to then link it with shepherd imagery.

In Chapter 4 I offered a comprehensive analysis of the fiery trials imagery of 1 Peter (1.6–7/4.12) and Zech. 13.8–9. I showed how a relationship between the two texts has been hinted at in the secondary literature, but that the discussion has never moved beyond noting a few parallel features. In my analysis I underscored that when the fiery trials imagery of 1 Peter (1.6/4.12) is compared to Zech. 13.9 and the wider themes that are developed in each of those texts, five striking parallels emerge which on the one hand eliminate other proposed precursor texts from consideration, and on the other hand point to several unique features of the eschatological programme of Zechariah 9–14. First, in both texts, the fiery trials imagery is used with a strong emphasis on it being a necessary part of a larger sequence of events that must take place before consummation. Second, in both texts the fiery trials are likened to a second exodus journey. Third, both texts express confidence in the positive outcome of the fiery trials for the remnant or elect. Fourth, in both texts the fiery trials period follows the death of a shepherd figure, and is prior to eschatological salvation/consummation. And finally, and perhaps most significantly, both texts downplay the purifying, educational benefits of 'fiery trials', and instead highlight their authenticating purposes.

In Chapter 5 I argued that there are three additional compelling reasons to suppose a relationship between 1 Peter and Zechariah 9–14. First, Zechariah 9–14 provides a framework for understanding why the addressees of 1 Peter are described both as returned from exile (see 2.25), as well as elect-sojourners of the διασπορά (1.1). Second, Zechariah 9–14 offers a compelling explanation for why Peter associated a persecuted community of God with the promise of the spirit resting upon a messianic community, and why that community is described as the 'house of God'. And third, Zechariah 9–14 provides a rationale for the logic that brings together 1 Pet. 4.12–17 and 5.1–4.

More specifically, I argued that the best way to read διασπορᾶς in 1 Pet. 1.1 is as an ablative genitive. An ablative reading is not only grammatically possible but also coheres with the overall narrative of 1 Peter, which describes its addressees as elect-sojourners who have returned to the shepherd and are now journeying through fiery trials towards their prepared inheritance. I indicated that this distinctive description of the addressees is a unique feature of Zechariah 9–14 and is most likely an early indication in the letter of Peter's dependence upon its eschatological programme. Second, I argued that a number of unique features in the eschatological programme of Zechariah 9–14 explain Peter's modification of Isa. 11.2 in 1 Pet. 4.14 and his appropriation of the phrase οἶκος τοῦ θεοῦ in 1 Pet. 4.17. Finally, I proposed that the unique emphasis in Zechariah 9–14 on the restoration of a second tier of leadership in 'the house of God' explains why Peter has moved from a discussion of the to-be-expected fiery trials to an exhortation to the elders to shepherd and oversee the flock through these wilderness trials. This chapter, then, helped to show the recurrence of Zecharian themes outside of 1 Pet. 2.25 and 1 Pet. 1.6/4.12. What makes these proposed echoes significant, I argued, is their distinctiveness; that is, they are exclusive to both Zechariah 9–14 and 1 Peter. Additionally, these proposed echoes provide coherence to features of 1 Peter that are otherwise lacking.

In Chapter 6, I transitioned to the second phase of enquiry – seeking to determine whether or how Zechariah 9–14 undergirds, supports, animates, constrains the logic of and gives coherence to the argumentative strategy of 1 Peter. Although my analysis prior to Chapter 6 often included a discussion of the broader literary contours of the letter, I determined that it was necessary to survey the letter as whole. As a result, I was able to demonstrate that, broadly speaking, the argumentative strategy of 1 Peter unfolds in two moves. First, Peter orients his addressees theologically by offering an interpretative framework for making sense of the social alienation his addressees experience as a result of aligning themselves with Jesus Christ (1.1–2.10). More specifically, I noted that embedded within this theological orientation is an implicit narrative through which his addressees are to view their lives: Jesus Christ has caused something to happen – as a result of his sacrificial death, the addressees have been relationally restored to God and presently are awaiting an inheritance, which will be awarded at the return of Jesus Christ. In the meantime, as the renewed people of God, they now find themselves living in a transition period characterized both as fiery trials in which their fidelity to God will be tested as well as a wilderness/second exodus journey towards their prepared inheritance. Second, I showed the way in which Peter offers a variety of exhortations which instruct his addressees regarding how they are to live in light of this new theological orientation (2.11–5.14). As I indicated in my survey, these exhortations are undergirded by constant reference (in a variety of manners) to the theological orientation (including the implicit narrative) offered at the beginning of the letter.

In the second part of Chapter 6 I indicated that the implicit narrative found in 1 Peter parallels the distinct programme of Zechariah 9–14. What is most significant, perhaps even determinative, is that only 1 Peter and Zechariah 9–14 offer an eschatological programme that develops the notion of a transition period subsequent to the coming of YHWH's shepherd and prior to consummation that is described both as a period of fiery trials as well as a second exodus journey. In other words, Zechariah 9–14 offers the unique solution to the precise issue with which Peter and his addressees are struggling: if Jesus is in fact the Christ, the agent appointed by God to bring about restoration, then why are Christians suffering *after* his coming?

In addition to sharing a similar unique narrative pattern, I further demonstrated that thirteen key themes and features of 1 Peter's eschatological programme are also found in the distinctive eschatological programme of Zechariah 9–14. The unique narrative embedded within the discourse of 1 Peter along with these thirteen themes, I argued, strongly suggest that Peter's eschatological programme has been generated from Zechariah 9–14. I further argued that Zechariah 9–14 likely generated and provides a better explanation for Peter's appropriation of a number of OT passages in the letter. More specifically, I proposed that Peter drew upon particular OT passages (e.g. Lev. 11.44/19.2; the stone catena in 1 Pet. 2.6–8; Isa. 43.20–1 and Exod. 19.5–6; Hosea 1.6,9/2.25; LXX Ps. 33; Isaiah 53; and Isa. 11.2) in order to fortify, explain, illustrate and corroborate the very substructure (i.e. the eschatological programme of Zechariah 9–14) that undergirds and generates his eschatological programme. Additionally, I argued that Peter's fragmentary allusions (i.e. shepherd and fiery trials imagery) and echoes (e.g. 'house of God') derive coherence from their relation to the eschatological programme of Zechariah 9–14: they are allusive recollections of this foundational eschatological narrative.

In my analysis I also highlighted that Peter was not simply trying to reduplicate the eschatological programme of Zechariah 9–14 in a wooden fashion, nor was he looking for a one-to-one correspondence. There are, for example, new features that Peter included in his account (e.g. the resurrection of Jesus Christ, Christ's second coming and Jesus as the Passover Lamb). There also appear to be features of the eschatological programme of Zechariah 9–14 that have been omitted from Peter's discourse (e.g. the military imagery of Zechariah 9 and 14; the violent hostility of the nations; the restoration of the land; and any explicit mention of Jesus as the *Davidic* eschatological shepherd).

One of the principal outcomes of my proposal is that it provides a more satisfying account of a variety of features in the letter that have been noted by Primopetrine scholars (such as was indicated in §1.1). First, we get a thicker description of the embedded narrative (and the eschatological programme) of 1 Peter than has been detailed by other scholars, one that is appropriately rooted in Israel's scriptures and the Jewish eschatological expectations which were prevalent at the time of composition. Second, my proposal brings coherence to the letter that is discerned not by rhetorical and compositional analyzes, but rather in relation to the substructure of Peter's eschatological programme, which is also able to explain Peter's seemingly eclectic appropriation of scripture and such apparently fragmented imagery as fiery trials, sheep returning to the shepherd, house of God and second exodus. Third, we get a Messianic Woes type scenario, that is, an explanation for a transition period of suffering subsequent to Christ's first coming and prior to his return, but from a text that we know was available rather than from a problematic scholarly construct. And finally, and perhaps most significantly, we are able to discern that Peter's principal strategy for helping his addressees remain faithful to Jesus Christ in the midst of suffering and social alienation is to show them that what they are undergoing is κατὰ τὰς γραφάς, and in particular κατὰ Ζαχαρίαν 9–14. In other words, my proposal identifies what has shaped Peter to regard Christian suffering as a necessary (1.6) and to-be-expected (4.12) component of faithful allegiance to Jesus Christ, which ultimately was the aim of this study.

7.1   Beyond the scope of this study: further directions

The proposal I have put forth is in no way exhaustive, and instead clears the way for further investigation along a number of lines. First, more can and should be said about the theological impact of Zechariah 9–14 beyond the subject of Christian suffering. For example, is there an implicit Davidic Christology in the letter that is everywhere present and yet nowhere mentioned? Second, what light might recent research on Roman imperial ideology shed on the allusive nature of Peter's appropriation of Zechariah 9–14 and seemingly his refusal to make explicit mention of a Davidic king? That is, can James C. Scott's work on 'hidden transcripts' or the development in postcolonial research of the notion of 'hybridity', for example, shed light on Peter's covert usage of a text which ultimately projects YHWH's universal reign through a Davidic shepherd? Third, in light of some of the conclusions that I have made in this study, and given the fact that the overall narrative of Revelation depicts Christian suffering as a necessary part of a wider eschatological programme, it would perhaps be fruitful to revisit Jauhiainen's work on Zechariah in Revelation to see whether he has underestimated the influence of Zechariah 9–14 on the eschatological programme of the Apocalypse. Fourth, perhaps a wider discussion and exploration is called for with respect to the way in which Zechariah 9–14 has (and has not) shaped the theology of Christian suffering in the early church. For example, why is Zechariah 9–14 almost entirely absent from Luke's Gospel and Paul's letters? Apart from 1 Peter and Revelation, is Zechariah 9–14 appropriated elsewhere in the NT in order to understand Christian theology beyond the suffering and death of Jesus Christ? Additionally, is there evidence that Zechariah 9–14 has shaped in any way the theology of Christian suffering in the Ante-Nicene fathers, and if so how? That is, how has Zechariah 9–14 been received in the early church outside of the canon?

However fruitful these lines of study may or may not be, the principal contribution of this study is that it offers a comprehensive explanation for the source that has generated 1 Peter's theology of Christian suffering, which, as I indicated, is a lacuna in 1 Peter scholarship. If what I have proposed has been argued persuasively, then we can conclude that 1 Peter offers a unique vista into the way in which at least one early Christian witness came to conclude and to communicate that Christian suffering was a necessary feature of faithful allegiance to Jesus Christ.

WORKS CITED

Primary sources

The Bible and other Jewish texts

Biblia Hebraica Stuttgartensia. Edited by K. Elliger and W. Rudolph. 5th edition. Stuttgart: Deutsche Bibelgesellschaft, 1997 [1967].

The Dead Sea Scrolls. Hebrew, Aramaic, and Greek Texts with English Translations. Edited by C. H. Charlesworth. 10 vols. Tübingen: Mohr-Siebeck, 1994.

The Dead Sea Scrolls Study Edition. Edited by F. Garcia Martinez and E. J. C. Tigchelaar. 2 vols. Grand Rapids: Eerdmans, 2000.

Duodecim prophetae. Edited by J. Ziegler. Vol. 13. 2nd edition. Septuaginta. Göttingen: Vandenhoeck & Ruprecht, 1984.

The Holy Bible, Containing the Old and New Testaments with the Apocryphal/Deutero-canonical Books: New Revised Standard Version. New York and Oxford: Oxford University Press, 1989.

Novum Testamentum Graece. Edited by B. Aland, K. Aland, J. Karavidopoulos, C. M. Martini and B. M. Metzger. 27th edition. Stuttgart: Deutsche Bibelgesellschaft, 1993 [1898].

The Old Testament Pseudepigrapha. Edited by J. H. Charlesworth. 2 vols. Garden City, New York: Doubleday, 1983–5.

1 Enoch: A New Translation. Translated and edited by G. W. E Nickelsburg and J. C. VanderKam. Minneapolis: Fortress Press, 2004.

Sapientia Iesu Filii Sirach. Edited by J. Ziegler. Vol. 12.2. Septuaginta. Göttingen: Vandenhoeck & Ruprecht, 1965.

Sapientia Salomonis. Edited by J. Ziegler. Vol. 12.1. 2nd edition. Septuaginta. Göttingen: Vandenhoeck & Ruprecht, 1980.

Septuaginta: Id est Vetus Testamentum Graece iuxta LXX interpres. Edited by A. Rahlfs. 2 vols. in 1. Stuttgart: Deutsche Bibelgesellschaft, 1979 [1935].

The Targum of the Minor Prophets. Edited by K. J. Cathcart and R. P. Gordon. Vol. 14. Aramaic Bible. Edinburgh: T&T Clark, 1989.

Josephus, *Works*. Edited by H. St. J. Thackeray, R. Marcus, A. Wikgren and L. H. Feldman. 9 vols. LCL (Loeb Classical Library) Cambridge, Massachusetts: Harvard University Press, 1929–53.

Miscellaneous

Augustine, *De Doctrina Christiana*. Edited and translated by R. P. H. Green. Oxford Early Christian Texts. Oxford: Clarendon Press, 1995.
Gerolamo: Gli Uomini Ilustri. Edited by A. Ceresa-Gastaldo. Vol. 12. Biblioteca Patristica. Florence: Nardini Editore, 1988.

Secondary sources

Abasciano, B. J. 2007 'Diamonds in the Rough: A Reply to Christopher Stanley Concerning the Reader Competence of Paul's Original Audiences'. *NovT* 49: 153–83.
Achtemeier, P. J. 1990 'Omne Verbum Sonat: The New Testament and the Oral Environment of Late Western Antiquity'. *JBL* 109: 3–27.
1993 'Suffering Servant and Suffering Christ in 1 Peter' in *The Future of Christology: Essays in Honor of Leander E. Keck*. Edited by A. J. Malherbe and W. A. Meeks. Minneapolis: Fortress Press, 176–88.
1996 *1 Peter*. Hermeneia. Minneapolis: Fortress Press.
1999 'Newborn Babes and Living Stones: Literal and Figurative in 1 Peter' in *To Touch the Text: Biblical and Related Studies in Honor of Joseph A. Fitzmyer, S.J.* Edited by M. P. Horgan and P. J. Kobelski. New York: Crossroad, 207–36.
Ackroyd, P. R. 1962 *Zechariah*. Peake's Commentary. London: Nelson.
1968 *Exile and Restoration: A Study of Hebrew Thought of the Sixth Century BC*. London: SCM Press.
Adinolfi, M. 1988 *La Prima Lettera di Pietro nel Mondo Greco-Romano*. Vol. 26. Bibliotheca Pontificii Athenaei Antoniani. Rome: Antonianum.
Agnew, F. H. 1983 '1 Peter 1:2: An Alternative Translation'. *CBQ* 45: 68–73.
Ahearne-Kroll, S. P. 2007 *The Psalms of Lament in Mark's Passion: Jesus' Davidic Suffering*. Vol. 142. SNTSMS. Cambridge: Cambridge University Press.
Aitken, E. B. 2004 *Jesus' Death in Early Christian Memory: The Poetics of the Passion*. Vol. 53. NTOA. Fribourg: Academic Press.
Albl, M. C. 1999 *'And Scripture Cannot Be Broken': The Form and Function of the Early Christian Testimony Collections*. Vol. 96. NovTSup. Leiden: Brill.
Alexander, P. S. 1983 'Rabbinic Judaism and the New Testament'. *ZNW* 74: 237–46.
1984 'Midrash and the Gospels' in *Synoptic Studies: The Ampleforth Conferences of 1982 and 1983*. Edited by C. M. Tuckett. Sheffield: JSOT Press, 1–18.
Allison, D. C. 1985 *The End of the Ages Has Come: An Early Interpretation of the Passion and Resurrection of Jesus*. Philadelphia: Fortress Press.
Anderson, B. W. 1962 'Exodus Typology in Second Isaiah' in *Israel's Prophetic Heritage*. Edited by B. W. Anderson and W. Harrelson. New York: Harper and Bros, 177–95.
Argall, R. A. 1995 *1 Enoch and Sirach: A Comparative Literary and Conceptual Analysis of the Themes of Revelation, Creation and Judgment*. Vol. 8. Early Judaism and Its Literature. Atlanta: Scholars Press.

Aune, D. E. 1987 *The New Testament in Its Literary Environment*. Vol. 8. LEC. Philadelphia: Westminster.

Balch, D. L. 1981 *Let Wives Be Submissive: The Domestic Code in 1 Peter*. Vol. 26. SBLDS. Chico, California: Scholars Press.

Baldwin, J. 1972 *Haggai, Zechariah, Malachi*. Tyndale Old Testament Commentary. Downers Grove: InterVarsity Press.

Barclay, J. M. G. 1996 *Jews in the Mediterranean Diaspora: From Alexander to Trajan (323 BCE–117 CE)*. Edinburgh: T&T Clark.

2004 (ed.) *Negotiating Diaspora*. Vol. 45. Library of Second Temple Studies. London: T&T Clark.

Barnett, P. 2006 *1 Peter: Living Hope*. Sydney: Aquila Press.

Barrett, C. K. 1962 *The Gospel According to St. John*. London: SPCK.

Barstad, H. M. 1989 *A Way in the Wilderness: The 'Second Exodus' in the Message of Second Isaiah*. Vol. 12. JST. Manchester: Manchester University Press.

Barton, J. 1986 *Oracles of God: Perceptions of Ancient Prophecy in Israel After the Exile*. London: Darton, Longman & Todd.

Bauckham, R. J. 1988 'James, 1 and 2 Peter, Jude' in *It is Written: Scripture Citing Scripture: Essays in Honour of Barnabas Lindars*. Edited by D. A. Carson and H. G. M. Williamson. Cambridge: Cambridge University Press, 303–17.

1993 *Climax of Prophecy: Studies on the Book of Revelation*. London: T&T Clark.

1996 'James, 1 Peter, Jude and 2 Peter' in *A Vision for the Church: Studies in Early Christian Ecclesiology in Honour of J. P. M. Sweet*. Edited by M. Bockmuehl and M. B. Thompson. Edinburgh: T&T Clark, 153–66.

1998 'John for Readers of Mark' in *The Gospels for All Christians: Rethinking the Gospel Audiences*. Edited by R. Bauckham. Grand Rapids: Eerdmans, 147–71.

2006 *Jesus and the Eyewitnesses: The Gospels as Eyewitness Testimony*. Grand Rapids: Eerdmans.

Baumgarten, J. M. 2000 'Damascus Document' in *Encyclopedia of the Dead Sea Scrolls*. Vol. 1. Edited by L. H Schiffman and J. VanderKam. New York: Oxford University Press, 166–70.

Beare, F. W. 1970 *The First Epistle of Peter*. 3rd edition. Oxford: Basil Blackwell.

1981 *The Gospel According to Matthew*. Oxford: Blackwell.

Beasley-Murray, G. R. 1999 *John*. Vol. 36. 2nd edition. Word Biblical Commentary. Nashville: Thomas Nelson.

Bechtler, S. R. 1998 *Following in His Steps: Suffering, Community, and Christology in 1 Peter*. Vol. 162. SBLDS. Atlanta: Scholars Press.

Beentjes, P. C. 1997 *The Book of Ben Sira in Hebrew*. Leiden: Brill.

Beker, J. C. 1986 'The Method of Recasting Pauline Theology: The Coherence-Contingency Theme As Interpretive Model' in *SBL 1986 Seminar Papers*. Edited by K. H. Richards. Atlanta: Scholars Press, 596–602.

1990 *The Triumph of God: The Essence of Paul's Thought*. Minneapolis: Fortress Press.

1993 'Echoes and Intertextuality: On the Role of Scripture in Paul's Theology' in *Paul and the Scriptures of Israel*. Edited by C. A. Evans and J. A. Sanders. JSNTSup 83. Sheffield: JSOT Press, 64–9.

1994 *Suffering and Hope: The Biblical Vision and the Human Predicament.* 2nd edition. Grand Rapids: Eerdmans.

Bellinger, W. H. and W. R. Farmer (eds.) 1998 *Jesus and the Suffering Servant: Isaiah 53 and Christian Origins.* Harrisburg, Pennsylvania: Trinity Press.

ben-Hayyim, Z. 1973 *The Book of Ben Sira: Text, Concordance, and an Analysis of the Vocabulary.* Jerusalem: Academy of the Hebrew Language and the Shrine of the Book.

Ben-Porat, Z. 1976 'The Poetics of Literary Allusions'. *PTL* 1: 105–28.

Best, E. 1965 *The Temptation and the Passion: The Markan Soteriology.* Vol. 2. SNTSMS. Cambridge: Cambridge University Press.

1970 '1 Peter and the Gospel Tradition'. *NTS* 16: 95–113.

1971 *1 Peter.* London: Oliphants.

Betz, O. 1960 *Offenbarung und Schriftsforschung in Der Qumransekte.* Vol. 6. WUNT. Tübingen: Mohr-Siebeck.

Bigg, C. 1901 *Epistles of St. Peter and St. Jude.* ICC. Edinburgh: T&T Clark.

Black, C. C. 1995 'Rhetorical Criticism' in *Hearing the New Testament: Strategies for Interpretation.* Edited by J. B. Green. 1st edition. Grand Rapids: Eerdmans.

Black, M. 1971 'The Christological Use of the Old Testament in the New Testament'. *NTS* 18: 1–14.

Black, M. C. 1990 'The Rejected and Slain Messiah Who Is Coming With His Angels: The Messianic Exegesis of Zechariah 9–14 in the Passion Narratives'. Doctoral dissertation. Emory University.

2008 'The Messianic Use of Zechariah 9–14 in Matthew, Mark and the Pre-Markan Tradition' in *Scripture and Tradition: Essays on Early Judaism and Christianity in Honor of Carl R. Holladay.* Edited by P. Gray and G. R. O'Day. Leiden: Brill, 97–114.

Blenkinsopp, J. 2002 *Isaiah 40–55.* Vol. 19A. Anchor Bible. New York: Doubleday.

2003 *Isaiah 56–66.* Vol. 19B. Anchor Bible. New York: Doubleday.

Bloomquist, L. G. 1993 *The Function of Suffering in Philippians.* Vol. 78. JSNTSup. Sheffield: Academic.

Bockmuehl, M. 2005 'Simon Peter and Bethsaida' in *The Missions of James, Peter, and Paul: Tensions in early Christianity.* Edited by B. Chilton and C. A. Evans. Leiden: Brill, 53–91.

2007 'Peter's Death in Rome? Back to Front and Upside Down'. *SJT* 60: 1–23.

Boda, M. J. and M. H. Floyd (eds.) 2004 *Bring Out the Treasure: Inner Biblical Allusion in Zechariah 9–14.* London: T&T Clark.

Boff, L. 1987 *Passion of Christ, Passion of the World: The Facts, Their Interpretation, and Their Meaning Yesterday and Today.* Maryknoll, New York: Orbis.

Boismard, M.-É. 1961 *Quatre Hymnes Baptismales dans la Première épître de Pierre.* Paris: Cerf.

Boomershine, T. E. 1994 'Jesus of Nazareth and the Watershed of Ancient Orality and Literacy'. *Semeia* 65: 7–36.

Boring, M. E. 1999 *1 Peter.* Abingdon New Testament Commentaries. Nashville: Abingdon Press.

2007 'Narrative Dynamics in First Peter: The Function of Narrative World' in *Reading First Peter with New Eyes: Methodological Reassessments of the*

Letter of First Peter. Edited by R. L. Webb and B. Bauman-Martin. London: T&T Clark, 8–40.

Bornemann, W. 1919 'Der erste Petrusbrief: Eine Taufrede des Silvanus?' *ZNW* 19: 143–65.

Bosetti, E. 1990 *Il Pastore: Cristo e la Chiesa Nella Prima Lettera di Pietro*. Vol. 21. Supplementi alla Rivista Biblica. Bologna: Edizioni Dehoniane.

Bowman, A. K. and G. Woolf (eds.) 1994 *Literacy and Power in the Ancient World*. Cambridge: Cambridge University Press.

Box, G. H. and W. O. E. Oesterley. 1913 'Sirach' in *Apocrypha and Pseudepigrapha of the Old Testament in English*. Edited by R. H. Charles. Vol. 1. Oxford: Clarendon Press, 268–517.

Boyarin, D. 2000 'Midrash' in *Handbook of Postmodern Biblical Interpretation*. Edited by A. K. M Adam. St Louis: Chalice Press, 167–73.

Bradshaw, P. F. 1992 *The Search for the Origins of Christian Worship*. London: SPCK.

2009 *Reconstructing Early Christian Worship*. London: SPCK.

Brewster, H. 1993 *Classical Anatolia: The Glory of Hellenism*. New York: Tauris.

Brooke, G. J. 2000 'Pesharim' in *The Dictionary of New Testament Backgrounds*. Edited by C. A. Evans and S. E. Porter. Downers Grove, Illinois: InterVarsity Press, 778–82.

Brown, G. and G. Yule 1983 *Discourse Analysis*. Cambridge Textbooks in Linguistics. Cambridge: Cambridge University Press.

Brown, J. 1855 *Expository Discourses on the First Epistle of the Apostle Peter*. 2nd edition. New York: Robert Carter.

Brown, R. E. 1966 *The Gospel According to John*. Vol. 29. Anchor Bible. New York: Doubleday.

1994 *The Death of the Messiah: A Commentary on the Passion Narratives in the Four Gospels*. 2 vols. Anchor Bible. New York: Doubleday.

Brox, N. 1986 *Der erste Petrusbrief*. Vol. 21. EKKNT. Zurich: Benzinger.

Bruce, F. F. 1961 'The Book of Zechariah and the Passion Narrative'. *Bulletin of the John Rylands Library* 43: 336–53.

1968 *This Is That: The New Testament Development of Some Old Testament Themes*. Devon: Paternoster.

1979 *Peter, Stephen, James, and John: Studies in Early Non-Pauline Christianity*. Grand Rapids: Eerdmans.

1988 *The Book of Acts*. NICNT. Revised edition. Grand Rapids: Eerdmans.

Brueggemann, W. 1986 *Hopeful Imagination: Prophetic Voices in Exile*. Philadelphia: Fortress Press.

1990 *First and Second Samuel*. Louisville: John Knox Press.

1993 'Preaching to Exiles'. *Journal for Preachers* 16: 3–15.

Buse, I. 1960 'St John and the Passion Narratives of St Matthew and St Luke'. *NTS* 7: 65–76.

Butterworth, M. 1992 *Structure and the Book of Zechariah*. Vol. 130. JSOTSup. Sheffield: JSOT Press.

Bynum, W. R. 2009 'The Citation of Zechariah 12:10 in John 19:37'. Doctoral dissertation. University of Manchester.

Byrskog, S. 2000 *Story as History – History as Story: The Gospel Tradition in the Context of Ancient Oral History*. Vol. 123. WUNT. Tübingen: Mohr-Siebeck.

Campbell, B. 1998 *Honor, Shame, and the Rhetoric of 1 Peter*. Vol. 160. SBLDS. Atlanta: Scholars Press.

Campbell, J. G. 1995 *The Use of Scripture in the Damascus Document 1–8, 19–20*. Vol. 228. BZAW. Berlin: de Gruyter.

Carter, W. 2006 *The Roman Empire and the New Testament: An Essential Guide*. Nashville: Abingdon Press.

Casey, M. 1991 *From Gentile Prophet to Jewish God: The Origins and Development of New Testament Christology*. Louisville: Westminster/John Knox Press.

Cervantes Gabarrón, J. 1991a *La Pasión de Jesucristo en la Primera Carta de Pedro: Centro Literario y Teológico de la Carta*. Vol. 22. Institución San Jerónimo. Estella, Navarra: Verbo Divino.

1991b 'El Pastor en La Teología de 1 Pedro'. *EstBib* 49: 331–51.

Chae, Y. S. 2006 *Jesus as the Eschatological Davidic Shepherd*. Vol. 216. WUNT II. Tübingen: Mohr-Siebeck.

Charlesworth, J. H. 2002 *The Pesharim and Qumran History: Chaos Or Consensus?* Grand Rapids: Eerdmans.

Chester, A. and R. P. Martin. 1994 *The Theology of the Letters of James, Peter, and Jude*. New Testament Theology. Cambridge: Cambridge University Press.

Childs, B. 1979 *Introduction to the Old Testament as Scripture*. Philadelphia: Fortress Press.

Chilton, B. 1983 'Varieties and Tendencies of Midrash: Rabbinic Interpretations of Isaiah 24.23' in *Gospel Perspectives III: Studies in Midrash and Historiography*. Edited by R.T. France and D. Wenham. Sheffield: JSOT Press, 289–99.

1992 *The Temple of Jesus: His Sacrificial Program within a Cultural History of Sacrifice*. University Park: Penn State Press.

Chin, M. 1991 'A Heavenly Home for the Homeless'. *TynBul* 42: 96–112.

Clements, R. E. 1998 'Isaiah 53 and the Restoration of Israel' in *Jesus and the Suffering Servant: Isaiah 53 and Christian Origins*. Edited by W. H. Bellinger and W. R. Farmer. Harrisburg: Trinity Press, 39–54.

Coggins, R. J. 1987 *Haggai, Zechariah, Malachi*. Old Testament Guides. Sheffield: Sheffield Academic Press.

1998 *Sirach: Guides to Apocrypha and Pseudepigrapha*. Sheffield: Sheffield Academic Press.

Collins, J. J. 1974 *The Sibylline Oracles of Egyptian Judaism*. Vol. 13. SBLDS. Missoula, Montana: Scholars Press.

1979 'Introduction: Towards the Morphology of a Genre'. *Semeia* 36: 1–20.

1984a *The Apocalyptic Imagination: An Introduction to Jewish Apocalyptic Literature*. 2nd edition. Grand Rapids: Eerdmans.

1984b *Jewish Writings of the Second Temple Period*. Philadelphia: Fortress Press.

1993 'Wisdom, Apocalypticism and Generic Compatibility' in *In Search of Wisdom: Essays in Memory of John G. Gammie*. Edited by L. Purdue, B. B. Scott and W. J. Wiseman. Louisville: Westminster/John Knox Press, 165–85.

1995 *The Scepter and the Star: The Messiahs of the Dead Sea Scrolls and Other Ancient Literature*. New York: Doubleday.

2000 *Between Athens and Jerusalem: Jewish Identity in the Hellenistic Diaspora*. 2nd edition. Grand Rapids: Eerdmans.

Colwell, E. C. 1939 'Popular Reactions against Christianity in the Roman Empire' in *Environmental Factors in Christian History*. Edited by J. T. McNeill, M. Spinka and H. R. Willoughby. Port Washington, New York: Kennikat, 53–71.

Conrad, E. W. 1999 *Zechariah*. Readings: A New Biblical Commentary. Sheffield: Sheffield Academic Press.

Conzelmann, H. 1975 *1 Corinthians*. Hermeneia. Philadelphia: Fortress Press.

Cook, J. G. 2010 *Roman Attitudes toward the Christians*. Vol. 261. WUNT. Tübingen: Mohr-Siebeck.

Cook, S. L. 1993 'The Metamorphosis of a Shepherd: The Tradition History of Zechariah 11.17 + 13. 7–9'. *CBQ* 55: 453–66.

Cousar, C. B. 1990 *A Theology of the Cross: The Death of Jesus in the Pauline Letters*. Minneapolis: Fortress Press.

Crenshaw, J. L. 1997 'The Book of Sirach' in *Introduction to Wisdom Literature; Proverbs; Ecclesiastes; Song of Songs; Book of Wisdom*. Vol. 5. New Interpreter's Bible. Nashville: Abingdon Press, 1997, 603–867.

Cross, F. L. 1954 *1 Peter: A Paschal Liturgy*. London: Mowbray.

Crossan, J. D. 1988 *The Cross That Spoke: The Origins of the Passion Narrative*. San Francisco: Harper & Row.

Crossan, J. D. and J. L. Reed 2004 *In Search of Paul: How Jesus' Apostle Opposed Rome's Empire With God's Kingdom*. New York: HarperCollins Publishers.

Cunliffe-Jones, H. 1973 *A Word for Our Time? Zechariah 9–14, the New Testament and Today*. The Ethel M. Wood Lecture. London: The Athlone Press.

Dalton, J. W. 1965 *Christ's Proclamation to the Spirits*. Rome: Pontifical Biblical Institute.

Danker, F. W. (ed.) 2000. *A Greek–English Lexicon of the New Testament and Other Early Christian Literature* (BDAG). 3rd edition. Chicago: University of Chicago Press.

Daube, D. 1949 'Rabbinic Methods of Interpretation and Hellenistic Rhetoric'. *HUCA* 22: 239–65.

1977 'Alexandrian Methods of Interpretation and the Rabbis' in *Essays in Greco-Roman and Related Talmudic Literature*. Edited by H. A. Fischel. New York: Ktaw, 165–82.

Davids, P. H. 1990 *The First Epistle of Peter*. NICNT. Grand Rapids: Eerdmans.

2004 'The Use of Second Temple Traditions in 1 and 2 Peter and Jude' in *The Catholic Epistles and the Tradition*. Edited by J. Schlosser. Leuven: Leuven University Press, 409–31.

Davies, W. D. 1983 'Reflections about the Use of the Old Testament in the New in Its Historical Context'. *JQR* 74: 105–36.

Davila, J. R. 2001 'The Perils of Parallels: "Parallelomania" Revisted'. Unpublished paper accessible at www.st-andrews.ac.uk/divinity/rt/dss/abstracts/parallels/.

2005a *The Provenance of the Pseudepigrapha: Jewish, Christian, or Other?* SJSJ. Leiden: Brill.

2005b 'The Old Testament Pseudepigrapha as Background to the New Testament'. *ExpTim* 117: 53–7.

de Jonge, M. (ed.) 1975 *Studies on the Testament of the Twelve Patriarchs*. Leiden: Brill.

de Ste Croix, G. E. M. 1963 'Why Were the Early Christians Persecuted?' *Past and Present* 26: 6–38.

1964 'Why Were the Early Christians Persecuted?–a Rejoinder'. *Past and Present* 27: 28–33.

Delcor, M. 1951 'Un Problème de Critique Textuelle et d'Exegese: Zach 12:10'. *Revue biblique* 58: 189–99.

Dentan, R. C. 1956 *Zechariah*. Interpreter's Bible. Nashville: Abingdon Press.

Derrett, J. D. M. 1968 'The Stone That the Builders Rejected'. *Studia Evangelica* 4: 180–6.

Deterding, P. E. 1981 'Exodus Motifs in 1 Peter'. *Concordia Journal* 7: 58–65.

Di Lella, A. A. 1987 *The Wisdom of Ben Sira*. Vol. 39. Anchor Bible. New York: Doubleday.

Dodd, C. H. 1952 *According to the Scriptures: The Sub-structure of New Testament Theology*. London: Nisbet & Co.

Doering, L. 2009 'First Peter as Early Christian Diaspora Letter' in *The Catholic Epistles and Apostolic Tradition: A New Perspective on James to Jude*. Edited by K.-W. Niebuhr and R. W. Wall. Waco: Baylor Press, 215–36.

Donaldson, T. L. 1983 'Parallels: Use, Misuse and Limitations'. *EvQ* 55: 193–210.

Dryden, J. W. 2006 *Theology and Ethics in 1 Peter: Paraenetic Strategies for Christian Character Formation*. Vol. 209. WUNT. Tübingen: Mohr-Siebeck.

Dubis, M. 2002 *Messianic Woes in First Peter: Suffering and Eschatology in 1 Peter 4:12–19*. Vol. 33. Studies in Biblical Literature. New York: Lang.

Duguid, I. 1995 'Messianic Themes in Zechariah 9–14' in *The Lord's Anointed: Interpretation of Old Testament Messianic Texts*. Edited by P. E. Satterhwaite, R. S. Hess and G. J. Wenham. Grand Rapids: Baker, 265–80.

Dunn, J. D. G. 1980 *Christology in the Making: An Inquiry into the Origins and Development of New Testament Christology*. London: SCM Press.

Edwards, C. and G. Woolf (eds.) 2003 *Rome the Cosmopolis*. Cambridge: Cambridge University Press.

Edwards, J. R. 2002 *The Gospel According to Mark*. The Pillar New Testament Commentary. Grand Rapids: Eerdmans.

Elliott, J. H. 1966 *The Elect and the Holy: An Exegetical Examination of 1 Peter 2:4–10 and the Phrase 'Basileion Hierateuma'*. Leiden: Brill.

1970 'Ministry and Church Order in the NT: A Traditio-Historical Analysis'. *CBQ* 32: 367–91.

1981 *A Home for the Homeless: A Sociological Exegesis of 1 Peter, Its Situation and Strategy*. Philadelphia: Fortress Press.

1985 'Backward and Forward "In His Steps": Following Jesus From Rome to Raymond and Beyond: The Tradition, Redaction, and Reception of 1 Peter 2.18–25' in *Discipleship in the New Testament*. Edited by F. Segovia. Philadelphia: Fortress, 184–209.

1992 'First Epistle of Peter' in *The Anchor Bible Dictionary*. Edited by D. N. Freedman, 269–78.

2000 *1 Peter: A New Translation with Introduction and Commentary*. Vol. 37B. Anchor Bible. New York: Doubleday.

Ellis, E. E. 1988 'Biblical Interpretation in the New Testament Church' in *Mikra: Text, Translation, Reading and Interpretation of the Hebrew Bible in Ancient*

Judaism and Early Christianity. Edited by M. J. Mulder. Philadelphia: Fortress Press, 691–725.

Ellul, D. 1990 'Un Exemple de Cheminement Rhétorique: 1 Pierre'. *Revue d'Historie et de Philosophie Religieuses* 70: 17–34.

Evans, C. A. 1992 'Midrash' in *Dictionary of Jesus and the Gospels*. Edited by J. B. Green, S. McKnight and I. H. Marshall, 544–8.

1999 'Jesus and Zechariah's Messianic Hope' in *Authenticating the Activities of Jesus*. Edited by B. Chilton and C. A. Evans. Leiden: Brill, 373–88.

Evans, C. A. and J. A. Sanders (eds.) 1993 *Paul and the Scriptures of Israel*. Vol. 83. JSNTSup. Sheffield: JSOT Press.

1997 *Early Christian Interpretation of the Scriptures of Israel: Investigations and Proposals*. Vol. 148. JSNTSup. Sheffield: Sheffield Academic Press.

Evans, C. F. 1954 'I Will Go Before You into Galilee'. *JTS* 5: 3–18.

Fagbemi, S. A. A. 2007 *Who Are the Elect in 1 Peter? A Study in Biblical Exegesis and Its Application to the Anglican Church of Nigeria*. Vol. 104. Studies in Biblical Literature. Oxford: Peter Lang.

Fee, G. D. 1987 *The First Epistle to the Corinthians*. NICNT. Grand Rapids: Eerdmans.

Feldmeier, R. 1992 *Die Christen als Fremde: Die Metapher der Fremde in der antiken Welt, im Urchristentum und im 1. Petrusbrief*. Vol. 64. WUNT. Tübingen: Mohr-Siebeck.

1996 'The "Nation" of Strangers: Social Contempt and Its Theological Interpretations in Ancient Judaism and Early Christianity' in *Ethnicity in the Bible*. Edited by M. G. Brett. Leiden: Brill, 240–70.

2008 *The First Letter of Peter*. Waco: Baylor Press.

Filson, F. V. 1955 'Partakers with Christ: Suffering in First Peter'. *Interpretation* 9: 404.

Fishbane, M. 1985 *Biblical Interpretation in Ancient Israel*. Oxford: Clarendon Press.

Forster, R. S. 1970 *The Restoration of Israel: A Study of Exile and Return*. London: Darton, Longman, and Todd.

Foster, P. 2003 'The Use of Zechariah in Matthew's Gospel' in *The Book of Zechariah and Its Influence*. Edited by C. Tuckett. Burlington, Vermont: Ashgate, 65–85.

France, R. T. 1971 *Jesus and the Old Testament: His Application of Old Testament Passages to Himself and His Mission*. London: Tyndale.

2002 *The Gospel of Mark*. NIGTC. Grand Rapids: Eerdmans.

Furnish, V. P. 1975 'Elect Sojourners in Christ: An Approach to the Theology of 1 Peter'. *Perkins School of Theology Journal* 28: 1–11.

Gamble, H. Y. 1995 *Books and Readers in the Early Church*. New Haven: Yale University Press.

Gan, J. 2007 *The Metaphor of Shepherd in the Hebrew Bible: A Historical-Literary Reading*. Lanham, Maryland: University Press of America.

Garcia Martinez, F., M. Verbenne and B. Doyle (eds.) 2005 *Interpreting Translation: Studies on the LXX and Ezekiel in Honour of Johan Lust*. Vol. 192. Bibliotheca Ephemeridum theologicarum Lovaniensium. Leuven: Peeters.

Garland, D. E. 1993 *Reading Matthew: A Literary and Theological Commentary on the First Gospel*. London: SPCK.

Gempf, C. 1994 'The Imagery of Birth Pangs in the New Testament'. *TynBul* 45: 119–35.

Gerhardsson, B. 1998 *Memory and Manuscript: Oral Tradition and Written Transmission in Rabbinic Judaism and Early Christianity with Tradition and Transmission in Early Christianity.* Grand Rapids: Eerdmans.

Gertner, M. 1962a 'Midrashim in the New Testament'. *JSS* 7: 267–92.

1962b 'Terms of Scriptural Interpretation'. *BSOAS* 25: 1–27.

Gignilliat, M. 2008 'Who Is Isaiah's Servant? Narrative Identity and Theological Potentiality'. *SJT* 61: 125–36.

Gilbert, M. 1984 'Wisdom Literature' in *Jewish Writings of the Second Temple Period.* Edited by M. E. Stone. Philadelphia: Fortress, 301–13.

Goldingay, J. 1989 *Daniel.* Vol. 30. Word Biblical Commentary. Dallas: Word Books.

Goldingay, J. and D. Payne 2006 *Isaiah 40–55.* Vols. 1–2. ICC. Edinburgh: T&T Clark.

Goodacre, M. 2002 *The Case against Q: Studies in Markan Priority and the Synoptic Problem.* Harrisburg: Trinity Press.

2006 'Scripturalization in Mark's Crucifixion Narrative' in *The Trial and Death of Jesus: Essays on the Passion Narrative in Mark.* Edited by G. van Oyen and T. Shepherd. Leuven: Peeters, 33–47.

Goodman, M. 1997 *The Roman World 44 BC–AD 180.* New York: Routledge.

1998 *Jews in a Graeco-Roman World.* Oxford: Clarendon Press.

Goppelt, L. 1982 *Typos: The Typological Interpretation of the Old Testament in the New.* Translated by Donald H. Madvig. Grand Rapids: Eerdmans.

1993 *A Commentary on 1 Peter.* Translated by J. E. Alsup. Grand Rapids: Eerdmans.

Gowan, D. E. 1977 'The Exile in Jewish Apocalyptic' in *Scripture in History and Theology: Essays in Honour of J. Coert Rylaarsdam.* Edited by A. L. Merrill and T. W. Overholt. Pittsburg: Pickwick, 205–22.

Grant, R. M. 1948 'The Coming of the Kingdom'. *JBL* 67: 297–303.

Green, G. 1989 *Imagining God: Theology and the Religious Imagination.* Grand Rapids: Eerdmans.

Green, G. L. 1990 'The Use of the Old Testament for Christian Ethics in 1 Peter'. *TynBul* 41: 276–89.

Green, J. B. 1987 'The Gospel of Peter: Source for a Pre-Canonical Passion Narrative?' *ZNW* 78: 293–301.

1988 *The Death of Jesus: Tradition and Interpretation in the Passion Narrative.* Vol. 33. WUNT II. Tübingen: Mohr-Siebeck.

1992a 'Death of Jesus' in *Dictionary of Jesus and the Gospels.* Edited by J. B. Green, S. McKnight and I. H. Marshall. Downers Grove: InterVarsity Press, 146–63.

1992b 'Passion Narrative' in *Dictionary of Jesus and the Gospels.* Edited by J. B. Green, S. McKnight and I. H. Marshall. Downers Grove: InterVarsity Press, 601–4.

2004 'Faithful Witness in the Diaspora: The Holy Spirit and the Exiled People of God According to 1 Peter' in *The Holy Spirit and Christian Origins: Essays in Honor of James D. G. Dunn.* Edited by G. N. Stanton, B. W. Longenecker and S. C. Barton. Grand Rapids: Eerdmans, 282–95.

2007a *1 Peter*. The Two Horizons New Testament Commentary. Grand Rapids: Eerdmans.

2007b 'Living As Exiles: The Holy Church in the Diaspora in 1 Peter' in *Holiness and Ecclesiology in the New Testament*. Edited by K. E. Brower and A. Johnson. Grand Rapids: Eerdmans, 311–25.

Green, J. B. and J. T. Carroll (eds.) 1995 *The Death of Jesus in Early Christianity*. Peabody, Massachusetts: Hendrickson.

Greenberg, M. 1997 *Ezekiel 21–37*. Vol. 22A. Anchor Bible. New York: Doubleday.

Gruen, E. S. 2002 *Diaspora: Jews amidst Greeks and Romans*. Cambridge, Massachusetts: Harvard University Press.

Gundry, R. H. 1967 'Verba Christi in 1 Peter: Their Implications Concerning the Authorship of 1 Peter and the Authenticity of the Gospel Tradition'. *NTS* 13: 336–50.

1974 'Further Verba on Verba Christi in First Peter'. *Biblica* 55: 211–32.

Hafemann, S. J. 1990 *Suffering and Ministry in the Spirit: Paul's Defense of His Ministry in II Corinthians 2:14–3:3*. Grand Rapids: Eerdmans.

1993 'Suffering' in *The Dictionary of Paul and His Letters*. Edited by R. P. Martin, G. F. Hawthorne and D. G. Reid. Downers Grove: InterVarsity Press, 919–21.

Hagner, D. A. 1993 *Matthew 14–28*. Vol. 33b. Word Biblical Commentary. Dallas: Word Books.

Ham, C. A. 2005 *The Coming King and the Rejected Shepherd: Matthew's Reading of Zechariah's Messianic Hope*. Sheffield: Sheffield Phoenix Press.

Hanson, P. D. 1975 *The Dawn of Apocalyptic*. Philadelphia: Fortress Press.

Harland, P. 2003 *Associations, Synagogues, and Congregations: Claiming a Place in Ancient Mediterranean Society*. Minneapolis: Fortress Press.

2006 'Acculturation and Identity in the Diaspora: A Jewish Family and "Pagan" Guilds at Hierapolis'. *JJS* 57: 222–44.

Harrington, D. J. 1999 *Invitation to The Apocrypha*. Grand Rapids: Eerdmans.

Harris, W. V. 1989 *Ancient Literacy*. Cambridge: Harvard University Press.

Hatch, E. 1889 *Essays in Biblical Greek*. Oxford: Clarendon.

Hauerwas, S. and L. G. Jones (eds.) 1989 *Why Narrative? Readings in Narrative Theology*. Grand Rapids: Eerdmans.

Hays, R. B. 1983 *The Faith of Jesus Christ: The Narrative Substructure of Galatians 3:1–4:11*. Grand Rapids: Eerdmans.

1989 *Echoes of Scripture in the Letters of Paul*. New Haven: Yale University Press.

2004 'Is Paul's Gospel Narratable?' *JSNT* 27.2: 217–39.

2005 *The Conversion of the Imagination: Paul as Interpreter of Israel's Scripture*. Grand Rapids: Eerdmans.

Hegemann, H. 1999 'The Diaspora in the Hellenistic Age' in *The Cambridge History of Judaism*. Edited by W. D. Davies and L. Finkelstein. Cambridge: Cambridge University Press.

Hempel, C. 2000 *The Damascus Texts*. Sheffield: Sheffield Academic Press.

Hendrickx, H. 1977 *Passion Narratives: Studies in the Synoptic Gospels*. London: Geoffrey Chapman.

Hengel, M. 1981 *The Atonement: The Origins of the Doctrine in the New Testament*. Philadelphia: Fortress Press.

Hengel, M. and D. P. Bailey 2004 'The Effective History of Isaiah 53 in the Pre-Christian Period' in *The Suffering Servant: Isaiah 53 in Jewish and Christian Sources*. Edited by B. Janowski and P. Stuhlmacher. Grand Rapids: Eerdmans, 75–146.

Henzser, C. 2001 *Jewish Literacy in Roman Palestine*. Texts and Studies in Ancient Judaism. Vol 81. Tübingen: Mohr-Siebeck.

Hiebert, D. E. 1982 'The Suffering and Triumphant Christ: An Exposition of 1 Peter 3:18–22'. *Bibliotheca Sacra* 139: 146–58.

Hill, D. 1972 *The Gospel of Matthew*. New Century Bible. London: Butler and Tanner.

1976 'On Suffering and Baptism in 1 Peter'. *NovT* 18: 181–9.

1982 '"To Offer Spiritual Sacrifices . . ." (1 Peter 2:5): Liturgical Formulations and Christian Paraenesis in 1 Peter'. *JSNT* 16: 45–63.

Hillyer, C. N. 1969 'Spiritual Milk . . . Spiritual House'. *TynBul* 20: 126–7.

Hodgson, R. 1979 'The Testimony Hypothesis'. *JBL* 98: 361–78.

Hofius, O. 2004 'The Fourth Servant Song in the New Testament Letters' in *The Suffering Servant: Isaiah 53 in Jewish and Christian Sources*. Edited by B. Janowski and P. Stuhlmacher. Grand Rapids: Eerdmans, 163–88.

Holdsworth, J. 1980 'The Sufferings of 1 Peter and "Missionary Apocalyptic"' in *Papers on Paul and Other New Testament Authors*. Vol. 3. JSNTSup. Sheffield: Academic Press, 225–32.

Holloway, P. A. 2002 'Nihil Inopinati Accidisse – "Nothing Unexpected Has Happened": A Cyrenaic Consolatory Topos in 1 Peter 4.12ff.' *NTS* 48: 433–48.

2009 *Coping with Prejudice*. Vol. 244. WUNT. Tübingen: Mohr-Siebeck.

Holman Illustrated Study Bible. 2006. Nashville: B&H Publishing.

Horbury, W. 1988 'Old Testament Interpretation in the Writings of the Church Fathers' in *Mikra: Text, Translation, Reading and Interpretation of the Hebrew Bible in Ancient Judaism and Early Christianity*. Edited by M. J. Mulder. Philadelphia: Fortress Press, 727–87.

1998 *Jewish Messianism and the Cult of Christ*. London: SCM Press.

2003 *Messianism among Jews and Christians: Twelve Biblical and Historical Studies*. London: T&T Clark.

Horrell, D. G. 1997 'Whose Faith(fulness) Is It in 1 Peter 1:5?' *JTS* 48: 110–15.

1998 *The Epistles of Peter and Jude*. Epworth Commentaries. Peterborough: Epworth Press.

2002 'The Product of a Petrine Circle? Reassessment of the Origin and Character of 1 Peter'. *JSNT* 86: 29–60.

2003 'Who Are "The Dead" and When Was the Gospel Preached to Them?: The Interpretation of 1 Peter IV, 6'. *NTS* 49: 70–89.

2007 'Between Conformity and Resistance: Beyond the Balch–Elliott Debate towards a Postcolonial Reading of 1 Peter' in *Reading 1 Peter with New Eyes: Methodological Reassessments of the Letter of First Peter*. Edited by R. L. Webb and B. J. Bauman-Martin. London: T&T Clark, 111–43.

2008 *1 Peter*. New Testament Guides. London: T&T Clark.

2009 'Aliens and Strangers? The Socioeconomic Location of the Addressees of 1 Peter' in *Engaging Economics: New Testament Scenarios and Early Christian Reception*. Edited by B. W. Longenecker and K. D. Liebengood. Grand Rapids: Eerdmans, 176–202.

Humphrey, J. H. (ed.) 1991 *Literacy in the Roman World*. Vol. 3. SJRA. Ann Arbor: Department of Classical Studies, University of Michigan.

Hunziker-Rodewald, R. 2001 *Hirt und Herder: Ein Beitrag zum altetestamentlichen Gottesvertändnis*. Vol. 155. BWANT. Stuttgart: W. Kohlhammer.

Hunzinger, C.-H. 1965 'Babylon als Deckname für Rom und die Datierung des 1. Petrusbriefes' in *Gottes Wort und Gottes Land*. Edited by H. G. Reventlow. Hertzberg and Göttingen: Vandenhoeck and Ruprecht, 67–77.

Hurtado, L. 1998 *One God, One Lord: Early Christian Devotion and Ancient Jewish Monotheism*. Philadelphia: Fortress Press.

2003 *Lord Jesus Christ: Devotion to Jesus in Earliest Christianity*. Grand Rapids: Eerdmans.

Instone-Brewer, D. 1992 *Techniques and Assumptions in Jewish Exegesis before 70 CE*. Vol. 30. TSAJ. Tübingen: Mohr-Siebeck.

Jaffee, M. S. 1992 'How Much Orality in Oral Torah? New Perspectives on the Compilation and Transmission of Early Rabbinic Tradition'. *Shofar* 10: 53–72.

1994 'Writing and Rabbinic Oral Tradition: On Mishnaic Narrative, Lists and Mnemonics'. *Journal of Jewish Thought and Philosophy* 4: 123–46.

2001 *Torah in the Mouth: Writing and Oral Tradition in Palestinian Judaism 200 BCE–400 CE*. New York: Oxford University Press.

Jauhiainen, M. 2005 *The Use of Zechariah in Revelation*. Vol. 199. WUNT II. Tübingen: Mohr-Siebeck.

Jenson, P. P. 1992 *Graded Holiness: A Key to the Priestly Conception of the World*. Vol. 106. JSOTSup. Sheffield: Sheffield Academic Press.

Jeremias, J. 1958 *Jesus' Promise to the Nations*. Vol. 24. SBT. London: SCM Press.

1962 'ποιμήν, ἀρχιποίμην, ποιμαίνω' in *Theological Dictionary of the New Testament*. Vol. 3. Grand Rapids: Eerdmans, 485–99.

1977 *New Testament Theology: The Proclamation of Jesus*. London: Scribner.

Jobes, K. H. 2002 'Got Milk? Septuagint Psalm 33 and the Interpretation of 1 Peter 2:1–3'. *Westminster Theological Journal* 63: 1–14.

2005 *1 Peter*. Baker Exegetical Commentary on the New Testament. Grand Rapids: Baker Academic.

2006 'The Septuagint Textual Tradition in 1 Peter' in *Septuagint Research: Issues and Challenges in the Study of the Greek Jewish Scriptures*. Edited by W. Krause and R. G. Wooden. Leiden: Brill, 311–33.

Johnson, D. E. 1986 'Fire in God's House: Imagery From Malachi 3 in Peter's Theology of Suffering (1 Pet 4:12–19)'. *JETS* 29: 285–94.

Johnson, S. E. 1975 'Asia Minor and Early Christianity' in *Christianity, Judaism and Other Greco-Roman Cults: Studies for Morton Smith at Sixty*. Edited by J. Neusner. Leiden: Brill, 77–145.

Juel, D. H. 1988 *Messianic Exegesis: Christological Interpretation of the Old Testament in Early Christianity*. Philadelphia: Fortress Press.

Kähler, M. 1964 *The So-Called Historical Jesus and the Historic, Biblical Christ*. Philadelphia: Fortress Press.

Kasemann, E. 1969 *New Testament Questions of Today*. Philadelphia: Fortress Press.

Kelly, J. N. D. 1969 *A Commentary of the Epistles of Peter and of Jude*. London: Black.

Kilpatrick, G. D. 1986 '1 Peter 1.11 τίνα ἤ ποῖον καιρόν'. *NovT* 28: 91–2.

Kim, S. 1987 'Jesus–the Son of God, the Stone, the Son of Man, and the Servant: The Role of Zechariah in the Self-Identification of Jesus' in *Tradition and Interpretation in the New Testament: Essays in Honor of E. Earle Ellis for His Sixtieth Birthday*. Edited by O. Betz and G. F. Hawthorne. Grand Rapids: Eerdmans, 134–48.

Klausner, J. 1956 *The Messianic Idea in Israel: From Its Beginnings to the Completion of the Mishnah*. Translated by W. F. Stinespring. London: George Allen and Unwin.

Kloppenborg, J. and S. G. Wilson (eds.) 1996 *Voluntary Associations in the Graeco-Roman World*. New York: Routledge.

Knibb, M. A. 1976 'The Exile in the Literature of the Intertestamental Period'. *Heythrop Journal* 17: 253–72.
1987 *The Qumran Community*. Vol. 2. Cambridge Commentaries on Writings of the Jewish and Christian World 200 BC to AD 200. Cambridge: Cambridge University Press.

Koch, D.-A. 1986 *Die Schrift als Zeuge des Evangeliums: Untersuchungen zur Verwendung und zum Verständnis der Schrift bei Paulus*. Vol. 69. BHT. Tübingen: Mohr-Siebeck.

Kolarcik, M. 1997 'The Book of Wisdom' in *Introduction to Wisdom Literature; Proverbs; Ecclesiastes; Song of Songs; Book of Wisdom; Sirach*. Vol. 5. New Interpreter's Bible. Nashville: Abingdon Press, 437–600.

Kraft, R. A. 1960 'Barnabas' Isaiah Text and the "Testimony Book" Hypothesis.' *JBL* 79:336–350.

Kraft, R.A. and G. W. E. Nickelsburg 1986 *Early Judaism and Its Modern Interpreters*. Philadephia: Fortress Press.

Kraus, W. and R. G. Wooden. 2006 *Septuagint Research: Issues and Challenges in the Study of the Greek Jewish Scriptures*. Vol. 53. Society of Biblical Literature Septuagint and Cognate studies. Leiden: Brill.

Kümmel, W. G. 1975 *Introduction to the New Testament*. Translated by H. C. Kee. Nashville: Abingdon Press.

Laato, A. 1997 *A Star Is Rising: The Historical Development of the Old Testament Royal Ideology and the Rise of Jewish Messianic Expectations*. Vol. 5. International Studies in Formative Christianity and Judaism. Atlanta: Scholars Press.

Laato, A. and J. C. de Moor (eds.) 2003 *Theodicy in the World of the Bible*. London: Brill.

Lamarche, P. 1961 *Zacharie ix–xiv: Structure Littéraire et Messianisme*. Études bibliques. Paris: Librairie Lecoffre.
1966 *Christ Vivant: Essai sur La Christologie du Nouveau Testament*. Vol. 43. Lectio Divina. Paris: Les Éditions du Cerf.

Lamau, L. 1988 *Des Chrétiens dans le Monde. Communautés Pétriennes au I. Siècle*. Vol. 134. LD. Paris: Cerf.

Lamb, J. A. 1962 *The Psalms in Christian Worship*. London: Faith Press.

Langkammer, H. 1987 'Jes 53 und 1 Petr 2,21–25: Zur chirstologischen Interpretation der Leidenstheologie von Jes 53'. *BL* 60: 90–8.

Laniak, T. S. 2006. *Shepherds after My Own Heart*. Vol. 20. Studies in Biblical Theology. Downers Grove: InterVarsity Press.

236   *Works cited*

Larkin, K. J. A. 1994 *The Eschatology of Second Zechariah: A Study of the Formation of a Mantological Wisdom Anthology*. Kampen, the Netherlands: Pharos.

Leaney, A. R. C. 1967 *The Letters of Peter and Jude*. Cambridge: Cambridge University Press.

Lim, T. H. 1997 *Holy Scriptures in the Qumran Commentaries and Pauline Letters*. Oxford: Clarendon Press.

Lincicum, D. 2008 'Paul and the Testimonia: Quo Vadimus?' *JETS* 51: 297–308.

Lincoln, A. T. 2005 *The Gospel According to Saint John*. Peabody: Hendrickson Publishers.

Lindars, B. 1961 *New Testament Apologetic: The Doctrinal Significance of the Old Testament Quotations*. London: SCM Press.

  1977 'The Passion in the Fourth Gospel' in *God's Christ and His People*. Edited by N. A. Dahl. Oslo: Universitatätsverlaget, 71–86.

Lococque, A. 1981 *Zecharie 9–14 Commentaire de l'Ancien Testament*. Paris: Delachaux & Niestlé.

Lohse, E. 1954 'Paraenese und Kerygma im 1. Petrusbrief'. *ZNW* 45: 68–89.

Longenecker, B. W. 1995 'The Unbroken Messiah: A Johannine Feature and Its Social Functions'. *NTS* 41: 428–41.

  (ed.) 2002 *Narrative Dynamics in Paul: A Critical Assessment*. Louisville: John Knox Press.

Lowe, W. H. 1882 *Zechariah: Hebrew and LXX with Excursus on Syllable-Dividing, Metheg, Intial Dagesh, and Siman Rapheh*. The Hebrew Student's Commentary. London: Macmillan and Co.

Macaskill, G. 2007 *Revealed Wisdom and Inaugurated Eschatology in Ancient Judaism and Early Christianity*. Vol. 115. SJSJ. Leiden: Brill.

Maccoby, H. 1988 *Early Rabbinic Writings*. Cambridge: Cambridge University Press.

Maier, G. 1985 'Jesustradition im 1. Petrusbrief?' in *Gospel Perspectives: The Jesus Tradition outside the Gospels*. Vol. 5. Edited by D. Wenham. Sheffield: JSOT Press, 85–128.

Mantey, J. R. 1951a 'The Causal Use of *Eis* in the New Testament'. *JBL* 70: 45–8.

  1951b 'On Causal *Eis* Again'. *JBL* 70: 309–11.

Marcus, J. 1992 *The Way of the Lord: Christological Exegesis of the Old Testament in the Gospel of Mark*. Louisville: Westminster/John Knox Press.

  1995 'The Old Testament and the Death of Jesus: The Role of Scripture in the Gospel Passion Narratives' in *The Death of Jesus in Early Christianity*. Edited by J. T. Carroll and J. B. Green; Peabody: Hendrickson, 205–33.

Marcus, R. 1952 'The Elusive Causal *Eis*'. *JBL* 1: 43–4.

Martin, F. 1975 'The Image of the Shepherd in the Gospel of Saint Matthew *Science et esprit* 27: 261–301.

Martin, R. P. 1994 'The Theology of Jude, 1 Peter, and 2 Peter' in *The Theology of the Letters of James, Peter, and Jude*. Edited by A. Chester and R. P. Martin. Cambridge: Cambridge University Press, 63–133.

Martin, T. W. 1992 *Metaphor and Composition in 1 Peter*. Vol. 131. SBLDS. Atlanta: Scholars Press.

Mason, R. 1973 *The Use of Earlier Biblical Material in Zechariah IX–XIV*. London: University of London.

1977 *The Books of Haggai, Zechariah, and Malachi*. Cambridge Bible Commentary. Cambridge: Cambridge University Press.

Matera, F. J. 1986 *Passion Narratives and Gospel Theologies: Interpreting the Synoptics Through Their Passion Stories*. New York: Paulist.

Mbuvi, A. M. 2007 *Temple, Exile and Identity in 1 Peter*. Vol. 345. Library of New Testament Studies. London: T&T Clark.

McAfee Moss, C. 2008 *The Zechariah Tradition and the Gospel of Matthew*. Vol. 156. BZNW. Berlin: Walter de Gruyter.

McKenzie, J. L. 1968 *Second Isaiah*. Vol. 20. Anchor Bible. New York: Doubleday.

Menken, M. J. J. 1993 'The Textual Form and the Meaning of the Quotation From Zechariah 12:10 in John 19:37'. *CBQ* 55: 494–511.

Metzger, B. 1957 *An Introduction to the Apocrypha*. New York: Oxford University Press.

Metzner, R. 1995 *Die Rezeption des Matthäusevangelium im 1. Petrusbrief: Studien zum Traditionsgeschichtlichen und Theologishen Einfluß des 1. Evangeliums auf den 1. Petrusbrief*. Vol. 74. WUNT II. Tübingen: Mohr-Siebeck.

Meyers, C. L. and E. M. Meyers 1993 *Zechariah 9–14*. Vol. 25C. Anchor Bible. New York: Doubleday.

Michaels, J. R. 1988 *1 Peter*. Vol. 49. Word Biblical Commentary. Waco: Word Books.

2004 'St. Peter's Passion: The Passion Narrative in 1 Peter'. *WW* 4: 387–94.

Millard, A. R. 2000 *Reading and Writing in the Time of Jesus*. New York: Sheffield Academic Press.

Millauer, H. 1976 *Leiden als Gnade: Eine Traditionsgeschichtliche Untersuchung zur Leidenstheologie des ersten Petrusbriefes*. Europäische Hochschulschriften. Reihe 23, Theologie; Bd. 56. Frankfurt: Lang.

Miller, D. 1993 *Upon This Rock: A Commentary on 1 Peter*. Vol. 34. Princeton Theological Monograph Series. Allison Park, Pennsylvania: Pickwick Publications.

Mitchell, D. C. 1997 *The Message of the Psalter: An Eschatological Programme in the Book of Psalms*. Vol. 252. JSOTSup. Sheffield: Sheffield Academic Press.

Mitchell, H. G. 1912 *Haggai and Zechariah*. International Critical Commentary Series. Edinburgh: T&T Clark.

Mitchell, S. 1990 'Festivals, Games, and Civic Life in Roman Asia Minor'. *Journal of Roman Studies* 80: 183–93.

1993 *Anatolia: Land, Men, and Gods in Asia Minor*. Vol. 1. The Celts in Anatolia. Oxford: Clarendon Press.

Moo, D. J. 1983 *The Old Testament in the Gospel Passion Narratives*. Sheffield: Almond.

Moule, C. F. D. 1955 'Some Reflections on the Stone Testimonia in Relation to the Name of Peter'. *NTS* 2: 56–9.

1956 'The Nature and Purpose of 1 Peter'. *NTS* 3: 1–11.

Moyise, S. 2000 'Intertextuality and the Study of the Old Testament in the New Testament' in *The Old Testament in the New Testament: Essays in Honour of J. L. North*. Edited by S. Moyise. Vol. 189. JSNTSup. Sheffield: Sheffield Academic Press, 14–41.

238   *Works cited*

2001 *The Old Testament in the New: An Introduction.* Continuum Biblical Studies Series. London: Continuum.

Murphy-O'Connor, J. 1970 'An Essene Missionary Document? CD II, 14-VI, 1'. *Revue biblique* 77: 201–29.

Myllykoski, M. 1991 *Die letzen Tage Jesu: Markus und Johannes, ihre Traditionen und die historische Frage.* Vol. 1. Suomalainen Tiedeakatemian Toimituksia Annales Academiae Scientiarum Fennicae. Helsinki: Suomalainen Tiedeakatemia.

Nehamas, A. 1986 'What an Author Is'. *Journal of Philosophy* 83: 685–91.

Neusner, J. 1983 *Midrash in Context: Exegesis in Formative Judaism.* Philadelphia: Fortress Press.

1987 *What Is Midrash?* Philadelphia: Fortress Press.

Neusner, J. with W. S. Green and E. Frerichs (eds.) 1987 *Judaisms and Their Messiahs at the Turn of the Christian Era.* Cambridge: Cambridge University Press.

Newman, C. C., J. R. Davila and G. S. Lewis (eds.) 1999 *The Jewish Roots of Christological Monotheism: Papers From the St Andrews Conference on the Historical Origins of the Worship of Jesus.* Leiden: Brill.

Nickelsburg, G. W. E. 1981 *Jewish Literature between the Bible and the Mishnah: A Historical and Literary Introduction.* London: SCM Press.

2001 *1 Enoch 1: A Commentary on the Book of 1 Enoch, Chapters 1–36; 81–108.* Hermeneia. Minneapolis: Fortress Press.

Norris, F. W. 1991 *Faith Gives Fullness to Reasoning: The Five Theological Orations of Gregory Nazianzen.* Leiden: Brill.

Novakovic, L. 2003 *Messiah, the Healer of the Sick: A Study of Jesus As the Son of David in the Gospel of Matthew.* Vol. 170. WUNT II. Tübingen: Mohr-Siebeck.

Oakes, P. 2001 *Philippians: From People to Letter.* Vol. 110. SNTSMS. Cambridge: Cambridge University Press.

O'Brien, J. M. 2004 *Nahum, Habakkuk, Zephaniah, Haggai, Zechariah, Malachi.* Abingdon Old Testament Commentaries. Nashville: Abingdon Press.

Oesterley, W. O. E. 1935 *An Introduction to the Books of the Apocrypha.* London: SPCK.

Ollenburger, B. C. 1996 *Zechariah.* Vol. 7. The New Interpreter's Bible. Nashville: Abingdon Press.

Osborne, T. P. 1983 'Guide Lines for Christian Suffering: A Source-Critical and Theological Study of 1 Peter 2, 21–25'. *Biblica* 64: 381–408.

Perdelwitz, R. 1911 *Die Mysterienreligion und das Problem Des 1. Petrusbriefes: Ein Literarischer und Religionsgeshichtlicher Versuch.* Vol. 11.3. RVV. Giessen: Töpelmann.

Perkins, P. 1995 *First and Second Peter, James, and Jude.* Louisville: John Knox Press.

Perrin, N. 1965 'Mark XIV.62: The End Product of a Christian Pesher Tradition'. *NTS* 12: 150–5.

Petersen, D. L. 1984a *Haggai and Zechariah 1–8.* Old Testament Library. London: SCM Press.

1984b 'Zechariah's Visions: A Theological Perspective'. *VT* 34: 195–206.

1995 *Zechariah 9–14 and Malachi: A Commentary.* Louisville: Westminster/ John Knox Press.

Pitre, B. 2005 *Jesus, the Tribulation, and the End of Exile: Restoration Eschatology and the Origin of the Atonement.* Vol. 204. WUNT II. Tübingen: Mohr-Siebeck.

Porter, S. 1997 'The Use of the Old Testament in the New Testament: A Brief Comment on Method and Terminology' in *Early Christian Interpretation of the Scriptures of Israel.* Edited by C. A. Evans and J. A. Sanders. London: Continuum, 79–96.

(ed.) 2006 *Hearing the Old Testament in the New Testament.* MNTS. Grand Rapids: Eerdmans.

Porter, S. with M. J. Boda. 2005 'Literature to the Third Degree: Prophecy in Zechariah 9–14 and the Passion of Christ' in *Traduire le Bible hébraïque de la Septante à la Nouvelle Bible Segond/Translating the Hebrew Bible. From the Septuagint to the Nouvelle Bible Segond.* Edited by M. Jinbachian. Montreal: Médiaspaul, 215–54.

Porton, G. G. 1981 'Defining Midrash' in *Mishhah, Midrash, Siddur.* Study of Ancient Judaism 1. Hoboken: KTAV, 55–92.

Pritchard, J. B. 1969 *Ancient Near Eastern Texts Relating to the Old Testament.* Princeton: Princeton University Press.

Proctor, J. 1993 'Fire in God's House: Influence of Malachi 3 in the NT'. *JETS* 36: 9–14.

Quarles, C. L. 1998 *Midrash Criticism: Introduction and Appraisal.* New York: University Press of America.

Rabinowitz, L. I. 1954 'A Reconsideration of "Damascus" and "390 Years" ("Zadokite") Fragments'. *JBL* 73: 11–35.

Redditt, P. L. 1989 'Israel's Shepherds: Hope and Pessimism in Zechariah 9–14'. *CBQ* 51: 631–42.

1995 *Haggai, Zechariah, Malachi.* NCBC. Grand Rapids: Eerdmans.

2008 *Introduction to the Prophets.* Grand Rapids: Eerdmans.

Reicke, B. 1964 *The Epistles of James, Peter and Jude.* Vol. 37. Anchor Bible. Garden City: Doubleday.

Reinbold, W. 1994 *Der älteste Bericht über den Tod Jesu: literarische Analyse und historische Kritik der Passiondarstellungen der Evangelien.* Vol. 69. BZNW. Berlin: Walter de Gruyter.

Reiser, M. 1994 'Die Eschatologie des 1. Petrusbriefs' in *Weltgericht und Weltvollendung. Zukunftsbilder im Neuen Testament.* Edited by H.-J. Klauck. Freiburg: Herder, 164–81.

Rendtorff, H. 1951 *Getrostes Wandern: Eine Einführung in den ersten Brief des Petrus.* Hamburg: Furche.

Richard, E. 2000 *Reading 1 Peter, Jude and 2 Peter: A Literary and Theological Commentary.* Reading the New Testament. Macon, Georgia: Smyth & Helwys Publishing.

2004 'Honorable Conduct among the Gentiles – a Study of the Social Thought of 1 Peter'. *WW* 24: 412–20.

Richards, E. R. 2004 *Paul and First-Century Letter Writing: Secretaries, Composition and Collection.* Downers Grove: InterVarsity Press.

Richardson, P. 1969 *Israel in the Apostolic Church.* Vol. 10. SNTSMS. Cambridge: Cambridge University Press.

Roth, C. 1960 'The Cleansing of the Temple and Zechariah XIV 21'. *NovT* 4: 174–81.

Rowland, C. C. 1982 *The Open Heaven: A Study of Apocalyptic in Judaism and Early Christianity*. New York: Crossroad.

Russell, D. S. 1964 *The Method and Message of Jewish Apocalyptic: 200 BC–AD 100*. Philadelphia: Westminster.

Russell, R. 1975 'Eschatology and Ethics in 1 Peter'. *EvQ* 47: 78–84.

Safrai, S. 1976 'Education and the Study of Torah' in *The Jewish People of the First Century: Historical Geography, Political History, Social, Cultural and Religious Life and Institution*. Edited by S. Safrai and M. Stern. Philadelphia: Fortress Press, 945–70.

Sander, E. T. 1966 'Πύρωσις and the First Epistle of St. Peter 4:12'. Doctoral dissertation. Harvard University.

Sanders, E. P. 1977 *Paul and Palestinian Judaism*. Philadelphia: Fortress Press.

Sandmel, S. 1962 'Parallelomania'. *JBL* 81: 1–13.

Satterthwaite, P. E., R. S. Hess and G. J. Wenham (eds.) 1995 *The Lord's Annointed: Interpretation of Old Testament Messianic Texts*. Grand Rapids: Baker Books.

Scharlemann, M. H. 1976 'Exodus Ethics: Part One–1 Peter 1:13–16'. *Concordia Journal* 2: 165–70.

Schelkle, K. H. 1970 *Die Petrusbrief–der Judasbrief*. Freiber: Herder.

Schlosser, J. 1983 'Guide Lines for Christian Suffering: A Source-Critical and Theological Study of 1 Peter 2,21–25'. *Biblica* 64: 381–410.

Schnackenburg, R. 1990 *The Gospel According to St. John*. 3 Vols. New York: Crossroad.

Schreiner, T. R. 2003 *1, 2 Peter, Jude*. Vol. 37. The New American Commentary. Nashville: Broadman & Holman.

Schürer, E. 1973–87 *The History of the Jewish People in the Age of Jesus Christ*. 3 vols. Revised and edited by G. Vermes, F. Millar and M. Black. Edinburgh, T&T Clark.

Schutter, W. L. 1989 *Hermeneutic and Composition in 1 Peter*. Vol. 30. WUNT II. Tübingen: Mohr-Siebeck.

Schweizer, E. 1972 *Der erste Petrusbrief*. 3rd edition. Zürcher Bibelkommentare. Zurich: Theologischer Verlag.

Scott, C. A. 1905 'The Sufferings of Christ: A Note on 1 Peter i.11'. *Expositor*: 234–40.

Scott, I. W. 2006 *Implicit Epistemology in the Letters of Paul: Story, Experience and the Spirit*. Vol. 205. WUNT II. Tübingen: Mohr-Siebeck.

Scott, J. C. 1985 *Weapons of the Weak: Everyday Forms of Peasant Resistance*. New Haven: Yale University Press.

Scott, J. M. (ed.) 1997 *Exile: Old Testament, Jewish, and Christian Conceptions*. Leiden: Brill.

2001 *Restoration: Old Testament, Jewish, and Christian Perspectives*. Leiden: Brill.

Seland, T. 1995 'The "Common Priesthood" of Philo and 1 Peter: A Philonic Reading of 1 Peter 2:5,9'. *JSNT* 57: 87–119.

2005 *Strangers in the Light: Philonic Perspectives on Christian Identity in 1 Peter*. Vol. 76. BINS. Leiden: Brill.

Selwyn, E. G. 1958 *The First Epistle of St. Peter*. 2nd edition. London: Macmillan and Co Ltd.

Senior, D. 2003 *1 Peter, Jude, 2 Peter*. Sacra Pagina. Collegeville, Minnesota: The Liturgical Press.

Shimada, K. 1981 'A Critical Note on I Peter 1,12'. *Annual of the Japanese Biblical Institute* 7: 146–50.

Smith, D. M. 1992 *John among the Gospels: The Relationship in Twentieth-Century Research*. Minneapolis: Fortress Press.

Smith-Christopher, D. L. 1997 'Reassessing the Historical and Sociological Impact of the Babylonian Exile (597/587–539 BCE)' in *Exile: Old Testament, Jewish and Christian Conceptions*. Edited by J. M. Scott. Leiden: Brill, 7–36.

2002 *A Biblical Theology of Exile*. Minneapolis: Fortress Press.

Snaith, J. G. 1974 *Ecclesiasticus, Or the Wisdom of Jesus Son of Sirach*. Cambridge: Cambridge University Press.

Snodgrass, K. R. 1980 'Streams of Tradition Emerging From Isaiah 40:1–5 and Their Adaptation in the New Testament'. *JSNT* 8: 24–45.

Soards, M. L. 1994 'Appendix IX: The Question of a Premarcan Passion Narrative' in *The Death of the Messiah*. Edited by R. E. Brown. Vol. 2. New York: Doubleday, 1,492–524.

Sommer, B. D. 1998 *A Prophet Reads Scripture: Allusion in Isaiah 40–66*. Stanford, California: Stanford University Press.

Spicq, C. 1966 *Les Épitres de Saint Pierre*. Paris: Librairie Lecoffre.

Stanley, C. D. 1992 *Paul and the Language of Scripture: Citation Technique in the Pauline Epistles and Contemporary Literature*. Vol. 74. SNTSMS. Cambridge: Cambridge University Press.

Stanton, G. N. 2004 *Jesus and Gospel*. Cambridge: Cambridge University Press.

Stemberger, G., and H. L. Strack 1991 *Introduction to the Talmud and Midrash*. Translated by Markus Bockmuehl. Minneapolis: Fortress Press.

Stowers, S. K. 1986 *Letter Writing in Greco-Roman Antiquity*. Vol. 5. LEC. Philadelphia: Westminster.

Strathmann, H. 1976 'μάρτυς' in *Theological Dictionary of the New Testament*. Edited by G. Kittel. Vol. 4. Grand Rapids: Eerdmans, 474–514.

Streeter, B. H. 1929 *The Primitive Church*. New York: Macmillan.

Stuhlmacher, P. 1968 *Das Paulinische Evangelium I: Vorgeschichte*. Vol. 95. Forschungen zur Religion und Literatur des Alten und Neuen Testaments. Göttingen: Vandenhoeck & Ruprecht.

Stuhlmacher, P. and B. Janowski (eds.) 2004 *The Suffering Servant: Isaiah 53 in Jewish and Christian Sources*. Grand Rapids: Eerdmans.

Stuhmueller, C. 1970 *Creative Redemption in Deutero-Isaiah*. Vol. 43. Anchor Bible. Rome: Pontifical Biblical Institute.

Sweeney, M. A. 2000 *The Twelve Prophets: Micah, Nahum, Habakkuk, Zephaniah, Haggai, Zechariah, Malachi*. Vol. 2. Berit Olam: Studies in Hebrew Narrative and Poetry. Collegeville: The Liturgical Press.

Talbert, C. A. (ed.) 1986 *Perspectives on First Peter*. Vol. 9. NABPR Special Studies Series. Macon: Mercer University Press.

Taylor, C. 1989 *Sources of the Self: The Making of the Modern Identity*. Cambridge: Cambridge University Press.

Theissen, G. 2004 *The Gospels in Context*. London: Continuum.

Thiede, C. 1986 *Simon Peter, From Galilee to Rome*. Exeter: Paternoster.

Thompson, M. 1991 *Clothed With Christ: The Example and Teaching of Jesus in Romans 12.1–15.13*. Vol. 59. JSNTSup. Sheffield: JSOT Press.

Thurén, L. 1990 *The Rhetorical Strategy of 1 Peter: With Special Reference to Ambiguous Expressions*. Abo, France: Abo Academy.

1995 *Argument and Theology in 1 Peter: The Origins of Christian Paraenesis*. Vol. 114. JSNTSup. Sheffield: Sheffield Academic Press.

Thurston, R. W. 1974 'Interpreting First Peter'. *JETS* 17: 171–82.

Tigchelaar, E. J. C. 1996 *Prophets of Old and the Day of the End: Zechariah, the Book of Watchers and Apocalyptic*. Leiden: Brill.

Tite, P. L. 1997 *Compositional Transitions in 1 Peter: An Analysis of the Letter-Opening*. San Francisco: International Scholars Publications.

Tooley, W. 1964 'The Shepherd and Sheep Image in the Teaching of Jesus'. *NovT* 7: 15–25.

Tov, E. 1995 'Excerpted and Abbreviated Biblical Texts From Qumran'. *RevQ* 16: 581–600.

Trebilco, P. R. 1991 *Jewish Communities in Asia Minor*. New York: Cambridge University Press.

Trocmé, E. 1983 *The Passion as Liturgy: A Study in the Origin of the Passion Narratives in the Four Gospels*. London: SCM Press.

Tromp, J. 2001 'The Davidic Messiah in Jewish Eschatology of the First Century BCE' in *Restoration: Old Testament, Jewish, and Christian Perspectives*. Edited by J. M. Scott. Leiden: Brill, 179–201.

Tuckett, C. (ed.) 2003 *The Book of Zechariah and Its Influence*. Aldershot: Ashgate.

van Oyen, G. and T. Shepherd (eds.) 2006 *The Trial and Death of Jesus: Essays on the Passion Narrative in Mark*. Leuven: Peeters.

van Unnik, W. C. 1954 'The Teaching of Good Works in 1 Peter' *NTS* 1: 92–110.

Vancil, J. W. 1975 *The Symbolism of the Shepherd in Biblical, Intertestamental, and New Testament Materials*. Philadelphia: Dropsie University.

1992 'Sheep, Shepherd' in *The Anchor Bible Dictionary*. Edited by D. N. Freedman. Vol. 5. New York, Doubleday, 1,187–90.

Vermes, G. 1970 'Bible and Midrash: Early Old Testament Exegesis' in *The Cambridge History of the Bible: Vol.1, From the Beginnings to Jerome*. Edited by P. R. Ackroyd and C. F. Evans. Cambridge: Cambridge Press, 199–231.

1999 *An Introduction to the Complete Dead Sea Scrolls*. Minneapolis: Fortress Press.

Volf, M. 1994 'Soft Difference: Theological Reflections on the Relation between Church and Culture in 1 Peter'. *Ex Auditu* 10 :1–15.

von Rad, G. 1972 *Wisdom in Israel*. London: SCM Press.

Wacholder, B. 2007 *The New Damascus Document: The Midrash on the Eschatological Torah of the Dead Sea Scrolls: Reconstruction, Translation and Commentary*. Vol. 56. Studies on the Texts of the Desert of Judah. Leiden: Brill.

Wagner, J. R. 2002 *Heralds of the Good News: Isaiah and Paul 'In Concert' in the Letter of Romans*. Vol. 101. NovTSup; Leiden: Brill.

Wallace, D. 1996 *Greek Grammar beyond the Basics: An Exegetical Syntax of the New Testament*. Grand Rapids: Zondervan.

Watson, D. F. (ed.) 2002 *The Intertexture of Apocalyptic Discourse in the New Testament*. Vol. 14, Society of Biblical Literature Symposium Series. Leiden: Brill.

Watts, R. E. 1990 'Consolation or Confrontation: Isa. 40–55 and the Delay of the New Exodus'. *TynBul* 41: 31–59.

1997 *Isaiah's New Exodus in Mark*. Vol. 88. WUNT II. Tübingen: J. C. B. Mohr-Siebeck.

1998 'Jesus' Death, Isaiah 53, and Mark 10:45: A Crux Revisited' in *Jesus and the Suffering Servant: Isaiah 53 and Christian Origins*. Edited by W. H. Bellinger and W. R. Farmer. Harrisburg: Trinity Press, 125–51.

Webb, R. L. 2007 'Intertexture and Rhetorical Strategy in First Peter's Apocalyptic Discourse: A Study in Sociorhetorical Interpretation' in *Reading First Peter with New Eyes: Methodological Reassessments of the Letter of First Peter*. Edited by R. L. Webb and B. Bauman-Martin. London: T&T Clark, 72–110.

Westermann, C. 2001 *Isaiah 40–66*. Translated by D. M. G. Stalker. Philadelphia: John Knox Press.

White, S. A. 1990 '4QDta: Biblical Manuscript or Excerpted Text?' in *Of Scribes and Scrolls: Studies He Read on the Hebrew Bible, Intertestamental Judaism, and Christian Origins Presented to John Strugnell on the Occasion of His Sixtieth Birthday*. Edited by H. W. Attridge, J. J. Collins and T. H. Tobin. Vol. 5. New York: University Press of America, 13–20.

Willitts, J. 2006 'The Remnant of Israel in 4QpIsaiaha (4Q161) and the Dead Sea Scrolls'. *Jewish Studies Quarterly* 57: 11–25.

2007a *Matthew's Messianic Shepherd-King: In Search of 'The Lost Sheep of the House of Israel'*. Vol. 147. BZNW. Berlin: Walter de Gruyter.

2007b 'Matthew's Messianic Shepherd-King: In Search of the "Lost Sheep of the House of Israel"'. *Theological Studies* 63: 365–82.

Wilson, W. T. 1997 *The Hope of Glory: Education and Exhortation in the Epistle to the Colossians*. Vol. 88. NovTSup. Leiden: Brill.

Windisch, H. 1951 *Die katholischen Briefe*. Vol. 15. HNT. Tübingen: Mohr-Siebeck.

Winston, D. 1979 *The Wisdom of Solomon*. Vol. 43. Anchor Bible. Garden City: Doubleday.

Winter, B. 1988 'The Public Honoring of Christian Benefactors: Romans 13.3–4 and 1 Peter 2.14–15'. *JSNT* 34: 87–103.

Witherington, B. 2007 *Letters and Homilies for Hellenized Christians: A Socio-Rhetorical Commentary on 1–2 Peter*. Vol. 2. Downers Grove: InterVarsity Press.

Woan, S. 2004 'The Psalms in 1 Peter' in *The Psalms in the New Testament*. Edited by S. Moyise and M. J. J. Menken. London: T&T Clark, 213–29.

Wright, A. G. 1966 'The Literary Genre Midrash'. *CBQ* 28: 105–38.

Wright, N. T. 1992 *The New Testament and the People of God*. Vol. 1. Christian Origins and the Question of God. Minneapolis: Fortress Press.

1996 *Jesus and the Victory of God*. Vol. 2. Christian Origins and the Question of God. Minneapolis: Fortress Press.

2003 *The Resurrection of the Son of God.* Vol. 3. Christian Origins and the Question of God. Minneapolis: Fortress Press.

Wright, R. B. 2007 *The Psalms of Solomon: A Critical Edition of the Greek Text.* Vol. 1. Jewish and Christian Texts in Contexts and Related Studies; London: T&T Clark.

Zeitlin, S. 1953 'Midrash: A Historical Study'. *JQR* 44: 21–36.

INDEX OF NAMES

This is an index of modern authors discussed in the text or cited/paraphrased in the notes (passing references excluded).

INDEX OF SCRIPTURE AND OTHER REFERENCES

This is a selective index of Scripture and Other references discussed in the main text, avoiding passing mentions and – where possible – repetition and recapitulation

NB The non-OT and non-NT references are collected under 'Other' as there are rather few to classify conventionally.

CPSIA information can be obtained at www.ICGtesting.com
Printed in the USA
LVOW10s0410240915

455536LV00013B/105/P